MAO TSETUNG'S IMMORTAL CONTRIBUTIONS

RCP Publications
P.O. Box 3486
Merchandise Mart
Chicago, IL 60654

Paperback Edition ISBN 0-89851-046-5
Cloth Edition ISBN 0-89851-045-7
Library of Congress Catalog Card Number 79-88177

MAO TSETUNG'S IMMORTAL CONTRIBUTIONS

BY BOB AVAKIAN

RCP PUBLICATIONS
CHICAGO, IL

"Chairman Mao Delivering a Report at a Cadre's Meeting in Yenan on Rectifying the Party's Style of Work" (Chinese pencil sketch)

PUBLISHER'S NOTE

Mao Tsetung's Immortal Contributions was originally published as a series of seven articles in *Revolution,* Organ of the Central Committee of the Revolutionary Communist Party, USA. Written by Bob Avakian, Chairman of the RCP Central Committee, they appeared in the pages of *Revolution* between April, 1978 and January, 1979. The decision to write these articles was part of the process of making public the line of the RCP on the 1976 revisionist coup in China and was crucial in upholding the banner of Mao Tsetung at a time when he has come under attack from various quarters.

The first four chapters of the book were written prior to the publication of the Central Committee Statement and the Mao Tsetung Memorial Meetings of September 1978, where the Party's analysis of the 1976 revisionist coup in China against Mao's line and the Four (Wang Hung-wen, Chang Chun-chiao, Chiang Ching and Yao Wen-yuan) who led in upholding it was made public. The last three chapters were written after September 1978 and thus speak openly against the revisionist line of the current Chinese rulers. In preparing the articles for publication in book form, the author has made some minor changes in the original manuscript.

May Day, 1979

TABLE OF CONTENTS

Chapter 1

REVOLUTION IN COLONIAL COUNTRIES

Mao Tsetung was the greatest revolutionary, the greatest Marxist-Leninist leader, of our time. For more than 50 years he led the Chinese people in monumental struggles and provided inspiration and illumination to the working class and oppressed people in every country. Under his guidance China was transformed from a backward preserve of imperialism into the most advanced stronghold of the international proletariat in the fight against imperialism and reaction, the beacon and bastion of the world revolution. Mao Tsetung's contributions to the revolutionary movement worldwide, to the revolutionary science of the international working class, Marxism-Leninism, and to its historic mission of abolishing all class distinctions and ushering in the communist era are indeed immortal.

Making revolution in a country like China—a colonial (or semicolonial) country with the world's largest population and a vast territory, carved up by various imperialists and contending domestic reactionaries allied with them—and advancing that revolution to socialism was an unprecedented achievement of the Chinese people which radically changed not only China itself but the face of the entire world. This Mao led them in doing, through decades of arduous and tortuous struggle, by concretely applying the universal principles of Marxism-Leninism to the concrete situation in China, in the context of the world revolution. And in so doing he enriched these principles.

This, the first chapter of this book on Mao's contributions, will specifically focus on the basic questions of Marxist theory and strategy concerning revolution in colonial countries which Mao Tsetung applied and enriched in leading the Chinese people in winning liberation and advancing to socialism, in particular his development of the line of new-democratic revolution.

Marx and Engels

To better understand Mao's contributions, first it is necessary to review the development of Marxism and Leninism on the question of national and colonial oppression, national revolution and revolution in colonial countries. Marx and Engels founded scientific socialism in the middle of the 19th century. At that time they analyzed the development of capitalism and the penetration and influence of capitalist commodity production not only in the capitalist countries themselves but in all parts of the world. They pointed out in the *Communist Manifesto* that:

Modern industry has established the world market, for which the discovery of America paved the way. This market has given an immense development to commerce, to navigation, to communication by land. This development has, in turn, reacted on the extension of industry; and in proportion as industry, commerce, navigation, railways extended, in the same proportion the bourgeoisie developed, increased its capital, and pushed into the background every class handed down from the Middle Ages...

The need of a constantly expanding market for its products chases the bourgeoisie over the whole surface of the globe. It must nestle everywhere, settle everywhere, establish connections everywhere...

The bourgeoisie, by the rapid improvement of all instruments of production, by the immensely facilitated means of communication, draws all, even the most barbarian, nations into civilization. The cheap prices of its commodities are the heavy artillery with which it batters down all Chinese walls, with which it forces the barbarians' intensely obstinate hatred of foreigners to capitulate. It compels all nations, on pain of extinction, to adopt the bourgeois mode of production; it compels them to introduce what it calls civilization into their midst, *i.e.*, to become bourgeois themselves. In one word, it creates a world after its own image.[1]

Marx and Engels firmly supported the struggles of the oppressed nations and the masses of people in the colonial areas subjected to this form of capitalist colonialism—including the struggle of the Irish people, and mass rebellions in places such as India, Persia and China. For example, in an article entitled "Revolution in China and in Europe," written by Karl Marx in 1853 and analyzing the effects of what came to be called the Taiping Rebellion, Marx pointed out that England, through enforcing the opium trade in China and other means, humiliated and oppressed China and the masses of Chinese people, but at the same time this also tended to break down the isolation which contributed to the preservation of the old feudal system of China. In this article Marx pointed out that:

Complete isolation was the prime condition of the preservation of old China. That isolation having come to a violent end by the medium of England, dissolution must follow as surely as that of any mummy carefully preserved in a hermetically sealed coffin, whenever it is brought into contact with the open air. Now, England having brought about the revolution of China, the question is how that revolution will in time react on England, and through England on Europe. This question is not difficult of solution . . . if one of the great markets [of England] suddenly becomes contracted, the arrival of the crisis is necessarily accelerated thereby. Now, the Chinese rebellion must, for the time being, have precisely this effect upon England.[2]

Several decades later, in the 1880s and 1890s, Engels further made an important analysis of the development of colonial oppression in such countries as China and pointed to the reaction of this on conditions in Europe and to a basic relationship between revolution in the capitalist countries themselves and revolution in colonial countries. For example in a letter to Karl Kautsky in 1894 Engels noted that:

The war between China and Japan signifies the end of old China, the complete, if gradual, revolution of its entire economic foundation, including the abolition of the old bonds between agriculture and industry in the countryside by big industry, railways, etc., and thus also the mass exodus of Chinese coolies to Europe; consequently, a hastening for us of the debacle and the aggravation of antagonisms into a crisis. It is again the wonderful irony of history: China alone is still to be conquered for capitalist production, and in so doing at long last the latter makes its own existence at home impossible . . .[3]

But at that time Engels was not able to foresee the actual relation between revolution in the West and East, nor was he able to predict what specific form the revolution in such countries as China would take. He noted, for example, in a letter to Karl Kautsky earlier, in 1882, that "as to what social and political phases these countries will then have to pass through before they likewise arrive at socialist organization, I think we today can advance only rather idle hypotheses."[4]

In sum, then, Marx and Engels dealt with the colonial question during the first phase of the development of capitalism, pre-monopoly capitalism, before it had developed into imperialism. This was a period in which colonialism was characterized economically by the export of goods, finished products, rather than later, in the imperialist era, by the export of capital itself, as Lenin was to analyze in *Imperialism, the Highest Stage of Capitalism*.

Thus the process which Marx and Engels had described in the

Above—the Chintien Uprising—the spark that set off the Taiping Rebellion (1851-65), one of many powerful struggles waged over the centuries by the Chinese people against feudalism and, increasingly, against foreign domination. From one of the reliefs on the Monument to the People's Heroes, Peking.

Left—Betsey, called the International Gun by U.S. forces. This gun, used against the Chinese people's Yi Ho Tuan Movement (Boxer Rebellion) in 1900, symbolized how the imperialists had carved up China. The barrel had been left behind by the 1860 Anglo-French Expedition in China. The gun was mounted on an Italian carriage, loaded with Russian ammunition, and fired by a U.S. marine.

Communist Manifesto—the tendency for the introduction of commodities produced in the capitalist countries into backward areas of the world to transform these areas in the image of the capitalist countries—did not fully develop. Instead, especially with the advent of imperialism and the consequent change in the nature of the relations between the capitalist countries and their colonies (as summarized by Lenin), colonial domination by imperialism tended to retard the development of capitalism in the colonies and maintain them in an enforced state of backwardness.

Wars of National Liberation in Europe in the Period of Rising Capitalism

From the beginning Marx and Engels also devoted considerable attention to analyzing the development of the bourgeois national liberation movements in Western Europe, where such movements were then focused. Marx and Engels supported various bourgeois liberation movements insofar as and when they represented a struggle against feudal absolutism and against reactionary states holding back the development of capitalism, which was then still historically on the order of the day in a number of countries such as Italy and Germany and others.

For example, in 1870-1871, Germany, still not having completed the bourgeois-democratic revolution, waged a war against the France of Napoleon III, which together with Russian tsarism had been preventing the unification of Germany on a capitalist basis. Since such unification represented a progressive step at that time, Marx and Engels supported this struggle on the part of Germany. Lenin, in setting forth and fighting for the correct line on World War I in opposition to social-chauvinism (socialism in words, national chauvinism and support for one's own bourgeoisie in deeds), analyzed this policy of Marx and Engels', stating for example that:

The war of 1870-1871 was a historically progressive war on the part of Germany until Napoleon III was defeated; for the latter, together with the tsar, had oppressed Germany for many years, keeping her in a state of feudal disintegration. But as soon as the war developed into the plunder of France (the annexation of Alsace and Lorraine), Marx and Engels emphatically condemned the Germans. And even at the beginning of that war Marx and Engels approved of the refusal of Bebel and Liebknecht [socialist leaders in Germany] to vote for credits and advised the Social-Democrats [socialists] not to merge with the bourgeoisie, but to uphold the independent class interests of the proletariat. To apply the appraisal of this bourgeois-progressive and national-liberating war to the present imperialist war means mocking at truth . . .

Whoever refers today to Marx's attitude towards the wars of the epoch of the *progressive* bourgeoisie and forgets Marx's statement that "the workers have no fatherland," a statement that applies *precisely* to the epoch of the reactionary, obsolete bourgeoisie, to the epoch of the socialist revolution, shamelessly distorts Marx and substitutes the bourgeois for the socialist point of view.[5]

Lenin consistently explained why it was that Marx and Engels supported various bourgeois liberation movements in Western Europe during the latter half of the 19th century, even as late as 1891 when, as Lenin noted, Engels said that in the event of war against Russia and France it would be the duty of the German socialists to defend their fatherland.

Blasting the social-chauvinists who attempted to misuse these positions of Marx and Engels, Lenin sharply pointed out that in the circumstances where Marx and Engels took the approach of determining whose victory in a war between states in Europe would be more desirable, it was the case that *"no other* question could have been posed at the time except the following: the success of *which* bourgeoisie, the success of which combination of forces, the failure of which reactionary forces (the feudal-absolutist forces which were hampering the rise of the bourgeoisie) promised contemporary democracy more 'elbow room.' "[6]

In other words, Lenin stressed, " 'the success of which side is more desirable' meant asking 'the success of which *bourgeoisie* is more desirable.' " This was because, as noted before, bourgeois liberation movements in Western Europe still could play a progressive role at that time in certain conditions. But, Lenin hastened to add, "one cannot even imagine bourgeois progressive movements, whether modestly liberal or tempestuously democratic, in Britain, Germany, or France," for the era of such movements had passed with the development of these countries into imperialism.[7]

Again, Marx and Engels dealt with the national and colonial question and with the question of national liberation struggles in the period of rising capitalism, when liberation struggles against national oppression and feudal survivals could only lead, even if they were carried as far as possible, to the consolidation of bourgeois rule and capitalism. And in general while they analyzed and supported uprisings of the masses in the countries of the East, the attention of Marx and Engels on the national question was mainly concentrated on the bourgeois liberation movements in Western Europe, where such movements were then most developed and influential in determining world events.

Imperialism Changes Colonial Revolution

The development of capitalism into imperialism in a handful of capitalist countries brought tremendous changes not only in those countries themselves, but also internationally and specifically in their relations with their colonies and in the internal relations within the colonies themselves. While subjecting these colonies to even more savage oppression, and while overall retarding the development of their economies, the increased penetration and domination by imperialism in these colonies did lead to the further break-up of the more primitive forms of economic relations and to the transformation of feudal relations into semi-feudal relations of production, especially in the countryside in many countries of the East, such as China and others.

This gave an impetus to the further development of the proletariat in these colonial countries while at the same time restricting the development of the national bourgeoisie there, which continued to be under the domination of the imperialists. At the same time the broad masses of people, in most cases the great majority of the population, were still peasants locked in the countryside in feudal or semi-feudal relations under the crushing oppression and exploitation of the landlords, who were the mainstay of the imperialist overlords in the country. Thus, just as in the capitalist countries capitalist development created the conditions for its own overthrow and brought into being its own gravedigger, the proletariat, so, too, with the development of capitalism into imperialism, imperialist domination brought into being in the colonial countries the conditions which would lead to its defeat there.

In these colonies, the immediate struggle had to be waged against imperialism and feudalism, and the forces that could be united in this struggle included not only the leading class, the proletariat, but also the broad masses of peasantry, the petty bourgeoisie in the urban areas and sections of the bourgeoisie themselves, especially the patriotic sections of the national bourgeoisie who, while subordinate to and in many ways dependent on imperialism, were at the same time held back in significant ways by imperialist domination and feudal relations in the country and could under certain conditions be an ally in the struggle against imperialism and feudalism.

So with the development of capitalism into imperialism in a handful of capitalist countries, the situation and the role of national liberation movements changed accordingly. In these imperialist countries themselves there was, of course, no longer any progressive role for bourgeois liberation movements. Such were in fact a thing of the past.

In the colonies of these imperialist powers, not only were the liberation movements capable of playing a tremendously progressive and revolutionary role, and not only were the masses rising increasingly in resistance to the imperialists, but, in addition, with the changes summarized earlier, there was the possibility for the proletariat to march at the head of these national liberation movements and to lead them not only to the immediate goal of defeating the imperialists and their domestic lackeys, especially the feudal landlord class, but of advancing through and beyond that to the socialist stage of revolution. There were, then, two different and fundamentally opposed situations in Western Europe on the one hand and the colonial countries of the East on the other with regard to the national question.

But there was at the same time a third situation, in Eastern Europe. There the question of overthrowing national oppression and feudal domination had not yet been thoroughly resolved, and the national movements could continue to play a progressive role, unlike Western Europe, where that period had passed and capitalism had on the whole developed into imperialism.

Lenin not only thoroughly analyzed imperialism but also specifically analyzed the national question in the era of imperialism. In "A Caricature of Marxism" Lenin categorized the types of countries with regard to the national question as follows:

First type: the advanced countries of Western Europe (and America), where the national movement is a thing of the *past*. Second type: Eastern Europe, where it is a thing of the *present*. Third type: semi-colonies and colonies, where it is largely a thing of the *future*.[8]

Russia: An East-West Bridge

Russia itself was a kind of bridge between the West and East; that is, while capitalism had developed in Russia and had in fact reached the stage of monopoly capitalism, on the other hand in the countryside, where the great majority of the people still lived, feudal survivals were widespread and were the dominant form. At the same time, Russia until February, 1917, continued to be ruled by the tsarist autocracy. In short, the bourgeois-democratic revolution had not been completed in Russia, even though Russia had developed to the stage of imperialism. In addition, in Russia there were large numbers of oppressed nations whose struggle against tsarist autocracy and against Great Russian domination still played a progressive role and was an ally of the proletariat in its struggle. Lenin and Stalin raised and fought for the right of self-determination of these nations as a crucial part of the Russian revolution.

Also, as early as 1905, during the period of the revolutionary upsurge in Russia at that time, Lenin set forth in his famous work "Two Tactics of Social-Democracy in the Democratic Revolution" the need for the proletariat to unite with the masses of peasantry to overthrow the tsarist autocracy as the first step and necessary stage of the Russian revolution at that time. Lenin pointed out that the bourgeoisie in Russia could not and would not carry through the democratic revolution and only the united efforts of the workers and the masses of peasants, under the leadership of the proletariat and its Party, could accomplish this task. At the same time Lenin pointed out that the democratic revolution was, for the proletariat, not an end in itself, but a necessary step in order to be able to advance to the socialist revolution. In "Two Tactics," Lenin wrote:

The revolutionary-democratic dictatorship of the proletariat and the peasantry is unquestionably only a transient, temporary socialist aim, but to ignore this aim in the period of a democratic revolution would be downright reactionary . . . While recognizing the incontestably bourgeois nature of a revolution incapable of *directly* overstepping the bounds of a mere democratic revolution our slogan *advances* this particular revolution and strives to give it forms most advantageous to the proletariat; consequently, it strives to make the utmost of the democratic revolution in order to attain the greatest success in the proletariat's further struggle for socialism.[9]

Lenin summed up the road to socialism in Russia in this formulation: the working class must fight to carry through the democratic revolution with the mass of peasantry as its reliable ally in this struggle; then it must advance the struggle, fighting to achieve the proletarian-socialist revolution and the dictatorship of the proletariat, with the mass of poor peasants, and the semi-proletarian elements in the countryside in particular, as its most reliable ally.[10]

Although the 1905 Revolution in Russia was crushed, in February 1917 the tsarist autocracy was overthrown through a mass upsurge. At that point Lenin summed up that the bourgeois-democratic revolution had been carried as far as it could be in Russia and that the next, and immediate, stage of struggle was the fight for proletarian dictatorship and the establishment of socialism. And in fact in that year in October the proletarian-socialist revolution did succeed in Russia.

This brought basic changes in the world; it marked the establishment of the first socialist state and, together with the changes brought by imperialism, made possible the transformation of the national liberation movements in the colonies. Speaking of its general character, the national liberation struggle in colonial countries was no longer part of the old bourgeois-democratic movement, part of the old capitalist revolution leading to the rule of the bourgeoisie and the establishment of capitalism, but became a component part of the world proletarian socialist revolution, an ally of the proletariat in the capitalist countries in its struggle against imperialism and for socialism on a world scale. Writing in 1918, Stalin summed up this development:

The great world-wide significance of the October Revolution chiefly consists in the fact that:
1) It has widened the scope of the national question and converted it from the particular question of combating national oppression in Europe into the general question of emancipating the oppressed peoples, colonies and semi-colonies from imperialism;
2) It has opened up wide possibilities for their emancipation and the right paths towards it, has thereby greatly facilitated the cause of the emancipation of the oppressed peoples of the West and the East, and has drawn them into the common current of the victorious struggle against imperialism;
3) *It has thereby erected a bridge between the socialist West and the enslaved East*, having created a new front of revolutions *against* world imperialism, extending from the proletarians of the West, through the Russian revolution, to the oppressed peoples of the East.[11]

Lenin and Stalin Analyze Developments

In the several years following the victory of the October Revolution in Russia in 1917, Lenin and Stalin not only analyzed the change in the general character of the colonial movements, but paid particular attention to the development of these movements and the forging of the correct policies of the communists in relation to them. Lenin gave direction to the Third International (the Communist International or Comintern) in its first years in developing its line on the national colonial question and in particular its line and work in relation to the colonial liberation movements of the East.

The victory of the October Revolution in Russia had spread

Marxism-Leninism throughout the world and given impetus to the
formation of communist parties built in the Marxist-Leninist style
and with a Marxist-Leninist line, including in many of the colonial
countries. This was also a factor of tremendous significance and
strengthened the role of the proletariat in fighting for leadership of
the national liberation struggle in the colonies and directing it
through the completion of the bourgeois-democratic revolution to
the stage of socialism.

At the Second Congress of the Comintern Lenin led the commission on the national and colonial questions. In a report on that subject he stressed on the one hand the need for communists to give
full support to and strive to carry forward the national liberation
movement in the colonies and on the other hand the need to maintain the independence of the communists and strengthen the
revolutionary forces within these national liberation movements.

Further, the question was posed and answered by Lenin as to
whether or not it would be possible for these countries to advance
to socialism without having to go through the stage of capitalism.
In his report of the commission on the national and colonial questions at this Congress of the Comintern Lenin wrote the following:

The question was posed as follows: are we to consider as correct the
assertion that the capitalist stage of economic development is inevitable
for backward nations now on the road to emancipation and among whom a
certain advance towards progress is to be seen since the war? We replied
in the negative. If the victorious revolutionary proletariat conducts
systematic propaganda among them, and the Soviet governments come to
their aid with all the means at their disposal—in that event it will be
mistaken to assume that the backward peoples must inevitably go
through the capitalist stage of development. Not only should we create independent contingents of fighters and party organizations in the colonies
and the backward countries, not only at once launch propaganda for the
organisation of peasants' Soviets and strive to adapt them to the pre-
capitalist conditions, but the Communist International should advance
the proposition, with the appropriate theoretical grounding, that with the
aid of the proletariat of the advanced countries, backward countries can
go over to the Soviet system and, through certain stages of development,
to communism, without having to pass through the capitalist stage.[12]

At the same time Lenin concluded that, "The necessary means
for this cannot be indicated in advance."[13]

After Lenin's death, Stalin not only led in building socialism in
the Soviet Union, but in giving support to and helping to formulate the line for revolutionary struggles throughout the world,
including in the colonial countries, China in particular. In several
speeches and articles during the period of the revolutionary up-

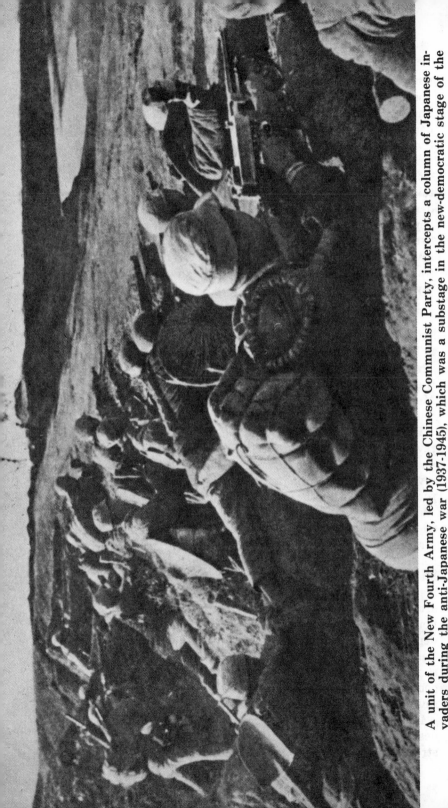

A unit of the New Fourth Army, led by the Chinese Communist Party, intercepts a column of Japanese invaders during the anti-Japanese war (1937-1945), which was a substage in the new-democratic stage of the Chinese revolution.

surge in China in the years 1924-27, Stalin helped to analyze the specific features of the Chinese revolution: the fact that it was an anti-imperialist struggle; the fact that the feudal domination of the countryside and the feudal exploitation of the peasantry played a central role in the Chinese economy, and therefore that the agrarian revolution in China was at the heart of the struggle and closely linked with the anti-imperialist struggle of the Chinese nation; and that the proletariat could and must lead the bourgeois-democratic revolution and advance the movement through and beyond that stage to the stage of socialist revolution. Further, Stalin pointed out that from the beginning in China the armed revolution was fighting the armed counter-revolution and that this was both a specific feature and a specific advantage in the Chinese revolution.

Mao on the Chinese Revolution

Thus Stalin helped to analyze some of the basic features of the Chinese revolution. But it was Mao Tsetung who, taking part in the Chinese revolution and applying the universal principles of Marxism-Leninism to it, fully developed and elaborated the basic line, theory and strategy of the new-democratic revolution.

From its earliest stages, Mao had recognized that the Chinese revolution would be characterized by the tremendously powerful and central role of the peasant uprisings and the peasant agrarian revolution. This was in opposition to various opportunist and erroneous lines within the Chinese Communist Party which wrote off the Chinese peasantry as a revolutionary force and which attempted to center the struggle in the cities and/or to make it a one-stage struggle of the proletariat against the bourgeoisie, thereby erroneously trying to bypass the stage of bourgeois-democratic struggle under the leadership of the proletariat. Mao's line was also in opposition to right-wing opportunists within the CCP who attempted to surrender leadership of the revolution to the bourgeois and landlord classes. They denied the need for the independence and initiative of the proletariat and its Communist Party and for the Communist Party to arm the masses and lead them as the mainstay of the armed struggle and in defeating the counter-revolutionary violence of the reactionary forces with the revolutionary violence of the masses.

In 1927, Mao wrote a very important work, "Report on an Investigation of the Peasant Movement in Hunan," in which he stressed the central role of the hundreds of millions of peasants in

China in the revolutionary movement. In that work he stated very powerfully:

For the present upsurge of the peasant movement is a colossal event. In a very short time, in China's central, southern and northern provinces, several hundred million peasants will rise like a mighty storm, like a hurricane, a force so swift and violent that no power, however great, will be able to hold it back. They will smash all the trammels that bind them and rush forward along the road to liberation. They will sweep away all the imperialists, warlords, corrupt officials, local tyrants and evil gentry into their graves. Every revolutionary party and every revolutionary comrade will be put to the test, to be accepted or rejected as they decide. There are three alternatives. To march at their head and lead them? To trail behind them, gesticulating and criticizing? Or to stand in their way and oppose them? Every Chinese is free to choose, but events will force you to make the choice quickly.[14]

"Terrible," this mass upsurge of the peasants, a question of "going too far," as some, including a number of people within the Communist Party, whimpered and complained? No, it was fine, for as Mao reminded these people in combatting their Confucian outlook:

. . .a revolution is not a dinner party, or writing an essay, or painting a picture, or doing embroidery; it cannot be so refined, so leisurely and gentle, so temperate, kind, courteous, restrained and magnanimous. A revolution is an insurrection, an act of violence by which one class overthrows another. A rural revolution is a revolution by which the peasantry overthrows the power of the feudal landlord class. Without using the greatest force, the peasants cannot possibly overthrow the deep-rooted authority of the landlords which has lasted for thousands of years. The rural areas need a mighty revolutionary upsurge, for it alone can rouse the people in their millions to become a powerful force. All the actions mentioned here which have been labelled as "going too far" flow from the power of the peasants, which has been called forth by the mighty revolutionary upsurge in the countryside.[15]

Correctly basing himself on the central role of the agrarian revolution and the upsurge of the peasants in China, as well as other specific features of Chinese society at that time which flowed from its semi-colonial, semi-feudal nature, Mao made the all-important strategic analysis that the road to the seizure of power through armed struggle lay not in insurrection in the cities followed by civil war but in establishing base areas in the countryside and, with the proletariat and its Party as the leading force, mobilizing the mass of peasants as the main force to wage a protracted people's war to encircle and finally seize the cities. This was, in fact, the road that Mao led the Chinese people in taking in winning nationwide victory, liberating China and advancing to socialism, through the course of more than 20 years. While, of course, this has all to do with the question of Mao's contributions in the area of military strategy—a subject which will be dealt with in the next chapter—it was an indispensable part of Mao's development of the overall line for revolution in China and still has great relevancy and importance today, especially for countries where conditions are the same as or very similar to those in China during its new-democratic revolution.

Firmly Based on Class Analysis

As early as 1926, Mao had posed and answered a crucial question in any revolutionary movement: "Who are our enemies? Who are our friends? This is a question of the first importance for the revolution."[16] Mao answered this by making an analysis of the classes in Chinese society, which he concluded as follows:

> To sum up, it can be seen that our enemies are all those in league with imperialism—the warlords, the bureaucrats, the comprador class, the big landlord class and the reactionary section of the intelligentsia attached to them. The leading force in our revolution is the industrial proletariat. Our closest friends are the entire semi-proletariat and petty bourgeoisie. As for the vacillating middle bourgeoisie, their right-wing may become our enemy and their left-wing may become our friend—but we must be constantly on our guard and not let them create confusion within our ranks.[17]

Mao pointed out in particular, not only at this point, but in leading the Chinese revolution through the entire stage of new democracy, that the question of the role of the Chinese bourgeoisie in the Chinese revolution was of special importance. He noted for example that in Russia, while there was a stage of bourgeois-democratic revolution, nevertheless even in that stage the bourgeoisie in Russia was not an ally of the proletariat as it was in China. Mao stated some years later, during the period of the anti-Japanese war when the united front was extended and larger sections of the bourgeoisie were included in it in order to unite all who could be united against the Japanese, that "It is through this kind of complex relationship with the Chinese bourgeoisie that the Chinese revolution and the Communist Party of China have progressed in their development. This is a special historical feature, a feature peculiar to the revolution in colonial and semi-colonial countries and not to be found in the revolutionary history of any capitalist country."[18]

Mao noted in the same work that the specific relation between the proletariat and the bourgeoisie in the Chinese revolution was such that at times the proletariat was able to establish a revolutionary united front with the bourgeoisie and at other times, owing to the actions of the imperialists and the Chinese bourgeoisie, it was forced to break off this united front. What characterized Mao's analysis and approach here and at all times was that it was firmly based on class analysis. Moreover, the various policies and lines that were adopted during the different phases of the new-democratic revolution were always rooted in this method of class analysis. At each point, within the Party, and as far as possible among the masses, the class basis of the actions of various forces in Chinese society was thoroughly explained.

When, in the revolution of 1924-27, Chiang Kai-shek turned traitor to the Chinese people and turned his guns against the Chinese masses, murdering tens of thousands of communists and other working people, Mao explained that Chiang's usurpation of the reins of the Kuomintang (previously a revolutionary organization made up of different class forces and including the Communists) and the overall treachery on the part of Chiang Kai-shek was due to the fact that he represented the big bourgeoisie and landlords in China who were allied with imperialism, in particular U.S. and British imperialism. Later, after the Japanese had invaded the northern provinces of China and were preparing to invade southward throughout China as a whole, the Chinese Communist Party proposed a truce and then a united front with the Kuomintang and even with Chiang Kai-shek at a certain point. Here again, the class basis for this was explained. Mao made clear that Chiang Kai-shek's nature had not changed, that he and the class forces he represented were still dependent on and lackeys of U.S. and British imperialism, but owing to the contradictions among the imperialists and in particular between British and U.S. imperialism on the one side and Japanese imperialism on the other, it was possible to build a united front with Chiang Kai-shek and the forces he represented. Further, Mao made clear that it was necessary to build such a united front in order to concentrate the struggle of the Chinese nation as a whole against Japan, which was attempting to reduce China from the status of a semi-colony to that of an outright colony of Japan.

For several years after the initial Japanese invasion in 1931, Chiang Kai-shek refused to enter into any united front and instead directed his main forces against the Communist Party, attempting time and again to "encircle and suppress" them—in fact to wipe them out. During this period, beginning with the betrayal by Chiang Kai-shek and his massacre of communists and other working people in 1927, the Chinese Communist Party was forced to and did wage a 10-year civil war, in which to a large degree it had to break off its united front with the bourgeoisie, since most sections of it followed and supported Chiang Kai-shek and his reactionary coup within the Kuomintang and his reactionary role within Chinese society as a whole.

Nevertheless, within the Communist Party Mao led a struggle against various erroneous and opportunist lines which, even after the initial Japanese invasion of 1931, refused to go along with the policy of developing the broadest possible united front to resist Japan and defeat its efforts to reduce China to its colony. Owing to these and other sectarian errors and "ultra-left" mistakes, the Communist Party, which under Mao's leadership had established base areas in the countryside, was during the period of the 10-year civil war weakened in its resistance to the continuous attacks by Chiang Kai-shek's forces; it was at various times isolated from sections of the people, including masses of people in the countryside.

Because of this in 1934 the Communist Party, together with the armed forces under its leadership, was forced to abandon its base areas and to embark on what became, as Mao called it, a "historic monument," the Long March, which in its course of about two years involved fighting on the average of more than one battle a day and carving a path of thousands of miles through China. This became a crucial turning point in the Chinese revolution. Though large numbers of the Communist Party and the armed forces under its leadership were lost during the course of the Long March, it was nevertheless brought to a victorious conclusion. As a result, during the course of the Long March, the basic line of Mao Tsetung and his leadership was consolidated within the Chinese Communist Party in early 1935.[19]

United Front Formed

It was on the basis of the triumph of Mao's line during the Long March that the Communist Party was able to formulate, struggle for and finally achieve the united front against Japan. Finally in late 1936, Chiang Kai-shek was kidnapped and held by two of his own generals who supported the Communist Party's call for a united front, and Chiang was forced to agree to this united front. Forming such a united front with the Kuomintang required certain adjustments in the struggle within China. In particular, in the countryside it required stepping back from the policy of confiscating the land of landlords and distributing this land among the peasants, replacing this policy with the more limited one of rent and interest reductions.

Mao led a struggle within the Communist Party to unite the Party around this adjustment, while at the same time opposing the line of class capitulation, of subordinating the Communist Party and the armed forces under its leadership to the Kuomintang and the Kuomintang's armed forces, a line which would in fact have led to defeat in the War of Resistance against Japan and the slaughter and suppression of communists and the masses of working people, including the peasants in the liberated areas, at the hands of Chiang Kai-shek.

Mao pointed out that on the one hand the class struggle within China had to be adjusted in conformity with the anti-Japanese war of resistance but on the other hand, as he stressed, the class struggle continued to exist independently of anyone's will. It could not be denied, still less could it be abolished, but it could and must be adjusted. And while it was absolutely necessary to form the broadest possible united front including sections of the big bourgeoisie and some landlords in order to defeat Japanese aggression, at the same time within that united front the Communist Party must continue to fight for and exercise its independence and initiative in every sphere, including the military sphere. It must in no way subordinate itself to the big bourgeosie, the landlords or any other class forces, but must instead fight for leadership of the united front.

Throughout this period of the united front, right up until the defeat of the Japanese aggressors in 1945, Chiang Kai-shek and those following him continued to direct their main fire against the Communist Party and the armed forces and liberated base areas under its leadership. The Kuomintang refused to even carry out the policy of rent and interest reduction, which represented, as noted before, a compromise, an adjustment, on the part of the Communist Party itself in the interests of the broad united front against Japan. The Kuomintang consistently attacked the Communist Party for carrying out such reforms in the countryside and for striving to establish the democratic rights of the masses of people throughout China as a whole.

In "On Coalition Government," the political report delivered by Mao to the 7th Congress of the Communist Party of China in 1945, on the eve of the victory of the anti-Japanese war, Mao summed up among other things the struggle around the question of reforms, particularly in the countryside. He noted that:

In the absence of political reforms all the productive forces are being ruined, and this is true both of agriculture and of industry.

By and large, it will be impossible to develop industry unless China is independent, free, democratic and united.[20]

In other words, everything then hinged on defeating the Japanese and carrying through the new-democratic revolution. For, as Mao went on to point out:

In semi-colonial, semi-feudal and divided China, many people have for years dreamed of developing industry, building up national defence, and bringing well-being to the people and prosperity and power to the nation, but all their dreams have been shattered. Many well-intentioned educators, scientists and students have buried themselves in their own work or studies and paid no attention to politics in the belief that they could serve the country with their knowledge, but this too has turned out to be a dream, a dream that has been shattered. This indeed is a good sign, for the shattering of these childish dreams marks a starting-point on China's road towards prosperity and strength. The Chinese people have learned many things in the war; they know that after the defeat of the Japanese aggressors they must build a new-democratic China enjoying independence, freedom, democracy, unity, prosperity and strength, all of which are interrelated and indispensable. If they do so, then a bright future lies before China. The productive forces of the Chinese people will be released and given every possibility to develop only when the political system of New Democracy obtains in all parts of China. More and more people are coming to understand this point every day.[21]

Here Mao emphasized the basic principle that revolution was the motive force in society and the basis for releasing the productive forces, that the liberation of the Chinese nation, and the Chinese working people in particular, and the building of a prosperous country meeting the needs of the masses of people all depended on "putting politics in command." This was a fundamental truth that Mao repeatedly emphasized, not only in carrying through the new-democratic revolution to victory but in the period of socialist revolution that followed upon this victory.

Combat Capitulationism

As pointed out before, there were forces within the Communist Party itself, some of whom had originally opposed the formation of the united front against Japan, who once that united front was formed flipped over to an outright capitulationist policy and advocated the virtual or even actual submission of the Communist

Party and the armed forces and even the liberated areas under its leadership to the control of the Kuomintang. In waging a very sharp struggle within the Communist Party to defeat these tendencies Mao pointed out the relationship between a line of class capitulation put forward within the Communist Party and a line of national capitulation to Japanese imperialism with regard to the struggle of the Chinese nation as a whole. Mao showed how these two capitulationist tendencies were linked together and mutually re-enforced each other.[22]

Only the proletariat and its Communist Party, as Mao repeatedly stressed and struggled for, could lead a thoroughgoing resistance to Japan and could carry the struggle through to complete victory. Only the proletariat and its Communist Party could, in the concrete historical conditions of China and the international situation, lead the bourgeois-democratic revolution in China to victory, let alone lead it forward to the stage of socialist revolution.

Throughout the period of the Anti-Japanese United Front and the war of resistance to Japan, as throughout the Chinese revolution as a whole, Mao not only based the line and policy of the Communist Party on the analysis of the class forces within China and the situation in the country as a whole but on an analysis of the international situation at each of its different stages and of the class forces involved in the struggle in the international arena. When, in September, 1939, World War 2 broke out, Mao immediately analyzed its imperialist character on both sides and stressed that:

On whichever side, the Anglo-French or the German, the war that has just broken out is an unjust, predatory and imperialist war. The Communist Parties and the people of all countries should rise up against it and expose the imperialist character of both belligerents, for this imperialist war brings only harm and no benefit whatever to the people of the world, and they should expose the criminal acts of the social-democratic parties in supporting the imperialist war and betraying the interests of the proletariat... Germany started the war in order to plunder the Polish people and smash one flank of the Anglo-French imperialist front. By its nature, Germany's war is imperialist and should be opposed, not approved. As for Britain and France, they have regarded Poland as an object of plunder for their finance capital, exploited her to thwart the German imperialist attempt at a world re-division of the spoils, and made her a flank of their own imperialist front. Thus their war is an imperialist war, their so-called aid to Poland being merely for the purpose of contending with Germany for the domination of Poland, and this war, too, should be opposed, not approved.[23]

On the other hand Mao continued to correctly apply the policy of making use of contradictions among the reactionary forces, including between the two imperialist blocs engaged in the imperialist war at that time. This made it possible to continue the united front with Chiang Kai-shek, the lackey of U.S. and British imperialism, and on the basis of the broadest possible unity to wage resistance to Japanese aggression in China without falling into the policy of siding with one imperialist bloc against the other. The fact that the overall character of the world war then was imperialist did not negate the revolutionary role of the Chinese nation's war of resistance against Japan, and vice versa.

Independence and Initiative in United Front

Crucial to maintaining a revolutionary line in this situation and correctly grasping and handling the relationship between the struggle in China and the international struggle was the question of maintaining the independence and initiative of the Communist Party and the armed forces and liberated areas under its leadership. Without this the Communist Party would have, in fact, led masses of Chinese people into joining with and depending upon one imperialist bloc in the situation of inter-imperialist war. Exactly by maintaining and fighting for initiative and independence was it possible for the Communist Party to continue to correctly maintain the united front and wage the war of resistance against Japan.

Later, the German attack on the Soviet Union in 1941 brought a change in the overall character of World War 2 from an inter-imperialist war to one whose main character and objective overall was the defense of socialism and the victory of those forces allied with the Soviet Union. In these circumstances Mao continued to oppose the line, which grew stronger during that period, of subordinating the Communist Party, and the armed forces and liberated areas under its leadership, to the Kuomintang and its British and U.S. masters. He continued to fight for the policy of maintaining independence and initiative and to struggle for the leadership of the proletariat in the anti-Japanese war. Once again, in doing this Mao based himself on a class analysis of the various forces in China and on an international level. And once again it is this correct method and this correct line which led to the victory of the Chinese people in the anti-Japanese war and prevented Chiang Kai-shek and his imperialist masters from seizing the fruits of victory of the Chinese people's heroic struggle.

As an important part of revolutionary strategy Mao knew how to take account of and utilize contradictions in the reactionary camp in order to advance the revolution at each point. But he also

knew and armed people with an understanding of the difference between such contradictions and the basic contradiction between the
people and the reactionaries. This was decisive both for carrying
through the revolution at the particular stage and for building up
the revolutionary forces of the masses and preparing to carry the
revolution forward to the next stage and ultimately to complete
victory.

New-Democratic Revolution

It was during the anti-Japanese war in particular that Mao further developed the theory and strategy of new democracy and its
application to the concrete conditions in China at that time. "The
Chinese Revolution and the Chinese Communist Party," written in
December, 1939, and "On New Democracy," written in January,
1940, are both major works of this period in which Mao further developed and elaborated the line of new-democratic revolution. In
"The Chinese Revolution and the Chinese Communist Party," in
particular, Mao further developed the class analysis he first made
in "Analysis of the Classes in Chinese Society" in 1926 and specifically applied class analysis to the situation at that time and to the
alignment of the various forces in China in the anti-Japanese war.

Further, in that same work, in setting forth the character of the
Chinese revolution, Mao thoroughly explained:

What, indeed, is the character of the Chinese revolution at the present
stage? Is it a bourgeois-democratic or a proletarian-socialist revolution?
Obviously, it is not the latter but the former . . .

However, in present-day China the bourgeois-democratic revolution is
no longer of the old general type, which is now obsolete, but one of a new
special type. We call this type the new-democratic revolution and it is
developing in all other colonial and semi-colonial countries as well as in
China. The new-democratic revolution is part of the world proletarian-socialist revolution, for it resolutely opposes imperialism, i.e., international
capitalism. Politically, it strives for the joint dictatorship of the revolutionary classes over the imperialists, traitors and reactionaries, and opposes the transformation of Chinese society into a society under bourgeois
dictatorship. Economically, it aims at the nationalization of all the big
enterprises and capital of the imperialists, traitors and reactionaries, and
the distribution among the peasants of the land held by the landlords,
while preserving private capitalist enterprise in general and not
eliminating the rich-peasant economy. Thus, the new type of democratic
revolution clears the way for capitalism on the one hand and creates the
prerequisites for socialism on the other. The present stage of the Chinese
revolution is a stage of transition between the abolition of the colonial,
semi-colonial and semi-feudal society and the establishment of a socialist

society, *i.e.*, it is a process of new-democratic revolution. This process, begun only after the First World War and the Russian October Revolution, started in China with the May 4th Movement of 1919. A new-democratic revolution is an anti-imperialist and anti-feudal revolution of the broad masses of the people under the leadership of the proletariat. Chinese society can advance to socialism only through such a revolution; there is no other way.[24]

In concluding this work, Mao sums up the development of the Chinese revolution as follows:

To complete China's bourgeois-democratic revolution (the new-democratic revolution) and to transform it into a socialist revolution when all the necessary conditions are ripe—such is the sum total of the great and glorious revolutionary task of the Chinese Communist Party... The democratic revolution is the necessary preparation for the socialist revolution, and the socialist revolution is the inevitable sequel to the democratic revolution. The ultimate aim for which all communists strive is to bring about a socialist and communist society. A clear understanding of both the differences and the interconnections between the democratic and the socialist revolutions is indispensable to correct leadership in the Chinese revolution.[25]

Proletarian Leadership Key

The link between the two revolutions and the necessary condition both for victory in the democratic revolution and the advance to the socialist revolution was the leadership of the proletariat. This is something which Mao consistently fought for and gave leadership in achieving. It was a basic point he explained over and over again, including in this work, and a condition he repeatedly and resolutely struggled inside and outside the Communist Party to realize and develop.

In "On New Democracy" Mao analyzed again the development of the bourgeois-democratic revolution in China and the line of new democracy. He explained that new democracy would be the stage of the Chinese revolution for a considerable period and that "In the course of its progress, there may be a number of further sub-stages, because of changes on the enemy's side and within the ranks of our allies, but the fundamental character of the revolution remains unchanged."[26]

Again, in this work Mao paid particular attention to analyzing the role of the bourgeoisie in the Chinese revolution and explained how it occupied a different place in the struggle than the bourgeoisie in tsarist Russia. This constituted an important aspect in which the Chinese revolution differed from the Russian revolution, even though in the latter there was a stage of bourgeois-democratic revolution preceding the proletarian-socialist revolution. At the same time Mao analyzed the tendency of the Chinese bourgeoisie to conciliate with the enemy and the fact that it was not even as thoroughgoing a revolutionary class in China at that time as were the bourgeoisies of the capitalist countries of the West in the period of the rise of capitalism there.[27]

Applying this to the situation in China at that time Mao summed up that, "Today, whoever can lead the people in driving out Japanese imperialism and introducing democratic government will be the saviours of the people. History has proved that the Chinese bourgeoisie cannot fulfil this responsibility, which inevitably falls upon the shoulders of the proletariat."[28] Mao went on to point out that "In present-day China, the anti-Japanese united front represents the new-democratic form of state."[29] This was in accordance not only with the correct analysis of the necessary stage of new democracy in general but also with the particular sub-stage at that time, represented by the struggle of the Chinese nation against Japan and those Chinese traitors who collaborated with it. But, again, in this specific sub-stage of the Chinese revolution, and more generally, overall what gave the united front its revolutionary character and what defined this overall stage of struggle as *new* democracy was, as Mao insisted, the leadership of the proletariat and its Communist Party.

It was this line, this theory and strategy of new democracy, which guided the Chinese proletariat and masses of people and the Chinese nation as a whole in winning victory in the war of resistance against Japan. This victory represented the end of the particular sub-stage within the general stage of new democracy. The defeat of the Japanese could not and did not mean an end to the new-democratic revolution in China because it did not yet represent the complete victory of the Chinese people over imperialism and its domestic lackeys, in particular the feudal landlord class and the big bourgeoisie (specifically the bureaucrat-capitalists whose accumulation of capital was merged with their ruling position in the state and the one-party dictatorship of the Kuomintang).

Civil War Against KMT

Naturally, with the defeat of Japanese imperialism, the U.S. imperialists, together with and through their lackey Chiang Kai-shek, attempted to seize the fruits of this victory. Mao led the

Chinese Communist Party in skillfully negotiating with the
Kuomintang, even making certain concessions while refusing to
compromise basic principles—giving up certain liberated areas but
refusing to give up arms and disband its armed forces and refusing
to capitulate to and subordinate itself to U.S. imperialism and its
lackeys represented by Chiang Kai-shek.

The line of the Chinese Communist Party under Mao's leadership, during and with the victory of the anti-Japanese war, had
been to bring about the dismantling of Chiang Kai-shek's one-
party dictatorship, representing the interests of imperialism,
feudalism and bureaucrat-capitalism, and replace it with the joint
dictatorship of the revolutionary classes in China, led by the proletariat. This was the form of state power corresponding to the
stage of new democracy. And it was the basic form of rule that was
exercised in the liberated areas under the leadership of the Communist Party.

But Chiang Kai-shek, with his imperialist backers, especially in
the U.S., refused to accept this. Not only did they continue to attack the Communist Party and the armed forces and liberated
areas under its leadership all during the anti-Japanese war, but
right after the victory in that war they made preparations for and
launched an all-out assault, attempting to impose their reactionary
rule throughout China. But the result was exactly the opposite.
Because of the correct line and leadership of Mao Tsetung, when
Chiang Kai-shek did unleash civil war the Chinese Communist Party was able to expose and increasingly isolate and defeat Chiang
Kai-shek's forces, to expand the liberated areas and, through a battle of three years, drive Chiang Kai-shek from the mainland and
liberate almost all of China, bringing the new-democratic revolution to a triumphant conclusion and ushering in the socialist era in
China.

But, once more, in the period between the defeat of Japan and
the beginning of this final battle for the completion of the new-
democratic revolution, there was considerable and intense struggle
within the Chinese Communist Party over the question of whether
or not it was possible to wage struggle against and defeat Chiang
Kai-shek, backed as he was by U.S. imperialism. Mao led this
struggle within the Chinese Communist Party against those who
overestimated the strength of U.S. imperialism, put too much
stock in the atom bomb and believed it to be all-powerful and
decisive and who doubted the ability of the Chinese people and the
Chinese revolutionary forces to wage a successful war of liberation
against U.S. imperialism and its lackey Chiang Kai-shek.

Struggle for Revolutionary Victory

As part of this important and decisive inner-Party struggle Mao wrote an article, "Some Points in Appraisal of the Present International Situation," in April of 1946, in which he stressed that while the Soviet Union would correctly come to certain agreements and compromises with the victorious imperialist states, specifically Britain, France and the United States, nevertheless, "Such compromise does not require the people in the countries of the capitalist world to follow suit and make compromises at home. The people in those countries will continue to wage different struggles in accordance with their different conditions."[30]

There is no doubt that here Mao had in mind not only the struggle in the capitalist countries themselves, such as Britain, France and the United States, but also in those areas where these imperialist powers, and the U.S. in particular, were striving to maintain colonial domination in one form or another. As a footnote to this article by Mao Tsetung explained, this document was written "since some comrades overestimated the strength of imperialism, underestimated the strength of the people, feared U.S. imperialism and feared the outbreak of a new world war," and therefore "showed weakness in the face of the armed attacks of the U.S.-Chiang Kai-shek reactionary gang and dared not resolutely oppose counter-revolutionary war with revolutionary war. In this document Comrade Mao Tsetung was combatting such erroneous thinking."[31]

It is also the case that Mao was countering the opinion of Stalin, who at that time advised the Chinese Communist Party not to wage an all-out struggle for power against Chiang Kai-shek but instead to make the best possible agreement with him for the time being. In this respect Stalin also overestimated the strength of U.S. imperialism and underestimated the strength of the people, and this re-enforced those inside the Chinese Communist Party who "dared not resolutely oppose counter-revolutionary war with revolutionary war." It should be noted, however, that (as he himself later commented) Stalin was glad to be proved wrong by the successful revolutionary struggle in China. And there was nothing to say that Chinese communists had to accept Stalin's wrong advice. Whether they did or not depended on their own line, as shown by Mao's rejection of this advice, his daring to lead the war of liberation against Chiang Kai-shek and U.S. imperialism—and to carry it through to victory.

This ideological struggle within the Chinese Communist Party was crucial in laying the basis for successfully leading the masses in waging the war of liberation and bringing to a victorious conclusion the new-democratic revolution in China. On October 1, 1949 Mao proclaimed the founding of the People's Republic of China. The Chinese revolution had thus entered the socialist stage through the road of the new-democratic revolution. The question of how to advance from a colonial or semi-colonial and semi-feudal society to a socialist society had in fact been answered. And it was Mao Tsetung who, by taking part in the concrete practice of the Chinese revolution and applying the universal principles of Marxism-Leninism to it, had developed the theory and strategy of this historic revolutionary advance.

On the eve of the complete victory of the new-democratic revolution, in reviewing its triumphant course and preparing for the next stage of the revolution, Mao summed up the crucial question of proletarian leadership. He recalled how earlier Chinese progressives had looked to the West for China's salvation and took up "the new learning" imported and adopted from there as a weapon against the old feudal culture in China.

"For quite a long time," Mao said, speaking especially of the period from the 1840s to the beginning of the 20th century,

those who had acquired the new learning felt confident that it would save China, and very few of them had any doubts on this score, as the adherents of the old learning had. Only modernization could save China, only learning from foreign countries could modernize China. Among the foreign countries, only the Western capitalist countries were then progressive, as they had successfully built modern bourgeois states. The Japanese had been successful in learning from the West, and the Chinese also wished to learn from the Japanese. . .

Imperialist aggression shattered the fond dreams of the Chinese about learning from the West. It was very odd—why were the teachers always committing aggression against their pupil? The Chinese learned a good deal from the West, but they could not make it work and were never able to realize their ideals. Their repeated struggles, including such a countrywide movement as the Revolution of 1911, all ended in failure. Day by day, conditions in the country got worse, and life was made impossible. Doubts arose, increased and deepened. World War I shook the whole globe. The Russians made the October Revolution and created the world's first socialist state. Under the leadership of Lenin and Stalin, the revolutionary energy of the great proletariat and labouring people of Russia, hitherto latent and unseen by foreigners, suddenly erupted like a volcano, and the Chinese and all mankind began to see the Russians in a new light. Then, and only then, did the Chinese enter an entirely new era in their thinking and their life. They found Marxism-Leninism, the universally applicable truth, and the face of China began to change.[32]

In this way, Mao concluded, China was able to embark on the revolutionary road of new democracy. In this way it was able to advance to "a people's republic led by the working class," to socialism, the real salvation of the Chinese people.

Philosophical Contributions

Not only did Mao elaborate the line of new democracy in terms of the political struggle and lead the battle on all fronts to establish the leadership of the proletariat in order to carry through the new-democratic revolution and advance to the socialist stage, but he also made important contributions in the sphere of Marxist philosophy as a necessary part of developing, defending and applying the line of new-democratic revolution.

In 1937, in the early period of the united front against Japan and the anti-Japanese war, Mao wrote two profound philosophical works, "On Practice" and "On Contradiction." These works made a tremendous contribution to Marxist philosophy in general. But more specifically they were aimed at combatting erroneous tendencies within the Chinese Communist Party at that time regarding the current struggle: both the tendency to deny the need for the united front and the failure to recognize the current stage of struggle characterized by the war of resistance to Japan, on the one hand; and, on the other hand, the tendency to deny the need for the leading role of the proletariat in the united front, to subordinate the proletariat and the Communist Party to the Kuomintang and the class forces it represented and therefore to fail to make preparations in the current stage of struggle for the future advance to the completion of the new-democratic revolution and the beginning of the socialist revolution.

In "On Practice" Mao set forth the philosophical basis, in particular with regard to the theory of knowledge, for both these right and "left" errors:

It often happens, however, that thinking lags behind reality; this is because man's cognition is limited by numerous social conditions. We are opposed to die-hards in the revolutionary ranks whose thinking fails to advance with changing objective circumstances and has manifested itself historically as Right opportunism. These people fail to see that the struggle of opposites has already pushed the objective process forward while their knowledge has stopped at the old stage. This is characteristic of the thinking of all die-hards. Their thinking is divorced from social practice, and they cannot march ahead to guide the chariot of society; they simply trail behind, grumbling that it goes too fast and trying to drag it back or turn it in the opposite direction.

We are also opposed to "Left" phrase-mongering. The thinking of "Left-
ists" outstrips a given stage of development of the objective process;
some regard their fantasies as truth, while others strain to realize in the
present an ideal which can only be realized in the future. They alienate
themselves from the current practice of the majority of the people and
from the realities of the day, and show themselves adventurist in their actions.[33]

Process of Development

Further, Mao analyzed from a philosophical standpoint the basis
for the change in China's bourgeois-democratic revolution from the
old-democratic to the new-democratic revolution, the basis for the
sub-stages within the new-democratic revolution, as well as the
basis for the advance through the new-democratic to the socialist
revolution:

The fundamental contradiction in the process of development of a thing
and the essence of the process determined by this fundamental contradiction will not disappear until the process is completed; but in a lengthy process the conditions usually differ at each stage. The reason is that,
although the nature of the fundamental contradiction in the process of
development of a thing and the essence of the process remain unchanged,
the fundamental contradiction becomes more and more intensified as it
passes from one stage to another in the lengthy process. In addition,
among the numerous major and minor contradictions which are determined or influenced by the fundamental contradiction, some become intensified, some are temporarily or partially resolved or mitigated, and some
new ones emerge; hence the process is marked by stages. If people do not
pay attention to the stages in the process of development of a thing, they
cannot deal with its contradictions properly...
Take the process of China's bourgeois-democratic revolution, which
began with the Revolution of 1911; it, too, has several distinct stages. In
particular, the revolution in its period of bourgeois leadership and the
revolution in its period of proletarian leadership represent two vastly different historical stages. In other words, proletarian leadership has fundamentally changed the whole face of the revolution, has brought about a
new alignment of classes, given rise to a tremendous upsurge in the peasant revolution, imparted thoroughness to the revolution against imperialism and feudalism, created the possibility of the transition from the
democratic revolution to the socialist revolution, and so on. None of these
was possible in the period when the revolution was under bourgeois
leadership. Although no change has taken place in the nature of the fundamental contradiction in the process as a whole, i.e., in the anti-
imperialist, anti-feudal, democratic-revolutionary nature of the process
(the opposite of which is its semi-colonial and semi-feudal nature),
nonetheless this process has passed through several stages of development in the course of more than twenty years.
...These stages are marked by particular features such as the inten-

sification of certain contradictions (*e.g.*, the Agrarian Revolutionary War and the Japanese invasion of the four northeastern provinces), the partial or temporary resolution of other contradictions (*e.g.*, the destruction of the Northern warlords and our confiscation of the land of the landlords), and the emergence of yet other contradictions (*e.g.*, the conflicts among the new warlords, and the landlords' recapture of the land after the loss of our revolutionary base areas in the south).[34]

While, as noted before, "On Practice" and "On Contradiction" have enduring and general application and have greatly enriched Marxist philosophy, they were of specific and critical importance in the Chinese revolution at that particular stage in laying the basis for the advance through the anti-Japanese war to the completion of the democratic revolution in China on a new basis and the advance in this way to socialism. As noted at the start of this chapter, the victory of the new-democratic revolution in China and the advance of China to socialism represented a great leap forward not only for the people of China but for the people of the whole world in their struggle against imperialism and reaction and for socialism and ultimately communism. It brought profound changes not only in China but in the entire international situation and in the class struggle internationally. As the statement from the leading bodies of the Chinese Party and state on the death of Mao Tsetung summed up:

During the period of the new-democratic revolution, Chairman Mao, in accordance with the universal truth of Marxism-Leninism and by combining it with the concrete practice of the Chinese revolution, creatively laid down the general line and general policy of the new-democratic revolution, founded the Chinese People's Liberation Army and pointed out that the seizure of political power by armed force in China could be achieved only by following the road of building rural base areas, using the countryside to encircle the cities and finally seizing the cities, and not by any other road. He led our Party, our army and the people of our country in using people's war to overthrow the reactionary rule of imperialism, feudalism and bureaucrat-capitalism, winning the great victory of the new-democratic revolution and founding the People's Republic of China. The victory of the Chinese people's revolution led by Chairman Mao changed the situation in the East and the world and blazed a new trail for the cause of liberation of the oppressed nations and oppressed people.[35]

Upholding Proletarian Internationalism

As a socialist country, the People's Republic of China, as well as the Chinese Communist Party, under the leadership of Mao Tsetung continued to support the revolutionary struggles of the

people of the world, including the struggle for national liberation
of the peoples of the colonial countries. Having only just achieved
its own liberation, China united with the Korean people in the war
against U.S. aggression in the early 1950s. At the same time China
supported the struggles of the peoples of Indochina and peoples of
other areas against imperialism and reaction. Further, in the mid
and late 1950s and afterward, with the degeneration of the Soviet
party into revisionism, the betrayal by Khrushchev, Brezhnev and
others, and the restoration of capitalism in the USSR, the Chinese
Communist Party led by Mao Tsetung waged decisive struggle
against the Soviet bourgeois ruling class, including an active
ideological struggle to expose and combat the sham Marxism and
counter-revolutionary treachery of these Soviet revisionists.

A most important issue in this struggle was the question of
whether or not to support the revolutionary movements of the
peoples of Asia, Africa and Latin America, which had swelled into
a mighty anti-imperialist torrent following World War 2. *Apologists of Neo-Colonialism* was a major article written by the
Chinese Communist Party as a polemic against the Soviet revisionists on this decisive question.

This article was written in 1963, when the Soviet revisionists
were only in the process of carrying out the all-around restoration
of capitalism in the USSR and their overall relationship with U.S.
imperialism then was characterized by capitulation to and collaboration with it. Still, *Apologists of Neo-Colonialism* sets forth
basic analysis and basic principles which retain great importance
and validity today in the situation where there have been significant changes in the world, where contention has clearly replaced
collusion as the principal aspect of the relationship between the
USSR and the U.S., and where U.S. imperialism is no longer alone
the chief world exploiter and oppressor and bulwark of colonialism.
Today the two superpowers, both of which practice neo-colonialism, are the main enemies of the people of the world and
must overall be the main target of the national liberation struggles
in Asia, Africa and Latin America.

In this article the Chinese Communist Party sharply pointed out
that with regard to the struggles in Asia, Africa and Latin
America:

An important line of demarcation between the Marxist-Leninists and
the modern revisionists is the attitude taken towards this extremely
sharp issue of contemporary world politics. The Marxist-Leninists firmly
side with the oppressed nations and actively support the national liberation movement. The modern revisionists in fact side with the imperialists

and colonialists and repudiate and oppose the national liberation movement in every possible way.[36]

Attitude Toward Revolutionary Movements

The Soviet revisionists attempted to subvert and actually suppress the revolutionary movements of the people in the colonial countries because they feared, and rightly so, that these movements would interfere with their collaboration with U.S. imperialism and their attempts to emerge as a superpower. Khrushchev and Co. claimed that the colonial system was on the verge of extinction in Asia, Africa and Latin America and that there was no longer any significant revolutionary mass struggle to be waged for national liberation in these areas. In fact Khrushchev regarded such struggles as extremely dangerous.

In answer to this the Chinese Communist Party pointed out that:

> The facts are clear. After World War II the imperialists have certainly not given up colonialism, but have merely adopted a new form, neo-colonialism. An important characteristic of such neo-colonialism is that the imperialists have been forced to change their old style of direct colonial rule in some areas and to adopt a new style of colonial rule and exploitation by relying on the agents they have selected and trained. The imperialists headed by the United States enslave or control the colonial countries and countries which have already declared their independence by organizing military blocs, setting up military bases, establishing "federations" or "communities," and fostering puppet regimes. By means of economic "aid" or other forms, they retain these countries as markets for their goods, sources of raw material and outlets for their export of capital, plunder the riches and suck the blood of the people of these countries. Moreover, they use the United Nations as an important tool for interfering in the internal affairs of such countries and for subjecting them to military, economic and cultural aggression. When they are unable to continue their rule over these countries by "peaceful" means, they engineer military *coups d'etat*, carry out subversion, or even resort to direct armed intervention and aggression . . .
> This neo-colonialism is a more pernicious and sinister form of colonialism.[37]

The Chinese Communist Party thoroughly exposed the bankruptcy of the revisionist leaders of the Communist Party of the Soviet Union (CPSU) on these vital questions. It pointed out that:

> The leaders of the CPSU have also created the theory that the national liberation movement has entered upon a "new stage" having economic

tasks as its core. Their argument is that, whereas "formerly, the struggle was carried on mainly in the political sphere," today the economic question has become the "central task" and "the basic link in the further development of the revolution.". . .

The primary and most urgent task facing these countries is still the further development of the struggle against imperialism, old and new colonialism, and their lackeys. This struggle is still being waged fiercely in the political, economic, military, cultural, ideological and other spheres. And the struggles in all these spheres still find their most concentrated expression in political struggle, which often unavoidably develops into armed struggle when the imperialists resort to direct or indirect armed suppression. It is important for the newly independent countries to develop their independent economy. But this task must never be separated from the struggle against imperialism, old and new colonialism, and their lackeys.

Like "the disappearance of colonialism," this theory of a "new stage" advocated by the leaders of the CPSU is clearly intended to whitewash the aggression against and plunder of Asia, Africa and Latin America by neo-colonialism, as represented by the United States, to cover up the sharp contradiction between imperialism and the oppressed nations and to paralyze the revolutionary struggle of the people of these continents.

According to this theory of theirs, the fight against imperialism, old and new colonialism, and their lackeys is, of course, no longer necessary, for colonialism is disappearing and economic development has become the central task of the national liberation movement. Does it not follow that the national liberation movement can be done away with altogether?. . .

The wrong line of the leaders of the CPSU completely abandons the task of fighting imperialism and colonialism and opposes wars of national liberation; this means that it wants the proletariat and the Communist Parties of the oppressed nations and countries to roll up their patriotic banner of opposing imperialism and struggling for national independence and surrender it to others. In that case, how could one even talk about an anti-imperialist united front or of proletarian leadership?

Another idea often propagated by the leaders of the CPSU is that a country can build socialism under no matter what leadership, including even that of a reactionary nationalist like Nehru. This is still farther removed from the idea of proletarian leadership.[38]

Continued Need for Proletarian Leadership

This did not mean, of course, that China did not support countries in Asia, Africa and Latin America, even those under the leadership of types like Nehru and others, in resisting imperialist domination. China assisted them in this resistance in many ways and encouraged them to strengthen such resistance. But the point being stressed was that such resistance could not substitute for nor certainly be raised above the revolutionary struggle of the masses and the need for the proletariat and its Communist Party to lead the national liberation movement to complete victory and

美帝国主义必须从它侵占的一切地方滚出去！

"U.S. imperialism must get out of all the places it has occupied!" (Chinese poster)

then lead the masses in building socialism.

And the Chinese Communist Party reaffirmed the all-important principle of the link between the national liberation struggles in the colonial countries and the struggle of the proletariat in the advanced capitalist countries, their common unity in the fight against imperialism and for the ultimate goal of socialism and finally communism:

> No one can deny that an extremely favourable revolutionary situation now exists in Asia, Africa and Latin America. Today the national liberation revolutions in Asia, Africa and Latin America are the most important forces dealing imperialism direct blows. The contradictions of the world are concentrated in Asia, Africa and Latin America.
>
> The centre of world contradictions, of world political struggles, is not fixed but shifts with changes in the international struggles and the revolutionary situation. We believe that, with the development of the contradiction and struggle between the proletariat and the bourgeoisie in Western Europe and North America, the momentous day of battle will arrive in these homes of capitalism and heartlands of imperialism. When that day comes, Western Europe and North America will undoubtedly become the centre of world political struggles, of world contradictions.[39]

Adhering to and firmly upholding proletarian internationalism, the Chinese Communist Party and the People's Republic of China under the leadership of Mao Tsetung opposed this to the stand of the revisionist rulers of the Soviet Union, pointing to the duties and responsibilities of the proletariat and its Communist Party in power in the socialist countries:

> According to Marxism-Leninism and proletarian internationalism, every socialist country which has achieved victory in its revolution must actively support and assist the liberation struggles of the oppressed nations. The socialist countries must become base areas for supporting and developing the revolution of the oppressed nations and peoples throughout the world, form the closest alliance with them and carry the proletarian world revolution through to completion.
>
> But the leaders of the CPSU virtually regard the victory of socialism in one country or several countries as the end of the proletarian world revolution. They want to subordinate the national liberation revolution to their general line of peaceful coexistence and to the national interests of their own country.[40]

At this time and in the following years Mao continued to lead the Chinese Communist Party and the Chinese people in supporting the struggles of the people in various parts of the world, especially in the countries of Asia, Africa and Latin America, since these areas had become the focal point of the contradictions of the imperialist system worldwide and the storm center of the revolutionary movement in the world. Throughout the 1960s, Mao made a number of statements at crucial points in support of key struggles in the world, especially in these areas, which rallied the Chinese people's support and called on the revolutionary people and the broad masses in all countries to stand with these struggles. Then, in 1970, during the height of U.S. aggression in Indochina, Mao issued another statement, in support of the Indochinese people as well as the people of the whole world, and especially of Asia, Africa and Latin America, in the fight against U.S. imperialism and its running dogs. During this period and after, Mao also increasingly warned the people throughout the world of the reactionary nature and role of Soviet social-imperialism, including its intensifying efforts to infiltrate and subvert revolutionary movements aimed against U.S. imperialism and pervert these into instruments of its growing contention with U.S. imperialism.

A Great Internationalist

Regardless of specific changes in the situation, Mao Tsetung continued to fight for the basic stand and line of support for the revolutionary struggle of the people in all countries, including the vital national liberation movements in Asia, Africa and Latin America, and to combat revisionism and revisionist subversion of this struggle down to his last breath. From all this we can see that Mao Tsetung's great role in relation to revolution in colonial countries lay first in developing the basic theory and strategy for advancing through the bourgeois-democratic revolution to the socialist revolution in such countries, and then in continuing to champion support for the revolutionary struggles of the people of the world, including, as a decisive part of this, assistance to the struggle of the people in the colonial countries, ideologically, politically and practically.

Today, although the situation in the various countries of Asia, Africa and Latin America varies and although the concrete conditions may differ in some ways from those during China's new-democratic revolution, nevertheless the basic theory, strategy, line and leadership provided by Mao Tsetung for revolutions in these countries stands as one of Mao's truly great and immortal contributions to Marxism-Leninism and the revolutionary struggle toward the ultimate goal of communism worldwide.

Mao talks with young fighters of the Eighth Route Army in Yenan, 1939.

Chapter 2

REVOLUTIONARY WAR AND MILITARY LINE

Introduction

The first chapter, dealing with Mao's development of the line for revolution in colonial countries, and in particular with the theory and strategy of new-democratic revolution, pointed out that Mao's contributions in that area were closely linked with those he made in the field of warfare and military strategy. This chapter takes up Mao's development of the line of people's war in China and his general contributions to Marxist military line, theory and strategy.

Basis, Fundamental Principles of Mao's Military Line

In formulating a revolutionary line on warfare and Marxist military strategy and theory, Mao summed up and learned from the contributions and writings on this subject of both Marxist revolutionary leaders and other writers and thinkers from various ages, both in China and in other countries. China itself, with its thousands of years of history and repeated uprisings of the masses and revolutionary wars, was rich in experience of warfare, both ancient and more contemporary. Also in the brief period since the proletariat had emerged on the historical scene it had been engaged in a number of countries in revolutionary wars, sometimes together with, even under the leadership of, other classes, including the bourgeoisie, against feudalism, reactionary monarchies or other forces holding back the development of capitalism, and sometimes as an independent force fighting together with other oppressed masses for the seizure of power and the establishment of a workers' state.

From the first, the leaders of the class conscious workers' movement paid considerable attention to the question of armed struggle and the role of revolutionary violence in advancing society from one historical stage to the next, in particular from capitalism to socialism and ultimately communism. Marx and Engels followed closely and wrote extensively on such historical events as the Civil War in the U.S. as well as various progressive wars in Europe and elsewhere. And in particular they followed closely and gave advice to the uprising of the workers in Paris which established the first, though short-lived, workers' government in 1871, the Paris Commune. They firmly established the basic principle of Marxism that the abolition of capitalism required as a first step the forcible overthrow of the capitalist state and the forcible suppression of the overthrown capitalist class and capitalist elements in order to advance to classless society, communism.

Engels, in such works as his "Introduction" to Marx's *The Class Struggles in France, 1848 to 1850* and his famous *Anti-Duhring* as well as in other works, summed up the recent developments in armaments and other developments which gave rise to necessary changes in the strategy and tactics of modern warfare. And he summed up political lessons from this and their application to the question of the armed uprising of the working class against the rule of capital.

Lenin, in the beginning of the 1905 Revolution in Russia, which he later would term a "dress rehearsal" for the successful seizure of power in 1917, paid particular attention to the question of the tactics of street fighting and armed insurrection which had to be developed in order to confront the military power of the Tsar. In leading the successful insurrection in Russia in October 1917, Lenin and Stalin developed Marxist theory and practice with regard to insurrection and warfare in a capitalist country—though one with backward features such as large-scale survivals of feudalism and backward conditions in the countryside. Lenin and Stalin further developed Marxist theory, strategy and tactics on revolutionary war, specifically in the civil war that followed the victorious insurrection in October 1917. It was in this war that the Russian workers and peasants, led by the Bolshevik Party and Lenin and Stalin, defeated not only the overthrown capitalists and landlords in Russia but fourteen reactionary powers that intervened on the side of counter-revolution.

And of course, in World War 2, in the great patriotic war of the USSR which ended in the defeat of the German Nazis, Stalin brilliantly led the Soviet Red Army and the Soviet people as a whole in waging revolutionary war to defeat the invasion and war of aggression of the Nazis, which became the turning point and decisive factor in the war and the defeat of the fascist axis. In the course of this, Stalin made great contributions to the revolutionary movement internationally and to communist strategy and tactics of warfare and their concrete application.

First Comprehensive Marxist Military Line

But it was Mao Tsetung who was the first among the great Marxist leaders to develop a comprehensive and complete Marxist military line and system of thought on military affairs. For over 20 years Mao Tsetung led the Chinese Communist Party, the Chinese people and the armed forces under the Communist Party's leadership in waging revolutionary warfare against the warlords, against the reactionary regime of Chiang Kai-shek, then in the united front against Japan in the anti-Japanese war, and finally in the war of liberation against Chiang Kai-shek and his U.S. backers, which resulted in the liberation of China in 1949.

Mao's development of Marxism-Leninism with regard to warfare was closely linked with the character of the Chinese revolution. For, as pointed out in the preceding chapter, from the beginning the armed revolution was fighting the armed counter-revolution in China. And this was both a specific feature and a specific advantage of the Chinese revolution.

In other words, as Mao pointed out and fought for, from the beginning warfare was the main form of the revolutionary movement in China. This was a truth that Mao established as a basic principle of the Party only through fierce struggle against right opportunists within the Party at the early stages of the Chinese revolution. It was in the course of leading the armed struggle through the various stages of the revolution that Mao fully developed his Marxist military line and strategy and system of thought on military affairs, which guided the Chinese revolution to complete victory and made lasting contributions in greatly enriching Marxism-Leninism on the question of warfare. As Mao himself was to say, for himself as well as the Communist Party and the Chinese masses which it led, it was a question of learning warfare through making warfare.

At the same time, as pointed out earlier, Mao studied and absorbed the rich lessons of warfare, especially progressive wars in China and other countries, and the thinking and analysis of revolutionary leaders, and particularly Marxist leaders, on the question of warfare. Furthermore, Mao brilliantly applied materialist dialectics to the question of warfare and the development of revolutionary strategy for warfare in China through the various stages of the Chinese revolution. Mao's military works, then, are a rich treasure house not only of Marxist thought on the question of war but also in the application of basic principles of Marxism, in particular Marxist philosophy.

Mao's military line was rooted in the basic fact that revolutionary war depends on the masses of people and can only succeed on the basis that it enjoys their support and enlists them actively in the struggle against the counter-revolutionary forces. In other words, as Mao said, a people's war is a war of the masses. This has important application not only in countries like China but universally for the revolutionary struggle in all countries. And while the military tactics Mao developed have specific relevancy and importance for countries like China during the period of the new-democratic revolution, the basic principles of Mao's military line have general application to revolutionary warfare in all countries.

From the very beginning, Mao fought for, and through the course of the revolution further deepened and forged, some of these basic principles. Of great importance among these is the principle that the Party must command the gun, and not the other way around—in other words, that the Party must lead the revolutionary armed forces and the armed struggle, and the army must never be allowed to become at the same time the political leading force of the revolution or a force independent from the political leadership of the Party; and, linked to this, that man, not weapons, is decisive in warfare, a fundamental truth that Mao fought for, defended and developed in opposition to the opportunism of old and new revisionists, from Bernstein and Kautsky to Khrushchev and Khrushchev-types in China itself.

Further, Mao developed the basic orientation which has application for oppressed nations and for socialist countries subjected to imperialist aggression, and further for all revolutionary armed forces which start off small and/or weak in opposition to their adversary—the orientation of first proceeding from the strategic defensive and waging the war in such a way as to prepare for and finally go over to the strategic offensive and on that basis carry the warfare through to victory.

In developing his line on revolutionary war, Mao based himself on and forcefully reaffirmed the fundamental Marxist analysis of the question of war. For example, in "Problems of Strategy in China's Revolutionary War," written in December 1936, Mao pointed out that "*War* is the highest form of struggle for resolving contradictions, when they have developed to a certain stage, between classes, nations, states, or political groups, and it has existed ever since the emergence of private property and of classes."[1]

Mao made clear that the purpose of the proletariat in waging war was to defeat imperialism and reaction and advance society toward the stage of communism, where war would finally be eliminated with the elimination of classes. He vividly showed that it is necessary to wage warfare in order to end warfare; as he graphically put it, in order to get rid of the gun it is necessary to pick up the gun. This was a stinging refutation of revisionist and other bourgeois trash that preaches passivity and pacifism to the masses in order to set them up for slaughter by the reactionaries and hold back the revolutionary struggle.

Further, in "Problems of War and Strategy," written in November 1938, Mao explained that "The seizure of power by armed force, the settlement of the issue by war, is the central task and the highest form of revolution. This Marxist-Leninist principle of revolution holds good universally, for China and for all other countries."[2] Mao immediately added, however, "But while the principle remains the same, its application by the party of the proletariat finds expression in varying ways according to the varying conditions."[3] As on other questions, with regard to the Marxist military line for revolutionary war, Mao concretely analyzed the concrete conditions, combatted dogmatism as well as revisionism and on this basis developed the correct military line in opposition to various opportunist military lines.

The correct military line for China's revolution was based on the correct analysis of Chinese society and the character of the Chinese revolution in general, which flowed from the basic semi-colonial, semi-feudal nature of China and its specific conditions, including its relation to various imperialist powers, during the course of this revolution. It was on this basis that Mao developed the strategy of establishing base areas, waging protracted war to surround the cities from the countryside and finally capture the cities and win nationwide political power, the correct road on which Mao led the Chinese masses in waging the successful revolutionary struggle in China.

Revolutionary Base Areas

At the very early stages of the Chinese revolution, Mao made and defended the analysis of why red political power could exist in China—that is, why it was possible to establish liberated base areas and use them as the foundation for waging revolutionary war. Mao provided leadership in carrying this out, not only in theory but in practice. In 1927 he led the Autumn Harvest Uprising, from which the armed forces were developed which established the first revolutionary base area in China in the Chingkang Mountains. The basic line of establishing base areas and waging warfare with them as the foundation was itself a brilliant application of Marxist materialist dialectics and provided the means for turning weakness and backwardness in China into a strength for the revolutionary struggle. Mao pointed out that not only was China subjected to imperialist aggression and domination, but that various imperialist powers were contending for control of China and the various reactionary forces in China were aligned with and lackeys of these contending imperialists. Therefore the reactionary forces in China were divided. Further, he pointed out that in the vast countryside of China there was "a localized agricultural economy (not a unified capitalist economy)" and this provided the economic base for relatively self-sufficient base areas to exist.[4] From the beginning Mao stressed that the armed struggle in China must be integrated with the agrarian revolution and that it was generally linked to the democratic revolution in China. He stressed that "the regions where China's Red political power has first emerged and is able to last for a long time have not been those unaffected by the democratic revolution...but regions...where the masses of workers, peasants and soldiers rose in great numbers in the course of the bourgeois-democratic revolution of 1926 and 1927."[5]

Mao pointed out that the existence and survival of such base areas was an unprecedented event in the history of the world, and he consistently pointed to the material and political reasons why such base areas could exist and could be expanded in the course of revolutionary struggle. In this he had to wage a fierce ideological struggle against putschists in the Chinese Communist Party who wanted to wage big attacks on the cities, rather than establish base areas, who wanted to attempt to seize nationwide power right away and all at once. But even more he had to wage struggle against pessimism and right opportunism, including that of Lin Piao even at this early stage of the Chinese Revolution, in the late 1920s. Such people were raising the question, "How long can we keep the red flag flying?" and doubting and challenging the strategy of establishing base areas and waging protracted warfare. Instead, such people, not believing that a revolutionary high tide in the country was imminent and being despondent in the face of temporary setbacks, wanted to go in for roving guerrilla actions and act as roving rebel bands. Mao pointed out that such an approach would isolate the revolutionary forces and the revolutionary army from the broad masses and was bound to lead to defeat. In refuting this line Mao stressed that "there will soon be a high tide of revolution" throughout the country as a whole, and specifically in response to the question of what was meant by "soon" Mao, in a now famous and powerfully poetic statement, explained it as follows:

But when I say that there will soon be a high tide of revolution in China, I am emphatically not speaking of something which in the words of some people "is possibly coming", something illusory, unattainable and devoid of significance for action. It is like a ship far out at sea whose mast-head can already be seen from the shore; it is like the morning sun in the east whose shimmering rays are visible from a high mountain top; it is like a child about to be born moving restlessly in its mother's womb.[6]

The establishment of base areas was, of course, not an end in itself, but the means and the foundation for waging revolutionary warfare. It was a question of establishing the political power of the masses through armed struggle and then using this as a support and rear area for engaging the enemy in revolutionary warfare. Here again, the role and struggle of the masses was decisive. In establishing the first base area in the Chingkang Mountains as early as 1927, Mao chose an area where the mass struggle was at a high level, and this was a most decisive factor in terms of not only establishing but being able to maintain an independent regime, a liberated base area. With this as a foundation, Mao led not only in formulating but in applying:

the policy of establishing base areas; of systematically setting up political power; of deepening the agrarian revolution; of expanding the people's armed forces by a comprehensive process of building up first the township Red Guards, then the district Red Guards, then the county Red Guards, then the local Red Army troops, all the way up to the regular Red Army troops; of spreading political power by advancing in a series of waves, etc., etc. Only thus is it possible to build the confidence of the revolutionary masses throughout the country, as the Soviet Union has built it throughout the world. Only thus is it possible to create tremendous difficulties for the reactionary ruling classes, shake their foundations and hasten their internal disintegration. Only thus is it really possible to create a Red Army which will become the chief weapon for the great revolution of the future. In short, only thus is it possible to hasten the revolutionary high tide.[7]

It was in this way that the workers' and peasants' army was in fact built up and the armed struggle against the counter-

revolutionary forces of Chiang Kai-shek was developed. From very
early on, Mao had developed some of the basic principles that were
to form the foundation of his military line. He concentrated the
many complexities of war into the formulation that the basic principle in war is to "preserve oneself and destroy the enemy." On the
other hand he applied materialist dialectics not only to
demonstrate how, overall, destroying the enemy is the principal
aspect, but to develop out of an understanding of the basic principle in war a whole series of strategic and tactical lines as well as
particular methods for waging revolutionary war and specific campaigns and battles within such a war in the concrete conditions of
the Chinese revolution at each of its stages, leading to the successful seizure of nationwide political power.

Mao stressed that in fighting battles and attacking the enemy it
was necessary to concentrate the forces of the revolutionary army,
while in order to develop and spread revolutionary struggle among
the masses it was correct to disperse the armed forces of the
revolution. Both of these were important, for unless the masses
were aroused and unless the armed struggle was integrated with
the revolutionary struggle of the masses, in particular the agrarian
revolution in the countryside, then despite its heroism and even
despite clever tactics in fighting, the Red Army would degenerate
into banditry and warlordism. It would lack both a political and
economic basis for waging revolutionary war, relying on the
masses of people. On the other hand, unless the revolutionary army adopted and successfully carried out correct military strategy
and tactics, and in particular the principle of concentrating its
forces, amassing a superior force in any particular battle against
the enemy, then it would not be able to sustain the base areas it
had established and to further arouse and mobilize the masses in
revolutionary struggle, build up the armed forces of the revolution
and gradually expand the revolutionary war. In "A Single Spark
Can Start a Prairie Fire," Mao summed up the military principles
which had been developed through the course of three years of
armed struggle:

> The tactics we have derived from the struggle of the past three years are
> indeed different from any other tactics, ancient or modern, Chinese or
> foreign. With our tactics, the masses can be aroused for struggle on an
> ever-broadening scale, and no enemy, however powerful, can cope with us.
> Ours are guerrilla tactics. They consist mainly of the following points:
> "Divide our forces to arouse the masses, concentrate our forces to deal
> with the enemy."
> "The enemy advances, we retreat; the enemy camps, we harass; the

enemy tires, we attack; the enemy retreats, we pursue."

"To extend stable base areas, employ the policy of advancing in waves; when pursued by a powerful enemy, employ the policy of circling around."

"Arouse the largest numbers of the masses in the shortest possible time and by the best possible methods."

These tactics are just like casting a net; at any moment we should be able to cast it or draw it in. We cast it wide to win over the masses and draw it in to deal with the enemy. Such are the tactics we have used for the past three years.[8]

Of particular importance was what came to be called "the sixteen-character formula: 'The enemy advances, we retreat; the enemy camps, we harass; the enemy tires, we attack; the enemy retreats, we pursue.' " Several years later, Mao was to point out that "The sixteen-character formula covered the basic principles for combating 'encirclement and suppression'; it covered the two stages of the strategic defensive and the strategic offensive, and within the defensive, it covered the two stages of the strategic retreat and the strategic counter-offensive. What came later was only a development of this formula."[9] Through the development and application of these principles Mao led the revolutionary armed forces in defeating four successive "encirclement and suppression" campaigns launched by Chiang Kai-shek in an attempt to wipe out the revolutionary armed forces and the revolutionary base areas. All during this period, however, there was sharp opposition and interference within the Communist Party itself from various "left" opportunist lines. Most damaging of these lines was the "left" opportunism of Wang Ming, who was later to flip over into outright right opportunism and capitulationism during the anti-Japanese war and the united front against Japan.

Combatting Opportunist Lines

In this period of the early 1930s Wang Ming's "left" opportunist line with regard to military affairs underestimated the enemy and insisted on the strategy of attacking large cities in opposition to the correct line of establishing and linking up base areas and luring the enemy in deep in order to strike at it, concentrate superior forces in particular battles and wipe out its troops, and in this way break through the encirclement and in the particular campaign go from the defensive to the offensive. Owing to the interference of Wang Ming's "left" opportunist line, the Chinese Communist Party and the revolutionary army under its leadership were finally unable to defeat the fifth "encirclement and suppression" campaign launched

Chinese peasants from the liberated areas mobilize to support the People's Liberation Army in the war for national liberation.

by Chiang Kai-shek against them, and were forced in 1934 to abandon the central base area in the south. Mao Tsetung, summing up
these developments, led the Chinese Communist Party's Red Army
in carrying out what became a historical event without precedent,
the Long March. For two years, fighting on the average of more
than one battle a day, and winding over several thousand miles, the
Red Army was finally able to break through the encirclement of
Chiang Kai-shek's forces and advance to the northwest,
establishing base areas there. The advance to the northwest was not
simply a question of fighting through, breaking the encirclement
and avoiding suppression and annihilation by Chiang Kai-shek's
forces, but was directly linked to the question of waging warfare
against the Japanese, who had invaded the northeast of China and
were preparing to advance into the rest of the country.

In January 1935, a decisive turning point took place in the
history of the Chinese Communist Party and the Chinese revolution. An expanded meeting of the Political Bureau of the Party's
Central Committee was held in which Mao Tsetung's military line
was upheld in opposition to the opportunist line of Wang Ming and
others, and Mao's leadership of the Chinese Communist Party and
the Red Army was affirmed. This laid the basis for correctly carrying out the armed struggle against Japan, which was posing itself
as the urgent requirement of the revolutionary struggle at the
time.

In solidifying Mao's revolutionary line and leadership with
regard to the armed struggle and within the Chinese Communist
Party a sharp struggle also had to be waged against the flightism
and splittism of Chang Kuo-tao, who attempted to set up a bogus
Central Committee in opposition to Mao's leadership and refused
to unite his armed forces with those under Mao's leadership to
wage the struggle against Japan. Looking at the temporary and
superficial phenomenon that the Communist Party and the Red
Army under its leadership had lost a large part of their forces
through the course of the Long March, and acting in the manner of
a warlord attempting to carve out territory for himself, Chang
Kuo-tao insisted on retreating away from the task of establishing
base areas and using them to engage in revolutionary warfare
against the Japanese aggressors. Mao, in opposition to this, insisted that it was through the establishment of these base areas
and the waging of the war against Japan and the full mobilizing
and arousing of the masses for this struggle that the Chinese Communist Party and the revolutionary armed forces would grow and
become stronger. Through this struggle Chang Kuo-tao was

defeated and soon after defected to the Kuomintang reactionaries. Through the course of the Long March, keeping firmly in mind the objective of establishing the base areas for waging the struggle against Japan as well as the immediate objective of breaking through and defeating the "encirclement and suppression" of Chiang Kai-shek, Mao brilliantly applied military strategy. In particular, he led the revolutionary armed forces in gaining the initiative and exercising flexibility under extremely difficult circumstances. Mao pointed out in his military writings that the question of initiative was closely linked to the question of superiority, and it was the case during the Long March that the reactionary forces of Chiang Kai-shek enjoyed strategic superiority in terms of numbers and training as well as armaments. But, taking that into account and applying materialist dialectics and specific principles of military strategy and tactics based on them, Mao led the revolutionary armed forces in establishing tactical superiority in certain battles and in seizing the initiative tactically within the situation where the enemy strategically had superiority. At the same time, Mao also correctly handled the dialectical relationship between the main direction and secondary directions—that is, he led the Red Army in shifting its directions tactically in order to fight battles in the most favorable circumstances, in order to be able to launch surprise attacks on the enemy, while at the same time adhering to the main direction of advancing to the north in order to be able to wage revolutionary warfare against Japanese aggression.

"Problems Of Strategy In China's Revolutionary War," written by Mao in December 1936, summed up the experience of revolutionary war in China under the leadership of the Chinese Communist Party up to that point and laid the basis for waging revolutionary war in resistance to Japanese aggression. In this work Mao reaffirmed the fundamental principle that he had fought for and set forth in earlier works, such as "The Struggle In The Chingkang Mountains," in November of 1928, and "On Correcting Mistaken Ideas In The Party," written in December 1929—the principle that the Party must lead the army and the armed struggle and that the revolutionary struggle must have the ideological and political leadership of the proletariat.

This leadership was not only established through the vanguard role of the Communist Party—which was overall the most important aspect of the proletariat's leading role—but also (if secondarily) was realized through the active participation of a number of class-conscious workers as backbone forces in the Communist Party and the revolutionary army founded by Mao. In fact, Mao had taken with him to the first base area in the Chingkang Mountains many workers who had been recruited out of various struggles of the working class. Thus it is fundamentally wrong to argue that the Chinese revolution, in proceeding from the countryside to the cities, represented the hegemony of the petty bourgeoisie (specifically the peasantry) rather than the leadership of the proletariat in the revolutionary movement. Such a position fails to grasp the dialectics of the revolution in China in its new-democratic stage, and in particular the fact that the peasantry was the *main* force but the working class—principally through the line and policies of its Party and secondarily through the backbone role of class-conscious workers—remained the *leading* force.

In "Problems of Strategy in China's Revolutionary War" Mao emphasized that: "Therefore, in an era when the proletariat has already appeared on the political stage, the responsibility for leading China's revolutionary war inevitably falls on the shoulders of the Chinese Communist Party."[10] This work was written to combat various erroneous tendencies within the Chinese Communist Party and in particular against various forms of dogmatism and mechanical thinking—either to regard it as sufficient to study and understand the laws of war in general, making no distinction between reactionary and progressive or revolutionary wars; or to mechanically copy the experience of the Civil War in Russia leading to the establishment of the Soviet Union; or to regard the early experience of the Chinese Communist Party when it was still within the Kuomintang as the only valid or most valuable experience, negating the rich lessons of the revolutionary war of ten years against Chiang Kai-shek's reactionary forces that followed the breakup of the alliance with the Kuomintang after Chiang's coup in 1927.

In answering this Mao pointed out that the laws of war, the laws of revolutionary war, and the laws of China's revolutionary war were all problems which required study, analysis, and solution, and that while there were certain basic principles to warfare in general, to revolutionary warfare in particular, and specifically to China's revolutionary war, it was necessary to continue to apply concrete analysis to concrete conditions and continue to develop the correct military strategy. While the line for waging revolutionary warfare could, of course, not be divorced from an overall analysis of the character of the Chinese revolution in general as well as at the particular stage of resistance against Japan, and while it could not be divorced from a correct political line in general, it was also necessary to study and develop specific lines and policies on warfare itself. As Mao explained, "Our revolutionary war has proved that we need a correct Marxist military line as well as a correct Marxist political line."[11]

Reviewing the experience of ten years of warfare against the Kuomintang reactionaries, Mao pointed out that a specific feature of the Chinese revolution and revolutionary war in China was that China was a very large country and that this afforded the revolutionary forces room for maneuver. Secondly, with regard to the war against Chiang Kai-shek's forces, it had been necessary to take into account the important characteristic that the enemy was big and powerful while, at the beginning of the war, the revolutionary forces, and the Red Army, were small and weak. At the same time, showing the interpenetration and close link between political and military questions, Mao pointed out that an important characteristic of the struggle against the Kuomintang was that the Communist Party firmly upheld and carried out the agrarian revolution, whereas the Kuomintang opposed the agrarian revolution and therefore it lacked support from the peasantry, which the Communist Party was able to mobilize as the main force for the revolution and the main support for revolutionary war.

Summing up these points, Mao showed that it was the case that because of large territory and maneuvering room in China and because of the leadership of the Communist Party and its integration of the agrarian revolution with the armed struggle, it was possible for the Red Army to grow and eventually defeat the enemy. On the other hand he stressed that because of the fact that at the beginning the enemy was big and powerful while the Red Army was small and weak, it was impossible to rapidly defeat the enemy and therefore the revolutionary war in China must of necessity assume a protracted character. Mao's purpose in summing up and analyzing these important characteristics was not only to arm Party members and the masses with a correct understanding of the military line in general, but also to lay the basis for waging the war of resistance against Japan. As he pointed out, "China's revolutionary war, which began in 1924, has passed through two stages, the first from 1924 to 1927, and the second from 1927 to 1936; the stage of national revolutionary war against Japan will now commence."[12] Lessons which had been learned at the cost of great sacrifice and paid for in blood had to be applied concretely to the present struggle against the Japanese aggressors.

Offensive and Defensive

Certain specific characteristics of the war against the Kuomintang might not entirely apply in the war against Japan. For example, in the short run in the war against the Kuomintang the enemy
(Chiang Kai-shek's forces) had a large population from which to
draw, or press-gang, its troops, whereas in the war against
Japanese aggression it was the Chinese nation that had a large
population from which to draw its troops while Japan was not
capable of fielding as large an army. Nevertheless, the basic principles of revolutionary war which had been forged in the course of
the struggle against the Kuomintang must now be applied in waging the revolutionary war against Japan.

And this was true for most of the specific characteristics of the
revolutionary war against the Kuomintang. For example, a most
important factor which Mao pointed to in summing up the struggle against the "encirclement and suppression" campaigns was
that in these battles "the two forms of fighting, offensive and
defensive, are both employed, and here there is no difference from
any other war, ancient or modern, in China or elsewhere. The
special characteristic of China's civil war, however, is the repeated
alternation of the two forms over a long period of time."[13]

At the same time, Mao stressed the special importance of the
strategic defensive in waging revolutionary war. He emphasized
that "In every just war the defensive not only has a lulling effect
on politically alien elements, it also makes possible the rallying of
the backward sections of the masses to join in the war."[14] He
noted that:

The military experts of the newer and rapidly developing imperialist
countries, namely, Germany and Japan, trumpet the advantages of the
strategic offensive and come out against the strategic defensive. This
kind of military thinking is absolutely unsuited to China's revolutionary
war. These military experts assert that a serious weakness of the defensive is that it shakes popular morale, instead of inspiring it. This applies
to countries where class contradictions are acute and the war benefits only
the reactionary ruling strata or the reactionary political groups in power.
But our situation is different.[15]

And Mao summed up the serious errors of those in the Chinese
Communist Party who had insisted on not giving up any territory
in the face of enemy attacks and wanted to fight the enemy "outside the gates," who advocated striking out in two directions, relying on positional warfare and following the policy of pitting a small

force against a larger one rather than the correct policy of concentrating a larger force against a numerically inferior force to wipe it out in any particular battle or campaign. Such people opposed the absolutely correct and necessary policy of luring the enemy in deep, surrounding it with the masses, cutting off its forces into various parts and annihilating them bit by bit. Mao noted that such erroneous arguments were raised in opposition to "guerrillaism" but that they would certainly lead to defeat, not victory, and that, where they held sway, they had led to exactly that.

Mao emphatically stated that:

> Without a doubt these theories and practices were all wrong. They were nothing but subjectivism. Under favorable circumstances this subjectivism manifested itself in petty-bourgeois revolutionary fanaticism and impetuosity, but in times of adversity, as the situation worsened, it changed successively into desperate recklessness, conservatism and flightism. They were the theories and practices of hotheads and ignoramuses; they did not have the slightest flavor of Marxism about them; indeed they were anti-Marxist.[16]

Those who held such wrong and opportunist theories had in fact been responsible for the defeat of the Red Army during the fifth "encirclement and suppression" campaign of Chiang Kai-shek. Mao recalled that they had incorrectly argued that, "Even though luring the enemy deep into our territory might have been useful in the past, it would be useless against the enemy's fifth 'encirclement and suppression' campaign in which he adopted the policy of blockhouse warfare. The only way to deal with this campaign, they said, was to divide up our forces for resistance and make short swift thrusts at the enemy."[17]

At the same time Mao pointed out that passive defense was also wrong and would lead to defeat. He stressed that the point in fighting defensive warfare, and of strategic retreat as a key part of defensive warfare, was in fact to prepare to go over to the counteroffensive. He summed this point up in this way: "Strategic retreat is aimed solely at switching over to the counter-offensive and is merely the first stage of the strategic defensive. The decisive link in the entire strategy is whether victory can be won in the stage of the counter-offensive which follows."[18]

Once again Mao emphasized the crucial importance of concentrating superior forces tactically within the situation where strategically the enemy had superior numbers as well as superior training and armaments. This came to be capsulized in the formula: "strategy, one against ten; tactics, ten against one." In other words, in the strategic situation where the revolutionary forces were still greatly outnumbered by the counter-revolutionary forces it was necessary in particular battles and campaigns to apply the principle of concentrating an overwhelming force to wipe out a numerically inferior section of the enemy force.

Mao also pointed out that another important characteristic of the operations of the revolutionary army which flowed from the fact that the enemy had technical superiority over it was that it fought with fluid and not fixed battle lines. And through analyzing the opportunist line which had led to defeat in the face of Chiang Kai-shek's fifth "encirclement and suppression" campaign and had forced the Chinese Communist Party and the Red Army to embark on what became the Long March, Mao pointed out, with a brilliant application of dialectics, that "The mistaken rejection of guerrilla warfare and fluidity on a small scale had led to guerrilla warfare and fluidity on a great scale."[19]

Mao insisted on a dialectical approach to what was called "guerrilla-ism." He rejected "guerrilla-ism" insofar as it meant opposition to building a regular army. At the same time he stressed the importance of guerrilla warfare and defended this against those who denounced the use of guerrilla warfare as "guerrilla-ism." He pointed out that in this sense "guerrilla-ism" had two aspects, and that while the revolutionary army and revolutionary warfare in China had developed to a much higher level than in the early stages of the first formation of armed units (the first building up of the Red Army) still it was necessary to retain and continue to apply some of the principles which had been forged through the waging of guerrilla war. He summed this up by saying:

> At present we oppose the wrong measures of the period of the domination of "left" opportunism on the one hand and on the other the revival of many of the irregular features which the Red Army had in its infancy but which are now unnecessary. But we should be resolute in restoring the many valuable principles of army building and of strategy and tactics by which the Red Army has consistently won its victories.[20]

Finally in this work, Mao reaffirmed the all-important principle of waging warfare of annihilation, that is fighting battles and campaigns not merely to rout the enemy but to thoroughly wipe it out and achieve a quick victory in battles. This, again, was a masterful application of dialectics, of applying the tactics of quick victory and annihilation to the situation where the strategic orientation must be a protracted war and a war of attrition to gradually and over a fairly long period of time wipe out large numbers of enemy forces and in this way wear down and finally defeat the enemy.

Guerrilla Warfare

A year and a half later, after almost a year of experience in the war of resistance against Japan, Mao wrote "Problems of Strategy in Guerrilla War Against Japan" in May 1938. As a note to this article explained, it was written as part of a struggle against those inside and outside the Party who "belittled the important strategic role of guerrilla warfare and pinned their hopes on regular warfare alone, and particularly on the operations of the Kuomintang forces. Comrade Mao Tse-tung refuted this view and wrote this article to show the correct road of development for anti-Japanese guerrilla warfare."[21]

In this work Mao reiterated the basic principle that the war must be fought at its beginning stages and throughout most of its duration as a strategically defensive war and that it must be a protracted war. This was necessary and also could be turned to the advantage of the revolutionary war, owing to the fact that on the one hand Japan was a strong country and was waging a war of aggression, an unjust war, while China was weak in terms of technical ability and level of development of its productive forces but was waging a just war of resistance which could and must rely upon the strength of the masses of people. Because of these factors it was the case that Japan could and would occupy large parts of Chinese territory. This increased the necessity and importance of waging guerrilla warfare, especially within the areas generally occupied by the Japanese aggressors.

Mao pointed out that "the basic principle of guerrilla warfare must be the offensive, and guerrilla warfare is more offensive in its character than regular warfare."[22] He stressed, however, that the offensive in guerrilla warfare must take the form of surprise attacks. He further emphasized that in guerrilla warfare it was even more important than in regular warfare to fight battles of quick decision. Guerrilla warfare is by its nature more dispersed than even mobile warfare but, Mao insisted, at the same time the principle of concentrating a superior force to strike at a small part of the enemy remains valid and important in guerrilla warfare.

In the overall sense, during the entire war, Mao said, regular warfare would be principal and guerrilla warfare secondary. However, regular warfare meant principally mobile warfare and only secondarily positional warfare. Mobile war refers to warfare fought by regular units with rear base areas and on a relatively large scale, applying the principle of moving and fighting, moving in order to fight; guerrilla warfare is generally fought by more irregular units, mainly for the purpose of harassing the enemy in its own territory. Mao summed up that, mainly through regular—and principally mobile—warfare but with guerrilla warfare playing an important though secondary role, the road to victory lay in "the accumulation of many minor victories to make a major victory."[23] In other words, in both regular as well as guerrilla warfare it was necessary to stress the principles of fighting battles of quick decision, of concentrating a big force to strike at a small section of the enemy forces and to annihilate the enemy forces piece by piece, thus through a protracted process carrying out a war of attrition against the enemy until it was weakened to the point where the final *coup de grace* could be delivered to it.

Mao also gave emphasis to the question of developing guerrilla war into mobile war through the course of the anti-Japanese war. He pointed out:

Since. the war is protracted and ruthless, it is possible for the guerrilla units to undergo the necessary steeling and gradually to transform themselves into regular forces, so that their mode of operations is gradually regularized and guerrilla warfare develops into mobile warfare. The necessity and possibility of this development must be clearly recognized by the guerrilla commanders if they are to persist in, and systematically carry out, the policy of turning guerrilla warfare into mobile warfare.[24]

In formulating this principle Mao criticized those who took the purely military approach, pointing out:

They do not realize that the development of guerrilla warfare into mobile warfare means not the abandonment of guerrilla warfare, but the gradual formation, in the midst of widespread guerrilla warfare, of a main force capable of conducting mobile warfare, a force around which there must still be numerous guerrilla units carrying on extensive guerrilla operations. These guerrilla units are powerful auxiliaries to the main force and serve as inexhaustible reserves for its continuous growth.[25]

And Mao went on to add that the principle of decentralized command in campaigns or battles should be applied to regular as well as guerrilla war—in short, that it was necessary to have unified strategy and overall a centralized strategic command but at the same time decentralized command and initiative and flexibility in waging particular campaigns and battles.

"On Protracted War"

Written at the same time as "Problems of Strategy in Guerrilla War Against Japan" Mao's "On Protracted War" was a broader and more general statement summing up the principles of war and revolutionary war in particular and setting down the policies and overall strategic orientation for the war of resistance against Japan. Mao pointed out that the war of the Chinese nation in resistance to Japan was a war "which has no precedent in the history of the East, and which will go down as a great war in world history too."[26]

In this work Mao forcefully combatted and refuted the theory of China's inevitable subjugation as well as the theory of quick victory, both of which had considerable currency within China generally as well as in the Chinese Communist Party itself, though the former, the theory of subjugation and its outlook of capitulation, constituted overall the greater danger. Mao analyzed once again and in a thorough way the factors which explained both why it was possible for China to wage a victorious war of resistance against Japan and why on the other hand it must be a protracted war. He criticized both the notion that since Japan was superior to China in arms and technology therefore China could not wage a successful war of resistance and the notion, which he described as groundlessly optimistic, that Japan could be easily defeated, a notion which, he pointed out, belittled the strategic role of guerrilla warfare in the war against Japan.

Mao thoroughly and all-sidedly answered the argument that China would not be able to achieve victory. He concretely analyzed the specific features of the anti-Japanese war and the international situation in which it was taking place. He pointed out that Japan, while temporarily powerful and enjoying technical superiority over China, was after all an imperialist power and therefore moribund, while on the other hand China was historically in an era of progress—the proletariat and its Party had emerged on the scene and was leading the war of resistance against Japan. Mao further pointed out that internationally there was the existence of the Soviet Union and wide-scale progressive and revolutionary movements in various countries throughout the world which were opposed to Japan's war of aggression against China.

On the basis of a concrete analysis of the different strengths and weaknesses of Japan and China Mao summed up once again that:

Japan can ride roughshod over China for a certain time and to a certain extent, that China must unavoidably travel a hard stretch of road, and that the War of Resistance will be a protracted war and not a war of quick decision; nevertheless, it follows from the other contrast—a small country, retrogression and meagre support versus a big country, progress and abundant support—that Japan cannot ride roughshod over China indefinitely but is sure to meet final defeat, while China can never be subjugated but is sure to win final victory.[27]

This was a sharp ideological struggle which had decisive effect in relation to the military struggle against Japan. At that time, at the beginning of the war, it was not at all clear, looking only on the surface and without examining the essence of things, that backward China could defeat advanced Japan. Because of this the tendencies to capitulate and to attempt to avoid protracted war were greatly strengthened.

Mao forcefully combatted those who wanted to adopt a policy of capitulation and concession to Japan and who promoted the erroneous notion that this would halt Japan's advances throughout China and induce Japan to rest content with its seizure of only certain parts of northern China. Mao pointed to the imperialist nature of Japan, which was in fierce rivalry with other imperialist powers, and he showed how Japan could not stand still with a partial seizure of China but must push deeper into the interior of China.

Basing himself on a class analysis of the forces not only within China but internationally and the relationship between the internal and external forces, Mao pointed out that the Kuomintang "depends on Britain and the United States and hence will not capitulate to Japan unless they tell it to."[28] Thus, Mao pointed out, the tendency to capitulate and compromise with Japanese imperialism, while great and dangerous, could and would be overcome by relying on the masses of Chinese people and the Chinese nation as a whole, which overwhelmingly favored and demanded resistance against Japan.

At the same time Mao refuted the erroneous arguments of the theorists of quick victory and pointed to the fundamental unity between the theory of subjugation and the theory of quick victory. Speaking of those who advocated quick victory Mao said pointedly, "they lack the courage to admit that the enemy is strong while we are weak," and base their strategy on this subjectivism.[29] Further about such people Mao said:

Unable to endure the arduous trials of a protracted war and eager for an early triumph, the impetuous theorists of quick victory clamor for a strategically decisive engagement the moment the situation takes a slightly favorable turn. To do what they want would be to inflict incalculable damage on the entire war, spell finis to the protracted war, and land us in the enemy's deadly trap; actually, it would be the worst policy. Undoubtedly, if we are to avoid decisive engagements, we shall have to abandon territory, and we must have the courage to do so when (and only when) it becomes completely unavoidable. At such times we should not feel the slightest regret, for this policy of trading space for time is correct.[30]

Mao answered those who called such a policy one of non-resistance, pointing to the truth that unless the strategy of protracted war and the various principles that were inevitably part of it were applied, and if in place of these the strategy of the theorists of quick victory was adopted, then this would inevitably land the Chinese nation in the position of subjugation. Mao summed this point up in the following way:

Not to fight at all but to compromise with the enemy—that is non-resistance, which should not only be denounced but must never be tolerated. We must resolutely fight the War of Resistance, but in order to avoid the enemy's deadly trap, it is absolutely necessary that we should not allow our main forces to be finished off at one blow, which would make it difficult to continue the War of Resistance—in brief, it is absolutely necessary to avoid national subjugation. To have doubts on this point is to be shortsighted on the question of the war and is sure to lead one into the ranks of the subjugationists. We have criticized the desperate recklessness of "only advance, never retreat" precisely because, if it became the fashion, this doctrine would make it impossible to continue the War of Resistance and would lead to the danger of ultimate national subjugation.[31]

Summing up the basis of the two erroneous kinds of thinking—the theory of subjugation and the theory of quick victory—and formulating in opposition to both of these the correct understanding, Mao made the following concise formulation:

In the eyes of the subjugationists the enemy are supermen and we Chinese are worthless, while in the eyes of the theorists of quick victory we Chinese are supermen and the enemy are worthless. Both are wrong. We take a different view; the War of Resistance Against Japan is a protracted war, and the final victory will be China's. These are our conclusions.[32]

Three Stages in War of Resistance

In this work Mao also analyzed the basic stages which the war of resistance to Japan would pass through. He explained that there would be three basic stages, the first covering the period in which

Japan would be on the strategic offensive and the Chinese war of resistance would be one of the strategic defensive. This would be a period in which mobile warfare would be the main form while guerrilla warfare, and secondarily to guerrilla warfare positional warfare, would be supplementary to mobile warfare.

The second stage of the war, Mao said, would be a strategic stalemate. In this period guerrilla warfare would assume the position of the main form, supplemented by mobile warfare, because the objective would be to threaten the enemy's consolidation of the areas it occupied and to harass it in its occupied areas.

The third stage would be that of the strategic counter-offensive by the forces of resistance to Japan. To go over to this stage would require the accumulation of strength of the forces of the Chinese nation in resistance to Japan as well as a shift in the international situation to one more favorable to China's war of resistance. In this stage mobile warfare would again become principal, but guerrilla war would continue and positional warfare would increase in importance.

Overall this analysis of Mao's of the development of the war was proved correct by the actual events in the war itself. As he was later to sum up after the victory of the anti-Japanese war and at the start of the war of liberation against Chiang Kai-shek and his U.S. imperialist masters, it proved to be the case during the anti-Japanese war that "the dispersal of our forces for guerrilla warfare was primary, and the concentration of our forces for mobile warfare was supplementary."[33] By this Mao meant that, taking the course of the anti-Japanese war as a whole and analyzing the succession of battles which accumulated to lay the basis for final victory, guerrilla warfare assumed the first place while mobile warfare assumed an important but secondary place. This was linked to the fact that the stage of stalemate in the war proved to be fairly lengthy. In "On Protracted War," Mao had already formulated the principle that would form the basis for the fact that guerrilla warfare actually proved to be primary: " 'With regard to the whole, mobile warfare is primary and guerrilla warfare supplementary; with regard to the parts, guerrilla warfare is primary and mobile warfare supplementary.' "[34]

People, Not Weapons, Decisive

While setting forth in "On Protracted War" the basic orientation and strategic principles for the war of resistance against Japan , and as a necessary part of this, Mao also criticized and refuted a number of other erroneous concepts. Crucial to defeating the theory of national subjugation was the criticism of the mistaken notion that "weapons decide everything." This upside-down view was naturally a powerful prop in support of the argument that Japan, superior in weapons and technology, was bound to defeat China, which was inferior in these things.

Mao forcefully answered the arguments of those who put forward such a line:

> At this point, the exponents of national subjugation and of compromise will again rush in and say, "To move from inferiority to parity China needs a military and economic power equal to Japan's, and to move from parity to superiority she will need a military and economic power greater than Japan's. But this is impossible, hence the above conclusions are not correct."
> ...This is the so-called theory that "weapons decide everything," which constitutes a mechanical approach to the question of war and a subjective and one-sided view. Our view is opposed to this; we see not only weapons but also people. Weapons are an important factor in war, but not the decisive factor; it is people, not things, that are decisive. The contest of strength is not only a contest of military and economic power, but also a contest of human power and morale. Military and economic power is necessarily wielded by people. If the great majority of the Chinese, of the Japanese and of the people of other countries are on the side of our War of Resistance Against Japan, how can Japan's military and economic power, wielded as it is by a small minority through coercion, count as superiority? And if not, then does not China, though wielding relatively inferior military and economic power, become the superior?[35]

Against the technical superiority of Japan, Mao stressed that the strength of the Chinese masses, led and mobilized politically to wage a war of resistance, could, in combination with the correct military line based on the principle of people's war, lead to victory. Mao put it this way: "The mobilization of the common people throughout the country will create a vast sea in which to drown the enemy, create the conditions that will make up for our inferiority in arms and other things, and create the prerequisites for overcoming every difficulty in the war."[36]

Speaking further of the relationship between people and weapons and of the need for the Chinese people and the revolutionary army, and the Chinese Communist Party leading them, to correctly handle this relationship, Mao emphasized that:

> The reform of our military system requires its modernization and improved technical equipment, without which we cannot drive the enemy back across the Yalu River. In our employment of troops we need progressive, flexible strategy and tactics, without which we likewise cannot

win victory. Nevertheless, soldiers are the foundation of an army; unless they are imbued with a progressive political spirit, and unless such a spirit is fostered through progressive political work, it will be impossible to achieve genuine unity between officers and men, impossible to arouse their enthusiasm for the War of Resistance to the full, and impossible to provide a sound basis for the most effective use of all our technical equipment and tactics.[37]

Closely linked to this, Mao stressed the importance of what he termed "man's conscious dynamic role," specifically in relation to war. He pointed out that though the objective conditions—the objective strengths and weaknesses of opposing sides in a war—set the possibility for victory or defeat, yet they don't determine the outcome of the war. The actual achievement of victory or actual defeat will also depend on the subjective factor, namely the concept of directing and the waging of the war. Hence the importance of a correct military line, in close connection with a correct overall political line, and hence also the importance of studying the laws of war and the concrete features of the particular war being waged and, as Mao stressed, of learning warfare through warfare.

Mao emphasized both that in the overall sense war could not be separated from politics nor military line from an overall political line, and on the other hand that war has its own particular features and laws, which cannot be simply equated with politics in general but must be concretely studied, acted on, summed up and developed in the course of waging a revolutionary war. In short, Mao stressed that it was impossible to win a revolutionary war without on the one hand widespread political mobilization and arming the masses to consciously wage and support the struggle, and on the other hand without concretely applying a correct military line. This military line must be based on the fact that the war was a just war, a people's war, and at the same time it must be rooted in the concrete conditions of China at that time in the context of the international situation and the international struggle.

Following exactly this method, Mao not only formulated and fought for the basic strategy of protracted war, but summarized and concentrated fully the tactics for carrying out such a war:

In a word, the above operational principle for fighting campaigns and battles is one of "quick-decision offensive warfare on exterior lines." It is the opposite of our strategic principle of "protracted defensive warfare on interior lines," and yet it is the indispensable principle for carrying out this strategy.[38]

"Interior lines" refers to a situation in which one's army is surrounded by the enemy. Strategically this was the situation for most of China's war of resistance against Japan. However, brilliantly applying materialistic dialectics, Mao developed the operational principles for tactically reversing this situation—that is, in fighting battles or campaigns surround parts of the enemy and force them into battles at a disadvantageous situation where they have only interior lines. Carrying this out depended on the strategy of establishing base areas and on the crucial principle of luring the enemy in deep.

At the same time, because strategically the enemy was more powerful and surrounded the revolutionary army, it was necessary to launch offensive battles of annihilation and to fight battles of quick victories. Otherwise the reserves of the overall superior forces of the enemy could be brought to bear and the tactical advantage of the revolutionary army would be turned into its opposite, with defeat rather than victory being the result. Further, as he had done all during the Long March and in the battles before it, Mao developed and applied the principle of achieving initiative and flexibility within the situation where the enemy was strategically superior. Applying again the principle of "man's conscious dynamic role," Mao pointed out:

In the struggle, correct subjective direction [i.e., correct direction by the subjective factor, leadership in the war] can transform inferiority into superiority and passivity into initiative, and incorrect subjective direction can do the opposite. The fact that every ruling dynasty was defeated by revolutionary armies shows that mere superiority in certain respects does not guarantee the initiative, much less the final victory. The inferior side can wrest the initiative and victory from the superior side by securing certain conditions through active subjective endeavor in accordance with the actual circumstances.[39]

Applying Marxism to China's Conditions

These analyses of Mao's of the essential basic principles of revolutionary war in China's conditions then were indispensable for victory in the war of resistance against Japan and the advance of the Chinese revolution overall. In formulating and fighting for a correct military line for the war of resistance against Japan and for revolutionary war in China in general, Mao, as noted earlier, had to not only concretely apply Marxist principles to the situation in China, but had to combat various erroneous tendencies, in particular those that attempted to mechanically copy and apply in China the experience of the October Revolution in Russia, which set the general strategic orientation for revolution and the seizure of power in the capitalist countries.

"Problems of War and Strategy" was written by Mao in November of 1938 to combat these erroneous lines. In it he stressed the difference between a country like China—a colonial or semicolonial and semi-feudal country—and the capitalist countries. Specifically he pointed out that:

On the issue of war, the Communist Parties in the capitalist countries oppose the imperialist wars waged by their own countries; if such wars occur, the policy of these Parties is to bring about the defeat of the reactionary governments of their own countries. The one war they want to fight is the civil war for which they are preparing. But this insurrection and war should not be launched until the bourgeoisie becomes really helpless, until the majority of the proletariat are determined to rise in arms and fight, and until the rural masses are giving willing help to the proletariat. And when the time comes to launch such an insurrection and war, the first step will be to seize the cities, and then advance into the countryside, and not the other way about. All this has been done by Communist Parties in capitalist countries, and it has been proved correct by the October Revolution in Russia.

China is different however. The characteristics of China are that she is not independent and democratic but semi-colonial and semi-feudal, that internally she has no democracy but is under feudal oppression and that in her external relations she has no national independence but is oppressed by imperialism. It follows that we have no parliament to make use of and no legal right to organize the workers to strike. Basically, the task of the Communist Party here is not to go through a long period of legal struggle before launching insurrection and war, and not to seize the big cities first and then occupy the countryside, but the reverse.[40]

Summing up the history of the Chinese revolution to that point, Mao forcefully drew the basic lesson that without armed struggle as the main form it would have been impossible to advance the revolutionary movement. He noted that the Chinese Communist Party at first failed to fully grasp this and that, even after this basic understanding was achieved, erroneous lines, political and military, led to setbacks in the armed struggle against Chiang Kaishek after his complete betrayal in 1927 and to serious defeats and setbacks in fighting the fifth "encirclement and suppression" in particular. It was in this work that Mao formulated his now famous statement that "political power grows out of the barrel of a gun" and stressed that it was necessary for all communists to fully grasp this principle.

At the same time he reaffirmed the decisive principle that the Party must lead the armed struggle and the revolutionary army and not the other way around. Or, as he formulated it then, "Our principle is that the party commands the gun, and the gun must never be allowed to command the party." Mao linked this to the all-important question of waging successful guerrilla warfare, emphasizing that only with the leadership of the Communist Party could guerrilla warfare be persevered in and both supplement regular war and at a certain point develop into regular warfare. In line with this Mao concluded this work by stressing once again the importance of studying military theory and strategy and the further strengthening of the whole Party in its grasp not only of the correct political line in general but in particular of military affairs and the laws and principles of revolutionary war. This was decisive in developing and implementing the correct policies and tactics for, and leading the masses in, waging the protracted war of resistance against Japan.

During the course of this war Mao not only summed up and gave further guidance to the development of the revolutionary war in China itself but followed closely and analyzed the development of the international struggle and the world war which broke out in 1939. In particular, at an early point in the historic battle of Stalingrad in the Soviet Union, Mao summed up that this would in fact be the turning point in the whole of WW2. On October 12, 1942 Mao wrote an editorial for *Liberation Daily* in Yenan (where the Communist Party leadership was headquartered), in which he analyzed the development of the battle of Stalingrad and predicted the victory of the Soviet army and the shift in the whole war in favor of the Soviet Union, the Chinese people and the forces worldwide who were allied with them. This article was written as a further refutation of pessimism and ended with the clear-cut statement: "All those who take a pessimistic view of the world situation should change their point of view."[41]

In fact, within three years the defeat of the fascist imperialists of Japan and Germany, and of the whole fascist Axis, was achieved. In China it was achieved on the basis of carrying out Mao Tsetung's revolutionary political line and military line. In "On Coalition Government," a report to the 7th Congress of the Chinese Communist Party delivered by Mao Tsetung on the eve of the victory of the anti-Japanese war, he summed up the victorious course of the war and the role of the armed forces under the leadership of the Communist Party in that war. Mao noted that at the beginning of the war, even within the Communist Party itself, "there were some who looked down on this army and thought that the main reliance for resistance to Japan should be placed on the Kuomintang."[42] He emphasized that the revolutionary army under the leadership of the Party "is powerful because all its

members have a discipline based on political consciousness; they
have come together and they fight not for the private interests of a
few individuals or a narrow clique, but for the interests of the
broad masses and of the whole nation. The sole purpose of this army is to stand firmly with the Chinese people and to serve them
wholeheartedly."[43]

Mobilizing the Masses

Mao summed up and stressed once again the importance of
mobilizing the masses broadly for the war and organizing the
masses into militia to fight in coordination with the regional forces
of the People's Liberation Army, while at the same time having a
main force of the army capable of fighting in different regions according to the different requirements of the war. In other words, it
was the full mobilization of the Chinese nation for people's war, for
carrying out the strategic line of protracted war and the various
tactics and principles of operation that Mao developed for fighting
such a war, that resulted in victory in the war of resistance to
Japan. Mao sharply pointed out that a force representing reactionary classes and therefore incapable of fundamentally relying
on the masses could not carry out, let alone lead, such a war. In
short: "Only by waging such a people's war can we defeat the national enemy. The Kuomintang has failed precisely because of its
desperate opposition to a people's war."[44]

In fact, as noted in the previous chapter, during the anti-
Japanese war, while nominally fighting the Japanese, Chiang Kai-
shek adopted a passive and defeatist stance towards the Japanese
aggressors and concentrated most of his fire against the Communist Party and the armed forces and base areas under its leadership. But, under Mao Tsetung's leadership, the Chinese Communist Party beat back such attacks and at the same time maintained the united front against Japan, while also maintaining its
independence and initiative. It carried out Mao's political line and
military line and on this basis greatly expanded the armed forces
and base areas under its leadership and played the leading and
decisive part in mobilizing the Chinese nation to wage people's
war, in the form of a protracted war of resistance, and finally
defeat Japan.

Summing up, on the eve of the victorious conclusion of this war,
its main lessons and the underlying causes of the policies and actions of the various forces involved in it, Mao looked ahead and
politically armed the Chinese Communist Party, and laid the basis

for arming the broad masses of people, with the understanding that they could not give up their weapons and subordinate themselves to the Kuomintang, which was attempting to seize the fruits of the victory the Chinese people had paid for in blood in the anti-Japanese war. It was in this work that Mao made another of his now famous statements, "Without a people's army the people have nothing."[45] This was a crucial point to stress not only in summing up the whole course of the anti-Japanese war and the Chinese revolution up to that point, but in waging struggle then and preparing to continue the revolution in the situation right after that war and carry the struggle forward in the next stage.

When Chiang Kai-shek refused to carry out democratic reform and to dismantle his one-party regime, and instead attempted to usurp power throughout China, launching a civil war against the Chinese Communist Party and the armed forces and base areas under its leadership, Mao led the Chinese Communist Party and the Chinese masses in waging revolutionary war against this counter-revolutionary war of Chiang Kai-shek and his U.S. backers. In guiding this armed struggle Mao applied the principles and strategy of revolutionary war that had been developed under his leadership in the Chinese revolution up to that point.

Concentrate a Superior Force

In an article written in September 1946, "Concentrate a Superior Force to Destroy the Enemy Forces One by One," Mao set the orientation for the Chinese Communist Party, the revolutionary army and the Chinese masses in carrying forward the strategy of people's war and in particular fighting battles of annihilation to defeat an enemy that at the beginning of the war was superior in numbers and had superior weapons and superior technology. Basing himself on the same principles of people's war as they applied to the concrete situation then, Mao wrote:

In the present civil war, since conditions have changed, the method of fighting should change too. The concentration of our forces for mobile warfare should be primary, and the dispersal of our forces for guerrilla warfare should be supplementary. Now that Chiang Kai-shek's army has acquired more powerful weapons, it is necessary for our army to lay special stress on the method of concentrating a superior force to wipe out the enemy forces one by one.[46]

In October 1946 Mao wrote "A Three Months' Summary" in which he analyzed the development of the war of liberation against

Chiang Kai-shek and the U.S. imperialists in its beginning phase up to that point. As was noted in the preceding chapter, at this point in the development of the Chinese revolution there was an intense struggle within the Chinese Communist Party over the question of whether or not it was possible to wage a successful revolutionary war against Chiang Kai-shek, backed as he was by U.S. imperialism. Mao began this "Summary" with the forceful reiteration of the Central Committee's directive of July 20 of that year—that indeed it was possible to defeat Chiang Kai-shek and that the whole Party must be confident about this.

Mao then proceeded to analyze the "fundamental political and economic contradictions which Chiang Kai-shek cannot resolve and which are the basic cause rendering our victory certain and Chiang's defeat inevitable..."[47] He went on to analyze the specific contradictions in the military sphere which would be the direct cause of the victory of the revolutionary forces and the defeat of Chiang Kai-shek—namely the fact that Chiang's battle lines were overextended and he had, from a long-term point of view, a shortage of troops.

However, to translate this into actual victory it was necessary to uphold and strictly apply the basic principles of fighting by the method of concentrating a superior force to wipe out the enemy forces one by one; fighting battles of decisive victory; fighting, as Mao said, when conditions were favorable and moving away when they were not favorable; fighting in a tactical way on exterior lines, offensively and in quick-decision battles. These and other basic principles which Mao had developed through the course of the revolutionary wars in China, and in particular the war of resistance against Japan, were still valid and had to be applied to the war against Chiang Kai-shek's forces at that time in order to bring about the actual victory.[48]

In a telegram, "The Concept of Operations for the Northwest War Theatre," sent by Mao Tsetung to the Northwest Field Army in April 1947, he stressed the importance of keeping the enemy on the run, tiring him out, wearing him down, reducing him to extreme fatigue and conditions of starvation and then launching the offensive to destroy him. Without doing this, Mao said, it would be impossible to win final victory.

Again, during this war of liberation against Chiang Kai-shek and the U.S. imperialists behind him, a struggle arose within the Chinese Communist Party over the question of whether or not to temporarily give up some territory in order to lure Chiang Kai-shek's forces in, divide them up and defeat them one by one.

Specifically, in 1947 Chiang Kai-shek amassed large forces for a direct attack on the area of Yenan, the base area where the Chinese Communist Party leadership and the leadership of the People's Liberation Army was headquartered. In the face of this there were some in the Chinese Communist Party who argued that it was wrong to retreat temporarily from the Yenan area and that instead an all-out fight should be waged to defend it.

Mao defeated this erroneous line and gave leadership and direction to the liberation forces in waging a tactical retreat, circling around and isolating, chopping up and annihilating large forces of Chiang Kai-shek's army one by one, using the methods of mobile warfare and the basic principle of concentrating a superior force in battles, fighting offensively and wiping out the enemy in quick-decision warfare.

Going on the Offensive

The tremendous success in this campaign marked the turning point in the war of liberation. In September of 1947 Mao wrote an inner-Party directive entitled "Strategy for the Second Year of the War of Liberation," which set forth the task of carrying the war into the Kuomintang areas and switching from the strategic position of fighting on interior lines to fighting on exterior lines—that is, going over from the strategic defensive in which the enemy was encircling and attacking to the strategic offensive in which the liberation army was encircling and attacking the enemy.

During that period the liberation army launched the countrywide offensive which was, in the space of two years, to lead to complete victory in the war of liberation. In setting forth the strategy for this offensive Mao stressed that "the operational principles of our army remain the same as those laid down before . . ."[49] In "The Present Situation and Our Tasks," written in December of 1947, Mao set down in more fully developed form these basic operational principles, which have come to be known as the ten major principles of operation (see p. 72).

Once again in this work ("The Present Situation and Our Tasks") written at the point when the liberation army had gone over to the strategic offensive and victory could be clearly seen on the horizon, Mao summed up the crucial importance at an earlier point in this war, in fact at its very beginning, of correctly assessing the domestic and international situation and on this basis recognizing the possibility for successfully waging a revolutionary war against the counter-revolutionary war that Chiang Kai-shek

TEN MAJOR PRINCIPLES OF OPERATION

(1) Attack dispersed, isolated enemy forces first; attack concentrated, strong enemy forces later.

(2) Take small and medium cities and extensive rural areas first; take big cities later.

(3) Make wiping out the enemy's effective strength our main objective; do not make holding or seizing a city or place our main objective. Holding or seizing a city or place is the outcome of wiping out the enemy's effective strength, and often a city or place can be held or seized for good only after it has changed hands a number of times.

(4) In every battle, concentrate an absolutely superior force (two, three, four and sometimes even five or six times the enemy's strength), encircle the enemy forces completely, strive to wipe them out thoroughly and do not let any escape from the net. In special circumstances, use the method of dealing the enemy crushing blows, that is, concentrate all our strength to make a frontal attack and an attack on one or both of his flanks, with the aim of wiping out one part and routing another so that our army can swiftly move its troops to smash other enemy forces. Strive to avoid battles of attrition in which we lose more than we gain or only break even. In this way, although inferior as a whole (in terms of numbers), we shall be absolutely superior in every part and every specific campaign, and this ensures victory in the campaign. As time goes on, we shall become superior as a whole and eventually wipe out all the enemy.

(5) Fight no battle unprepared, fight no battle you are not sure of winning; make every effort to be well prepared for each battle, make every effort to ensure victory in the given set of conditions as between the enemy and ourselves.

(6) Give full play to our style of fighting—courage in battle, no fear of sacrifice, no fear of fatigue, and continuous fighting (that is, fighting successive battles in a short time without rest).

(7) Strive to wipe out the enemy when he is on the move. At the same time, pay attention to the tactics of positional attack and capture enemy fortified points and cities.

(8) With regard to attacking cities, resolutely seize all enemy fortified points and cities which are weakly defended. At opportune moments, seize all enemy fortified points and cities defended with moderate strength, provided circumstances permit. As for strongly defended enemy fortified points and cities, wait till conditions are ripe and then take them.

(9) Replenish our strength with all the arms and most of the personnel captured from the enemy. Our army's main sources of manpower and *matériel* are at the front.

(10) Make good use of the intervals between campaigns to rest, train and consolidate our troops. Periods of rest, training and consolidation should not in general be very long, and the enemy should so far as possible be permitted no breathing space.

(*SMW*, "The Present Situation And Our Tasks," pp. 349-350)

Crossing the Snow Mountains on the Long March.

had unleashed. Mao pointed out that at the beginning of the war, when Chiang Kai-shek initially seized certain cities and grabbed territory, he became swelled with arrogance; he mistook the strategy of the liberation army—of fighting first from the strategic defensive—for strategic weakness on the part of the liberation army. Mao pointed out that:

We said then that Chiang Kai-shek's superiority in military forces was only transient, a factor which could play only a temporary role, that U.S. imperialist aid was likewise a factor which could play only a temporary role, while the anti-popular character of Chiang Kai-shek's war and the feelings of the people were factors that would play a constant role, and that in this respect the People's Liberation Army was in a superior position. Patriotic, just and revolutionary in character, the war waged by the People's Liberation Army was bound to win the support of the people of the whole country. This was the political foundation for victory over Chiang Kai-shek. The experience of eighteen months of war has fully confirmed our judgement.[50]

Mao not only insisted that the major principles of operation for the revolutionary army developed through the course of earlier warfare were still correct and applicable but stressed again that it would be impossible for Chiang Kai-shek's army to make use of these principles. He noted that Chiang Kai-shek and the U.S. imperialists were fully aware of the strategy and principles of the People's Liberation Army but that this knowledge could not save Chiang Kai-shek. Mao pointedly said that "The reason is that our strategy and tactics are based on a people's war; no army opposed to the people can use our strategy and tactics."[51] A revolutionary war, a war of the masses, can and must be fought only according to military principles which are in conformity with relying upon the masses and mobilizing their strength as the backbone of the war. A reactionary war can never be fought on this basis.

Masses Are Bastion of Iron

And the reverse is also true. A revolutionary war can never be fought without relying on the masses of people and mobilizing them as the strength and bastion of iron, as Mao said, of the revolutionary war. For example, such things as launching surprise attacks, evading the enemy, circling around, retreating and then turning a retreat into a counter-offensive, concentrating superior forces for attack in battles and campaigns and in general conducting guerrilla and mobile warfare—all these depend upon the firm support of the masses of people. Without that support the enemy will be able to upset the element of surprise through gaining intelligence, he will be able to thwart attempts at surprise attacks and evasion, to determine the point where a retreat is to be turned into a counter-offensive, etc., and will be able to defeat the attempts of carrying out mobile warfare as well as guerrilla warfare.

So, too, a regime which does not depend on the masses of people to support it and supply it both with provisions and with soldiers, but which, like the army of Chiang Kai-shek, is forced to press-gang soldiers into its service and has its technical base resting upon the exploitation of the masses, is bound to be riddled with internal contradictions. Its army is bound to be characterized by low morale, particularly in circumstances where it is very difficult to engage the enemy on your own terms and where there is no quick victory. This is an expression of the truth that people, not weapons, are decisive in warfare.

Three Decisive Campaigns

When the People's Liberation Army had entered into the country-wide counter-offensive and was approaching the hour of victory, Mao developed specific principles of operation for three decisive campaigns in the Chinese people's war of liberation against Chiang Kai-shek and U.S. imperialism. These were the Liaohsi-Shenyang campaign, the Huai-Hai campaign and the Peiping-Tientsin campaign. Mao drafted the telegrams to the armed forces of the People's Liberation Army involved in these campaigns. In fact "The Concept of Operations for the Liaohsi-Shenyang Campaign" and "The Concept of Operations for the Peiping-Tientsin Campaign" were not only general instructions for carrying out these decisive campaigns but also represented sharp struggle against opportunists, including most especially Lin Piao, in the leadership of these particular forces of the People's Liberation Army. Lin Piao, showing his right deviationism, wanted to drag his feet and was afraid to launch the all-out attack to carry through these decisive campaigns—in particular of Liaohsi-Shenyang and Peiping-Tientsin.

This stemmed from Lin Piao's rightist view and his tendency to overestimate the enemy, which had occurred several times at decisive points in the history of the Chinese revolution and which had been criticized by Mao at several key junctures, including as far back as 1930 when Mao wrote "A Single Spark Can Start a Prairie Fire" to counter the pessimism of Lin Piao and others who were committing right deviations. In the telegram on "The Concept of Operations for the Peiping-Tientsin Campaign," drafted on December 11, 1948, Mao emphatically warned Lin Piao and others that "You should on no account overrate the enemy's combat effectiveness."[52]

With the carrying out of Mao's specific directives on these decisive campaigns and with the achievement of victory in these campaigns, the success of the war of liberation became fundamentally assured. Still, of course, it was necessary to vigorously carry the war against Chiang Kai-shek's reactionary forces through to the end and to resolutely, thoroughly, completely and wholly wipe them out, as Mao put it. At this point, in late 1948—early 1949, the U.S. imperialists and their Kuomintang lackeys, facing imminent defeat, began to make attempts to politically maneuver and employ new dual tactics—that is, to continue the war against the People's Liberation Army while at the same time attempting to organize an opposition faction within the revolutionary camp which would split that camp and conclude a "peace" with the Kuomintang, leaving it still in power. Again, Mao led the Chinese Communist Party, the revolutionary army and the Chinese masses in successfully continuing and carrying forward the revolutionary war while at the same time exposing the maneuvers of officials within the Kuomintang, backed by U.S. imperialism, who were attempting to secure an "honorable peace" on reactionary terms.

In this way the broadest masses of the Chinese people were won to unity with the revolutionary movement, and the enemy—imperialism, feudalism and bureaucrat-capitalism, as represented by the Kuomintang and its U.S. backers—was isolated to the extreme and finally dealt a crushing and thorough defeat. Thus, after more than 20 years of almost continual warfare, China had finally achieved national liberation and the Chinese people had been emancipated from the rule of imperialism, feudalism and bureaucrat-capitalism. On October 1, 1949 the People's Republic of China, led by the working class and its Communist Party, was founded as the crowning victory of the revolutionary armed struggle of the Chinese people.

Worldwide Significance of Mao's Military Line

In sum, it was the leadership of Mao Tsetung, his revolutionary political line and his revolutionary military line, which guided the Chinese people in winning this great victory. And the political and military lines of Mao Tsetung, though forged through the application of Marxism-Leninism to China's concrete conditions during

its new-democratic revolution, and though involving certain
policies specifically related to those conditions, are, in their basic
principles, of great significance not only for the Chinese revolution
and not only historically, but for revolutions in colonial and semi-
colonial countries today and more generally for revolutionary
struggles for the seizure of power and revolutionary wars. Through
leading the Chinese revolution, which was (as noted before) from
its beginning to the seizure of state power an armed struggle, Mao
developed and enriched Marxist theory and strategy on warfare
and developed a comprehensive Marxist system of military thinking which is of great value and significance for the international
proletariat.

As noted in the preceding chapter, almost immediately after the
victory of the Chinese revolution, starting in the year following the
founding of the People's Republic, China aided the Korean people
in resisting the war of aggression by U.S. imperialism, and Chinese
volunteers took part in this war on a broad scale.

There was struggle within the Chinese Communist Party and army over what military line to carry out in the war to resist U.S. aggression and aid Korea. Mao, while taking into account the specific
features of that war, argued that the basic line, strategy and principles that had been developed in the course of the various stages
of the revolutionary armed struggle in China basically applied. In
1953, at the conclusion of the war, Mao made a speech which
stressed that, while the factor of leadership was important in the
victories scored in the war, "the most important factor is the contribution of ideas by the masses." And he added that "Our experience is that reliance on the people together with a fairly correct
leadership enables us to defeat a better-equipped enemy with our
inferior equipment."[53]

At the same time, while stressing and explaining the vital importance for China to carry out its internationalist tasks and aid
Korea in resisting U.S. aggression, Mao emphasized that "we will
invade no one anywhere. But if others invade us, we will fight back
and fight to a finish."[54] Here again Mao was reaffirming the basic
principles of people's war upon which the successful armed struggle of the Chinese people in liberating China had been founded.

Throughout the 1950s, while U.S. imperialism, with its atomic
weapons, continued to threaten the socialist countries including
China and the people of other countries with aggression in various
parts of the world, Mao continued to uphold the orientation which
he had set forth years earlier—that U.S. imperialism was a paper
tiger and specifically that even the atom bomb could not enable

U.S. imperialism to win in a war of aggression against China. Mao stood firmly by the principles which had guided the successful armed struggle of the Chinese people in winning their liberation. In a statement in July 1956, "U.S. Imperialism Is a Paper Tiger," Mao stressed once more that the reason that the Chinese Communist Party and the revolutionary armed forces under its leadership were able to triumph over the reactionary forces in China was because they were linked with, relied upon and mobilized the masses of people. He summarized this in the basic law that "small forces linked with the people become strong, while big forces opposed to the people become weak."[55]

A year later, in November 1957, at the Moscow meeting of representatives of Communist and Workers' Parties, Mao sharply combatted the revisionist betrayal by Khrushchev and his attempt to put over the line that U.S. imperialism was all-powerful because it had superior weapons, including atomic weapons, and that the development of new weapons, in particular atomic weapons, changed the basic principles of war. Mao reaffirmed the basic principle of strategically despising the enemy, including a big and powerful force like U.S. imperialism, while tactically respecting and taking it seriously, a principle that was applied in China's revolutionary war and found expression in the orientation of waging people's war and relying on the strength of the masses while carrying out the policy in campaigns and battles of concentrating a superior force to annihilate and defeat the enemy forces one by one.[56]

Combatting Revisionist Military Line

Mao continued to uphold this basic military line in opposition to revisionists in the Soviet Union and in China itself, who argued, as revisionists have historically argued, that weapons, not people, are decisive in warfare. While of course stressing that China should develop its national defense and achieve the most modern weapons possible, Mao insisted that the development of new weapons, including nuclear weapons, did not change the basic principles of war and revolutionary wars in particular. He continued to give emphasis to the development not only of a regular army, but also to the broad armed forces of the masses of people, as expressed organizationally in the development of the militia, which would be an important force in addition to the regular people's army in the waging of a revolutionary war against imperialist aggression in China.

In 1958, in a speech at the group leaders' forum of the enlarged meeting of the military affairs committee, Mao criticized the Soviets' military doctrine and military strategy because it was all based on the offensive and was opposed to the basic principles of waging people's war.[57]

Several years later, in the early 1960s, in criticizing a Soviet textbook on political economy Mao stressed that it was important to achieve modernization of the economy, and that this had particular significance in regard to the question of war and defending the country, but that it could not be made decisive in the development of military strategy. He noted that:

For now we are holding off on general automation. Mechanization has to be discussed, but with a sense of proportion. If mechanization and automation are made too much of, it is bound to make people despise partial mechanization and production by native methods. In the past we had such diversions, when everybody was demanding new technology, new machinery, the large scale, high standards; the native, the medium, or small in scale were held in contempt. We did not overcome this tendency until we promoted concurrently native *and* foreign, large *and* medium *and* small.[58]

Mao specifically drew the link between this and the question of warfare:

We will adopt advanced technology, but this cannot gainsay [negate] the necessity and the inevitability of backward technology for a period of time. Since history began, revolutionary wars have always been won by those whose weapons were deficient, lost by those with the advantage in weapons. During our civil war, our War of Resistance Against Japan, and our War of Liberation, we lacked nationwide political power and modernized arsenals. If one cannot fight unless one has the most modern weapons, that is the same as disarming one's self.[59]

Here, as before, Mao was basing himself on the rich experience of the Chinese revolution as well as the revolutionary struggles in other countries and on the basic principles of military line and strategy which he had developed over a long period in leading the armed struggle of the Chinese people and in summing up further the development of revolutionary wars in the world.

Later, Mao spoke to this basic principle immediately after the 9th National Congress of the Chinese Communist Party in 1969. This was a time when U.S. military action against Vietnam was at a high point, with the stationing of hundreds of thousands of troops in southern Vietnam and aggression against the North, while at the same time Soviet aggressive acts were intensifying on the northern border of China. Mao once again reaffirmed the basic

A women's detachment of the Cambodian liberation forces marching to the front during the war against U.S. imperialism.

strategic orientation and principles of warfare which, in opposition
to various revisionist lines, he insisted still applied to the situation
in China in the face of the threat of imperialist aggression at that
time. He pointedly declared:

> Others may come and attack us but we shall not fight outside our
> borders. We do not fight outside our borders. I say we will not be pro-
> voked. Even if you invite us to come out we will not come out, but if you
> should come and attack us we will deal with you. It depends on whether
> you attack on a small scale or a large scale. If it is on a small scale we will
> fight on the border. If it is on a large scale then I am in favor of yielding
> some ground. China is no small country. If there is nothing in it for them I
> don't think they will come. We must make it clear to the whole world that
> we have both right and advantage on our side. If they invade our territory
> then I think it would be more to our advantage, and we would then have
> both right and advantage. They would be easy to fight since they would
> fall into the people's encirclement. As for things like aeroplanes, tanks
> and armored cars, everywhere experience proves that they can be dealt
> with.[60]

One year later Mao issued his statement in support of the Indochinese peoples' struggle against U.S. aggression, which was also
a declaration of support for the revolutionary struggles of the
peoples of the world. In this statement Mao emphasized that a
small country can defeat a big country and a weak country can
defeat a strong country if the people dare to rise in struggle, take
up arms, rely on their own strength and fight to become masters of
their own country. This was not only based on a summation of the
heroic struggle and experience in revolutionary warfare of the
peoples of Indochina (which retain great value, despite the total
revisionist betrayal of the leaders of Vietnam today) but also a
summation of the long years of revolutionary armed struggle in
China itself, especially after the establishment of the first base
areas. For these revolutionary base areas represented in essence a
state, a revolutionary regime, and the historical experience of the
Chinese revolution exactly marked the process of a small and weak
state, the liberated base areas, defeating a more powerful state by
carrying out people's war. It marked the process of a revolutionary
army, relying on the masses of people, defeating a reactionary army which at the start of the war was superior technologically and
even in numbers. This has great significance for revolutionary warfare in all countries.

Down to the very end Mao Tsetung not only continued to champion and support revolution in China but also the revolutionary
struggles of the peoples of the world. And it can be clearly seen

that Mao Tsetung's overall analysis and basic line and theory on the question of warfare, as on other questions, is a powerful weapon for the revolutionary people in all countries and has enduring and universal significance, though its concrete application may differ from country to country. On the question of warfare and military line, as on other questions, Mao Tsetung has made truly immortal contributions to the revolutionary struggle of the working class and oppressed peoples throughout the world and to the cause of communism.

Chapter 3

POLITICAL ECONOMY,
ECONOMIC POLICY
AND SOCIALIST CONSTRUCTION

Introduction

As pointed out in the two previous chapters (dealing with Mao's line on revolution in colonial and semi-colonial countries and on revolutionary war and military line respectively), one of the specific features—and specific advantages—of the Chinese revolution was that from a very early stage the revolutionary forces, led by the Communist Party, established liberated areas which served as a base for waging war against the reactionary enemy. In order to maintain these liberated base areas and make them as powerful as possible a foundation for waging revolutionary war, in order to unleash the activism of the masses in these areas—and ultimately in the whole country—in the revolutionary struggle and as the backbone of that struggle, and in order to unite all real friends against the enemy at every point, it was necessary not only to have a correct political line generally, and not only to have in particular a correct military line; it was also necessary to forge and apply a correct line on questions of political economy, economic policy and construction.

As noted in the first chapter, at a very early point in the Chinese revolution (1926) Mao made a basic analysis of classes in Chinese society, exactly for the purpose of determining friends and enemies in the revolution at that stage. Such class analysis is an important part of Marxism and Marxist political economy in particular as well as an urgent task at each decisive stage in the development of the revolution. And throughout the various stages (and sub-stages) of the Chinese revolution Mao devoted serious attention to this problem.

In addition, from the time of the establishment of the first base area (1927) Mao, in leading the revolutionary struggle, had to and did devote serious attention to economic policy and to specific guidelines for economic construction. And through the course of more than 20 years, from the time of the establishment of the first base area to the winning of nationwide political power in 1949, Mao and the Chinese Communist Party accumulated rich experience in carrying out revolution on the economic battlefront and on that basis developing production. This was to serve as an important part of the foundation for Mao's development of a revolutionary line on these crucial questions during the socialist period following the seizure of power. Further, many of the basic principles of military line and strategy which Mao developed in guiding the Chinese people during the long years of revolutionary war leading up to the seizure of nationwide political power were applied by Mao to the problems of economic policy and construction both in the liberated areas during the period of the new-democratic revolution and in the country as a whole during the socialist stage which followed.

All this is another aspect of the phenomenon that the new-democratic revolution served as the preparation for and prologue to socialism in China. But, of course, upon entering the socialist period new tasks presented themselves, new problems which had to be solved in order to continue to advance. As always, in addressing himself to and providing solutions for these problems, Mao not only applied the rich lessons of the Chinese revolution but assimilated and applied the lessons of the positive and negative experience of other revolutions and in particular of the Soviet Union, the world's first socialist state. In this process he not only applied and defended but developed and enriched basic principles of Marxism-Leninism. This is certainly true with regard to the questions of political economy, economic policy and socialist construction.

These questions and Mao's great contributions in these areas constitute of course a big subject. To go fully into it is beyond the scope of this book. The closely related question of Mao's great theory of "continuing the revolution under the dictatorship of the proletariat" will be dealt with in a subsequent chapter. Here attention will be focused on summarizing the main points concerning Mao's line on political economy, economic policy and socialist construction.

Marxist Political Economy

As Mao himself was to say, "Political economy aims to study

the production relations."[1] Karl Marx, with the collaboration of Frederick Engels, in founding the revolutionary science of the proletariat, first developed socialist political economy as a key component part of this science. Marx penetrated beneath the thousands of surface phenomena of capitalism and analyzed the essential relations that characterize this form of society. As Mao pointed out, "Marx began with the commodity and went on to reveal the relations among people hidden behind commodities . . ."[2]

Proceeding from this, in his famous work *Capital* and elsewhere, Marx laid bare the basic contradiction of capitalism between socialized production and private ownership and the secret of capitalist accumulation—the exploitation of the wage-workers in the process of production by the capitalist owners of the means of production to create surplus value appropriated privately by these capitalists.

Marx showed that this capitalist mode of production was not, as its apologists proclaimed, the highest, most perfect and final stage of society, but merely represented the latest of *"particular historical phases in the development of production."*[3] It was bound to be superseded by a new, higher mode of production—communism—which would represent a qualitative leap for mankind, characterized by the elimination of all class distinctions and a tremendous and continuous advance of the social forces of production.

Communism was bound to replace capitalism, Marx demonstrated, not because communism represented a more "just" or a "utopian" form of society, but because the progress of mankind through all previous historical phases in the development of production, up to capitalism, had prepared the basis for communism, and because the fundamental contradiction of capitalism would continually throw society into ever greater chaos and crisis, with the development of the social productive forces straining to burst the confines of the relations of production—in particular private capitalist ownership—until this contradiction was resolved in the only way it could be: through the abolition of the capitalist system of private ownership and the conversion of all means of production into the common property of society.

To accomplish this required, Marx further showed, a political revolution in which the exploited proletariat overthrew the capitalist class, smashed the capitalists' state machinery, established its own state—the revolutionary dictatorship of the proletariat—and advanced to "the *abolition of class distinctions generally,* to the abolition of all the relations of production on which they rest, to the abolition of all the social relations that correspond to these relations of production, to the revolutionizing of all the ideas that result from these social relations."[4]

Unfortunately, however, neither Marx nor Engels lived to see the period when the proletariat, having seized power, began the process of carrying out this unprecedented transformation of society. With the exception of the Paris Commune in 1871, no proletarian state was established during their lifetimes and the Paris Commune itself lasted only a few months before it was smashed by the forces of counter-revolution.

Lenin's Contribution to Political Economy

But at that very time capitalism was, in a number of countries, beginning to develop towards its highest and final stage—imperialism. It was Lenin who thoroughly analyzed this development and proved in opposition to various opportunists—including Karl Kautsky, who had been a close collaborator of Engels but had turned into a counter-revolutionary in the latter part of his life—that imperialism did not eliminate or somehow dilute the basic contradiction of capitalism but raised it to a higher level. Imperialism, Lenin showed, was not only the highest stage of capitalism, it was also the eve of proletarian revolution. And Lenin led the proletariat of Russia in making the first successful proletarian revolution, in establishing the first socialist state which began the process of transition to communism.

Lenin developed Marxism—and, as a key component part of this, Marxist political economy—to a new and higher stage. Marxism became Marxism-Leninism.

Further, for the brief period between the seizure of power in Russia in 1917 and his death in 1924, Lenin applied these scientific principles to the concrete problems confronting the new socialist state, including in the crucial sphere of economic policy and construction. Lenin set forth the basic orientation and direction that would guide the proletariat of the Soviet Union in carrying out the transformation of ownership from capitalist to socialist in town and countryside and lead to the high-speed development of the socialist economy.

During the Civil War and the imperialist intervention following the October Revolution, Lenin developed the policy of War Communism. This immediately concentrated ownership and the lifelines of the economy in the hands of the proletarian state and enabled the victorious proletariat to maintain a sufficient material base to defeat the domestic and foreign reactionaries that had ganged up against it and to lay the basis for developing the economy following the war. At the same time, it required tremendous sacrifice on the part of the Russian workers and peasants and, with regard to the latter in particular, put severe strains on them in the form of state appropriation of their surplus grain.

After the civil war, Lenin recognized that the policy of War Communism, while it had contributed to victory in the war, had also raced ahead of the material as well as political, ideological and organizational conditions. He called for a retreat, to prepare the conditions for a future advance. This retreat was embodied in the New Economic Policy (NEP). This new policy abandoned the surplus grain appropriation policy and replaced it with a tax (the tax in kind) as the means for the state to secure grain.

The NEP embodied considerable concessions to capitalism—both domestic and foreign, in both city and countryside. It allowed foreign capitalists to operate in the country and even lured them with the prospect of high profits. It permitted domestic capitalists to operate certain businesses. Even within state-owned enterprises it involved the practices of one-man management, reliance on bourgeois experts, specialists and executives, and the widespread use of such things as piece-work and many rules and regulations similar to those in capitalist factories (many of these management policies had actually been part of War Communism as well).

All this was necessary to achieve in the shortest possible time the rehabilitation of the economy, which had been shattered and in many places nearly brought to a standstill during the course of the civil war, with many workers dislodged from production and becoming virtually declassed. It was necessary to strengthen the proletariat and the proletarian state politically as well as economically. At the same time, however, the proletariat, through its state power, maintained control over finance and trade and placed restrictions on the operation of private capital in town and countryside. And Lenin stressed the importance during this period of establishing and developing producers' and consumers' cooperatives to lay the basis for collectivization in the countryside and the general advance to socialist relations in the near future. In this way, the Soviet Union advanced economically through the state capitalism of the NEP to socialism.

Lenin was very open about the fact that the NEP represented a retreat and a concession in the short run to capitalism. It was justified and necessary, he argued, because of the specific conditions in the country at that time. It was not a grand plan for developing the country into a powerful modern socialist state, nor were its basic policies meant to apply to socialist construction, as revisionists since Khrushchev's time have been known to claim. It was the means for creating the conditions in a brief period for the advance to a socialist economy, for an assault on strategic economic positions of capitalism.

Socialist Construction Under Stalin

During the very last part of his life Lenin fell seriously ill and was no longer able to give leadership to the day to day affairs of the Party and state. It was Stalin who took the helm, carried forward the NEP and led in the advance to socialist industrialization and development of agriculture. In carrying this out, Stalin also led the fierce and continuing struggle within the Party against the likes of Trotsky, Kamenev, Zinoviev and Bukharin, opportunists who opposed now from one side and now the other the correct road forward.

Trotsky, and along with him Kamenev and Zinoviev, peddled the "theory of productive forces," arguing that it was impossible to construct socialism in the Soviet Republic because it was economically and technically too backward. This line had, in part, a thin "left" cover by insisting that immediate revolution in Europe was required for socialism to survive in Russia. However the rightist essence of this line was barely below the surface. On the other hand, Trotsky opposed the NEP by clamoring for policies of exploiting the peasants to achieve industrialization and organizing military-like conditions in the factories to force the workers to boost production; and he even called for extending the granting of foreign concessions to strategic plants and branches of industry, thus, as Stalin put it, trying to "throw ourselves on the tender mercies of foreign capitalists."[5]

Later, when the Party had formulated and embarked on the policy of carrying out socialist industrialization of the country on the basis of a revived agriculture, Trotsky, in league with Zinoviev and others, charged that industrialization was not being carried out fast enough. But in reality they were fully opposed to socialist industrialization and tried to undermine it by pitting the mass of peasants against the working class, calling in fact for reliance on the rich peasants, the capitalist forces in the countryside. From all this it can be seen that the distinguishing feature of Trotsky, and what enables one to recognize the real followers of Trotsky, is the consistent absence of principles except careerism and lack of faith in the masses and a fundamental unity with the right.

This was demonstrated in the fact that Trotsky's line of relying on capitalist forces with regard to industry and agriculture was very similar to that of Bukharin, who during the NEP and afterward pushed the line of building up the bourgeoisie according to the notion of "the peaceful growing of the bourgeoisie into Socialism, amplifying it with a 'new' slogan—'Get Rich!' "[6] Bukharin especially championed this right opportunism with regard to the countryside, arguing straight out for a policy which, like the essence of Trotsky's line, meant fostering and relying on the capitalist elements, the Kulaks.

Stalin led the Soviet Party in defeating these various bourgeois lines and in carrying out socialist industrialization and the step by step collectivization of agriculture. Neither of these, of course, had been accomplished before in history; and in particular the successful collectivization of agriculture, involving the most acute class struggle inside and outside the Party, was a monumental task and of decisive importance for the building of socialism in the Soviet Union. For Russia at the time of the October Revolution was largely a peasant country with a backward countryside, including large-scale survivals of feudal relations, even though it had been an imperialist country.

To bring about socialist collectivization together with socialist industrialization and transform the Soviet Union from a relatively backward to an advanced country economically—all of which was accomplished in the two decades between the end of the civil war in Russia and WW2—was a great achievement of the Soviet working class and people under the leadership of Stalin. And it had much to do with the Soviet Union's ability to defeat the Nazi invaders in WW2, another great achievement of the Soviet people carried out under Stalin's leadership.

At the same time, in giving leadership to an unprecedented task of such tremendous proportions—the socialization, transformation and rapid development of the economy of such a large and complex country as the Soviet Union under the conditions where it was the only socialist state in a world still dominated by imperialism—Stalin did make certain errors. To a significant degree this is explainable by the very fact that there was no historical precedent for this task, no previous experience (and previous errors) to learn from. On the other hand, as Mao has summed up, certain of Stalin's errors, including in the sphere of political economy,

economic policy and socialist construction, arose because and to
the extent that Stalin failed to thoroughly apply materialist dialectics to solving problems, including many genuinely new problems
that did arise.

Owing largely to this, especially in the period of the 1930s—after
collectivization in agriculture and socialist transformation of
ownership in industry had been essentially completed—Stalin
himself adopted aspects of the "theory of productive forces." He
developed first the slogan that "technique decides everything"
and then the related concept that, with modern technique, cadres
capable of mastering this technology decide everything.

This seriously downplays the question of politics, in fact goes
against the line of politics in command, and also downplays the
role of the masses and specifically the need to rely on the conscious
activism of the masses in socialist production as in everything
else. Along with this, while he led in carrying out collectivization
in the countryside in the late 1920s, Stalin tended to develop industry at the expense of agriculture, leaving the peasants too few
funds for accumulation through their own efforts.

Stalin also continued many of the policies that had been in-
troduced during the NEP (or before, during War Communism),
such as extensive use of piece-work, bonuses, one-man management, experts in command, and so forth. In essence Stalin put one-
sided emphasis on the question of ownership, which is the most
decisive but not the only aspect of the relations of production. He
failed to pay consistent attention to revolutionizing the other
aspects of the relations of production (relations between people in
production and distribution) and the superstructure.

To a large degree, Stalin proceeded from the assumption that
once the question of ownership was largely settled—that is, once
public ownership had basically replaced private ownership—then
all that was necessary was to achieve and master advanced
technology and efficient management and in this way socialism
would continue to achieve a more powerful material base and society would continue advancing toward communism. This incorrect
view went hand in hand with Stalin's erroneous analysis that by
the mid-1930s antagonistic classes had been eliminated in the
Soviet Union. It failed to recognize that the bourgeoisie is constantly regenerated out of the contradictions of socialist society
itself—such as between mental and manual labor, town and countryside, worker and peasant, as well as disparities in income arising from the application of the principle of "to each according to
his work"—and that so long as these inequalities left over from

capitalism persist there will continue to be classes and class struggle, including the antagonistic struggle between the proletariat and the bourgeoisie, which forms the principal contradiction under socialism.

Stalin himself repeatedly and resolutely fought against attempts to restore capitalism in the Soviet Union. But errors such as those briefly summarized above did take their toll. And the effects of these errors were greatly magnified during the Great Patriotic War against Germany, when a certain amount of compromise was necessary with bourgeois forces inside and outside the Soviet Union who were opposed to the fascist Axis. All this allowed more ground for bourgeois forces, especially the bourgeoisie within the Soviet Party and state (those whose counterparts in China Mao was later to call "capitalist-roaders") to prepare the ground for capitalist restoration while Stalin was still alive and then to carry out this retrogression not long after he died.

In his last few years Stalin did in fact address himself to some of the basic questions arising from the remnants of capitalism still surviving under socialism. Specifically, in *Economic Problems of Socialism in the USSR*, Stalin pointed out that, while it did not play a regulating role in the economy, the law of value continued to operate within a restricted sphere. This was due, Stalin said, to the fact that in the countryside the form of socialist ownership was not state but collective, which was an important aspect of the continuing disparity between the city and countryside, and because commodity exchange hadn't yet been entirely replaced by a higher form of exchange.

Further, Stalin addressed some of the major contradictions that would have to be resolved in order to advance to communism. Besides the disparity between town and country, he called particular attention to the mental/manual contradiction. Stalin stressed that in order to advance to communism it would be necessary to resolve these as well as other contradictions left over from capitalism—to eliminate the essential difference between town and country, mental and manual labor and so on.

But, at the same time, Stalin tended to treat the question of eliminating these differences almost entirely from the standpoint of developing production and raising the material and technical level of the masses and not very much from the standpoint of politics and ideology. In other words, Stalin did not put much emphasis on restricting these differences to the degree possible at

each point and how this was dialectically related to the tasks of
developing production, raising the material and technical level of
the masses, etc., nor on the question of waging struggle in the
ideological sphere to combat the bourgeois ideology which is
fostered by these disparities.

One of the strongest points in this work by Stalin is his refutation of the revisionist deviations of L.D. Yaroshenko. "Comrade
Yaroshenko's chief error," wrote Stalin, "is that he forsakes the
Marxist position on the question of the role of the productive
forces and of the relations of production in the development of
society, that he inordinately overrates the role of the productive
forces, and just as inordinately underrates the role of the relations
of production, and ends up by declaring that under socialism the
relations of production are a component part of the productive
forces."[7]

Stalin went on to point out that the contradiction between the
relations and forces of production continues to exist under
socialism, because "the development of the relations of production
lags, and will lag, behind the development of the productive
forces."[8] With a correct line in command, Stalin stressed, this contradiction would not become an antagonistic one. The opposite
would be the case, however, if an incorrect line were applied.

But a shortcoming of Stalin's analysis of this question was that
he still did not acknowledge the existence of the antagonistic class
contradiction between the proletariat and the bourgeoisie and the
fact that the correct handling of the contradiction between the
forces and relations of production depended principally on the correct handling of the contradiction between the proletariat and the
bourgeoisie, on the waging of the class struggle against the
bourgeoisie. In addition, as Mao emphasized, while Stalin insisted
on the continuing existence of the contradiction between the forces
and relations of production, he did not make the same point with
regard to the contradiction between the economic base and the
superstructure: "Stalin speaks only of the production relations,
not of the superstructure, nor of the relationship between
superstructure and economic base. . . . Stalin mentions economics
only, not politics." And "Stalin's book from first to last says nothing about the superstructure. It is not concerned with people; it
considers things, not people."[9]

In these criticisms, written in the late 1950s, Mao was not only
reflecting certain important differences he had developed with the
Soviet line even under Stalin, but he was also beginning to forge a
further advance in Marxist-Leninist theory and practice on the

question of political economy, in particular on the relationship between revolution and production. This was only forged, however, through sharp two-line struggle within the Chinese Communist Party around these same questions, struggle which was to continue and deepen over the remaining years of Mao's life.

In fact, from the time that political power was won there developed a struggle within the Chinese Communist Party over what road to take—the socialist or capitalist road. Opposition to the socialist road came from two directions. First were those who argued for the necessity of "assistance" from the United States, even though U.S. imperialism had been the most powerful backer of Chiang Kai-shek and was of course still intent on subjugating China. Such a line of looking to the U.S. for "assistance" amounted in fact to promoting dependence on and capitulation to U.S. imperialism and would have meant not only that socialism could not be built in China but even that the victories of the new-democratic revolution would be wiped out.

At the same time there were those who wanted to strictly apply in China the Soviet approach to economic construction, just as there had been those who earlier had wanted to blindly follow the Soviet model in the struggle leading up to the seizure of nationwide political power. The struggle against this deviation sharpened into an antagonism after the revisionist coup of Khrushchev & Co. in the mid-1950s, when the Soviet model became a model for restoring capitalism.

Economic Policy in Liberated Areas

In opposition to both these opportunist lines Mao increasingly developed a revolutionary line for building socialism, which was rooted both in the long experience and lessons of the Chinese revolution during the struggle for power and in a deepening summation of the Soviet experience and its positive and negative lessons, under Stalin's leadership and then with the triumph of revisionism. Some who had sided with Mao during the period of the new-democratic revolution came to regard his line and the basic principles guiding it as "outmoded" once political power was captured, and this became a more marked phenomenon the further China advanced into the socialist period. But Mao continued to fight for the understanding that the basic principles that had guided the successful, if protracted and complex, struggle for power must also guide revolution and construction in the socialist stage. Politics in command, reliance on the masses, recognizing the crucial role of the peasants and the importance of the countryside, combatting elitism and tendencies to bureaucratism—these and other points which reflected and flowed from the ideological and political line representing the outlook and interests of the proletariat continued to form the foundation of Mao's line.

From the first phases of the Chinese revolution, Mao stressed that, with regard to economic policy as in other fields, while carrying out the bourgeois-democratic revolution as the first stage and resisting "ultra-left" lines that would expropriate small-owning middle forces and drive them into the camp of the enemy, it was necessary during that stage to lay the basis economically as well as in other ways for the socialist future. In an article written in January 1934, addressing the question of the economic policy in the liberated areas, Mao formulated it this way:

The principle governing our economic policy is to proceed with all the essential work of economic construction within our power and concentrate our economic resources on the war effort, and at the same time to improve the life of the people as much as possible, consolidate the worker-peasant alliance in the economic field, ensure proletarian leadership of the peasantry, and strive to secure leadership by the state sector of the economy over the private sector, thus creating the prerequisites for our future advance to socialism.[10]

Later, in his major work "On New Democracy," written in January 1940 during the anti-Japanese war, Mao stressed that "we must never establish a capitalist society of the European-American type or allow the old semi-feudal society to survive." And he noted that as far as the economy of the new-democratic period was concerned, "In general, socialist agriculture will not be established at this stage, though various types of co-operative enterprises developed on the basis of 'land to the tiller' will contain elements of socialism."[11]

As explained in the first chapter of this book, in order to unite all possible forces against the Japanese aggressors, for the duration of the anti-Japanese war the Chinese Communist Party adjusted its policy on agrarian economic relations, pulling back from the policy of confiscating the landlords' holdings in most cases and substituting instead the campaign to reduce rent, taxes, etc. But this did not mean that such reduction could be achieved, nor certainly maintained, without a struggle.

Mao emphasized that "rent reduction is a mass struggle by the peasants," and that therefore "Party directives and government decrees [of the government in the base areas] should guide and help it instead of trying to bestow favours on the masses. To bestow rent reduction as a favour instead of arousing the masses to achieve it by their own action is wrong, and the results will not be solid."[12]

Mobilizing the masses was the key to carrying out rent (and tax) reduction, which in turn served as the basis for organizing the peasant masses to carry out production to support the revolutionary government and armed forces. And in this production drive, mobilizing the masses was also decisive. While insisting that "No one who fails to study production carefully can be considered a good leader," Mao sharply criticized those cadres who:

take a conservative and purely financial point of view which concentrates on revenue and expenditure to the neglect of economic development. It is wrong to have a handful of government functionaries busying themselves with collecting grain and taxes, funds and food supplies to the neglect of organizing the enormous labour power of the rank and file of the Party, the government and the army, and that of the people, for a mass campaign of production.[13]

Here a crucial question was at stake: how to ease the burden that the peasants had been forced to bear under the old rule while at the same time providing the necessary material base for maintaining the new regime and supporting the revolutionary armed forces in the war of resistance against Japan. The solution lay, Mao stressed, in mobilizing the Party rank and file and Party and government functionaries (cadre), as well as the army members as far as possible, together with the masses of people in mass campaigns of production. At the same time it was crucial to mobilize the masses both to transform production relations as far as possible—establish mutual-aid labor teams and other beginning forms of cooperation—and to make breakthroughs in developing new techniques in production, even with the still primitive means of production they possessed. Without this it would be impossible to unleash the activism and creativeness of the masses as the backbone of the war of resistance against Japan.

The participation of the troops in production was an important link in all this: it helped enable the burden of taxation by the revolutionary government to be lightened for the peasants. As Mao pointed out, if the soldiers spent three months of the year in production and devoted nine months to fighting and training, then the situation could be maintained where "Our troops depend for their pay neither on the Kuomintang government, nor on the Border Region Government [revolutionary government], nor on the people, but can fully provide for themselves."[14] This remained an important part of Mao's line on economic policy and specifically the relation between economic construction and warfare, resistance to aggression, in the socialist period as well.

In his well-known speech to labor heroes in the liberated areas ("Get Organized!") Mao again gave emphasis to the fact that there were two opposed methods of dealing with production problems:

> To organize the strength of the masses is one policy. Is there a contrary policy? Yes, there is. It is one that lacks the mass viewpoint, fails to rely on the masses or organize them, and gives exclusive attention to organizing the small number of people working in the financial, supply or trading organizations, while paying no attention to organizing the masses in the villages, the army, the government and other organizations, the schools and factories; it treats economic work not as a broad movement or as an extensive front, but only as an expedient for meeting financial deficits. That is the other policy, the wrong policy.[15]

Mao went on to show again the links between present economic policy and the future advance to socialism. "The cooperatives," he pointed out, "are now the most important form of mass organization in the economic field." They represented a cornerstone of the bridge leading from the individual economy of the peasants that had existed for thousands of years under feudalism to the collective economy of socialism. Mao noted:

> This scattered, individual form of production is the economic foundation of feudal rule and keeps the peasants in perpetual poverty. The only way to change it is gradual collectivization, and the only way to bring about collectivization, according to Lenin, is through co-operatives. We have already organized many peasant co-operatives in the Border Region [base area], but at present they are only of a rudimentary type and must go through several stages of development before they can become co-operatives of the Soviet type known as collective farms. Ours is a new-democratic economy, and our co-operatives are still organizations for collective labour based on an individual economy (on private property).[16]

Here Mao charted the basic course that cooperation in the Chinese countryside would undergo in advancing the peasant economy to socialist relations, with the first step, appropriate to the new-democratic period, being mutual-aid labor teams. As with everything else, Mao stressed that the success of these teams depended on the mobilization and conscious activism of the masses. In fact, Mao pointed out, "These methods of collective mutual aid are the inventions of the masses themselves...." and the task of the Party was to sum up and popularize them.[17]

Several years later, with victory approaching in the anti-Japanese war, Mao emphasized again the importance of correctly handling economic policy. In particular, he criticized those comrades who did not base economic policy on the concrete conditions of China's revolutionary struggle, specifically the fact that this struggle was then centered in the countryside and must proceed by advancing from the countryside to the cities:

We want to hit the Japanese aggressors hard and make preparations for seizing the cities and recovering our lost territories. But how can we attain this aim, situated as we are in a countryside founded on individual economy, cut up by the enemy and involved in guerrilla warfare? We cannot imitate the Kuomintang, which does not lift a finger itself but depends entirely on foreigners even for such necessities as cotton cloth. We stand for self-reliance. We hope for foreign aid but cannot be dependent on it; we depend on our own efforts, on the creative power of the whole army and the entire people. But how do we go about it? By launching large-scale production campaigns simultaneously among the troops and the people.[18]

This was akin to the principle Mao applied in warfare—concentrating forces for a battle of annihilation—a principle he continued to apply to economic construction, in particular with regard to key links and key projects in the economy, both in the new-democratic and the socialist periods.

While he was specifically dealing with the situation then facing the revolution, the emphasis Mao gives in the quote above—on the importance of the countryside, on mobilizing the masses, on the army taking part in production as well as fighting and training, and on self-reliance generally—all these were not only of vital importance in the conditions of that time. They remained basic principles even after nationwide political power was won and the socialist period was entered.

Similarly, in the same article, Mao says, "Since we are in the countryside, where manpower and material resources are scattered, we have adopted the policy of 'unified leadership and decentralized management' for production and supply."[19] This was closely linked with the military principle that Mao developed of combining unified strategy and strategic command with decentralized command and flexibility and initiative in particular campaigns and battles. (See the previous chapter.) And this principle, too, was upheld and applied by Mao in the socialist period—though again, not without sharp struggle within the Communist Party itself.

Immediately following the defeat of the Japanese imperialists,

Mao again reminded the Party and the masses that the victories won through their own efforts could only be defended, and new victories achieved, by continuing to practice self-reliance. Preparing for the counter-revolutionary attempt of Chiang Kai-shek to seize the fruits of this victory and re-establish reactionary rule throughout China, Mao insisted that "As for the reactionaries in China, it is up to us to organize the people to overthrow them."[20]

Using an example from an earlier period in the Chinese revolution, when a landlord in a particular area refused to surrender and held out in his fortified village until the revolutionary army swept in and cleaned him out, Mao called attention to the fact that there remained many such reactionary "fortified villages" in China and drew the lesson that "Everything reactionary is the same; if you don't hit it, it won't fall. It is like sweeping the floor; where the broom does not reach, the dust never vanishes of itself."[21]

What, then, could and must be relied on to sweep China clean of reactionary rule? Reliance must be placed, Mao said, on the masses of people led by the Communist Party. "On what basis should our policy rest?" he asked. "It should rest on our own strength, and that means regeneration through one's own efforts."[22] Again, this was also a basic principle that Mao fought for and applied not only in leading the Chinese new-democratic revolution to complete victory through successful revolutionary war against Chiang Kai-shek, but also in carrying forward socialist revolution and socialist construction following this victory. And, again, this Mao did only through waging sharp struggle within the Communist Party itself against those who opposed the policy of self-reliance and regeneration through one's own efforts.

Mao Analyzes New Tasks

On the other hand, policies adopted in the countryside during the long years of revolutionary struggle centered there could not be mechanically applied in the cities. And even in the countryside a distinction had to be drawn between agriculture and industry, between policies that guided the anti-feudal agrarian revolution and those that must be utilized with regard to capitalist production and commerce. To handle this correctly required more deeply arming the Party and the masses with the far-sighted outlook of the proletariat and educating them as to their general and long-term interests.

Mao addressed these questions in an article written in early 1948, when final victory in the war against Chiang Kai-shek could already be seen on the horizon and the question of capturing and administering larger cities was already an immediate one. Mao warned that "Precautions should be taken against the mistake of applying in the cities the measures used in rural areas for struggling against landlords and rich peasants." He further insisted that:

A sharp distinction should be made between the feudal exploitation practised by landlords and rich peasants, which must be abolished, and the industrial and commercial enterprises run by landlords and rich peasants, which must be protected. A sharp distinction should also be made between the correct policy of developing production, promoting economic prosperity, giving consideration to both public and private interests and benefiting both labour and capital, and the one-sided and narrow-minded policy of "relief," which purports to uphold the workers' welfare but in fact damages industry and commerce and impairs the cause of the people's revolution. Education should be conducted among comrades in the trade unions and among the masses of workers to enable them to understand that they should not see merely the immediate and partial interests of the working class while forgetting its broad, long-range interests.[23]

What Mao was upholding here was both the correct policy for the present new-democratic stage of the revolution and the correct basis for making the future advance from this to the socialist stage. This was directly in opposition to a line which would have made the democratic revolution an end in itself and would have promoted welfarism and economism among the workers, pitting immediate short-term improvement in their conditions—"relief" —against their basic interests in establishing the material as well as political and ideological conditions for advancing to socialism—including the achievement of final victory in the war against Chiang Kai-shek.

Struggle against this kind of erroneous line was becoming increasingly decisive exactly because the seizure of nationwide political power was on the horizon. And with the achievement of political power the question of whether to take the capitalist or socialist road came to the fore. In March of 1949, in a most important speech to the Central Committee of the Chinese Communist Party, Mao analyzed the situation and the tasks immediately confronting the Party with the capture of the big cities and the victorious conclusion of the war of liberation against Chiang Kai-shek and his U.S. imperialist backers.

The central task immediately following the seizure of power, Mao said, must be production and construction. Why? Because otherwise political power could not be consolidated and the advance to socialism would, of course, also be impossible. As Mao bluntly pointed out:

If we know nothing about production and do not master it quickly, if we cannot restore and develop production as speedily as possible and achieve solid successes so that the livelihood of the workers, first of all, and that of the people in general is improved, we shall be unable to maintain our political power, we shall be unable to stand on our feet, we shall fail.[24]

Here Mao was following a policy similar to that adopted by Lenin during the first few years of the Soviet Republic—the period of War Communism and then the NEP—when the rehabilitation of the national economy under the rule of the proletariat was decisive in determining whether or not the new state power of the proletariat would survive and be able to advance to take up the socialist transformation and development of the economy. But even under these conditions, as Lenin had insisted in fierce battle against Trotsky, Bukharin and other opportunists, the correct political line must lead, or else state power would be lost anyway by the proletariat and then of course it could not solve its production problems either.

So, too, Mao fought against incorrect lines that would either have given free rein to private capitalism and elevated its position above state enterprise in industrial policy or would have too severely restricted or even tried to eliminate private capitalism right away, not making use of it in rehabilitating and beginning to develop the economy. In opposition to both of these errors Mao insisted that:

all capitalist elements in the cities and countryside which are not harmful but beneficial to the national economy should be allowed to exist and expand. This is not only unavoidable but also economically necessary. But the existence and expansion of capitalism in China will not be unrestricted and uncurbed as in the capitalist countries. It will be restricted from several directions—in the scope of its operation and by tax policy, market prices and labour conditions.[25]

This policy of allowing but restricting capitalism and of gradually transforming private ownership in industry into socialist state ownership through a series of steps was essential to make the transition from new democracy to socialism. During this process of transition and transformation, Mao pointed out, "Restriction versus opposition to restriction will be the main form of class struggle. . ."[26]

Such a policy, while correct with regard to the national capitalists—the middle bourgeoisie—absolutely could not be applied to the imperialists nor to the big bourgeoisie in China, the bureaucrat-capitalists, whose holdings constituted roughly 80% of China's capitalism. These had to be immediately confiscated, both to break the economic and political basis of their power and to liberate the productive forces and make possible the rehabilitation and rapid development of the economy. As Mao said:

The confiscation of this capital and its transfer to the people's republic led by the proletariat will enable the people's republic to control the economic lifelines of the country and will enable the state-owned economy to become the leading sector of the entire national economy. This sector of the economy is socialist, not capitalist, in character.[27]

From New Democracy to Socialism

This, again, was crucial in making the transition from new democracy to socialism. As Mao was later to sum up, "The struggle against bureaucratic capitalism had a two-sided character: it had a democratic revolutionary character insofar as it amounted to opposition to comprador capitalism, but it had a socialist character insofar as it amounted to opposition to the big bourgeoisie."[28]

Establishing the primacy of the state sector and control of the economy generally by the state led by the proletariat and its Party—this was the essential condition for achieving the transition to socialism. It was the key to resolving the main contradictions as they posed themselves during the period immediately after the seizure of nationwide political power.

At this point Mao made the all-important analysis that with country-wide victory in the new-democratic revolution, "two basic contradictions will still exist in China. The first is internal, that is, the contradiction between the working class and the bourgeoisie. The second is external, that is, the contradiction between China and the imperialist countries."[29]

This analysis was to remain a decisive question of line and a sharp focus of two-line struggle within the Chinese Communist Party during the rest of Mao's life. Applying it then to the immediate situation and the task at hand, victory in the new-democratic revolution and the transition to socialism, Mao pointed out that "The two basic policies of the state in the economic struggle will be regulation of capital at home and control of foreign trade. Whoever overlooks or belittles this point will commit extremely serious mistakes."[30]

At the same time Mao pointed to the tremendous importance of the peasant question and of continuing the agrarian revolution beyond the bourgeois-democratic step of land reform—which had been carried out on a broad scale by the end of the war of liberation. Providing "land to the tiller" eliminated the basis of feudal but not of capitalist relations in the countryside. "The serious problem is the education of the peasantry," he noted. And, he said:

The peasant economy is scattered, and the socialization of agriculture, judging by the Soviet Union's experience, will require a long time and painstaking work. Without socialization of agriculture, there can be no complete, consolidated socialism. The steps to socialize agriculture must be co-ordinated with the development of a powerful industry having state enterprise as its backbone.[31]

Analyzing this in the realm of politics, the concentrated expression of economics, Mao pointed out that the people's democratic dictatorship, the form of the dictatorship of the proletariat corresponding to China's conditions with the victory of the new-democratic revolution:

is based on the alliance of the working class, the peasantry and the urban petty bourgeoisie, and mainly on the alliance of the workers and the peasants, because these two classes comprise 80 to 90 per cent of China's population. These two classes are the main force in overthrowing imperialism and the Kuomintang reactionaries. The transition from New Democracy to socialism also depends mainly upon their alliance.[32]

In a period of seven years from the founding of the People's Republic in October 1949, the socialist transformation of ownership in both industry and agriculture was basically completed. But, of course, this too was not accomplished without fierce class struggle both in society as a whole and within the Communist Party itself. During this period the class struggle—the struggle between the socialist and capitalist roads—focused mainly on the question of ownership. But there were also sharp struggles over questions of management, investment priority and other essential issues of economic policy.

Following the basic guidelines set forth by Mao, as outlined before, the Communist Party carried out the line in industry of immediately confiscating the holdings of imperialism and bureaucrat-capitalism while implementing the step by step transformation of national capitalism. This not only allowed the utilization of the positive role of national capital in rehabilitating and developing the economy but also the utilization of the national capitalists in management in the joint state-private enterprises that were set up as an important link in this transformation. At the same time the state enterprises themselves received the bulk of investment and were built up as the main sector. This was crucial in establishing and maintaining the dominance of the state component of the economy and in carrying through socialist transformation in industry.

Two Roads After Liberation

But of course all this gave rise to new contradictions and new struggles. In addition to the problems arising for the use of national capitalists in managerial and even planning positions, the former big capitalists and other reactionary elements not only carried out sabotage and direct resistance to socialist transformation, but a number of them actually succeeded in infiltrating key positions in the economy, including in the state sector. And as Mao had warned in his speech at the Second Plenary Session of the Seventh Central Committee in March 1949, a number of Party members who had stood up heroically to the actual bullets of the enemy during the long years of revolutionary warfare found it difficult to resist the sugar-coated bullets of the bourgeoisie in the new situation where these Party cadre were in positions of power.

To counter this, and as an essential part of carrying forward not only the rehabilitation of the economy but the policy for socialist transformation, the Party launched a struggle against the "three evils" of corruption, waste and bureaucracy in management and administration and the "five evils" of bribery, tax evasion, theft of state property, cheating on government contracts and stealing of economic information for private use. The seriousness with which these struggles had to be undertaken is indicated by the following statement by Mao in late 1951: "The struggle against corruption, waste and bureaucracy should be stressed as much as the struggle to suppress counter-revolutionaries."[33] And Mao called for linking the struggle against these "three evils" with that against the "five evils"—"This is both imperative and very timely," he insisted.[34]

This did not mean that in every case such struggle should be conducted as one between the people and the enemy, though in some cases that was necessary. Distinctions as to the seriousness of the cases should be drawn, but nevertheless the struggle must be sharply waged—"Only thus can we check the grave danger of many Party members being corroded by the bourgeoisie," and prevent the disruption of economic development and transformation in the direction of socialism.[35]

The successful waging of these struggles, however, could not be carried out only "at the top." It required the mobilization of the masses. And as Mao pointed out, an important part of combatting the "five evils" in particular was to "gradually establish a system under which the workers and shop assistants supervise production and management."[36]

But an even more decisive struggle during this period was that within the Party itself against those who promoted and fought for a line in opposition to carrying out socialist transformation. Such revisionists, including Liu Shao-chi and other similar types in top Party leadership, argued that instead of making the transition from the democratic to the socialist stage after seizing political power the task was to "consolidate new democracy."

In the economic sphere, as against the policy of utilizing but restricting and transforming those sections of capital that could contribute to the rehabilitation and development of the economy, these bourgeois-democrats-turned-capitalist-roaders insisted that capitalism should be encouraged and promoted without restriction, even arguing that "exploitation is a merit." They bitterly opposed Mao who, after several years of successful rehabilitation of the economy, in accordance with the basic orientation he had set forth nearly four years earlier, formulated at the end of 1952 the general line for the transition to socialism, calling for bringing about the step by step development of socialist industrialization and socialist transformation of agriculture and handicrafts as well as capitalist industry and commerce.

To rationalize their opposition, these revisionists, represented in the realm of theory and philosophy by some reactionary scholars, most notably one Yang Hsien-chen, "churned out the so-called theory of 'synthesized economic base,' thereby provoking the first big struggle on the philosophical front" in New China.[37]

This bogus, bourgeois theory argued that during the period of transition the economic base should consist of the capitalist and socialist sectors co-existing in harmony and that the superstructure should serve both of these sectors and even serve the bourgeoisie. This echoed Bukharin who, as noted earlier, argued in the Soviet Union in the 1920s that capitalism would peacefully grow into socialism and that therefore the former should be fostered without restriction.

Of course, as pointed out, during the period of transition to socialist ownership in China private capital was allowed to play a

The proclamation of the "Land Reform Law of the People's Republic of China," shortly after liberation, which took away the landlords' right to own land.

certain role, but in order to advance on the socialist road it was necessary to establish the primacy of the socialist sector through the proletarian state and to wage class struggle to achieve the triumph of socialist relations over capitalist relations and bring about socialist transformation. To preach some kind of "harmony" between capitalism and socialism and to even argue that the superstructure, including state power, should serve both sectors and even serve the bourgeoisie meant in fact to champion the victory of capitalism over socialism and the establishment of bourgeois state power enforcing the exploitation of the proletariat and broad masses of people.

With regard to agriculture specifically, Liu Shao-chi and other revisionists opposed and actively tried to stifle and sabotage cooperative transformation. They insisted that any attempt to carry out collectivization must depend on the prior development of heavy industry, which in turn could only be developed by relying on foreign technology according to this view, and that in the meantime the peasants should go it alone in private farming. This, of course, could only lead to widespread polarization and the strengthening of the capitalist forces in the countryside.

Mao sharply criticized and vigorously fought against this line. He showed that in China collectivization must precede mechanization in agriculture and that unless cooperative transformation was carried out the worker-peasant alliance, which had been built during the stage of new democracy on the basis of a bourgeois-democratic program, could not be maintained and developed on a new, socialist basis.

By 1955 this struggle had reached a crossroads. Mao pointed out then that despite the step by step advance from mutual-aid teams to small agricultural producers' cooperatives:

What exists in the countryside today is capitalist ownership by the rich peasants and a vast sea of ownership by individual peasants. As is clear to everyone, the spontaneous forces of capitalism have been steadily growing in the countryside in recent years, with new rich peasants springing up everywhere and many well-to-do middle peasants striving to become rich peasants. On the other hand, many poor peasants are still living in poverty for shortage of the means of production, with some getting into debt and others selling or renting out their land. If this tendency goes unchecked, it is inevitable that polarization in the countryside will get worse day by day.[38]

Mao answered those trumpeting the revisionist line on this question by turning their arguments back against them. In response to

the attack that he was advocating a rash advance in the countryside, and specifically in response to the statement, "if you don't
get off the horse quickly, there will be the danger of breaking up
the worker-peasant alliance," Mao replied:

[This] is probably an "argument" relayed down from the Rural Work
Department of the Central Committee. This department not only
manufactures rumours but also produces a lot of "arguments." I think
that this statement is in the main "correct"—only a single word needs to
be changed, that is, the word "off" be changed into "on." You comrades of
the Rural Work Department do not have to feel discouraged, for I have accepted almost all your words and changed only one. The difference lies in a
single word, our controversy is over just one word—you want to get off
the horse while I want to get on. "If you don't get on the horse quickly,
there will be the danger of breaking up the worker-peasant alliance," and
danger there certainly will be.[39]

The only road forward, Mao made clear, was to mobilize the
peasants "to combine further on the basis of these small semi-
socialist co-operatives and organize large fully socialist
agricultural producers' co-operatives." And there was every basis
for this, Mao said; in fact it was the erroneous line of certain Party
authorities that was holding things back. "We must now realize,"
he declared, "that there will soon be a nation-wide high tide of
socialist transformation in the countryside."[40]

And Mao was correct. His line triumphed over the revisionist
line; in a tremendous upsurge, socialist cooperative transformation triumphed over capitalist ownership in the countryside.

It was through this kind of struggle in society as a whole and in
a concentrated way within the Communist Party itself that
socialist ownership was in the main established in city and countryside, in industry and agriculture—and also in the same way in
handicrafts and commerce—by 1956. But this did not mean the
end of class struggle in society or in the Communist Party; it merely advanced socialist revolution and socialist construction and the
struggle between the socialist and capitalist roads to a new stage.

Learning From Negative Experience of Soviets

By this time the People's Republic of China was well into its
First Five-Year Plan, initiated in 1953. This plan was largely
modelled after and incorporated extensive aid from the Soviet
Union. It put too much emphasis on the development of heavy industry at the expense of agriculture and light industry and on
highly centralized planning at the expense of local initiative. It

called for such things as one-man management, reliance on specialists, and other measures such as extensive rules and regulations which suppressed rather than unleashed the activism of the workers—who were supposed to memorize and strictly abide by scores of such rules and regulations.

This was all to the liking of conservative forces and increasingly encrusted bureaucrats and especially so to those revisionists in the Chinese Communist Party who refused to draw correct conclusions from and insisted instead on repeating the negative experiences of the Soviet Union. But it was more and more not to the liking of Mao, who insisted on summing up these errors while learning from the positive experience of the first socialist state.

In opposition to the Soviet model, Mao had already begun to chart a different path for China's socialist development, one which was suited to its own conditions and, more than that, one which would avoid the errors and shortcomings of the Soviet Union even under Stalin's leadership. In charting this course, it should be noted, Mao was in no way joining with or following those like the Yugoslav revisionists who took a so-called "independent" road in economics and politics—that is, who took the capitalist road under the banner of opposing Stalin and the Soviet Union under his leadership. What these renegades opposed in Stalin was not his errors—for example his tendency toward adopting aspects of the "theory of productive forces," to put experts in command, etc. What they opposed in Stalin and the Soviet Union under his leadership was exactly what was correct and overall the main thing about them—the fundamental upholding of Marxism-Leninism and the building of genuine socialism on this basis.

Mao's approach, as indicated, was to sum up the shortcomings of the Soviet Union under Stalin and the errors in Stalin's line—from the standpoint of Marxism-Leninism, not revisionism—and to also learn from the real achievements and advances, which constituted the main aspect. Significant steps in applying this approach, and on this basis charting a path for China's socialist economic development, were embodied in a speech by Mao to an enlarged meeting of the Political Bureau of the Chinese Communist Party's Central Committee in April 1956, "On the Ten Major Relationships."

In this speech Mao criticized the one-sided emphasis on heavy industry which still characterized planning and investment in China. He stressed that while the development of heavy industry should overall have priority, "the proportion for agriculture and light industry must be somewhat increased."[41] Light industry and agriculture, he pointed out, bring about faster accumulation than heavy industry, and therefore an increase in investment in these spheres, on the basis of an overall and long-range priority to heavy industry, would actually "lead to a greater and faster development of heavy industry and, since it ensures the livelihood of the people, it will lay a more solid foundation for the development of heavy industry."[12]

Here Mao was characteristically applying materialist dialectics in a throughgoing way. If too much priority was given to heavy industry at the expense of agriculture and light industry then both raw materials and the market for industry would be undercut, the cost of labor power in industry—in particular the cost of food—would be shoved up, and the release of labor power for industry would be obstructed by the retarding of agriculture. On the other hand, of course, if in the final analysis priority were not given to development of heavy industry, to the production of means of production, then agriculture and light industry would both suffer and stagnate, which in turn would further cripple the development of heavy industry, and the whole economy would be dragged down.

Mao expressed the dialectic this way:

Here the question arises: Is your desire to develop heavy industry genuine or feigned, strong or weak? If your desire is feigned or weak, then you will hit agriculture and light industry and invest less in them. If your desire is genuine or strong, then you will attach importance to agriculture and light industry so that there will be more grain and more raw materials for light industry and a greater accumulation of capital. And there will be more funds in the future to invest in heavy industry.[43]

This was the basis for the policy that was to be expressed in the formula that agriculture was the foundation of China's economy and industry the leading factor.

Mao was to apply the same kind of dialectical approach later in determining priorities within industry and agriculture. He developed the policy of taking steel as the key link in the former and grain as the key link in the latter, while ensuring on this basis all-around development in both industry and agriculture. This was also an example of politics in command, for left to spontaneity and the pursuit of profit both steel and grain and therefore ultimately the whole economy would suffer at the hands of more immediately "rewarding" pursuits.

In "On the Ten Major Relationships" itself Mao specifically criticized the policy in the Soviet Union which took too much of the product of the peasants and left them too few funds for further accumulation through their own efforts. "This method of capital accumulation," Mao said, "has seriously dampened the peasants' enthusiasm for production. You want the hen to lay more eggs and yet you don't feed it, you want the horse to run fast and yet you don't let it graze. What kind of logic is that!"[44]

Although there had been errors in China in the direction of developing heavy industry at the expense of agriculture (and light industry), Mao said that overall China's approach to agriculture had been more correct than the Soviet Union's: "Our policies towards the peasants differ from those of the Soviet Union and take into account the interests of both the state and the peasants."[45] He pointed out that the agricultural tax in China was relatively low and that in the exchange between agriculture and industry (through the state) conscious attention was paid to lowering the cost of machinery sold to the peasants and raising the price for their products, in order to begin reversing the dominance of town over country, industry over agriculture, inherited from the old society. But, sharply combatting tendencies within the Party and state to go against this correct policy, he warned that "In view of the grave mistakes made by the Soviet Union on this question, we must take greater care and handle the relationship between the state and peasants well."[46]

In a similar way Mao criticized the policy of putting too much stress on military construction and thereby undermining economic foundation construction. Again applying materialist dialectics to this question, he pointed out that it was necessary to cut back the proportion spent on military construction and give more emphasis to basic economic construction or else not only would the economy suffer overall but, as a consequence, military construction would actually suffer in the long run as well.

In this same speech Mao also criticized overemphasis on central control of the economy at the expense of local initiative. What was developing in China then was the tendency for the central ministries to exercise tight control over the sector of the economy they were reponsible for, right down to the local level. This not only stifled local initiative but actually undermined unified leadership over the economy as a whole.

In opposition to this Mao argued that:

Our territory is so vast, our population is so large and the conditions are so complex that it is far better to have initiative come from both the central and the local authorities than from one source alone. We must not follow the example of the Soviet Union in concentrating everything in the hands of the central authorities, shackling the local authorities and denying them the right to independent action.[47]

All this was to be carried out, of course, on the basis of—in dialectical unity with and not as an antagonism to—"strong and unified central leadership and unified planning and discipline throughout the country..."[48] In fact, if handled correctly, the kind of local initiative Mao was calling for would, as noted above, strengthen not weaken what must overall be the main thing —centralized leadership and unified planning, with the Party as the guiding force.

"On the Ten Major Relationships" began to chart a clearly different course from the Soviet Union—and from much of economic policy in the first few years of the People's Republic of China, which was heavily influenced by Soviet methods. But while this speech addressed new problems arising in socialist construction and economic relations emerging with the basic transformation of ownership, it did not specifically deal with the fundamental question of class relations after the transition to socialist ownership. This was a problem Mao was to begin to write about within the next year.

In the meantime, at the 8th Congress of the Chinese Communist Party in 1956, Liu Shao-chi and other revisionists in top leadership of the Party promoted and actually got adopted the theory that the principal contradiction in China had become that "between the advanced socialist system and the backward social productive forces." This was the application of their revisionist line to the new situation where socialist ownership had been in the main established and it was no longer possible to oppose socialist revolution on the basis of promoting the theory of the "synthesized economic base." This new theory of the principal contradiction represented "only another expression of the reactionary 'theory of productive forces' in the new circumstances."[49]

What this theory said was that the class struggle was over, socialist relations had been established and the thing now was to concentrate on raising the level of technology and economic development of the country. The role of the masses was simply to work hard. This merged nicely with the line on economic policy that these revisionists had all along pushed—promoting reliance on bureaucratic methods of management, specialists in command and the treatment of the workers as mere labor power.

Mao, other revolutionaries in the Chinese Communist Party and the Chinese masses struck back at this counter-revolutionary line both in theory and in practice. In early 1957 Mao made two very important speeches in which, for the first time in the history of the international communist movement, it was explicitly pointed out that even after the basic achievement of socialist ownership the bourgeoisie continues to exist in socialist society and that:

Class struggle is by no means over. The class struggle between the proletariat and the bourgeoisie, the class struggle between the various political forces, and the class struggle between the proletariat and the bourgeoisie in the ideological field will still be protracted and tortuous and at times even very sharp. The proletariat seeks to transform the world according to its own world outlook, and so does the bourgeoisie. In this respect, the question of which will win out, socialism or capitalism, is not really settled yet.[50]

Again, what Mao was emphasizing was that:

While we have won basic victory in transforming the ownership of the means of production, we are even farther from complete victory on the political and ideological fronts. In the ideological field, the question of who will win out, the proletariat or the bourgeoisie, has not yet been really settled.[51]

Here Mao gave tremendous emphasis to the role of the superstructure and struggle in this realm, politics and ideology in particular. At the same time he pointed not only to the continued existence of the contradiction between the economic base and the superstructure but also between the forces and relations of production. But he did not here give the same emphasis to continuing revolution on the economic front—to further transforming the relations of production—as he was to give in the next few years, both in theory and in practice.

Mao was clearly developing his thinking on contradiction and struggle in the socialist period in opposition to the revisionists in the Chinese Party and their counterparts in the Soviet Union who had already usurped supreme power there. The next year, 1958, saw these two fundamentally opposed lines, and the two opposed roads, come into even sharper conflict.

People's Communes and the Great Leap

That was the year that throughout the Chinese countryside the movement to establish people's communes erupted. Mao, in opposition to the revisionists in the Party, gave all-out support to and championed this earth-shaking event and the Great Leap Forward of which it was a decisive part. Not only was the scale and scope of land ownership raised to a higher level, but in the people's communes masses of peasants took up small scale industrial production, including of such basic materials as steel, as well as many and varied construction projects. This was a completely unprecedented event in the countryside of China—or any other country for that matter. It was of great importance not only in narrowing the differences between town and country and workers and peasants but also in regard to the question of waging people's war in resistance to aggression according to Mao's revolutionary line, which required the greatest possible degree of local self-sufficiency, especially in the face of invading enemy forces that might initially occupy significant parts of Chinese territory and cut off different parts of China from each other.

It was during this same time that Mao formulated the general line for socialist construction—which along with the Great Leap Forward and the people's communes came to be known as the "three red banners." This general line was one of "going all out, aiming high and achieving greater, faster, better and more economical results in building socialism."

This was not an abstract exhortation that everyone should try hard to get the best results. It gave concrete expression and support to the upsurge of the masses themselves as represented by the Great Leap Forward and the people's communes and upheld these in opposition to the line that the only way to develop the economy was through the big, the foreign, the advanced and the centralized, and that as for China and the Chinese people they could only "crawl behind at a snail's pace."

Further, this general line was an expression of politics and ideology in command. As Mao was to point out, the first two parts of the general line—"going all out" and "aiming high"—refer to ideological questions, to the subjective factor, to conscious initiative. The last part—"achieving greater, faster, better and more economical results in building socialism"—refers to the results from the conscious initiative of the masses. This was again a brilliant application of materialist dialectics as opposed to mechanical materialism.

So, too, as Mao pointed out, the second part of the general line must also be viewed dialectically. That is, "greater" and "faster"—which refer to quantity and speed—must be seen as a unity of opposites with "better" and "more economical"—which refer to quality and cost. If high quality and low cost are one-

sidedly stressed, in neglect of quantity and speed, then the needs
of the economy overall and the possibility of its rapid development
will be sacrificed. But, on the other hand, if quantity is one-sidedly
stressed at the expense of quality then quantity will itself be
undermined (low quality products don't last as long and therefore
actually represent less quantity in the long run). And, further, if
one-sided emphasis is placed on quantity and speed without regard
to cost then similarly the basis for expanding production and turning out more products will also be undermined in the long run.
Once again, the key to handling these contradictions is to arouse
and rely on the conscious activism of the masses themselves to correctly combine quantity, speed, quality and cost and in this way
push the whole economy forward.

All this drove the revisionists in the Party into frenzied opposition—it flew directly in the face of every bourgeois prejudice and
convention. They attacked Mao as an idealist—an attack that was
consistently launched against Mao by the revisionists—charging
that he "exaggerated man's conscious dynamic role."[52]

Things came to a head at the Central Committee meeting in
1959. The revisionists, spearheaded then by Peng Teh-huai, at that
time Defense Minister, seized on difficulties connected with the
Great Leap Forward and the people's communes—such as problems in transport, shortage of certain supplies and certain "left"
excesses that accompanied these revolutionary upsurges—to
launch an all-out attack on them and the whole revolutionary road
they represented. Peng Teh-huai also was a leading spokesman for
the demand that China's army be transformed into a "modern" army like that in the Soviet Union (and the Western capitalist countries), which went hand in hand with the demand that China's
economic development return to the policy of one-sided emphasis
on heavy industry and military construction at the expense of
agriculture, light industry and all-around economic construction.

Mao led the revolutionaries in the Party's leadership in beating
back this attack from the right at this famous Central Committee
meeting at Lushan in 1959. He declared that the mass upsurge of
the Great Leap Forward was fine, not terrible, even with its
dislocations and disruptions and even if in the short run the economic returns were not uniformly high.

"The chaos caused was on a grand scale and I take responsibility," he said, throwing down the gauntlet to the rightists. He
reminded them of what Marx's outlook had been on the Paris Commune. Marx did not take the standpoint that narrow and immediate results determine everything but reckoned from the view-

Demonstrators hold high the three red banners: The general line, the Great Leap Forward and the People's Communes. These three were the cutting edge of Mao's revolutionary line on socialist construction in the late 1950s, which took shape in struggle with the revisionist line of Peng Teh-huai and others.

point of the general and long-term interests of the proletariat, Mao said. When Marx realized that the Paris Commune "was the first proletarian dictatorship, he thought it would be a good thing even if it only lasted three months. If we assess it from an economic point of view, it was not worth while."[53]

Besides, Mao added, while the main thing about the Great Leap Forward was the fact that the masses had taken matters into their own hands and begun to make new breakthroughs—and thus it was wrong to assess it from the standpoint of immediate economic results—it was also true that, unlike the Paris Commune, the Great Leap Forward and the people's communes, despite certain difficulties, would not fail. In the face of this the revisionists were forced to beat a retreat.

At the same time, the Soviet Union, acting in coordination with these revisionists within the Chinese Communist Party itself, suddenly pulled out technicians and blueprints, leaving a number of vital construction projects unfinished and severely sabotaging the development of the Chinese economy. Following that, in the next several years China was hit by a series of natural disasters.

Taking advantage of all this the revisionists in the Chinese Communist Party's leadership launched another attack and, in fact, were able to gain the initiative in many areas, including in significant aspects of economic policy. It was during this period that Liu Shao-chi and others like him dished up "70 Articles" for the regulation of industry, which echoed earlier revisionist lines on the economy and which were to be echoed again later in the struggle over economic policy and its relation to class struggle.

These "70 Articles" called for reassertion of exclusive control by the central ministries, for cancellation of many construction projects, established the "market as the primary" object in production, and even called for the shutting down of factories that did not show a profit. They resurrected restrictive rules and regulations that had been reformed, called for instituting piece-work wherever possible—much of which had been criticized and eliminated—cut back the time workers were to spend in political study and demanded an end to political struggle in the factories. At the same time these regulations contained certain provisions supposedly dealing with the "well-being" of the masses—in other words promoting economism and welfarism. All this was necessary, the revisionists said, to put an end to disorder. At the same time these renegades did not fail to take credit for advances in the economy whose basis was laid in the mass upsurges and the shattering of convention in the Great Leap Forward—the very "chaos" they were condemning.

In the realm of the superstructure the revisionists also launched a number of attacks. Through literature and art works they clamored for the return to office of Peng Teh-huai—who had been dismissed following his defeat in 1959—and of course the return of the counter-revolutionary line he fought for in opposition to Mao's revolutionary line.

Two Line Struggle Sharpens

Mao counter-attacked. In 1962, at meetings of the leading bodies of the Party, he issued the call "never forget class struggle" and formulated what became the basic line of the Chinese Communist Party for the entire period of socialism:

Socialist society covers a considerably long historical period. In this historical period of socialism there are still classes, class struggle, there is the struggle between the socialist road and the capitalist road, and there is the danger of capitalist restoration. We must recognize the protracted and complex nature of this struggle. We must heighten our vigilance. We must conduct socialist education. We must correctly understand and handle class contradictions and class struggle, distinguish the contradictions between ourselves and the enemy from those among the people and handle them correctly. Otherwise a socialist country like ours will turn into its opposite and degenerate, and a capitalist restoration will take place. From now on we must remind ourselves of this every year, every month and every day so that we can have a rather sober understanding of this problem and have a Marxist-Leninist line.[54]

All this was a direct slap in the face to the revisionists, who preached the "dying out of class struggle" and argued that since there was socialist ownership there was no danger of capitalist restoration and only the necessity to boost production regardless of what methods were used to accomplish this. Mao championed the socialist education movement in opposition to this, to carry forward the class struggle and combat revisionist attempts at capitalist restoration.

During this same general period—the early 1960s—Mao also devoted serious attention to the questions of political economy and economic policy. This was a crucial part of both defending and developing his revolutionary line in opposition to the onslaughts of the revisionists.

Much of this was expressed in Mao's "Reading Notes on the Soviet Text *Political Economy.*" Here Mao not only criticized revisionist deviations in the Soviet Union but summarized the importance of policies and methods that had been developed in China in opposition to revisionism.

These included the line on the relation between agriculture and industry, and other questions touched on in "On the Ten Major Relationships," the general line for building socialism, the importance of self-reliance and regeneration through one's own efforts, and the whole series of policies described by the formula "walking on two legs." These latter meant simultaneously developing small and medium-sized enterprises as well as large ones; making use of native as well as foreign technology and technique, and the backward as well as the advanced; bringing into play the role of the masses as well as experts in technical innovation; and other similar combinations.

Further, Mao contrasted in these "Reading Notes" the correct versus the bourgeois-bureaucratic approach to planning. "A plan," he pointed out, "is an ideological form. Ideology is a reflection of realities, but it also acts upon realities . . . Thus, ideological forms such as plans have a great effect on economic development and its rate."[55]

Planning is not merely a technical question, nor does it involve simply the contradiction between ignorance and knowledge. It also involves class struggle in the ideological realm, between the world outlook and method of the proletariat and that of the bourgeoisie. Whether to rely on a handful of "experts" and on bureaucratic methods, or on the masses and the scientific summation of their experiences, ideas, etc.—this is a fundamental dividing line between the proletarian and the bourgeois outlook, which finds expression in planning as in other spheres. As Mao sharply put it, regarding "the mass struggle as 'one important factor' flies in the face of the principle that the masses are the creators of history. Under no circumstances can history be regarded as something the planners rather than the masses create."[56]

Mao also stressed that planning must take into account that development in everything, including in the economy, is not in the manner of a straight line but in spirals or waves. Further, Mao said:

Balance is relative to imbalance. Without imbalance there is no balance. The development of all things is characterized by imbalance. That is why there is a demand for balance . . . Plans constantly have to be revised precisely because new imbalances recur.[57]

Here Mao was making a clear repudiation of and delivering a

direct rebuff to the revisionist approach to planning, which in essence denies the dialectical movement of things and attempts to impose order and balance from the top, through bureaucratic methods and decrees divorced from and opposed to the masses and mass initiative as well as the actual laws of development of the economy. And Mao's whole approach to planning was another aspect in which Mao was emphasizing the tremendous importance of the superstructure and class struggle in this realm, in opposition to the revisionists, who regard all this as "idealism."

Further, Mao not only noted as Stalin had that the law of value continued to operate and must be taken into account in planning, without allowing it to play a regulating role. He also indicated, in disagreement with Stalin, that the means of production—and not simply means of consumption—continued to have certain properties of commodities.

Commodity exchange relationships were bound to be reflected in the exchange of products even within the state sector itself. And since the state enterprises were still required to maintain a relative independence in accounting, their exchanges with each other were still significantly influenced by the operation of the law of value, the basic law of commodity production and exchange.

All this was unavoidable and would be to varying degrees for some time. But it could also be made use of by the bourgeoisie, especially capitalist-roaders in positions of power, to excessively widen the scope of the law of value in relations within and between different economic units, as a decisive part of their attempts to actually transform socialist relations into capitalist relations and restore capitalism in the country as a whole.

In these "Reading Notes" Mao expresses a further development of his thinking on the question of revolutionizing the relations of production after socialist ownership is in the main achieved. He attaches particular importance to the relations among people in production.

In one of the most significant parts of this article he writes the following:

After the question of the ownership system is solved, the most important question is administration—how enterprises owned either by the whole people [the state] or the collective are administered. This is the same as the question of the relations among people under a given ownership system, a subject that could use many articles. Changes in the ownership system in a given period of time always have their limits, but the relations among people in productive labor may well, on the contrary, be in ceaseless change. With respect to administration of enterprises owned by the whole people, we have adopted a set of approaches: a combination of concentrated leadership and mass movement; combinations of party leaders, working masses, and technical personnel; cadres participating in production; workers participating in administration; steadily changing unreasonable regulations and institutional practices.[58]

These kinds of revolutionary steps were not just "good ideas" but were of great importance in the class struggle, in determining whether China would continue on the socialist road or be dragged down the capitalist road. If such revolutionary measures were not implemented, and beyond that if a revolutionary line was not in command overall, Mao warned in 1963,

then it would not be long, perhaps only several years, or a decade, or several decades at most before a counter-revolutionary restoration on a national scale would inevitably occur, the Marxist-Leninist party would undoubtedly become a revisionist party, a fascist party, and the whole of China would change its colour. Comrades, please think it over. What a dangerous situation this would be![59]

Obviously, all this, too, represented a line in direct opposition to the whole bourgeois line as well as the set of economic policies, represented by the "70 Articles," promoted by the revisionists and generally embraced by large numbers of bureaucratic-minded cadres. The two classes, two lines and two roads were again clearly on a collision course. The explosion that erupted from this was the Great Proletarian Cultural Revolution, which developed into a mass political struggle against the capitalist-roaders in 1966.

In the first few years of this revolutionary upsurge, which Mao not only championed but gave particular guidance to, the masses smashed the bourgeois headquarters of Liu Shao-chi in the Party, seized back power in various spheres of society where it had been usurped by the capitalist-roaders, upheld and carried out Mao's revolutionary line in opposition to the revisionist line and hit back at the reversals of the gains and correct verdicts of the Great Leap Forward. Through this process further revolutionary transformations were carried out in the superstructure and the economic base.

Revolution in education and culture was carried forward with the overthrow of bourgeois authority in those realms. The study of Marxist theory was promoted on a broad scale and active ideological struggle encouraged on all levels. Revolutionary committees, new organs of power and of administration in the basic units as well as at the higher levels, were set up combining the masses, cadres and technical personnel as well as old, middle-aged and young people. Mass movements in science and technology, combining workers and peasants with professional personnel in these fields, were developed. Similar changes were brought about in health work, in which the emphasis was shifted to the rural areas, where most of the people lived and conditions, including in health care, were more backward.

In management the kinds of revolutionary advances in relations among people in production which Mao had called attention to—such as cadres participating in collective labor, workers taking part in administration, the reform of irrational and restrictive rules and regulations—all these were further strengthened and developed. Also upheld and strengthened was the principle of politics leading vocational work and non-professionals armed with a correct line leading professionals. This was expressed in the slogan "red and expert"—with the "red" aspect in command. In most cases piece-work and bonuses were done away with and disparities in income were reduced to the degree possible in accordance with fostering comradely relations among different grades and types of workers and promoting socialist cooperation and activism in production. Similarly, socialist cooperation between different enterprises and economic units was developed to a higher level.

During the Cultural Revolution, Mao concentrated the experience of the Chinese masses in socialist revolution and socialist construction, expressing the dialectical relationship between the two in the slogan "grasp revolution, promote production." This principle correctly explains the relationship between revolution and production, between politics and economics, between consciousness and matter, between the superstructure and the economic base and between the relations of production and the productive forces.

In all these relationships the latter aspect is overall the principal one and is both the foundation and the ultimate point of determination for the other. But, on the other hand, in each case it is the former aspect that plays the initiating role in transforming the latter. Further, in each case the principal aspect tends to advance ahead of the secondary aspect and conscious action is required to bring this secondary aspect into correspondence with the principal one. Thus it can be seen that the overall secondary aspect has a tremendous reaction upon the overall principal aspect and at certain times can itself become principal.

Only by continuously unfolding revolution in the superstructure and making use of its initiating role—in particular the state power and ideology of the proletariat—is it possible for the proletariat to consolidate and develop the socialist economic base. Similarly, without continuing to revolutionize the relations of production, even after socialist ownership has in the main been accomplished, it is impossible to continue to liberate and thereby develop the social productive forces. And, as Mao had pointed out before, at those times when the relations of production and the super-structure act mainly as fetters on the further development of the forces of production and the economic base, then the relations of production and the superstructure become principal.[60]

And, at all times, only by commanding economics with politics is it possible for the proletariat to develop production along the socialist road. Only by arousing the conscious activism of the laboring masses is it possible to transform the material world in accordance with its objective laws and the revolutionary interests of the proletariat. In sum, this principle, "grasp revolution, pro-mote production," expresses the correct dialectical relationship between the two and promotes the role of revolution in command-ing production.

Naturally, while this principle was grasped and applied by the masses of Chinese people to transform the world, it has been con-sistently opposed and attacked by the revisionists, and this was certainly true even during the height of the Cultural Revolution. In fact, at the Ninth Congress of the Chinese Communist Party in 1969, in the midst of the Cultural Revolution, Lin Piao, who had masqueraded as a close comrade of Mao Tsetung and a leader of the masses in the Cultural Revolution, collaborated with other revisionists to oppose Mao's line on the relation between revolu-tion and production and substitute for it the "theory of productive forces."

This was done in the form of arguing that instead of class strug-gle the main task then was to develop production. Mao and other genuine revolutionary leaders rejected and defeated this line, em-phasizing that waging the class struggle against the bourgeoisie remained the key link for all work.

At the First Plenary Session of the Communist Party's Central Committee following the Ninth Congress, Mao spoke again to the relationship between revolution and production. He said then:

Apparently, we couldn't do without the Great Proletarian Cultural Revolution, for our base was not solid. From my observations, I am afraid that in a fairly large majority of factories—I don't mean all or the over-whelming majority—leadership was not in the hands of real Marxists and the masses of workers. Not that there were no good people in the leader-ship of the factories. There were. There were good people among the

In the movement to criticize Lin Piao and Confucius, the poor and lower-middle peasants and barefoot doctors of Leyuan Commune wrote big character posters to praise the cooperative medical service and denounce Lin Piao for negating the achievements of the Cultural Revolution and strangling socialist new things like these.

secretaries, deputy secretaries, and members of Party committees and among the Party branch secretaries. But they followed that line of Liu Shao-chi's, just resorting to material incentive, putting profit in command, and instead of promoting proletarian politics, handing out bonuses, and so forth . . . there are indeed bad people in the factories . . . [and all this] shows that the revolution is still unfinished.[61]

Here Mao was giving deeper analysis to the question of production relations and classes and class struggle after socialist transformation of ownership has in the main been completed. He focused on the fact that as regards the matter of ownership it is not enough to determine whether or not it is public as opposed to private in form, but what is the essence of the ownership, which after all is not a thing but a social relationship. If bourgeois forces and a bourgeois line are in command then public ownership will be merely the outer shell of bourgeois production relations. This is what happened in the Soviet Union as a whole with the seizure of supreme power by the revisionists in that country. And it is what happened to varying degrees in particular enterprises and other economic units controlled by the capitalist-roaders in China—this can and does happen even under the conditions where the proletariat holds political power in the country as a whole. This was what Mao was pointing out in speaking of factories—even a majority of them—which before the start of the Cultural Revolution were not under the command of a correct line and not under the leadership of real Marxists and the masses of workers.

All this is dialectically related to the fact that in society as a whole, while socialist ownership is in the main established, it is not completely established. In other words, in agriculture and even industry, the means of production have not yet been fully converted into the common property of all of society and therefore commodity production and the law of value still operate, though with a restricted scope. Until these and other vestiges of capitalism are eliminated in both the relations of production and the superstructure, the possibility of socialist relations and institutions—and even socialist society as a whole—being transformed into capitalist ones cannot be eliminated. This understanding represented a real contribution by Mao Tsetung to Marxist-Leninist theory on these all-important questions.

In immediate terms, Mao's analysis of this in 1969 was not only a summation of the situation before the start of the Cultural Revolution but represented a sharp rebuke right then to Lin Piao and others who were attempting to declare that the revolution was over—or should be—and the thing to do was to put production in first place. But these revisionists refused to unite with Mao's revolutionary line and continued to fight for their own counter-revolutionary line. As a result of this, Lin Piao and some others were exposed, isolated and defeated. Not long after the Ninth Congress Lin Piao himself died a traitor's death, fleeing toward the Soviet Union in September 1971.

But the attempt to substitute the theory of the "dying out of class struggle" and the "theory of productive forces" for Mao's revolutionary line did not, of course, die with Lin Piao. At the Tenth Congress of the Chinese Communist Party in 1973 it was pointed out that the program of making production the main task, which Lin Piao and another opportunist in leadership of the Party, Chen Po-ta, had pushed at the time of the Ninth Congress, represented nothing more than "a refurbished version under new conditions of the same revisionist trash that Liu Shao-chi and Chen Po-ta had smuggled into the resolution of the Eighth Congress, which alleged that the major contradiction in our country was not the contradiction between the proletariat and the bourgeoisie, but that 'between the advanced socialist system and the backward productive forces of society.' "[62] (This report was delivered by Chou En-lai, who, like Lin Piao four years earlier, found himself having to deliver a report to a Congress with whose line he was in fundamental disagreement. In fact, as the most powerful leader of the Right in China at that time, Chou was vigorously promoting precisely the line that production—or "modernization"—was the main task.)

Mao continued to lead the Chinese Communist Party and the masses in revolutionary struggle down to his last breath. In the course of this struggle, shortly before he died, Mao issued a statement which said in part:

You are making the socialist revolution, and yet don't know where the bourgeoisie is. It is right in the Communist Party—those in power taking the capitalist road. The capitalist-roaders are still on the capitalist road.[63]

This was yet another important contribution of Mao's to Marxist theory and Marxist political economy in particular. Here Mao was not only calling attention to the fact that even after socialist ownership is in the main established new bourgeois elements will be engendered and the bourgeoisie as a class will continue to exist throughout the socialist period, but in particular to the fact that in these conditions the bourgeoisie—not the whole but the heart of it—will emanate from within the Communist Party itself, especially its top ranks.

This is because of the position of the Party itself in socialist society and of the changes in class relations that arise with the development of socialism, especially after socialist ownership is in the main established. In this situation, those people who exercise leadership in the allocation of means of production and means of consumption are in the final analysis overwhelmingly Party members, particularly those at the top levels. Though in theory they exercise this leadership on behalf of the masses, nevertheless there is a contradiction here, which is a reflection of the fact that the means of production have not yet fully become the common property of all of society and the masses of people have not yet fully become the masters of production and all of society—the divisions, inequalities and other material and ideological remnants of bourgeois society have not yet been completely overcome.

Where a correct line is carried out by those in leadership, this contradiction will be moved in the direction of enabling the masses to increase their mastery of production and society. But where a revisionist line is in command, leadership will be transformed into a position of bourgeois domination and exploitation of the masses.

If, for example, the division of labor in an enterprise is not restricted—and therefore leading personnel do not participate in productive labor and the workers do not participate in management—and at the same time the share of income leading cadre receive relative to that of the mass of productive workers is expanded rather than restricted, and especially if along with this profit, not politics, is put in command, then in fact the relation of the leading people to the workers smacks of exploitation. In effect they are beginning to appropriate some of the surplus produced by the workers while they themselves have command over the workers and over production without taking part in production. Hence the importance of restricting as opposed to expanding bourgeois right in relations among people in work and in distribution. If this is not done, and instead an incorrect line and policies are applied, these two aspects of the relations of production can, together with the superstructure, exert a reactionary influence on what is overall the principal aspect of production relations—ownership—and can even transform the production relations from socialist to capitalist in essence.

This does not mean that the country has become capitalist if such a situation prevails in a large number or even a majority of enterprises at any given time; this will happen only through a change in the superstructure—only if the revisionists seize

The 10,000-ton freighter *Fengguang*, built entirely of Chinese parts on a 3,000-ton dock by Shanghai Shipyard workers, triumphantly returns to Shanghai Harbor from its maiden voyage to the Mediterranean.

supreme power—and overall a revisionist line is in command in society. But, on the other hand, this is not a static thing, and if bourgeois production relations are allowed to emerge and develop without opposition, then the basis for revisionists in positions of power to pull off a reactionary coup and restore capitalism will be greatly strengthened.

Mao had touched on this problem in his "Reading Notes" on the Soviet political economy text: "In our experience, if cadres do not set aside their pretensions and identify with the workers, the workers will never look on the factory as their own but as the cadres'."[64] And if a bourgeois line is in command and promoted and implemented by the leading cadres of the Party and state, the masses will look at not only the factories but the means of production as a whole and society in general as belonging not to them but to a privileged stratum—and the masses will be correct. This, again, stems from the transitional and contradictory nature of socialist society, and as such it will either be resolved in a revolutionary direction, in the advance toward communism, or, in the short run, in a counter-revolutionary direction, down the capitalist road to the restoration of the old order.

Mao's analysis here is an application of Lenin's statement that politics is the concentrated expression of economics. As pointed out earlier, in socialist society control over the economy is concentrated as the power of political leadership. Where this leadership is in the hands of revisionists, it is in actuality in the hands of the bourgeoisie, and bourgeois production relations will actually begin to be enforced. It is the power of leadership resting on this material basis which in the hands of capitalist-roaders enables them to build up strength and, if they succeed in seizing supreme political power, to carry off capitalist restoration, acting as the core and commanders of the social forces in society, inside and outside the Party, who can be mobilized to support such a restoration. It is for this reason that Mao also insisted shortly before his death that "if people like Lin Piao come to power, it will be quite easy for them to rig up the capitalist system."[65]

This is why Mao put so much emphasis on the superstructure and insisted that the decisive question was the correctness or incorrectness of the ideological and political line. For it is this that will determine whether the political leadership in power represents the revolutionary interests of the proletariat in advancing to communism or represents a new bourgeoisie and suppresses the masses in the interests of capitalist restoration. It is also why Mao put so much emphasis on arming the masses with a Marxist-

Leninist line and mobilizing them on this basis to struggle against the capitalist-roaders. For this is decisive in preventing a revisionist seizure of power and capitalist restoration and continuing instead the advance toward communism.

From all this can be seen the great significance of Mao's last major statement on this question: that the bourgeoisie "is right in the Communist Party—those in power taking the capitalist road." This analysis of Mao's is of life and death importance to the proletariat and Marxist revolutionaries in waging the class struggle under socialism for the ultimate aim of communism. It is a powerful new weapon of the proletariat in this struggle.

This is another important reason why Mao Tsetung's contributions in the field of political economy in particular, as well as in economic policy and socialist construction—and in other areas—represent a further advance for the proletariat and its revolutionary science. These contributions are truly immortal and can never be erased, denied or downgraded regardless of any events in the world.

Chapter 4

PHILOSOPHY

Introduction

The first three chapters of this book have dealt with Mao's contributions in the areas of revolution in colonial countries; revolutionary warfare and military strategy; and political economy, economic policy and socialist construction. But would it have been possible for Mao to develop his revolutionary line in these, and other, spheres and make such great contributions in these areas without the consistent application of Marxist philosophy, materialist dialectics? Impossible.

In fact, as the previous chapters have stressed, Mao's contributions in these fields are all based upon and characterized by the thoroughgoing application of materialist dialectics. At the same time Mao devoted great attention to and further developed and enriched Marxism-Leninism in the realm of philosophy in its own right. This itself was dialectically related to his contributions in other areas and most especially, as will be gone into later in this chapter, to what is overall his greatest contribution—the development of the theory and line of continuing the revolution under the dictatorship of the proletariat.

Struggle and development on the philosophical front are closely linked with struggle and development in society as a whole. This has always been the case and becomes all the more so with the emergence of Marxism and the development of the proletariat into a class for itself, that is, with the development of the class conscious movement of the working class. Under socialism this truth takes on even greater importance, because the task of the proletariat as master of socialist society is to consciously transform nature, society and the people according to its world outlook and advance to communism.

Class Basis of Philosophy

So long as there are classes, any kind of philosophy has a class nature. And "Philosophy always serves politics."[1]

As Mao himself insisted, the foundation of philosophy—in class society—is class struggle, and this is especially true of Marxist philosophy. Mao explained it this way:

There is a struggle between the proletariat and the bourgeoisie. . . . The oppressors oppress the oppressed, while the oppressed need to fight back and seek a way out before they start looking for philosophy. It was only when people took this as their starting point that there was Marxism-Leninism, and that they discovered philosophy. We have all been through this.[2]

In this same talk Mao pointedly asked a group of intellectuals: "If you don't engage in class struggle, then what is this philosophy you're engaged in?"[3]

But philosophy in turn exerts a tremendous reaction on the political struggle. This is the main reason why Mao not only devoted great attention to philosophy and to struggle in this realm himself but repeatedly insisted that philosophy must be liberated from the confines of the scholar's study and be taken up by the broad masses of people. For without consciously taking up Marxist philosophy and breaking the mental shackles of the philosophy of the exploiting classes it would be impossible for the proletariat and the broad masses to smash completely the fetters of capitalism and class society, emancipate mankind and bring about a qualitative leap in its mastery over nature.

Foundations of Marxist Philosophy

Mao systematized and enriched the understanding of the fundamental law of contradiction and armed masses of people, not only in China but worldwide, with this deepened understanding. This is the essence of Mao's tremendous contribution to Marxism-Leninism in the sphere of philosophy. To grasp this fully it is necessary first to summarize the basic principles of Marxist philosophy and their development beginning with Marx and Engels.

Marxist philosophy, like Marxism in general, did not, of course, spring full-blown from the head of Marx. As Mao was reported to have jokingly asked, when Marx was a very young man did he study any Marxism? Marxist philosophy was forged by Marx, in close collaboration with Engels, by concentrating, reconstructing and recasting what was correct in Hegel's dialectical method and the materialism of Feuerbach, both of whose schools of thought Marx successively passed through as a young man, before he became a Marxist.

In "Ludwig Feuerbach and the End of Classical German Philosophy," Engels summarizes this process. There he shows how the development of Hegel's philosophy, as well as that of Feuerbach—and that of Marx and Engels themselves—were closely linked to the development of capitalism and the rapid advances in science and technology as well as the dramatic social changes and upheavals that were associated with it, especially in the late 18th and early 19th centuries.

Engels explained with regard to Hegel's philosophy that:

> Just as the bourgeoisie by large-scale industry, competition and the world market dissolves in practice all stable time-honoured institutions, so this dialectical philosophy dissolves all conception of final, absolute truth and of absolute states of humanity corresponding to it. For it (dialectical philosophy) nothing is final, absolute, sacred. It reveals the transitory character of everything and in everything; nothing can endure before it except the uninterrupted process of becoming and of passing away, of endless ascendancy from the lower to the higher. And dialectical philosophy itself is nothing more than the mere reflection of this process in the thinking brain.[4]

But at the time Hegel developed his philosophy (the first few decades of the 19th century) capitalism was only weakly developing in Germany. The German state was not united under capitalist rule, the bourgeois revolution in Germany had not been completed and the rising bourgeoisie was forced to compromise with the feudal aristocracy and the monarchy in the person of Frederick William III, King of Prussia. All this had a great influence on Hegel's thinking, both philosophical and political.

Hegel endeavored to develop a complete philosophical system, which had its material basis in the contradictory conditions in Germany at that time. Owing to this, while Hegel's method was dialectical, his philosophical system ended up in metaphysics, in the proclamation of a realized absolute truth represented precisely by Hegel's philosophical system itself. Hegel was after all an idealist, whose philosophical system invented an Absolute Idea, existing prior to and independent of nature; this Idea then "alienated" itself into nature, to be progressively comprehended by man in society, leading up to its final and complete realization in the philosoph-

ical system of Hegel.
   As Engels expressed it,

the whole dogmatic content of the Hegelian system is declared to be absolute truth, in contradiction to his dialectical method, which dissolves
all dogmatism. Thus the revolutionary side is smothered beneath the
overgrowth of the conservative side. And what applies to philosophical
cognition applies also to historical practice. Mankind, which, in the person
of Hegel, has reached the point of working out the absolute idea, must also
in practice have gotten so far that it can carry out this absolute idea in
reality. Hence the practical political demands of the absolute idea on con-
temporaries may not be stretched too far. And so we find at the conclusion
of [Hegel's] *Philosophy of Right* that the absolute idea is to be realized in
that monarchy based on social estates which Frederick William III so per-
sistently but vainly promised to his subjects [i.e., a constitutional monar-
chy].[5]

   Especially after Hegel's death in 1831, however, there were
those, including Marx and Engels, who inherited the revolutionary
side of Hegel's philosophy—its dialectical method. Engels stressed
that while Hegel's *system* led to conservatism in both philosophy
and politics, "whoever regarded the dialectical *method* as the main
thing could belong to the most extreme opposition, both in politics
and religion."[6] And, Engels recalled, after 1840, when in Prussia
"orthodox pietism and absolute feudal reaction ascended the
throne with Frederick William IV," Marx—and Engels himself—took the field of opposition as part of those "Young
Hegelians" whose stand "revealed itself directly as the philosophy
of the aspiring radical bourgeoisie and used the meagre cloak of
philosophy only to deceive the censorship."[7]
   But Marx and Engels soon revealed themselves to be more
radical than bourgeois. Here is Engels' description of what happened next in their development:

Then came Feuerbach's *Essence of Christianity*... it placed materialism
on the throne again. Nature exists independently of all philosophy. It is
the foundation upon which we human beings, ourselves products of
nature, have grown up. Nothing exists outside nature and man, and the
higher beings our religious fantasies have created are only the fantastic
reflection of our own essence. The spell was broken; the [Hegelian] system
was exploded and cast aside...one must himself have experienced the
liberating effect of this book to get an idea of it. Enthusiasm was general;
we all became at once Feuerbachians. How enthusiastically Marx greeted
the new conception and how much—in spite of all critical reservations—he
was influenced by it, one may read in *The Holy Family*.[8]

   But Feuerbach was not a thoroughgoing materialist. Driven into isolation by the reactionary authorities, Feuerbach retreated philosophically as well. He rejected consistent materialism because he conceived of materialism as that kind characteristic of the 18th century—mechanical materialism, metaphysics as opposed to dialectics—as represented especially by the French materialists of that period. This materialism recognized only quantitative motion and treated the divisions in nature as absolute, reflecting the level of scientific discovery at that time and the fact that capitalism had not yet gained conquest of society (a major exception being England, where it involved the continuation of the monarchy and a landed aristocracy). Such materialism failed to grasp the fact that everything is contradiction; that the "natural order" is change, marked by leaps (qualitative change); that there is interconnection of contradictory things; and that there is only relative, not absolute, division between different kinds of matter in motion.

Finally Feuerbach himself ended up in idealism. While he had shown that religion represented merely the fantastic expression in the human mind of human and natural existence, he attempted not to abolish religion but to give human relations a religious character. As Engels characterized it:

> According to Feuerbach, religion is the relation between human beings based on the affections, the relation based on the heart, which relation until now has sought its truth in a fantastic mirror image of reality—in the mediation of one or many gods, the fantastic mirror images of human qualities—but now finds it directly and without any mediation in the love between "I" and "Thou." Thus, finally, with Feuerbach sex love becomes one of the highest forms, if not the highest form, of the practice of his new religion.[9]

And things turn out even worse when Feuerbach's philosophical and moral system is carried into the field of economic, social and political relations. Engels, with both sarcasm and regret, pointed out that the stock exchange indeed served as the perfect model and "temple" for Feuerbach's moral credo, for there everyone involved equally pursues his right to happiness, and ethics can be equated with doing well. In short, Feuerbach went no farther than the bourgeoisie itself in the final analysis—no farther than enshrining equality before the law as the highest principle of society. As Engels said, "Feuerbach's morality is cut exactly to the pattern of modern capitalist society, little as Feuerbach himself might desire or imagine it."[10]

Therefore, towards the oppressed classes, and the proletariat in capitalist society in particular, Feuerbach's philosophy/morality could only preach capitulation in the guise of "love" and "equality." Engels summed up that:

At this point the last relic of its revolutionary character disappears from his philosophy, leaving only the old cant: Love one another—fall into each other's arms regardless of distinction of sex or estate [class]—a universal orgy of reconciliation.[11]

Marx's Leap

Thus it was necessary to go beyond Feuerbach, who had evolved out of Hegelianism of an unorthodox sort but had been incapable of making an actual qualitative leap beyond Hegel and idealism in general. It was Marx who, more than anyone else, led in making this leap. As Engels summarized it, "Out of the dissolution of the Hegelian school, however, there developed still another tendency, the only one which has borne real fruit. And this tendency is essentially connected with the name of Marx."[12]

Marx did not completely cast aside Feuerbach, any more than he did Hegel. He criticized Feuerbach's failure to carry materialism forward and he critically assimilated the materialist side of Feuerbach. According to Engels, Marx' "Theses on Feuerbach," written in 1845, is "the first document in which is deposited the brilliant germ of the new world outlook."[13]

In these "Theses" Marx showed that Feuerbach was a contemplative materialist:

The chief defect of all hitherto existing materialism—that of Feuerbach included—is that the thing, reality, sensuousness, is conceived only in the form of the *object* or of *contemplation*, but not as *human sensuous activity, practice*, not subjectively. Hence it happened that the *active* side, in contradistinction to materialism, was developed by idealism—but only abstractly, since, of course, idealism does not know real, sensuous activity as such.[14]

For this reason, Marx said, Feuerbach "regards the theoretical attitude as the only genuinely human attitude. . . . Hence he does not grasp the significance of 'revolutionary,' of 'practical-critical' activity."[15]

Here, for the first time in history, Marx is insisting on the central and determining role of practice in the process of cognition, its decisive role in the movement of knowledge. Previously, including with Feuerbach, as Marx points out, materialism conceived of objective reality as things existing outside of and independently of human thought, but did not consider human activity itself as part of objective reality. Thus Marx says of Feuerbach that he "wants sensuous objects, really differentiated from the thought objects, but he does not conceive human activity itself as objective activity."[16] According to this view the relation of man to nature in the process of cognition is simply that man must reflect external reality in his thoughts, or contemplate it.

But this by itself cannot solve the question of whether man's thoughts correctly reflect nature. As Marx goes on to stress:

> The question whether objective truth can be attributed to human thinking is not a question of theory but is a *practical* question. In practice man must prove the truth, that is, the reality and power, the this-sidedness of his thinking. The dispute over the reality or non-reality of thinking which is isolated from practice is a purely *scholastic* question.[17]

In "Ludwig Feuerbach" Engels said that, "The great basic question of all philosophy, especially of more recent philosophy, is that concerning the relation of thinking and being."[18] Already in 1845, in his "Theses on Feuerbach," Marx had provided the basis for answering this question by identifying practice as the criterion of truth. "Social life" Marx said, "is essentially *practical*. All mysteries which mislead theory to mysticism find their rational solution in human practice and in the comprehension of this practice."[19]

As for society, Marx explained, contemplative materialism dealt at most with the role of *individuals* in relation to each other. It could not reveal the *social relations* that are the essential human relations, or the actual material conditions that establish the basis for these social relations. "Feuerbach," Marx noted, "consequently does not see that the 'religious sentiment' is itself a *social product*, and that the abstract individual whom he analyzes belongs in reality to a particular form of society."[20]

The problem with Feuerbach was that as far as he "is a materialist he does not deal with history, and as far as he considers history he is not a materialist. With him materialism and history diverge. . ."[21]

Finally, then, in opposition to Feuerbach and all previous materialists, the new—dialectical and historical—materialism is based on the understanding that "it is men that change circumstances," and that "the coincidence of the changing of circumstances and of human activity can be conceived and rationally understood only as *revolutionizing practice.*"[22] In other words, what Marx emphasizes here is that just as people relate to each other in and through society and are generally shaped by the society in which they exist, so, too, on the other hand, people can and must change society—and through it nature. Hence Marx' famous statement: "The philosophers have only *interpreted* the world, in various ways; the point, however, is to *change* it."[23]

Of course, Marx repeatedly stressed, people cannot change things as they wish but only in accordance with their objective laws. And this is true with regard to society as with regard to nature. Society is ultimately determined by the level of development of the productive forces, which each successive generation inherits. But society does not simply go through a series of quantitative changes, characterized only by addition of productive forces. The material life of society, in particular the economic relations, forms the base upon which arise political institutions, customs, laws, ideology, culture, etc.; these (the superstructure) in turn exert a tremendous reaction on the economic base and at particular times become decisive. At certain points the development of the productive forces itself brings them into conflict with the economic relations which people have entered into in using the productive forces. At such times a social revolution—a change in the superstructure—is required to replace the old production relations with new ones which can liberate the productive forces.

As Marx put it in criticizing the French anarchist of his time, M. Proudhon, "In acquiring new productive forces men change their mode of production; and in changing their mode of production, in changing their way of earning their living, they change all their social relations."[24] But, again, to change their social relations requires a social revolution. Society therefore develops, from a lower to a higher level, through a series of such revolutions (qualitative leaps). This occurs (in class society) through the overthrow of one class by another after a certain point in the development of the struggle between them; thus the history of society, since classes first emerged, is the history of class struggle.

Marxist philosophy recognizes in society, as in nature, the dialectical law of development. And in fact, recognizing the importance of changing the world—of acting in accordance with the world, especially society, in its changingness, in its motion and development, and helping to hasten the revolutionary leap from capitalism to communism—Marx and Engels emphasized dialectics. As Lenin put it:

Marx and Engels, as they grew out of Feuerbach and matured in the fight against the scribblers, naturally paid most attention to crowning the structure of philosophical materialism, that is not to the materialist epistemology but to the materialist conception of history. That is why Marx and Engels laid the emphasis in their works rather on *dialectical* materialism than on dialectical *materialism,* and insisted on *historical* materialism rather than on historical *materialism.*[25]

Hence, in developing their revolutionary philosophy Marx and Engels did not simply discard Hegel. Instead they retained the revolutionary side of Hegel, his dialectical method, and as Engels said, "freed [it] from the idealist trimming which with Hegel had prevented its consistent execution."[26] Now it was not a case of the dialectical movement of an absolute idea, of spirit as the creator and shaper of the material world, but the reverse. Now it was recognized that it is matter that is eternally moving and changing, and transforming itself into different particular forms which themselves come into being and go out of existence; and more that ideas, consciousness, spirit are but the reflection in the human mind (itself matter) of this process and follow the same laws of development. This was dialectical materialism—or materialist dialectics—and, as applied to history, historical materialism, as it was developed and systematized by Marx and Engels.

But, as indicated before, this philosophy was not simply, or fundamentally, the product of the brains of Marx and Engels. It was the result of the development of capitalism, of natural science and of the class struggle. And it was the product of a dialectical process of development of philosophy itself, reflecting these changes and upheavals in society and in man's comprehension and mastery of the natural world. Nor did dialectical and historical materialism represent Marx and Engels and a few others alone; it was, and is, the revolutionary philosophy of the proletariat, both objective and partisan, reflecting both the objective laws of natural and historical development and the interests and historic mission of the proletariat, which are fully in accord with these laws. For, unlike all other classes in human history which have previously risen to the ruling position and remolded society in their image, the proletariat aims not merely to seize power; its mission is not to establish an "eternal" unchanging system representing the "end point" of human development, but to abolish all class distinctions and enable mankind to continuously overcome barriers to the development of human society and its transformation of nature.

Lenin Defends, Develops Marxist Philosophy

Here it has been possible to give only the briefest and most general outline of the development of the philosophical thinking of Marx and Engels and their founding of dialectical materialism and historical materialism through this process. But it should be pointed out that, with the forging of this scientific view of nature, society and thought, philosophy as it had been in the past—as a branch of thought which could only attempt to fashion in the imagination all-encompassing principles for nature, society and thought and to bridge the gap between seemingly unconnected phenomena, unifying them into a complete system—such philosophy came to an end, except as the persistence of outmoded thinking representing the interests of reactionary forces in society.

As Engels forcefully put it, historical materialism "puts an end to philosophy in the realm of history, just as the dialectical conception of nature [i.e., dialectical materialism] makes all natural philosophy both unnecessary and impossible. It is no longer a question anywhere of inventing interconnections from out of our brains, but of discovering them in the facts."[27] Or as he explained it in another famous work:

... modern materialism is essentially dialectic, and no longer requires the assistance of that sort of philosophy which, queen-like, pretended to rule the remaining mob of sciences. As soon as each special science is bound to make clear its position in the great totality of things and of our knowledge of things, a special science dealing with this totality is superfluous or unnecessary. That which still survives of all earlier philosophy is the science of thought and its laws—formal logic and dialectics. Everything else is subsumed in the positive science of Nature and history.[28]

But it hardly needs saying that putting an end to such outmoded philosophy is not so easy. This is not only, or even mainly, because this greatly displeases the professional philosophers, but because, as suggested earlier, such outmoded philosophy serves the reactionary forces in society. Marxist philosophy has had to fight every step of the way against the decadent philosophies of the reactionary classes and has developed in opposition to them, to one form or another of idealism and metaphysics. This is not only a reflection of the practical struggle between the proletariat and the bourgeoisie (and other exploiting classes) but is also an important part of the overall struggle between these classes.

And such struggle in the philosophical realm, reflecting and going hand in hand with practical struggle, has taken place very intensely within the working class movement, between Marxists and opportunists of various kinds. This remained true throughout the lives of Marx and Engels, and one of the results of it was a further systematizing and deepening of Marxist philosophy, as for example in Engels' outstanding work *Anti-Duhring*.

Such was also the case with Lenin, and in particular the sharp struggle he waged to expose and combat renegades within the Marxist movement. The most severe of these in the philosophical field, and the one which produced the most extensive work by Lenin in defending and developing Marxist philosophy, was Lenin's scathing criticism of the philosophical and political opportunists who rallied around the thinking of Ernst Mach, Austrian physicist and philosopher, in the early 1900s, especially in the period between the 1905 and the 1917 revolutions in Russia.

Essentially, Machism (the most popular variety of empiriocriticism at that time) was a form of idealism. It was linked with the general positivist trend in philosophy that developed then and was closely akin to pragmatism, which was the specifically American form of positivism that arose with the development of U.S. capitalism into imperialism.[29]

As Lenin showed, Machism basically attempted to resurrect the reactionary philosophical concoctions of Lord George Berkeley, an 18th century British bishop. The Machists ridiculed the materialists because, as Lenin put it, the materialists "recognize something unthinkable and unknowable—'things-in-themselves'— matter 'outside of experience' and outside of our knowledge."[30] Instead, the Machists insisted, the real world consists only of "sensations," it consists of things which exist only as they are realized in our knowledge of them and which have no existence outside of our knowledge of them. According to the Machists, the materialists err because they "hold that beyond the appearance there is the thing-in-itself; beyond the immediate sense data there is something else, some fetish, an 'idol,' an absolute, a source of 'metaphysics,' a double of religion ('holy matter,' as Bazarov says)."[31]

In thoroughly refuting the Machist view, Lenin demonstrated not only its fundamental unity with but its near exact copying of Berkeley's arguments two centuries earlier. Berkeley had to attempt to square his blatant idealism—his insistence that things apparently existing outside us are merely extensions of the mind—with the difficult-to-dismiss sensation that these things not only exist for different people (different minds) but are used by these different people according to laws which pertain to these things. To cite a simple example, two different people in a room prove repeatedly capable not only of recognizing but of sitting on one and the same chair (though usually not at the same time).

Even Berkeley could not deny this. But how to explain it, consistent with his idealism? Berkeley's answer, surprising to few if any, was to attribute all this to God, a spiritual force which has created and unifies all existing things, including different people themselves, into one great whole—one extension of this spirit. This having been set right, Berkeley was quite content to allow for the existence of the reality commonly perceived by ordinary mortals and even of natural laws pertaining to this reality. As Lenin sarcastically summarized it:

Berkeley does not deny the existence of real things! Berkeley does not go counter to the opinion of all humanity! Berkeley denies 'only' the teaching of the philosophers, viz., the theory of knowledge, which seriously and resolutely takes as the foundation of all its reasoning the recognition of the external world and the reflection thereof in the minds of men.[32]

And such, in essence, was the denial of the Machists, though they did not insist on the invention of God in the same way as Berkeley. Lenin noted that "Berkeley's train of thought... correctly expresses the essence of idealist philosophy and its social significance, and we shall encounter it later when we come to speak of the relation of Machism to natural science"; and further that "the 'recent' Machists have not adduced a single argument against the materialists that had not been adduced by Bishop Berkeley."[33]

But why did these "recent" opponents of materialism—many of whom had been Marxists and some of whom still claimed to be at least "critical supporters" of Marxism—make such a retreat? In part this was due to some recent discoveries in natural science, among which was the discovery that the atom is not an indivisible whole but can be divided into different particles (the existence of electrons became known at this time). These discoveries brought about a "crisis in physics," exposing the limitations of theories previously held as basic premises. In fact such discoveries provided further proof of the dialectics of nature. But among many scientists, philosophers, etc., who did not adhere, at least consistently, to *dialectical* materialism, they presented "proof" of the incorrectness of materialism.

Experiments indicated that mass was capable of being transformed into energy. From this many concluded that "matter disappears." And it seemed a logical step philosophically to deduce from this that matter cannot be the substance of reality and the basis for consciousness.

In criticizing and refuting this, Lenin not only reaffirmed

materialism—dialectical materialism—but developed the understanding of it by integrating these advances of science into this revolutionary philosophy, whose basic principles fully embraced the new discoveries and were in turn enriched by them. "Matter disappears," explained Lenin, means actually that "the limit within which we have hitherto known matter disappears and that our knowledge is penetrating deeper; properties of matter are likewise disappearing which formerly seemed absolute, immutable, and primary . . . and which are now revealed to be relative and characteristic only of certain states of matter."[34] And Lenin explained the critical criterion regarding the role of matter in materialist philosophy: "the sole 'property' of matter with whose recognition philosophical materialism is bound up is the property of *being an objective reality*, of existing outside the mind."[35]

In other words, what is decisive in drawing the fundamental distinction between materialism and idealism in philosophy is not what state particular matter exists in at any time, but that, in whichever state, matter *exists* and exists independently of and as the foundation for human consciousness, ideas. In Lenin's words,

dialectical materialism insists on the approximate, relative character of every scientific theory of the structure of matter and its properties; it insists on the absence of absolute boundaries in nature, on the transformation of moving matter from one state into another . . . dialectical materialism insists on the temporary, relative, approximate character of all these *milestones* in the knowledge of nature gained by the progressing science of man. The electron is as *inexhaustible* as the atom, nature is infinite, but it infinitely *exists*.[36]

Mechanical materialism, metaphysics, is, of course, incapable of grasping this and so, sooner or later, is forced to concede to and degenerate into idealism. "It is mainly because the physicists did not know dialectics that the new physics strayed into idealism." [37] Relating this specifically to the Machists, Lenin exposed that:

The error of Machism in general, as of the Machist new physics, is that it ignores the basis of philosophical materialism and the distinction between metaphysical materialism and dialectical materialism. The recognition of immutable elements, "of the immutable essence of things," and so forth, is not materialism, but *metaphysical*, i.e., anti-dialectical, materialism.[38]

And so it ends up being not materialism at all, as with the Machists.

Such, generally, was the basis in scientific discovery for the desertion of many erstwhile materialists, including a number of

Marxists, and their degeneration into idealists and opponents of Marxism. But more important was the advent of imperialism, the highest stage of capitalism, which internationally led many to abandon Marxism, proclaiming that the laws of development of society and of capitalism in particular don't apply. In Russia, this was sharply manifested with the defeat of the 1905 revolution and the subsequent Stolypin reaction. This was a time of vicious political repression and of temporary lull in the working class movement in Russia particularly, a period of regrouping and reconstituting the shattered forces of the revolutionary party of the Russian working class, the Bolsheviks. It proved to be a brief period indeed, but in the depth of it, between 1908 and 1912, desertions from the revolutionary ranks and outright degeneracy were marked phenomena, especially among formerly revolutionary intellectuals and others who had joined the revolutionary movement in its period of upsurge but abandoned and even attacked it in the period of reaction and regrouping.

Revisionism was strengthened. Denying materialism, objective truth and so on was part and parcel of denying that Marxism is a science, that its analysis of capitalism, capitalist crisis, the inevitability of proletarian revolution, etc., are valid, true. During this period especially it was of the greatest importance to defend the basic principles of Marxism against open attacks and to guard against their being adulterated with all manner of bourgeois junk. If this were not done then not only would the proletariat have suffered a severe setback in the short run but it would be robbed of a revolutionary vanguard. What a loss that would have been, especially with the upheaval that followed this temporary ebb!

It was Lenin who led the way in exposing and combatting the revisionists. He criticized them in an all-around way, pointing out that since the beginning Marxism had to wage a most determined struggle against the enemies of the working class within the socialist movement and that this was an urgent requirement right then. He laid bare the fundamental features of revisionism:

To determine its conduct from case to case, to adapt itself to the events of the day and to the chopping and changing of petty politics, to forget the primary interests of the proletariat and the basic features of the whole capitalist system, of all capitalist evolution, to sacrifice these primary interests for the real or assumed advantages of the moment—such is the policy of revisionism. And it patently follows from the very nature of this policy that it may assume an infinite variety of forms, and that every more or less "new" question, every more or less unexpected and unforeseen turn of events, even though it changes the basic line of development only to an insignificant degree and only for the briefest period, will always inevitably give rise to one variety of revisionism or another.[39]

The battle against revisionism in the philosophical sphere was closely tied to the struggle against it politically. But at that time the fight against philosophical revisionism assumed tremendous significance itself. In fact, without upholding dialectical and historical materialism and answering in a thoroughgoing way the "revisions" of and outright attacks on it, particularly in the revival of idealism as represented by Machism, it would have been impossible to maintain a Marxist movement and preserve the proletarian vanguard. Such is the great importance of ideology, and philosophy as a crucial part of it, in general. And such was the great importance of Lenin's *Materialism and Empirio-Criticism* in particular.

As noted before, the purpose and substance of that great work was the defense of materialism against "recent" idealist assaults and inventions. But as also noted, such a defense had to and did stress and apply dialectics in opposition to metaphysics, for only *dialectical* materialism could explain the recent developments in natural science and thoroughly refute idealist interpretations of them. And in doing this Lenin not only upheld but enriched modern, dialectical materialism, Marxist philosophy.

In general Lenin attached great importance to dialectics, to its study and application. His "Philosophical Notebooks," which span more than two decades, devote considerable attention to the question of dialectics. Included within them is a manuscript, "On The Question of Dialectics," written in 1915. Here Lenin said that "The splitting of a single whole and the cognition of its contradictory parts... is the *essence* (one of the 'essentials,' one of the principal, if not the principal, characteristics or features) of dialectics."[40]

Lenin went on to say that recognition of the identity, or unity, of opposites is the key to understanding the movement of all processes. This he sharply opposed to the metaphysical conception of movement as merely mechanical, mere quantitative increase and decrease, repetition. This latter conception he described as "lifeless, pale and dry," while the dialectical conception "alone furnishes the key to the 'leaps,' to the 'break in continuity,' to the 'transformation into the opposite,' to the destruction of the old and the emergence of the new."[41]

And more, Lenin concisely summarized the relationship between the unity (or identity) and the struggle of opposites. The former, he said, "is conditional, temporary, transitory, relative," while the struggle of opposites "is absolute, just as development and motion are absolute."[42]

These were extremely important points which represented basic elements of the further development of Marxist philosophy. As Lenin said in this same manuscript, "Dialectics *is* the theory of knowledge of (Hegel and) Marxism."[43] Yet, he noted, this had not received sufficient attention in Marxist philosophy, not only in the profound early writings of Plekhanov (around 1900) but even in Engels. Lenin specifically pointed out that not only Plekhanov but Engels as well had given insufficient attention to the central, or essential, point of dialectics, the unity of opposites.[44] This fundamental question was to be later taken up and more fully developed by Mao Tsetung.

Stalin: Marxism and Metaphysics

But before turning to Mao's enrichment of Marxist philosophy, it is important to briefly summarize Stalin's role in this area. As Mao himself was to write, such works as *The Foundations of Leninism* demonstrated a grasp and application by Stalin of important principles of dialectics and of historical materialism. As Mao put it, Stalin, in *The Foundations of Leninism:*

... analysed the universality of contradiction in imperialism, showing why Leninism is the Marxism of the era of imperialism and proletarian revolution, and at the same time analysed the particularity of tsarist Russian imperialism within this general contradiction, showing why Russia became the birthplace of the theory and tactics of proletarian revolution and how the universality of contradiction is contained in this particularity. Stalin's analysis provides us with a model for understanding the particularity and the universality of contradiction and their interconnection.[45]

In 1924, at the time Stalin wrote *The Foundations of Leninism*, he was, as leader of the Soviet Communist Party, locked in a life and death struggle with Trotsky and other opportunists. *The Foundations of Leninism* played a crucial part in that struggle, in educating the broad ranks of Party members and the masses and helping to expose and defeat Trotsky's counter-revolutionary line in particular. Compelled to wage struggle like this to win over the Party rank and file and the masses broadly, Stalin was impelled to apply dialectics.

Later, however, when the Soviet Union had become more powerful and Stalin's leadership was generally acknowledged and his prestige great, Stalin, while remaining a great revolutionary leader of the working class, did not as consistently and thoroughly rely on the masses and was not as consistently or thoroughly dialectical in his approach to problems. As Mao commented later, "At that time [the 1920s] Stalin had nothing else to rely on except the masses, so he demanded all-out mobilization of the party and the masses. Afterward, when they had realized some gains this way, they became less reliant on the masses."[46]

In the preceding chapter of this book, some of Stalin's main errors, particularly during the period of the 1930s, were discussed. It was indicated that the most central and serious of these errors was his mistaken assessment that there were no longer antagonistic classes in the Soviet Union after socialist transformation of ownership had been basically achieved. Obviously this is bound up with the philosophical question of contradiction, and specifically with an understanding of the particular forms and development of contradictions in socialist society. And Stalin's mistaken assessment on classes and class struggle in the Soviet Union beginning in the 1930s was closely linked with errors in philosophy, particularly on the question of dialectics.

This is evident in what is perhaps Stalin's major philosophical work, *Dialectical and Historical Materialism*, written in the late 1930s (as part of *History of the Communist Party of the Soviet Union (Bolshevik)*[*HCPSU*]). While this work presents in concentrated form a largely correct summation of Marxist philosophy, and while it specifically applies some principles of dialectics to development in nature and society, it is also marred by a certain amount of metaphysics. Although Stalin introduces the subject of dialectics by speaking of contradiction, he does not focus on contradiction as the *basic law* of materialist dialectics. When he lists four points of dialectics as opposed to metaphysics, he mentions contradiction only as the fourth and doesn't say it is the main point. And further, while he speaks of the struggle of opposites and of the interconnection of things, he does not link these together; he makes them separate features of dialectics instead of showing how they are both part of contradiction. And when, in his fourth point on dialectics, Stalin does emphasize the struggle of opposites he does not speak at the same time of the identity between them. Stalin even quotes Lenin when he says that "Development is the 'struggle' of opposites."[47] But Stalin does not quote the sentence in Lenin that appears right before the one above— "The condition for knowledge of all processes of the world in their '*self-movement,*' in their spontaneous development, in their real life, is the knowledge of them as a unity of opposites."[48]

This is important because, as Lenin also says, "In brief, dialectics can be defined as the doctrine of the unity of opposites. This embodies the essence of dialectics, but it requires explanations and development."[49] And Lenin further states that, "The identity of opposites . . . is the recognition (discovery) of the contradictory, *mutually exclusive,* opposite tendencies in *all* phenomena and processes of nature (*including* mind and society)."[50] In other words, contradiction is inconceivable without the *identity,* or *unity,* of *opposites.* And, having such identity, there is the basis for the contradictory aspects to transform themselves into each other.

At the same time there is not only identity but also struggle between the opposites of a contradiction. In this way identity and struggle themselves form a contradiction, in which struggle is principal and is absolute, while identity is secondary and relative. But, forming a contradiction, identity and struggle are dependent on each other for their existence; and to leave out the identity of opposites means to eliminate in fact the possibility of struggle between them as well.

The tendencies in Stalin toward metaphysics, as evidenced in his treatment of dialectics in *Dialectical and Historical Materialism,* also show themselves in how that work deals with the development of society. This is indicated not only in its rather wooden treatment of the different phases of society leading up to socialism, but also in the way that socialism is treated more or less as an absolute.

Stalin quite correctly emphasizes, in combatting apologists of capitalism and exploiting systems generally, that "there can be no 'immutable' social systems, no 'eternal principles' of private property and exploitation, no 'eternal ideas' of the subjugation of the peasant to the landlord, of the worker to the capitalist."[51] And he draws the correct conclusion that, "Hence the capitalist system can be replaced by the Socialist system, just as at one time the feudal system was replaced by the capitalist system."[52] But there is no sense that the law that "there can be no 'immutable' social systems," is being applied, at least in a thoroughgoing way, to socialism itself.

Similarly, Stalin draws from the law that internal contradiction is the basis of development of things the conclusion that, "Hence we must not cover up the contradictions of the capitalist system, but disclose and unravel them; we must not try to check the class struggle but carry it to conclusion."[53] But, again, there is not the sense that the need to disclose rather than cover up the contradictions of society is being applied in any thoroughgoing way to socialism, and no sense of the necessity to carry the class struggle forward under socialism and carry it through—through socialism to the abolition of classes.

As noted, *Dialectical and Historical Materialism* was written by Stalin during the period when he had concluded that antagonistic classes no longer existed in the Soviet Union. The previous article in this series pointed out that toward the end of his life Stalin's analysis of socialist society was somewhat more dialectical, as reflected especially in his *Economic Problems of Socialism in the USSR*. In that important work Stalin dealt with a number of contradictions in socialist society which would have to be resolved in order to advance to communism. In particular he insisted that the contradiction between the forces and relations of production continued to exist in the USSR and that if not handled correctly this could turn into an antagonistic contradiction.

But Stalin did not examine the contradiction between the base and superstructure under socialism or point to its continuing existence, which is also a basic feature and an extremely important question in socialist society. In fact, as Mao pointedly commented several times, Stalin seriously underestimated the importance of the superstructure and of struggle in this realm.

And, as discussed in the previous chapter, Stalin still did not recognize the existence of antagonistic classes in the Soviet Union, he did not grasp that the contradiction between the proletariat and the bourgeoisie was still the driving force in socialist society and that correctly handling this contradiction was the key to correctly handling the contradiction between the forces and relations of production under socialism.

In general, then, after socialist ownership was basically achieved in the Soviet Union, Stalin did not take contradiction as the motive force of development of socialist society. And he failed to recognize the existence of the antagonistic contradiction between the proletariat and the bourgeoisie in particular and to grasp that this is the main motive force under socialism and in the advance to communism.

Dialectical Development of
Mao's Philosophical Contributions

Mao's development of Marxist-Leninist philosophy was itself a demonstration of the laws of materialist dialectics. It proceeded in

dialectical relationship to the overall development of the Chinese
revolution and through the analysis of the experience of the Soviet
Union and the synthesis of its positive and negative lessons, including in the realm of philosophy.

This was a reflection of the law that Mao summarized in 1957:

> Truth stands in opposition to falsehood. In society as in nature, every en-
> tity invariably divides into different parts, only there are differences in
> content and form under different concrete conditions. There will always be
> wrong things and ugly phenomena. There will always be such opposites as
> the right and the wrong, the good and the evil, the beautiful and the ugly.
> The same is true of fragrant flowers and poisonous weeds. The relation-
> ship between them is one of unity and struggle of opposites. Only by com-
> paring can one distinguish. Only by making distinctions and waging
> struggle can there be development. Truth develops through its struggle
> against falsehood. This is how Marxism develops. Marxism develops in
> the struggle against bourgeois and petty-bourgeois ideology, and it is only
> through struggle that it can develop.[54]

This was true of Mao's development of Marxism, including in
philosophy, both before and after the seizure of nationwide
political power, during both the new-democratic and the socialist
revolutions. And in both periods, through the various stages and
sub-stages of the Chinese revolution, the struggle on the
philosophical front, in which Mao led the proletarian forces, was of
tremendous importance in determining the direction and outcome
of the overall revolutionary struggle.

In the first chapter of this book (on revolution in colonial countries), it was pointed out that as a crucial part of developing, defending and applying the line of new-democratic revolution, and
specifically the policies for the anti-Japanese struggle which constituted a sub-stage within the stage of new democracy, Mao took
up the struggle in the philosophical realm. This struggle was particularly aimed against dogmatic (and secondarily empiricist)
tendencies which reflected idealist and metaphysical thinking in
opposition to materialist dialectics. Mao's criticism of this was embodied especially in "On Practice" and "On Contradiction," both
written in 1937 and constituting two (the first two) of Mao's major
philosophical works. In the earlier chapter in this book (referred to
just above), while it was pointed out that these works enriched
Marxist philosophy, the political significance of these works and
their role in the inner-party struggle and the overall revolutionary
struggle at that time were stressed. Here attention will be focused
on the principles of Marxist philosophy elaborated and enriched by
Mao in these works, while also reviewing their relationship to the

Mao writing in a cave in Yenan, 1938.

overall ideological and political struggle at that time.

"On Practice" was subtitled "On the Relation Between Knowledge and Practice, Between Knowing and Doing." It reaffirmed and concentrated the Marxist, dialectical materialist, theory of knowledge, with its emphasis on the centrality of practice, and in particular *social* practice. Continuing and developing what Marx had first set forth in his "Theses on Feuerbach," Mao pointed out that "Before Marx, materialism examined the problem of knowledge apart from the social nature of man and apart from his historical development, and was therefore incapable of understanding the dependence of knowledge on social practice, that is, the dependence of knowledge on production and the class struggle."[55] Here, as throughout this work, Mao upholds and applies the materialist view of the relation between thinking and being (which Engels said was the basic question of philosophy). Mao goes on to explain that "It was not until the modern proletariat emerged along with the immense forces of production (large-scale industry) that man was able to acquire a comprehensive, historical understanding of the development of society and turn this knowledge into a science, the science of Marxism."[56]

But it is also clear that what is presented here is not merely a materialist but a dialectical approach. What applies to society, as well as nature, also applies to thought. Cognition itself is a dialectical process and follows the same laws of motion as matter in nature and man's actions and relations in society.

Specifically and most importantly, Mao analyzes the stages in the process of cognition and the leaps from one stage to another. Basing himself again on the decisive role of practice, and addressing the question of how knowledge both arises from and serves practice, Mao points out that "In the process of practice, man at first sees only the phenomenal side, the separate aspects, the external relations of things . . . . This is called the perceptual stage of cognition, namely, the stage of sense perceptions and impressions."[57] But "As social practice continues, things that give rise to man's sense perceptions and impressions in the course of his practice are repeated many times; then a sudden change (leap) takes place in the brain in the process of cognition, and concepts are formed."[58]

These concepts, Mao stresses, "are no longer the phenomena, the separate aspects and the external relations of things; they grasp the essence, the totality and the internal relations of things. Between concepts and sense perceptions there is not only a quantitative but also a qualitative difference."[59] Further, Mao says,

"This stage of conception, judgment and inference is the more important stage in the entire process of knowing a thing; it is the stage of rational knowledge."[60]

Such rational knowledge is abstract in the scientific sense. And it is therefore not farther from the truth but in fact closer to it. Or, as Lenin said (in a statement Mao quotes in "On Practice"), "The abstraction of *matter*, of a *law* of nature, the abstraction of *value*, etc., in short, *all* scientific (correct, serious, not absurd) abstractions reflect nature more deeply, truly and *completely*."[61]

Mao further explains this by noting that "Perception only solves the problem of phenomena; theory alone can solve the problem of essence."[62] Perception only represents the knowledge of the appearance of things as they are reflected by the senses and registered in the brain as impressions; conception, rational knowledge, theory, represents the synthesis of these perceptions, the concentration of the essential aspects of them and their internal relations. From this can be understood the tremendous importance and role of theory in general and in the revolutionary movement in particular.

But does this mean, then, that theory is, after all, more important than practice? No. Mao explains how practice is primary and overall more important than theory in several ways. "The perceptual and the rational," he notes, "are qualitatively different, but are not divorced from each other; they are unified on the basis of practice. Our practice proves that what is perceived cannot at once be comprehended and that only what is comprehended can be more deeply perceived."[63] Further, Mao explains that, while the leap from perceptual to rational knowledge is more important than the leap to perceptual knowledge, nevertheless the movement of knowledge does not stop there. There remains what is an even more important leap—to apply the rational knowledge, or theory, in practice. And this represents a further leap not only in doing but in *knowing* as well. It is only when these rational ideas are applied in practice that their validity can be verified; and only when such ideas (theories) can be translated into fact can "the movement of knowledge...be considered completed with regard to this particular process."[64] Here Mao gives further expression and development to the famous statement of Marx that the philosophers have only interpreted the world in various ways but the point is to change it. And, again, this is not a vulgar statement that doing is what counts, who cares about knowing; nor is it of course a metaphysical separation of doing and knowing; it is a dialectical materialist explanation of the relationship between doing and knowing, with practice as the key link.

Theory of Knowledge

Practice is the source of theory, theory is a concentration of practice; perception is the raw material of conception, conception is the product of the synthesis of perception. But conception, rational knowledge, theory, must also be returned to practice, in which process not only is the rational knowledge tested, but new raw materials are gathered for deepening rational knowledge . . . and so on in an endless upward spiral. This is why Mao states that, on the one hand, when the anticipated results can be achieved in practice, then the particular process of cognition or a particular stage of the process (perception-conception-practice) can be considered complete, but on the other hand, "the movement of human knowledge is not completed."[65]

Nor is the movement of human knowledge ever completed. As Mao explains, summing up the laws of the process:

> Discover the truth through practice, and again through practice verify and develop the truth. Start from perceptual knowledge and actively develop it into rational knowledge; then start from rational knowledge and actively guide revolutionary practice to change both the subjective and the objective world. Practice, knowledge, again practice, and again knowledge. This form repeats itself in endless cycles, and with each cycle the content of practice and knowledge rises to a higher level. Such is the whole of the dialectical-materialist theory of knowledge, and such is the dialectical-materialist theory of the unity of knowing and doing.[66]

But the fact that the movement of knowledge is unending should not be taken to mean that it is impossible at any point to distinguish the true from the false. A fundamental tenet of Marxism has always been that there is objective truth, and that it is possible to know it. Without this understanding it is impossible to be a materialist.

But there is not only objective truth, there is also such a thing as *absolute truth*. And in fact, as Lenin pointed out, to acknowledge the one is to acknowledge the other:

> To be a materialist is to acknowledge objective truth, which is revealed to us by our sense-organs. To acknowledge objective truth, i.e., truth not dependent upon man and mankind, is, in one way or another, to recognize absolute truth.[67]

But at the same time, most truths will turn out to be not absolute, but *relative*. Marxism holds that there is both relative and absolute truth. Marxists believe in the relativity of most truths, yet Marxists are not *relativists*. Relativists say that all truths are relative, and then argue that you can therefore pick and choose what "truths" to believe. In other words, they deny that there is objective truth. This was a major argument that Lenin was combatting in *Materialism and Empirio-Criticism*, and he there contrasts the relativism of these Machists with the Marxism of Engels:

For Bogdanov (as for all the Machists) recognition of the relativity of our knowledge *excludes* even the least admission of absolute truth. For Engels absolute truth is compounded from relative truths. Bogdanov is a relativist. Engels is a dialectician.[68]

So absolute truth is made up of relative truths. But what is the relation between them? Mao explains it as follows:

Marxists recognize that in the absolute and general process of development of the universe, the development of each particular process is relative, and that hence, in the endless flow of absolute truth, man's knowledge of a particular process at any given stage of development is only relative truth. The sum total of innumerable relative truths constitutes absolute truth.[69]

In other words, absolute truth in its fullest sense is the sum total of truth, the whole truth. But this whole is made up of innumerable parts. These are relative truths; they are only partial.

But what about ideas which were held to be true at one time and are later proven to be untrue or only partially true (for example, certain laws of physics)? This happens because man acquires and sums up more experience, discovers new processes and laws and develops and refines his understanding of things. But this obviously does not go against the fact that man's knowledge is proceeding from the lower to the higher level, that he is acquiring more and more knowledge of the objective world. Nor does it change the fact that man's knowledge *must* proceed from the lower to the higher level; that at any point he can only apply what knowledge of the truth then exists to the process of changing the world, in which process he tests those ideas and acquires the basis for making a further leap in his knowledge. He cannot apply today what he will only know tomorrow; he will only know more tomorrow if today he applies what he already knows and then sums up the results.

Mao also says that:

In social practice, the process of coming into being, developing and passing away is infinite, and so is the process of coming into being, developing and passing away in human knowledge. As man's practice which
changes objective reality in accordance with given ideas, theories, plans or
programmes, advances further and further, his knowledge of objective
reality likewise becomes deeper and deeper. The movement of change in
the world of objective reality is never-ending and so is man's cognition of
truth through practice.[70]

Some people try to use this to promote the idea that, since
knowledge is continually deepened, it is not necessary to
thoroughly uphold and systematically apply the basic principles of
Marxism-Leninism, Mao Tsetung Thought. Their position in
essence says: since tomorrow we may discover that some things
held true by Marxism-Leninism, Mao Tsetung Thought are not
true, or only partially true, there is no need to apply this science in
a systematic way; instead we will take what is useful to us and put
aside what is not. This is outright eclecticism, relativism, empirio-
criticism and pragmatism; it is metaphysics and idealism.

Such people pose as big upholders of materialism and of practice
as the criterion of truth. But who are they fooling? The fact is that
such a line goes against the Marxist theory of knowledge with its
correct emphasis on practice. To put it plainly, if a line is not carried out thoroughly, if Marxism-Leninism, Mao Tsetung Thought
is not systematically applied, then there is no way to test in practice the correctness of the line, policies, etc., and also no way to acquire more knowledge in the process of changing the world "in accordance with given ideas, theories, plans or programmes."

Such an opportunist line as described above "forgets" that the
movement of knowledge proceeds in cycles, each involving leaps
from practice to theory and back to practice. Absolute truth is, as
Mao says, an "endless flow," but man's cognition of the truth is
not a straight line, but proceeds as a spiral. To say at any point,
"Well, tomorrow we will know more than today so let's not
(dogmatically) apply what is known as truth today," is to deny and
disrupt the process by which more knowledge is actually acquired.
This is metaphysical because it goes against the actual dialectical
relationship between theory and practice; it is idealist because it
actually denies objective truth. It is not in accordance with or a
defense of "On Practice"; it is a violation of and attack on this
great work of Mao's.

"On Practice," and particularly its emphasis on both the
primacy of practice and the continuous development of human
knowledge and practice through an endless series of stages or

cycles, was of great importance in combatting erroneous tendencies in thinking and doing within the Chinese Communist Party at
the time it was written, 1937, a time when the anti-Japanese
united front had just been formed and the anti-Japanese struggle
was only in its beginning stages. At that point there were many
not only outside but inside the Communist Party who opposed the
Party's policies and, knowingly or unknowingly, were sabotaging
the united front and the war of resistance against Japan.

Most pronounced within the Party itself was the dogmatist
deviation which failed to make a concrete analysis of the actual
conditions in China and the objective stage of the struggle, and
treated theory not in its correct dialectical relationship to practice,
but as a set of eternal unchanging truths which must be imposed
on the objective world rather than drawn from and returned to it
as a guide to revolutionary practice. On the other hand, as a secondary problem at that time, there were those who denied the importance of theory and thus, proceeding from the opposite side from
the dogmatists, broke the link between theory and practice and
adopted a metaphysical view of the relation between thinking and
doing.

Both of these erroneous tendencies were incapable of recognizing
the dialectical unity between the present stage (or sub-stage) of the
struggle and its future development. The dogmatists generally
refused to recognize the necessity of proceeding through the anti-
Japanese united front to the completion of the new-democratic
revolution and the advance to socialism, or they posed "left"
policies that would wreck the united front (though at certain
points many of them dogmatically applied in China the policies of
the Soviet Union toward Chiang Kai-shek and advocated reliance
on and capitulation to the Kuomintang in the anti-Japanese struggle). The empiricists generally failed to recognize the aspects of the
future that existed within the stage of the anti-Japanese struggle—the mobilization of the masses as the main force, the continuation, with adjustment, of agrarian reform and the primitive
cooperatives of the peasants, the independence and initiative of
the Communist Party in the united front and the necessary struggle on its part to win and maintain leadership of the united front,
etc.

While the dogmatist tendency generally posed the greater
danger, it was obviously necessary to combat both of these deviations in order both to carry the struggle through in the present
stage (or sub-stage) and to move forward to the future stages, the
completion of the new-democratic revolution and the advance to

socialism.

Beyond its immediate great significance for the Chinese revolution, "On Practice" has more general and long-term importance as a contribution to Marxist-Leninist philosophy and a weapon in the ongoing revolutionary struggle. This is especially so with regard to its explanation of how Marxism-Leninism has not exhausted truth but "ceaselessly opens up roads to the knowledge of truth in the course of practice"[71] —in other words, in its opposition to metaphysics and the tendency to "absolutism" in particular. This point will be returned to later, in discussing struggle on the philosophical front in socialist China and its relation to the class struggle as a whole.

"On Contradiction"

A more lengthy work, dealing more specifically with dialectics, "On Contradiction" was written just after "On Practice," and with the same immediate purpose—to combat erroneous thinking in the Party, in particular dogmatism. At the very start of this essay Mao presents a concentration of the principles of Marxist philosophy: "The law of contradiction in things, that is, the law of the unity of opposites, is the basic law of materialist dialectics."[72] At the end of the essay, in summarizing its main points, he makes it clear that this law "is the fundamental law of nature and of society and therefore also the fundamental law of thought."[73]

Why is this so? And since the law of contradiction is a law of dialectics, does Mao, in identifying it as the fundamental law of nature, society and thought, raise dialectics above materialism, does he in fact lapse into idealism? Of course the accusation that Mao is an idealist has been constantly hurled by the revisionists, both in China and in other countries, who have consistently charged him with exaggerating the role of consciousness and with distorting dialectics. Let's look deeper into these basic questions.

Why does Mao identify the law of contradiction as the basic law of nature, society and thought? Is it not an equally important question of philosophy that matter exists independently of and as the basis for consciousness, human thought? Is not the primacy of matter over ideas as important as the law of contradiction, and doesn't it open the door to idealism to single out the law of contradiction in this way?

The primacy of matter over ideas as described above is indeed a fundamental question and a fundamental dividing line in philosophy. But this cannot be said to be a basic law of the universe on the same level as the unity of opposites. It does not tell us anything about matter in and of itself, in the absence of consciousness. And as materialism teaches us, matter not only exists independently of consciousness but exists even where there is no consciousness—that is, where there is no matter that has developed to a state where it is capable of consciousness. The primacy of matter over ideas tells us the correct relationship between matter and consciousness and as such is a fundamental question of philosophy—remember Engels' statement that the basic question of philosophy is the relationship of thinking and being. But, again, the primacy of matter over consciousness does not reveal anything about unthinking matter and, with regard to conscious matter, describes its relationship to matter outside of it but does not tell us more than that.

On the other hand, the law of contradiction universally applies to unthinking matter and to conscious matter, and to the relationship between them. It is thus correct to say that it is the fundamental law of nature, of men's organized interaction with nature and with themselves in the process—society—and therefore of thought.

As Mao summarized it, "This dialectical world outlook teaches us primarily how to observe and analyze the movement of opposites in different things and, on the basis of such analysis, to indicate the methods for resolving contradictions. It is therefore most important for us to understand the law of contradiction in things in a concrete way."[74] Mao goes on to explain what the universality of contradiction means and what its importance is:

The universality or absoluteness of contradiction has a twofold meaning. One is that contradiction exists in the process of development of all things, and the other is that in the process of development of each thing a movement of opposites exists from beginning to end.[75]

And:

The interdependence of the contradictory aspects present in all things and the struggle between these aspects determine the life of all things and push their development forward. There is nothing that does not contain contradiction; without contradiction nothing would exist.[76]

Here Mao is not only summarizing basic points of materialist dialectics, but countering various incorrect ideas that had their source in the Soviet Union and found their way into the Chinese Communist Party. The first was the opportunist theory of the

Deborin school in the Soviet Union, which denied the universality of contradiction, particularly the fact that contradiction exists from beginning to end in the process of development of each thing. According to this theory, contradiction only appears when the process has reached a certain stage. This is, of course, metaphysical and also idealist, because it necessarily involves the conclusion that at the start of a process the motive force is external, not internal. This opens the door to the notion of some external force providing the "initial impulse" to the universe—that is, to the notion of God.

Further, in the political sphere it leads to class collaboration and conciliation, for if contradiction is not always present then struggle need not be the means for resolving differences. One example of this which Mao cites is that "the Deborin school sees only differences but not contradictions between the kulaks and the peasants in general under existing conditions in the Soviet Union, thus agreeing with Bukharin."[77]

Stalin led in exposing and defeating the counter-revolutionary philosophical theory of the Deborin school as an important part of waging the overall class struggle in the Soviet Union, especially in the late 1920s. But, as noted earlier, Stalin himself failed to thoroughly apply materialist dialectics. This was expressed in *Dialectical and Historical Materialism* in particular in the failure to focus on the law of contradiction as the basic law of materialist dialectics and to link together the struggle and the identity of opposites. Thus, when Mao states in "On Contradiction" that both the interdependence and the struggle of the contradictory aspects determine the life of all things and push their development forward, he is putting forward a different, and more correct, understanding than Stalin. (*Dialectical and Historical Materialism* itself was written about the same time as "On Contradiction," but the same views, including the erroneous ones, that characterize it were known and circulated in the Chinese Communist Party before Mao wrote "On Contradiction.")

Identity and Struggle of Opposites

A lengthy section of "On Contradiction" is devoted to this problem of the identity and struggle of the aspects of a contradiction. Here Mao explains that there are two meanings to the identity of opposites. The first is their interdependence and their coexistence in a single entity. But, Mao says, the matter does not end there; "what is more important is their transformation into each other.

That is to say, in given conditions, each of the contradictory aspects within a thing transforms itself into its opposite, changes its position to that of its opposite."[78]

The importance of this can be seen by taking the example of the proletariat and the bourgeoisie. If it were not recognized that these two aspects are not only interdependent but can transform themselves into their opposite, then it would not be seen how the proletariat could undergo the change from the secondary to the principal aspect of the contradiction, from being the ruled to being the ruling class, while the bourgeoisie underwent the contrary change. In the concrete conditions of China at that time, in the midst of the anti-Japanese war of resistance, such an erroneous, metaphysical view on the part of communists would lead either to refusing to enter into a united front with the Kuomintang or, as the mirror opposite, to failing to struggle for the leading role of the proletariat in the united front. In either form—"left" or right—this would amount to seeing a united front with the Kuomintang as meaning the inevitable and continual subordination of the Communist Party to the Kuomintang, since the Kuomintang would start out in the stronger, dominant position, being the ruling party in the country.

In this same section of "On Contradiction" Mao also emphasized, however, that in the relation between the identity and struggle of opposites, identity is relative but struggle is absolute. He pointed out that "struggle between opposites permeates a process from beginning to end and makes one process transform itself into another. . . . The combination of conditional, relative identity and unconditional, absolute struggle constitutes the movement of opposites in all things."[79] The two things which form a contradiction and have identity do so only under certain conditions; but from the beginning to the end of that particular contradiction there will be struggle and this struggle will eventually lead to the resolution of that contradiction and the emergence of another.

If this were not grasped then it would not be recognized that struggle is the basis for resolving a particular contradiction and moving from one stage to the next. The importance of this can be readily grasped by applying it to the contradiction between the proletariat and the bourgeoisie, or, as in the case of China during the new-democratic stage, the contradiction between the broad masses on the one hand and imperialism and feudalism on the other (and in the sub-stage of the anti-Japanese war of resistance, the contradiction between the Chinese nation and Japanese imperialism).

In combatting erroneous tendencies, particularly dogmatism, within the Chinese Communist Party, Mao devoted more attention in "On Contradiction" to the particularity of contradiction than to the universality of contradiction. The dogmatists, Mao noted, did not recognize or at least give proper weight to the problem of the particularity of contradiction. In combatting this dogmatism Mao stressed that while there is nothing in the world except matter in motion, "this motion must assume certain forms. . . .[and] what is especially important and necessary, constituting as it does the foundation of our knowledge of a thing, is to observe what is particular to this form of motion of matter, namely, to observe the qualitative difference between this form of motion and other forms."[80] This applies not only to nature, but to society (and thought) as well. Each particular form of matter in motion has its own particular essence which is "determined by its own particular contradiction."[81]

The dogmatists, failing to base themselves on this, were incapable of recognizing the actual features of the Chinese revolution at that time, of determining the motive forces, target and tasks of the revolution at that stage and therefore of uniting all possible forces against the main enemy while maintaining the independence and initiative of the proletariat and its Party. Many wanted to blindly follow the model of the Russian revolution. This was not applicable in the concrete conditions of China, a semi-colonial, semi-feudal country, which at that time Japan was attempting to reduce to an outright colony.

Part of Mao's answer to this in "On Contradiction" was also contained in the section on antagonism and its role in contradiction. Mao noted that "antagonism is one form, but not the only form, of the struggle of opposites."[82] And he insisted that:

we must make a concrete study of the circumstances of each specific struggle of opposites and should not arbitrarily apply the formula discussed above [the need to violently overthrow the reactionary classes] to everything. Contradiction and struggle are universal and absolute, but the methods of resolving contradictions, that is, the forms of struggle, differ according to the differences in the nature of the contradictions. Some contradictions are characterized by open antagonism, others are not. In accordance with the concrete development of things, some contradictions which were originally non-antagonistic develop into antagonistic ones, while others which were originally antagonistic develop into non-antagonistic ones.[83]

This was of particular importance then because it had become necessary to change from warfare against the Kuomintang to a united front with it, because of the primacy of the struggle against the Japanese aggressors. This did not mean that the fundamentally reactionary nature of the Kuomintang and the class forces it represented had changed, but it did mean that in the concrete conditions of the struggle at that time the contradiction with the Kuomintang had been temporarily mitigated and had been temporarily transformed from an antagonistic to a non-antagonistic one. Struggle against the Kuomintang must continue, particularly over the question of leadership in this united front, but the policy of the Party must be to wage this struggle non-antagonistically, in the form of political and ideological struggle within the context of maintaining the united front (of course, when the Kuomintang militarily attacked the Communist Party and the revolutionary armed forces, then this had to be rebuffed, but the objective even here was to maintain the united front while exercising independence and initiative and fighting for leadership of the united front). And more generally in the conditions of China's new-democratic revolution, the contradiction between the proletariat and the bourgeoisie (or parts of it) was not antagonistic (at least at times) and should not be incorrectly handled as such when conditions called for dealing with it non-antagonistically.

In fully criticizing and opposing erroneous lines within the Party at that time, especially dogmatist deviations, Mao not only upheld but concretely applied the principle of the particularity of contradiction. He explained the philosophical basis for the correctness of the strategy of new-democratic revolution as the necessary prelude to and preparation for the socialist revolution in China:

Qualitatively different contradictions can only be resolved by qualitatively different methods. For instance, the contradiction between the proletariat and the bourgeoisie is resolved by the method of socialist revolution; the contradiction between the great masses of the people and the feudal system is resolved by the method of democratic revolution; the contradiction between the colonies and imperialism is resolved by the method of national revolutionary war.... Processes change, old processes and old contradictions disappear, new processes and new contradictions emerge, and the methods of resolving contradictions differ accordingly. In Russia, there was a fundamental difference between the contradiction resolved by the February Revolution and the contradiction resolved by the October Revolution, as well as between the methods used to resolve them. The principle of using different methods to resolve different contradictions is one which Marxist-Leninists must strictly observe. The dogmatists do not observe this principle; they do not understand that conditions differ in different kinds of revolution and so do not understand that different methods should be used to resolve different contradictions; on the contrary, they invariably adopt what they imagine to be an

unalterable formula and arbitrarily apply it everywhere, which only
causes setbacks to the revolution or makes a sorry mess of what was
originally well done.[84]

Universality and Particularity

Mao also took up the question of the relationship between the
particularity and universality of contradiction, which was of great
importance in combatting the dogmatists in particular. He noted
that:

Of course, unless we understand the universality of contradiction, we
have no way of discovering the universal cause or universal basis for the
movement or development of things; however, unless we study the particularity of contradiction, we have no way of determining the particular
essence of a thing which differentiates it from other things, no way of
discovering the particular cause or particular basis for the movement or
development of a thing, and no way of distinguishing one thing from
another or of demarcating the fields of science.[85]

The dogmatists, who failed to seriously study the particularity
of contradiction, did not grasp the correct, dialectical relationship
between the universality and particularity of contradiction. They
did not understand that the movement of man's cognition is from
the particular to the universal (or general)—to the recognition of
the common essence of things—and then back to the particular (on
a higher basis) and so on in an endless upward spiral. They did not
understand that man's knowledge of things in general must consist of his knowledge of many different things in particular, and
that in this way the general (or universal) resides in the particular—not the whole universal residing in and reducible to one or
a few particulars but the universal residing in an endless number
of particulars, each with its specific essence, and therefore, in that
sense, residing in every particular. Hence they treated theory as
"general truth," neither drawn from particular things nor needing
to be applied to them—in short, as dogma.

Moreover, the dogmatists failed to understand that, as universality and particularity of contradiction themselves form a contradiction, they have identity and can be transformed into each
other. They did not grasp that:

Because the range of things is vast and there is no limit to their development, what is universal in one context becomes particular in another. Con-
versely, what is particular in one context becomes universal in another.[86]

To illustrate this, Mao used the example of the contradiction between socialized production and private ownership. Under
capitalism this constitutes the universality of contradiction—it is
fundamental to and runs throughout capitalist society as a whole.
But with regard to society in general it is only a particular form of
the contradiction between the forces and relations of production.
This was obviously important in exposing the erroneous thinking
that China's revolution must be the same as that in capitalist
countries; in China at that stage the fundamental contradiction
and the particular form of the contradicton between the forces and
relations of production was of a different nature than in the
capitalist countries.

On the other hand, of course, being particular, this contradiction
and the nature of the process determined by it—the new-democratic revolution—was only temporary. It would be necessary at a certain point, with the resolution of this contradiction, to move on to
the next stage, the socialist revolution, characterized by the fundamental contradiction between the proletariat and the
bourgeoisie. The basis for this was also explained and emphasized
by Mao in analyzing the relationship between the universality and
particularity of contradiction. Here is Mao's summation of this
point and its extreme importance:

> The relationship between the universality and the particularity of con-
> tradiction is the relationship between the general character and the indivi-
> dual character of contradiction. By the former we mean that contradiction
> exists in and runs through all processes from beginning to end; motion,
> things, processes, thinking—all are contradictions. To deny contradiction
> is to deny everything. This is a universal truth for all times and all coun-
> tries, which admits of no exception. Hence the general character, the ab-
> soluteness of contradiction. But this general character is contained in
> every individual character; without individual character there can be no
> general character. If all individual character were removed, what general
> character would remain? It is because each contradiction is particular that
> individual character arises. All individual character exists conditionally
> and temporarily, and hence is relative.
> This truth concerning general and individual character, concerning ab-
> soluteness and relativity, is the quintessence of the problem of contradic-
> tion in things; failure to understand it is tantamount to abandoning
> dialectics.[87]

In this same section of "On Contradiction," Mao also made clear
the philosophical basis for the fact that in the Chinese revolution
there were sub-stages within the overall stage of new democracy,
and specifically the basis for the necessary policies and adjust-

ments characteristic of the united front against Japan. This particular point was gone into at some length in the first chapter of this book, hence it will only be briefly summarized here. The fundamental contradiction in the process of development of anything runs throughout that entire process and determines the essence of the process from beginning to end. Only with the resolution of the fundamental contradiction characterizing and determining the essence of the particular process will that process transform itself into another and a new fundamental contradiction emerge. But within the process characterized by a particular fundamental contradiction there are stages because "among the numerous major and minor contradictions which are determined or influenced by the fundamental contradiction, some become intensified, some are temporarily or partially resolved or mitigated, and some new ones emerge."[88] These other contradictions react upon the fundamental contradiction and, while in the main they are determined by its development, they in turn play a role in affecting its development; hence the development of the fundamental contradiction proceeds in a spiral, through stages.

As applied to the Chinese revolution in that period, this meant that the nature of the Chinese revolution would remain fundamentally unchanged until imperialism and feudalism (and bureaucrat-capitalism) were overthrown in China. This would mark the end of the new-democratic revolution and the beginning of the socialist revolution. But within the general stage of the new-democratic revolution there would be stages; during the anti-Japanese war in particular, the contradiction between the masses of Chinese people and the domestic reactionaries receded temporarily, while the contradiction between the Chinese nation and Japan came to the forefront. This was part of and not separate from the process of the new-democratic revolution and its fundamental contradiction but marked a particular stage within it.

Principal Contradiction

Clearly this was closely linked with the question of principal contradiction, the next main question addressed by Mao in "On Contradiction." As Mao explained:

There are many contradictions in the process of development of a complex thing, and one of them is necessarily the principal contradiction whose existence and development determine or influence the existence and development of the other contradictions....at every stage in the development of a process, there is only one principal contradiction which plays the leading role . . . . Therefore, in studying any complex process in which there are two or more contradictions, we must devote every effort to finding its principal contradiction. Once this principal contradiction is grasped, all problems can be readily solved.[89]

What is the relationship between the principal contradiction and the fundamental contradiction, which determines the essence of the process as a whole? The principal contradiction at any time is the main contradiction in the particular stage of development of the process defined by the fundamental contradiction; it cannot represent the switch from one whole (or fundamental) process to another, for only the resolution of the fundamental contradiction can bring that about. The principal contradiction may be exactly the same as the fundamental contradiction, but need not be; it may represent the fundamental contradiction at a certain stage in its development without representing the fundamental contradiction in its entirety, as it fully determines the essence of the process as a whole. But only when the principal contradiction represents the fundamental contradiction as a whole can the resolution of the principal contradiction bring about the transformation of the old process into a new one, the resolution of the old fundamental contradiction and the emergence of a new one.

Obviously this is a complicated question. And as applied to the new-democratic revolution in China it was particularly complicated. The principal contradiction during the anti-Japanese war was that between the Chinese nation as a whole and Japanese imperialism (together with those elements of Chinese society that sided with Japan). This represented a particular stage within the development of the whole process of the new-democratic revolution, which process was determined by the fundamental contradiction between the broad masses on the one hand and imperialism and feudalism (and bureaucrat-capitalism) on the other.

During the stage of the anti-Japanese war certain contradictions were "temporarily or partially resolved or mitigated," including that between the broad masses and the feudal system, but this did not mean that the process of new-democratic revolution and its fundamental contradiction had been resolved and transformed into a new process. With the defeat of the Japanese imperialists, the fundamental contradiction developed to a new stage and was intensified. The principal contradiction once again fully represented the fundamental contradiction, only now on a higher level, and the resolution of this contradiction—between the broad masses and imperialism and feudalism (and bureaucrat-capitalism)—meant the transformation of the old process (the new-democratic revolution) into a new one, the socialist revolution.

From all this we can see why Mao had to write "On Contradiction," and can begin to get a better sense of the depth and importance of it. And after analyzing the question of principal contradiction, Mao went on to analyze the question of the principal aspect of a contradiction. What is the heart of this question? Mao wrote:

In any contradiction, the development of the contradictory aspects is uneven. Sometimes they seem to be in equilibrium, which is however only temporary and relative, while unevenness is basic. Of the two contradictory aspects, one must be principal and the other secondary. The principal aspect is the one playing the leading role in the contradiction. The nature of a thing is determined mainly by the principal aspect of a contradiction, the aspect which has gained the dominant position.[90]

Mao went on to add immediately, however, that "this situation is not static; the principal and the non-principal aspects of a contradiction transform themselves into each other and the nature of the thing changes accordingly."[91] This, as noted earlier, is the most important part of the identity of opposites and occurs because of the struggle between them.

Mao attached tremendous importance to this point. He pointed both to the contradiction between the proletariat and the bourgeoisie and to the contradiction between China and the Chinese masses on the one side and imperialism and feudalism on the other. The position of the aspects in both these contradictions was bound to change, he affirmed; the proletariat was bound to transform itself into the dominant position over the bourgeoisie, and old China, dominated by imperialism and feudalism, was bound to be transformed into new China ruled by the masses of people, led by the proletariat and its Communist Party.

Mao emphasized this to struggle against defeatism with regard to the Chinese revolution and class capitulationism with regard to the relationship between the proletariat and the bourgeoisie in the united front. The proletariat was bound to gain the dominant, leading position in this united front through struggle and, dialectically related to this, the Chinese revolution was bound to advance through the war of resistance against Japan and beyond this to the complete defeat and overthrow of imperialism and feudalism (and bureaucrat-capitalism). But this would happen only through struggle.

Mao powerfully expressed this principle in the following passage:

We often speak of "the new superseding the old." The supersession of the old by the new is a general, eternal and inviolable law of the universe. The transformation of one thing into another, through leaps of different forms in accordance with its essence and external conditions—this is the process of the new superseding the old. In each thing there is contradiction between its new and old aspects, and this gives rise to a series of struggles with many twists and turns. As a result of these struggles, the new aspect changes from being minor to being major and rises to predominance, while the old aspect changes from being major to being minor and gradually dies out. And the moment the new aspect gains dominance over the old, the old thing changes qualitatively into a new thing. It can thus be seen that the nature of a thing is mainly determined by the principal aspect of the contradiction, the aspect which has gained predominance. When the principal aspect which has gained predominance changes, the nature of a thing changes accordingly.[92]

Such was the relationship between the masses of people and the reactionary forces, the proletariat and the bourgeoisie, and the new society and the old.

The Socialist Period

"On Contradiction" was, along with "On Practice," a tremendous weapon in the Chinese revolution at that time and played a great part in charting the course of the Chinese revolution through new democracy to socialism. And more than that it was a treasure house of Marxist theory, philosophy in particular, of great and enduring value in the overall and ongoing revolutionary struggle not only in China but worldwide.

But Mao's greatest development and application of Marxism-Leninism came after the seizure of nationwide political power, in the period of socialist revolution. And a crucial part of this was his development and application of Marxist-Leninist philosophy, materialist dialectics.

In the preceeding chapter the relationship between the struggle on the philosophical front and the struggle on the economic and political fronts was touched on. Particular attention was focused on the struggle against the reactionary theory of the "synthesized economic base" cooked up by the revisionists in the Chinese Communist Party and in particular a leading philosopher of this camp, Yang Hsien-chen.

Yang's reactionary theory that the superstructure should serve capitalist relations as well as socialist ones in the economic base and should even "serve the bourgeoisie" was part and parcel of the "theory of productive forces." It argued that China's productive forces were too backward to allow for the advance to socialism and the elimination of capitalist relations and that instead capitalism must be allowed to develop without restriction and for a long period before the basis would exist to make the transition to socialism. Hence, according to this view, the task was to "consolidate new democracy," and it was even said that in these conditions "exploitation is a merit."

Mao formulated the general line for the transition from new democracy to socialism in opposition to the revisionist program of "consolidating new democracy." And he led the fight on the philosophical front to demolish the ideological basis for this counter-revolutionary line.

In fact, Mao had already anticipated this in "On Contradiction." In speaking of the transformation of the aspects of a contradiction into their opposite, Mao gave special emphasis to the fact that this applied among other things to the contradiction between the forces and relations of production and the base and superstructure, thus striking a sharp blow against mechanical materialism. This was of extreme importance even then, in showing how China did not have to pass through the capitalist stage but could advance through the new-democratic revolution to socialism, despite the fact that its productive forces were not highly developed. Mao wrote then that:

Some people think that this [the transformation of contradictory aspects into their opposite] is not true of certain contradictions. For instance, in the contradiction between the productive forces and the relations of production, the productive forces are the principal aspect; . . . in the contradiction between the economic base and the superstructure, the economic base is the principal aspect; and there is no change in their respective positions. This is the mechanical materialist conception, not the dialectical materialist conception. True, the productive forces . . . and the economic base generally play the principal and decisive role; whoever denies this is not a materialist. But it must also be admitted that in certain conditions, such aspects as the relations of production . . . and the superstructure in turn manifest themselves in the principal and decisive role. When it is impossible for the productive forces to develop without a change in the relations of production, then the change in the relations of production plays the principal and decisive role . . . . When the superstructure (politics, culture, etc.) obstructs the development of the economic base, political and cultural changes become principal and decisive. Are we going against materialism when we say this? No . . . . This does not go against materialism; on the contrary, it avoids mechanical materialism and firmly upholds dialectical materialism.[93]

Applying this principle to the situation in China right after the seizure of nationwide political power, Mao showed that unless socialist production relations were established, China's productive forces could not continue to develop. "Consolidating new democracy"—that is, capitalism—would hinder, not help, this development; "only socialism can save China." And unless a socialist superstructure was established and strengthened—unless the proletariat, together with its allies, held power and exercised dictatorship over the reactionary classes, and unless the ideology, politics, culture, etc., of the proletariat were in command—then the socialist economic base could not be developed and "eat up" the remaining capitalist relations through the period of transition. The superstructure could not serve both capitalism and socialism, it certainly could not "serve the bourgeoisie." This was an extremely sharp and decisive struggle, and only by waging it on the philosophical as well as the political and economic battlefronts was it possible for the proletariat to prevail and continue to advance along the socialist road.

But after the transition had been basically completed, after socialist ownership had been in the main achieved, in 1956, the class struggle did not die down nor certainly die out. And it was in leading the proletariat and broad masses in waging the class struggle under these conditions that Mao made his greatest contributions to Marxism-Leninism and the cause of communism.

Deepening Dialectics

As noted earlier, Mao's development and application of Marxist-Leninist philosophy was a decisive part of this. And, as also stated at the start of this chapter and indicated throughout it, the heart of Mao's contributions to Marxist-Leninist philosophy was his concentration and development of the understanding and application of the law of contradiction. What Mao unceasingly stressed, and even more intensely so in the socialist period, was dialectics, motion, change, upheavals, leaps, the transformation of things into their opposites, the supersession of the old by the new—all in opposition to tendencies to stagnation, "absolutism," "settling down," permanent "great order," etc., in short, metaphysics. As Mao emphasized in 1966, with his characteristic and classic style of understatement, " . . . diligently study dialectics, its efficacy is very great."[94]

In early 1958, at the time when Mao was beginning to develop the basis for his great theory of continuing the revolution under the dictatorship of the proletariat, he commented that:

To talk all the time about monolithic unity, and not to talk about struggle, is not Marxist-Leninist. Unity passes through struggle, only thus can unity be achieved. It is the same within the party, as regards classes, and among the people. Unity is transformed into struggle, and then there is unity again. We cannot talk of monolithic unity alone, and not talk about struggle, about contradictions. The Soviet Union does not talk about the contradiction between the leaders and the led. If there were no contradictions and no struggle, there would be no world, no progress, no life, there would be nothing at all. To talk all the time about unity is "a pool of stagnant water"; it can lead to coldness. We must destroy the old basis for unity, pass through a struggle, and unite on a new basis. Which is better—a stagnant pool, or "the inexhaustible Yangtse comes roaring past"?[95]

At several points in this chapter it has been noted that Mao summed up that Stalin deviated in some significant ways from dialectics. In 1957, a year before he made the comments cited just above, Mao made a rather thorough analysis of this, and it is worth quoting at length here."Stalin had a fair amount of metaphysics in him and he taught many people to follow metaphysics," Mao states flatly. He notes that in *HCPSU:*

Stalin says that Marxist dialectics has four principal features. As the first feature he talks of the interconnection of things, as if all things happened to be interconnected for no reason at all. What then are the things that are interconnected? It is the two contradictory aspects of a thing that are interconnected. Everything has two contradictory aspects. As the fourth feature he talks of the internal contradiction in all things, but then he deals only with the struggle of opposites, without mentioning their unity. According to the basic law of dialectics, the unity of opposites, there is at once struggle and unity between the opposites, which are both mutually exclusive and interconnected and which under given conditions transform themselves into each other.

Stalin's viewpoint is reflected in the entry on "identity" in the *Shorter Dictionary of Philosophy,* fourth edition, compiled in the Soviet Union. It is said there: "There can be no identity between war and peace, between the bourgeoisie and the proletariat, between life and death and other such phenomena, because they are fundamentally opposed to each other and mutually exclusive.".... This interpretation is utterly wrong.... War and peace are both mutually exclusive and interconnected and can be transformed into each other under given conditions. If war is not brewing in peace-time, how can it possibly break out all of a sudden? If peace is not brewing in wartime, how can it suddenly come about?

If life and death cannot be transformed into each other, then please tell me where living things come from.... All living matter undergoes a process of metabolism; it grows, reproduces and perishes. While life is in progress, life and death are engaged in a constant struggle and are being transformed into each other all the time.

If the bourgeoisie and the proletariat cannot transform themselves into each other, how come that through revolution the proletariat becomes the

ruler and the bourgeoisie the ruled? . . . .
     Stalin failed to see the connection between the struggle of opposites and
the unity of opposites.[96]

     This was of particular importance at that time because it was a
period when in China as well as a number of other socialist countries there were a number of disturbances, arising from the
resistance of reactionaries to socialism and from bureaucratic
tendencies and other defects in the policies of the party and state
in these countries. Thus it was very important to distinguish and
correctly deal with two different types of contradictions—those
among the people and those between the people and the reactionaries—which interpenetrated. Antagonistic and non-
antagonistic contradictions are opposites, but as such they also
have identity and can be transformed into each other.
     In particular Mao was stressing at that time that non-
antagonistic contradictions could be transformed into antagonistic ones if they were not handled properly. In the same
"Talks" quoted at length above, Mao makes a point of stating that
in the circumstances at that time the class struggle in China found
expression on a great scale in contradictions among the people.[97]
What he was emphasizing was that the reactionaries, the enemies,
were taking advantage of certain defects and difficult conditions
to stir up broad-scale unrest and even rebellion on the part of sections of the people against the party and state.
     Here he was not attempting to negate the fact that the principal
contradiction was still that between the proletariat and the
bourgeoisie, which is overall an antagonistic contradiction (though
in China's conditions it was correct to attempt to handle the contradiction with the national bourgeoisie non-antagonistically so
far as it was possible). In fact, later that year (1957) Mao explicitly
criticized the formulation adopted at the Eighth Congress of the
Chinese Communist Party (in 1956) that the principal contradiction was that between the advanced socialist system and the
backward productive forces, a revisionist formulation opposed to
the correct line that the principal contradiction was between the
proletariat and the bourgeoisie and that the spearhead of the
revolution was directed against the latter.[98] What Mao was getting at in focusing on the fact that the class struggle found expression on a vast scale in contradictions among the people was that in
order to carry the revolution forward and defeat the resistance of
the enemy it was necessary to distinguish and correctly handle the
two different types of contradictions in society. As he said in the
above-mentioned "Talks," in January, 1957, "How to handle the

contradictions between the people and the enemy and those among the people in socialist society is a branch of science worthy of careful study."[99]

And Mao made a major speech on this question the next month (February 1957), "On the Correct Handling of Contradictions Among the People." In that speech Mao reiterated that "Marxist philosophy holds that the law of the unity of opposites is the fundamental law of the universe. This law operates universally, whether in the natural world, in human society, or in man's thinking."[100] He went on to re-emphasize that "Between the opposites in a contradiction there is at once unity and struggle, and it is this that impels things to move and change."[101] And he criticized "Many [who] do not admit that contradictions still exist in socialist society, with the result that they become irresolute and passive when confronted with social contradictions; they do not understand that socialist society grows more united and consolidated through the ceaseless process of correctly handling and resolving contradictions."[102]

Mao applied to the situation at that time the law that, in given conditions, the aspects of a contradiction can be transformed into their opposite. This meant that the disturbances occurring then must be viewed dialectically. They were a bad thing—that was their principal aspect, which determined the nature of them. But they could be turned into a good thing, because they contained a positive aspect within them. They revealed shortcomings and mistakes on the part of the party and state, making it possible to correct these. Through this process, if handled correctly, the unity among the people, including the relations between the leadership and the led, would be strengthened and the socialist state further consolidated, while the counter-revolutionaries would be further isolated and more effectively suppressed. But, if it was handled incorrectly, disunity would grow among the people and the enemy would be strengthened, while the socialist state would be weakened—and perhaps even overthrown.

The law that opposites can be transformed into each other also means not only that the proletariat can become the dominant force in society while the bourgeoisie becomes the dominated, but the reverse as well. In other words, the proletariat could still lose power and the bourgeoisie could replace it as the ruling class. "Correct Handling" points to this danger and in fact, as noted in the preceding chapter, it was in this speech that for the first time in the history of the international communist movement it was explicitly pointed out that even after the basic achievement of socialist ownership the bourgeoisie continues to exist, class struggle continues and the question of whether socialism or capitalism will win out is still not settled.[103]

This also represented, of course, a further development of Mao's own understanding, including in philosophy. Specifically it represented a different—and more advanced and correct—view than what he had put forward in "On Contradiction" concerning contradiction and antagonism in socialist society. In that earlier work Mao had quoted (and obviously expressed agreement with) a statement by Lenin that under socialism contradiction will remain but antagonism will disappear.[104] This was, of course, the prevailing line in the Soviet Union and the international communist movement at the time "On Contradiction" was written. But it was incorrect—it is an accurate analysis of *communism* and not of socialism. This Mao determined by continuing to apply materialist dialectics to the actual contradictions in socialist society and on the basis of summing up experience in China itself as well as the (positive and negative) experience of the Soviet Union. "On the Correct Handling of Contradictions Among the People" contained, as noted, the first explicit and unequivocal recognition in the history of the international communist movement of the continuation of classes and class struggle, including specifically the antagonistic contradiction between the proletariat and the bourgeoisie, in socialist society—after the basic transformation of ownership. All this is itself further proof of the truth of materialist dialectics and of the fact that Mao's understanding and development of Marxist philosophy was founded on and proceeded in dialectical unity with developments in society—and in particular the class struggle, which in fact continues under socialism.

Man's Conscious, Dynamic Role

Indeed the class struggle in China was very sharp at that time and was further intensified the next year, 1958. As also pointed out in the previous chapter, that was the year that the movement to establish people's communes erupted throughout the Chinese countryside as a decisive part of the Great Leap Forward. In opposition to the revisionists within the Communist Party, Mao championed these mass movements and formulated the general line for building socialism, which both summed up early experience in these movements and gave further direction and impetus to them. The struggle within the Communist Party, focused on these questions, was extremely sharp. And this was true on the philosophical front, where the revisionists, again hurling the accusation of idealism at Mao, stepped up their attack on the principle of the identity between thinking and being.

Yang Hsien-chen, the leading revisionist philosophical "authority," stated straight out that "there is no identity between thinking and being."[105] He accused Mao and other revolutionaries of contending that "thinking and being are the same."[106] And further, he:

totally denied the necessity of a process for man's cognition of objective phenomena. In his eyes, it was "idealism" when the subjective could not readily conform with the objective. Proceeding from this fallacy, he used the tactics of attacking one point to the total disregard of the rest and grossly exaggerated the temporary, isolated shortcomings which were difficult to avoid in our actual work, labelling them all "idealism." He wildly went for so-called "mistakes" in the great leap forward and ascribed the cause to "the identity between thinking and being," to "man's conscious dynamic role which makes a mess of things," etc. He made a big show of upholding materialism, while actually using metaphysics and idealism to oppose the active and revolutionary theory of reflection.[107]

We have seen that the identity of the two aspects of a contradiction is one of the two features of a contradiction, the other being the struggle of opposites. And as we have also seen, identity between the aspects does not at all mean that they are the same; it means rather that they are interconnected, interdependent and interpenetrate with each other. And more than that, it means that under given conditions they can be transformed into each other. In the relation between thinking and being this means that being can be transformed into thinking and vice versa. To deny this is obviously metaphysics, for it makes the two aspects absolutes and absolutely separated from each other. But it is also idealist, for if being cannot be transformed into thinking, matter into consciousness, then where does thinking (consciousness) come from, what is its source?

Mao directly addressed this question in a counter-attack on the philosophical front, concentrated in a short essay (actually a passage in a Central Committee circular), "Where Do Correct Ideas Come From?" written in 1963. Here Mao reviewed the stages in the process of cognition and pointedly stated that:

Among our comrades there are many who do not yet understand this theory of knowledge. When asked the source of their ideas, opinions, policies, methods, plans and conclusions, eloquent speeches and long articles, they consider the question strange and cannot answer it. Nor do they comprehend that matter can be transformed into consciousness and consciousness into matter, although such leaps are phenomena of everyday life.[108]

Speaking to the question of the subjective conforming to the objective, of consciousness correctly reflecting the material world and being capable therefore of guiding the practice of changing the world, Mao not only noted that there must be the accumulation of perceptual knowledge before it can be analyzed and synthesized into rational knowledge, but also that in translating this into action, in making the leap from consciousness back to matter, there is the resistance of reactionary forces, especially in changing society. "In social struggle," he wrote, "the forces representing the advanced class sometimes suffer defeat not because their ideas are incorrect but because in the balance of forces engaged in struggle, they are not as powerful for the time being as the forces of reaction; they are therefore temporarily defeated, but they are bound to triumph sooner or later."[109]

While there were shortcomings and mistakes in the Great Leap Forward, the main reason for the difficulties during that period was the resistance of the reactionary forces in China, and in the Chinese Communist Party in particular, as well as in the Soviet Union (the Soviet revisionists actively attempted to sabotage the Great Leap Forward by pulling out assistance and blueprints, leaving many projects unfinished, etc.). To attribute these difficulties to "man's conscious dynamic role" and to the "subjective idealism" of the revolutionaries, including Mao, was to turn things upside down and inside out, to attack the conscious activism of the masses and deny the decisive role of a revolutionary line in leading the masses in transforming society and nature. This, of course, was the aim of the revisionists—who also, of course, took credit for the real gains that actually resulted from the upsurge of the Great Leap Forward.

Mao had actually addressed the basic philosophical principle involved here in "On Contradiction," where, in combatting mechanical materialism, he showed that the law of the transformation of opposites into each other applies not only to the forces and relations of production and the base and superstructure but also to practice and theory. He specifically pointed out that, although practice is principal over theory in general, there are certain times when the relationship is reversed. And "When a task, no matter which, has to be performed, but there is as yet no guiding line, method, plan or policy, the principal and decisive thing is to decide

During the Cultural Revolution Mao's works, as well as Marxist-Leninist classics, were first printed and distributed on a large scale in the main language in China and many minority languages. Here, distributors carrying these books across mountains are greeted by the Miao people in Kweiting County, Kweichow Province.

on a guiding line, method, plan or policy."[110] Here Mao stressed the tremendous importance of line, policy, etc., which belong to the category of consciousness, and which can be transformed into matter, into revolutionary practice. And in general the dialectical relationship between consciousness and matter, the identity between them and therefore the possibility of the one being transformed into the other—this is an extremely important principle of Marxism-Leninism and was a focus of fierce struggle in the Chinese Communist Party, especially from the time of the Great Leap Forward.

In 1959, during the struggle against Peng Teh-huai over the Great Leap Forward (see the previous chapter), Mao declared that empiricism had become the main danger. Actually, for several years before that he had been stressing that revisionism, right opportunism, was a greater danger than dogmatism. This revisionism was reflected in the attacks on "man's conscious dynamic role," on "the identity of thinking and being" and in general on the importance of theory, line, consciousness. All this was an attempt to suffocate the mass movements that in fact represented the transformation of Mao's revolutionary line—drawn from the experience of struggle in China and internationally—into a tremendous material force changing the face of China, especially its vast countryside.

Struggle and Synthesis

During the several-year period of intense struggle over the Great Leap Forward, Mao made in 1962 the historic analysis that socialist society was a long transition period during the entire course of which there are classes and class struggle and the danger of capitalist restoration (as well as the threat of attack from external class enemies). This became the basic line of the Chinese Communist Party for the entire period of socialism. It represented a historic advance in Marxism-Leninism, and it was the result of the brilliant application of the fundamental law of contradiction to socialist society. Mao applied this law to the material and ideological conditions under socialism, showing how the bourgeoisie would constantly be regenerated out of these conditions, out of the contradictions that characterized socialism from beginning to end (for more on this see the previous chapter in this book). And, if the bourgeoisie and the proletariat both existed and formed a contradiction—in fact the principal contradiction—throughout the socialist period, then not only must there be struggle between them but the possibility must also exist that they could be transformed into their opposites—in other words, that the bourgeoisie could usurp power from the proletariat, that capitalist restoration could take place.

Again the revisionists viciously attacked this pathbreaking theory and line of Mao's. As early as 1958 Yang Hsien-chen, taking up a new tactic, had attacked Mao and the proletarian headquarters in the party for talking "only about the struggle between opposites, but not their unity." Here Yang became a champion of the unity of opposites and clamored for "using identity of contradiction."[111]

Yang's babbling became especially intense during the early 1960s, particularly in 1961-1962, when Soviet sabotage, natural calamities and revisionist treachery within the Chinese Communist Party were all at a high point and combined to pose great obstacles to the advance along the socialist road in China. At this time Yang insisted that unity of opposites meant "common points," and that the Chinese people and the Chinese revolution had "common points" with U.S. imperialism and "common points with some differences" with Soviet revisionism. This was the theory of "two combines into one" (or two into one) in direct opposition to Mao's concentrated expression of dialectics, one divides into two, which he had formulated some time earlier. In 1964 Yang, Liu Shao-chi and other top revisionists in the Chinese Communist Party leadership openly proclaimed their reactionary theory of two combines into one. This was aimed at providing a philosophical rationalization for their revisionist line of "the dying out of class struggle."

To counter Mao's line and in an attempt to confuse people, Yang Hsien-chen combined two into one on the question of one divides into two vs. two combines into one. That is, he claimed that " 'combine two into one' and 'one divides into two' had 'the same meaning'...."[112]

Here the question of synthesis and its role in contradiction is of particular importance. Yang Hsien-chen argued that "analysis means 'one divides into two' while synthesis means 'combine two into one.' "[113] That is, in analyzing a contradiction it is correct to divide it into its contradictory aspects, but in seeking the resolution—or really, reconciliation—of the contradiction the two aspects should be combined into one, united into a "common point" so to speak. This is the opposite of the correct, dialectical materalist understanding which holds that:

Marxist philosophy tells us that analysis and synthesis are an objective law of things and at the same time a method for people to understand things. Analysis shows how an entity divides into two different parts and how they are locked in struggle; synthesis shows how, through the struggle between the two opposite aspects, one prevails, defeats and eliminates the other, how an old contradiction is resolved and a new one emerges, and how an old thing is eliminated and a new thing triumphs. In plain words, synthesis means one "eats up" the other.[114]

The difference here, the heart of this struggle in the realm of philosophy, is no mere academic debate but the struggle between two fundamentally opposed lines, the revolutionary line of resolving contradiction through struggle versus the reactionary line of attempting to reconcile contradiction through the subordination of the progressive to the reactionary, the advanced to the backward, the new to the old, the correct to the incorrect, etc. And under socialism in particular, this assumes its most concentrated political expression as the struggle between the Marxist-Leninist line of taking class struggle as the key link and the revisionist line of "the dying out of class struggle."

This law of synthesis applies in all contradictions, both antagonistic and non-antagonistic. In either case the new, rising aspect eventually "eats up" the old, decadent aspect. Only the means of "eating up" is different. The proletariat "eats up" the bourgeoisie by waging class struggle against it, wresting political power from it, exercising dictatorship over it and continuing the class struggle against it under the conditions of this proletarian dictatorship. This is an antagonistic contradiction and is resolved by antagonistic means. On the other hand, with regard to the contradiction between right and wrong among the people, this is resolved by non-antagonistic means, through ideological struggle. But in this process right still "eats up" wrong. And so it is as well with other non-antagonistic contradictions. Synthesis through struggle is a universal law, flowing from the fundamental law of the unity of opposites.

Without this correct view of synthesis "one divides into two" turns into eclectics—into the recognition of the contradictory aspects but an attempt to reconcile them, to reconcile two mutually exclusive things. In other words it turns into "two into one." In popular terms in this country this is expressed as "there are two sides to every story"—meaning you can't tell right from wrong, good from bad, etc.

Mao spoke to this in his "Reading Notes" on the Soviet political economy text. He said that to talk of contradictions that are "not irreconcilable," even under socialism, "does not agree with the laws of dialectics, which hold that all contradictions are irreconcilable. Where has there ever been a reconcilable contradiction? Some are antagonistic, some are non-antagonistic, but it must not be thought that there are irreconcilable and reconcilable contradictions."[115]

Mao spoke to this question of synthesis and its political implications in a major talk on philosophy in 1964. "What is synthesis?" he asked. And he answered:

You have all witnessed how the two opposites, the Kuomintang and the Communist Party, were synthesized on the mainland. The synthesis took place like this: their armies came, and we devoured them, we ate them bite by bite. It was not a case of two combining into one as expounded by Yang Hsien-chen, it was not the synthesis of two peacefully coexisting opposites.... Having analysed, how do we synthesize? If you want to go somewhere, you go right ahead; we still swallow your army mouthful by mouthful.... This was synthesis.... One thing eating another, big fish eating little fish, this is synthesis. It has never been put like this in books. I have never put it this way in my books either. For his part, Yang Hsien-chen believes that two combine into one and that synthesis is the indissoluble tie between two opposites. What indissoluble ties are there in this world? Things may be tied, but in the end they must be severed. There is nothing which cannot be severed.[116]

As applied to the class struggle, such is the case with regard to the proletariat and the bourgeoisie; if, through struggle, the proletariat does not synthesize the bourgeoisie, if the two are not severed through the resolution of the contradiction between them—resulting, through the victory of the proletariat, in the elimination of both as classes and the emergence of classless society—then how can there ever be any communism?

Unity of Opposites is Basic

In this same talk on philosophy, Mao expresses a further development of Marxist dialectics. He says that "Engels talked about three categories, but as for me I don't believe in two of these categories." Here Mao was referring to the transformation of quantity and quality into each other and the negation of the negation, which, along with the unity of opposites, Engels speaks of as the three basic laws of dialectics (see for example *Anti-Duhring*, "Part I. Philosophy"). As to quantity and quality, Mao says that "The transformation of quality and quantity into one another is the unity of the opposites quality and quantity."[117] And, Mao argues, "the negation of the negation does not exist at all." In sum, he says:

> The juxtaposition, on the same level, of the transformation of quality and quantity into one another, the negation of the negation, and the law of unity of opposites is "triplism," not monism. The most basic thing is the unity of opposites.[118]

In other words, to say that these three things are all, equally, basic laws of dialectics is in essence a violation of the law that there must be a principal contradiction. One of these must be basic, and it is the unity of opposites. As Mao explains, the transformation of quantity into quality, and of quality into quantity, is itself a result of the contradiction between quantity and quality and cannot be placed on a par with the law of contradiction.

But why does Mao insist that, "There is no such thing as the negation of the negation"? His explanation is as follows:

> Affirmation, negation, affirmation, negation . . . in the development of things, every link in the chain of events is both affirmation and negation. Slave-holding society negated primitive society, but with reference to feudal society it constituted, in turn, the affirmation. Feudal society constituted the negation in relation to slave-holding society but was in turn the affirmation with reference to capitalist society. Capitalist society was the negation in relation to feudal society, but it is, in turn, the affirmation in relation to socialist society.[119]

Here it may seem that Mao is not so much denying the negation of the negation as making a dialectical application of it. But what he is applying is the law of one divides into two, and what he is getting at is that in the process he describes—the development of human society so far, through stages, from primitive communal society to socialism—the negation of the negation cannot be said to be a law. How, for example, does feudalism represent a negation of the negation with regard to primitive society? Or capitalism with regard to slavery? Or socialism with regard to feudalism?

It is true that in the development of society things can be found which could be described as the negation of the negation. An example is that which Marx uses in *Capital,* Volume 1, and Engels defends against Duhring: individual private property in the means of production is negated by capitalist ownership of the means of production, which is in turn negated by socialized ownership; this gives private property to the individual but in the means of consumption only and on the basis of socialized ownership of production, in conformity with socialized production. Or another example

pointed to by Engels can be described as the negation of the negation: the negation of common ownership in primitive society by the
emergence of class society and in turn the negation of class society
by classless society, leading again to common ownership, but on
the basis of a tremendous accumulation of productive forces during the period of class societies between primitive communal and
communist society. Other examples may be found in nature and
society and in thought.

But again, can these be said to demonstrate that the negation of
the negation is a *law* of dialectics, applicable to all processes in
nature, society and thought? No. In a certain process or a certain
stage of a process, the resolution of a contradiction might be
described as the negation of the negation, but even here this is not
the law underlying and defining the process. The law operating is
the unity of opposites, leading ceaselessly to the emergence and
resolution of new contradictions. This is what Mao means when he
says the negation of the negation does not exist.

Take the example of life and death. All particular things come into existence and go out of existence, all living things become living
and later cease to live. But how is their going out of existence, or
ceasing to live, a negation of the original negation that brought
them into existence, or to life? The negation of the negation may
describe what happens to certain things through their life cycle, as
for example the barley grain Engels cites in *Anti-Duhring* (which
becomes a plant, which in turn gives birth to many grains). But
Engels acknowledges even in this case that the grain is transformed into a plant only under certain conditions, and that the first
negation must be constructed so that the second is possible. All
this is not a demonstration of the negation of the negation as a law
of dialectics but in fact of the unity of opposites, the basic law of
materialist dialectics.

Grain-plant-grain(s) is the unity of opposites of grain and plant.
Engels says that, of course, if you grind the grain down it won't
become a plant. But a ground-down grain also demonstrates the
law of contradiction: there is the unity and struggle of opposites,
the grain and the force grinding it down; and there is the resolution, the ground-down grain. Here there is no negation of negation,
but there is the law of contradiction.

Beyond what has been cited before, Mao objects to the negation
of the negation as a law of dialectics because it leads to, or is part
of, an incorrect view of synthesis. In this view, synthesis is not the
"eating up" of one aspect by another through struggle, leading to
a new contradiction in which even the principal aspect of the old

has been changed; instead synthesis becomes something which resurrects elements of the thing first negated (but on a different and qualitatively higher level) and tends to be viewed as an end product of development—or at most the starting point of the same process once again (though on a higher level). And if the negation of the negation is made a law of development, for example the development of society from primitive communalism to communism, then what would be focused on as the motive force in advancing to communism would not be the basic internal contradiction of capitalism (and socialism) between the proletariat and the bourgeoisie (nor the basic contradictions internal to previous systems), but the process: thesis—primitive communalism; antithesis—class society; synthesis—communism. Again, this is not a correct view of the process and motive force of development of society to communism, nor of synthesis.

Immediately after citing the development of society as an example of why the negation of the negation is not a law of dialectics, Mao returns to the question: "What is the method of synthesis?"[120] And he answers: "In a word, one devours another, one overthrows another, one class is eliminated, another class rises, one society is eliminated, another society rises."[121] This is the law of contradiction, the basic law of materialist dialectics, and this is the real nature and role of synthesis, in moving things constantly from one process to another, from the lower to the higher level in an endless spiral.

Finally on this matter of the negation of the negation, if this is made a law of dialectics, it will actually tend to promote metaphysics. Of course it should be clearly said that Engels promoted dialectics as opposed to metaphysics and certainly overall he promoted a dialectical, not a metaphysical, view of historical development; but Marxist dialectics have been further developed since Engels' time—especially by Mao. Specifically in regard to the development of society, the concept of negation of the negation will tend to present a "closed system" of development leading to communism and promote a static, "absolutist" view of communism itself as the end product of the negation of the negation and the kingdom of "great harmony." As opposed to this, Mao declares in his 1964 talk on philosophy: "Communism will last for thousands and thousands of years. I don't believe that there will be no qualitative changes under communism, that it will not be divided into stages by qualitative changes! I don't believe it! ... This is unthinkable in the light of dialectics."[122]

The importance of this, particularly at that time in China, was more directly in relation to socialism than communism; for some communists were making an absolute, static thing out of socialism, regarding it in effect as the end product of the development of society, the final negation of previous society. On this Mao comments: "Socialism, too, will be eliminated, it wouldn't do if it were not eliminated, for then there would be no communism."[123]

Cultural Revolution and the Continuing Struggle

The revisionists, too, wanted to eliminate socialism, but not through the advance to communism. They were actively promoting and working for capitalist restoration. And the specific revisionist clique grouped around Liu Shao-chi and other top leaders aligned with him had a powerful headquarters within the Communist Party and in the state apparatus. They controlled important parts of the superstructure and had dominance, or a very strong influence, over much of the economy. If this situation were allowed to continue much longer, these revisionists would succeed in usurping power in the country as a whole and pulling off a counter-revolutionary restoration. Something had to be done. Something was done.

That something was the Great Proletarian Cultural Revolution, which in 1966 burst into a tremendous uprising of the Chinese masses, under the leadership of Mao and the proletarian headquarters in the Party, against the capitalist-roaders, headed then by Liu Shao-chi and others closely allied with him. This mass upsurge of the Cultural Revolution and its necessity was a dramatic demonstration of the dialectical materialist principle that Mao had expounded in "On Contradiction" in combatting mechanical materialism: "When the superstructure (politics, culture, etc.) obstructs the development of the economic base, political and cultural changes become principal and decisive." If the bourgeoisie's (the capitalist-roaders') domination of large parts of the superstructure—including culture, education and much of the Party and state apparatus—were not smashed, then the socialist economic base could not be defended and developed; instead the capitalist-roaders would make a thorough change in the superstructure—replace proletarian dictatorship with bourgeois dictatorship—and then proceed to transform the economic base into a capitalist one, replace socialist production relations with capitalist ones throughout society, and restore capitalism in an all-round way. This, Mao had summed up, was exactly the process that occurred in the Soviet Union with the rise to power of

Khrushchev & Co. and the implementation of their revisionist line in society as a whole.

The Cultural Revolution also represented a revolutionary line on and application of the principle of synthesis as opposed to the reactionary philosophy of two into one. It was "taking class struggle as the key link" as opposed to "the dying out of class struggle." It represented the masses, led by the proletarian headquarters in the Party, synthesizing, "eating up," the bourgeois headquarters within the Party.

But this represented only one stage in the long process of transition between capitalism and communism and could not resolve the fundamental contradiction between the proletariat and the bourgeoisie. One bourgeois headquarters was smashed, synthesized, but others were bound to emerge as the core and commander of the bourgeoisie in society so long as the bourgeoisie existed—in other words, throughout the transition period. This is why Mao said that not only would class struggle continue but that every few years there would be a major struggle, a showdown to determine who held power. In addition Mao said that one Cultural Revolution could not solve the problem of preventing capitalist restoration.

This was, again, a thoroughgoing application of materialist dialectics. And it was fully verified in practice, as first Lin Piao and then others rose to challenge the proletariat in a political struggle for power, seeking to reverse the gains of the Cultural Revolution in particular and reverse the socialist revolution in general in order to restore capitalism. Here the profound importance of Mao's great theory and basic line of continuing the revolution under the dictatorship of the proletariat shines brilliantly.

Some might argue that if capitalist restoration occurs in China then this would show that Mao's theory of continuing the revolution under the dictatorship of the proletariat—as well as the Cultural Revolution which was the transformation of this theory into a tremendous material force on a mass scale—was basically flawed. This kind of thinking is nothing but empiricism and relativism. The correctness of this theory does not depend on the immediate results in any particular situation; it has been verified in practice, in the mass struggle of hundreds of millions of Chinese people, and will be further verified in the future in the revolutionary struggle not only in China but in every country. Here it is useful to recall Mao's statement that:

In social struggle, the forces representing the advanced class sometimes suffer defeat not because their ideas are incorrect but because, in the balance of forces engaged in struggle, they are not as powerful for the time being as the forces of reaction; they are therefore temporarily defeated, but they are bound to triumph sooner or later.[124]

This remains absolutely true.

Another absolute truth is that Mao led the Chinese masses in continuing revolutionary struggle under the dictatorship of the proletariat, and continuing the Cultural Revolution through various forms of struggle, down to his last breath. And a crucial part of this was, once again, the struggle in the philosophical realm, particularly between dialectical materialism and metaphysics and mechanical materialism.

For example, one of the main questions focused on in the campaign to Criticize Lin Piao and Confucius during the last years of Mao's life was the exposure of and struggle against the "doctrine of the mean" peddled by Confucius and his followers in China down through the ages. This doctrine was in essence the same as the reactionary theory of "combining two into one." It opposed "going to extremes" and called for reconciling opposites rather than resolving the contradiction between them through struggle. The ideological defeat of this doctrine was obviously crucial to upholding class struggle as the key link and opposing "the dying out of class struggle" at home and reconciliation with and capitulation to the international class enemies.

Ceaseless Struggle

In general throughout this period of his last years Mao repeatedly stressed the need for struggle. He called attention to the fact that "without struggle, there is no progress" and sharply posed the question to which his answer was obvious: "Can 800 million people manage without struggle?" Blasting at those who denied the importance and necessity of the Cultural Revolution and exposing the real aims of those who preached "the dying out of class struggle" in opposition to continuing the revolution, Mao declared:

What is the Great Cultural Revolution for? To wage class struggle. Liu Shao-chi advocated the theory of the dying out of class struggle, but he himself never ceased to wage class struggle. He wanted to protect his bunch of renegades and sworn followers. Lin Piao wanted to overthrow the proletariat and attempted a coup. Did the class struggle die out?[125]

Giving this profound truth—the need to continue the revolution—an "extreme" expression, exactly in order to emphasize its great and long-term importance, Mao said:

Will there be need for revolution a hundred years from now? Will there still be need for revolution a thousand years from now? There is always need for revolution. There are always sections of the people who feel themselves oppressed; junior officials, students, workers, peasants and soldiers don't like bigshots oppressing them. That's why they want revolution. Will contradictions no longer be seen ten thousand years from now? Why not? They will still be seen.[126]

Here again Mao was calling attention to the fact that even under communism there will still be contradiction, struggle to resolve contradiction and qualitative change (leaps)—and in this sense revolution. As he had said in 1971:

We have been singing *The Internationale* for fifty years, yet on ten occasions certain people inside our Party tried to split it. As I see it, this may happen another ten, twenty or thirty times. You don't believe it? You may not believe it. Anyhow I do. Will there be no struggle when we get to communism? I just don't believe it. There will be struggles even then, but only between the new and the old, between what is correct and what is incorrect. Tens of thousands of years from now, what is wrong still won't get by, it won't stand up.[127]

Why was Mao giving such great emphasis then to the fact that even thousands of years from now there will still be contradiction and struggle? It was to strike at the line right then that contradiction, class struggle, revolution could and should come to an end. To the revisionists, the top Party persons in power taking the capitalist road in particular, the revolution had gone far enough; it had made them "bigshots" and nothing could be more important than this; development need not and must not proceed any farther.

This is closely linked with the question that Mao focused attention on two years before he died:

Why did Lenin speak of exercising dictatorship over the bourgeoisie? It is essential to get this question clear. Lack of clarity on this question will lead to revisionism. This should be made known to the whole nation.[128]

The essence of what Mao was getting at here is that the purpose of the dictatorship of the proletariat is to achieve the transition to communism. It is the form through which the proletariat rules *and* wages class struggle against the bourgeoisie in the socialist transition period in order to advance to communism. Without continuing the revolution, continuing to wage the class struggle against the

1975—Teachers and students of the international politics department of Futan University study the current economic crisis in the capitalist world together with worker-theoreticians at a Shanghai bakery. Groups like these were created and spread on a wide scale during the Cultural Revolution.

bourgeoisie under the dictatorship of the proletariat, the proletariat cannot continue to rule and cannot continue the advance to communism.

In opposition to this, if the dictatorship of the proletariat is viewed as an end in itself whose purpose is merely to ensure order and the development of production, then it will turn into its opposite, it will be transformed into a dictatorship of the (new) bourgeoisie. This is because of the transitional and contradictory nature of socialism and the persistence of remnants of exploiting class society throughout the socialist transition period, which continually give rise to the bourgeoisie and to a bourgeois headquarters in the Party as the concentration of this.

This is closely bound up with a correct understanding of what Marx wrote to J. Weydemeyer in 1852, in a famous statement where Marx gives a concise summation of the question of the dictatorship of the proletariat:

And now as to myself, no credit is due to me for discovering the existence of classes in modern society or the struggle between them. Long before me bourgeois historians had described the historical development of this class struggle and bourgeois economists the economic anatomy of the classes. What I did that was new was to prove: 1) that the *existence of classes* is only bound up with *particular historical phases in the development of production,* 2) that the class struggle necessarily leads to the *dictatorship of the proletariat,* 3) that this dictatorship itself only constitutes the transition to the *abolition of all classes* and to a *classless society.*[129]

All three points Marx makes here are of great importance; but, after the dictatorship of the proletariat has been established and in the conditions where the necessity for maintaining it are generally acknowledged (in words even by the revisionists), the last point above takes on special importance and will become the focus of sharp struggle. The revisionists will try to deny this last point, or the substance and meaning of it, especially as this has been developed by Mao—namely, the need to continue the revolution to carry through the transition to communism.

The revisionists, of course, will talk about communism and the need to achieve it, but they will treat this metaphysically and according to mechanical materialism—that is, as a question of simply developing the productive forces. They will not deal with socialism itself as a contradiction which, as such, can be moved one way or the other in the short run—though its final resolution can only be in the advance to communism. They will not recognize that socialism represents a struggle between the new, rising aspects of communism within it and the old, declining aspects of capitalism retained in the socialist period. In short, they will wall off socialism from communism: "Communism, that's for later and the way to get there is to maintain strict order and do everything to boost production so that someday the economy is developed enough and we can then talk of introducing communism." Such is the revisionist view, and in particular its "theory of productive forces" and "dying out of class struggle," its metaphysics and mechanical materialism, in the form which all this takes where the dictatorship of the proletariat has been established and its necessity has become part of popular consciousness.

Socialism as an Absolute Means Capitalist Restoration

In the first part of this article it was shown how Engels analyzed the ways in which Hegel's dialectics turned into metaphysics. Hegel's philosophical *system*, in contradiction to his dialectical method, pronounced the end of the dialectic in the realization of the Absolute Idea in Hegel's philosophical system itself. Politically, this was expressed in the idea that the constitutional monarchy promised by Frederick William III of Prussia was the highest and final form of society. Observing a similar phenomenon, Mao had summed up that there was the recurring tendency for communists to turn Marxism and the socialist system into absolutes and that this leads to revisionism. As Mao said as early as 1957:

If it is asserted that the socialist system and its relations of production and superstructure will not die out, what kind of Marxism would that be. Wouldn't it be the same as a religious creed or theology that preaches an everlasting God?[130]

This was a theme Mao would hammer at again and again throughout the rest of his life. As he insisted in his "Reading Notes" on the Soviet political economy text, in criticizing the notion of "completely consolidating" socialism:

This socialist economy has had its own birth and development. Who would believe that this process of change has come to an end, and that we will say, "These two forms of ownership [state and collective] will continue to be fully consolidated for all time?" Who would believe that such formulas of a socialist society as "distribution according to labor," "commodity production," and "the law of value" are going to live forever? Who would believe that there is only birth and development but no dying away and transformation and that these formulas unlike all others are ahistorical?

Socialism must make the transition to communism. At that time there will be things of the socialist stage that will have to die out.[131]

It was precisely the revisionists who made an absolute out of these socialist categories and of socialism itself. They opposed the dialectical materialist understanding that for these things to die out there must be struggle and that the capitalist elements within these things must be restricted at every point to the degree possible in accordance with the material and ideological conditions. They cannot be expanded and built up and then one day, out of nowhere, suddenly die out. To think this is in essence the same as the Deborin school of philosophy summarized earlier—that contradiction appears only at a certain stage and that struggle is not necessary to deal with differences.

These questions became the focus of intense struggle in the last years of Mao's life, when he called for restricting such things as distribution according to work, the difference between mental and manual labor, the sphere of operation of the law of value, and so on—things generally described by the term "bourgeois right." The revisionists wanted instead to expand these things and actively resisted the attempts to restrict them. Such people, Mao said, were not genuine communists but capitalist-roaders.

As pointed out earlier, the tendency to view socialism as a static absolute can be found in Stalin and goes hand in hand with tendencies to metaphysics in his treatment of Marxist philosophy. But this tendency becomes a principle and fundamental characteristic with the revisionists in China and the Soviet Union itself (and other countries). Such people, therefore, regardless of good or bad intentions and regardless of pretensions of upholding socialism and even the eventual realization of communism, represent not the proletariat but the bourgeoisie in socialist society and stand not for the actual development of socialism as a transition to communism but for the restoration of capitalism. Such people become the bourgeoisie in the Party, the core and commanders of the reactionary forces in socialist society.

This process itself, of course, follows the laws of dialectics. There is a contradiction within all communists between proletarian and bourgeois ideology, and under certain conditions these aspects, too, can be transformed into their opposites. Communists can be turned into their opposite. People who are revolutionaries at a certain stage and under certain conditions can turn into counter-revolutionaries at another stage and under different conditions.

In the history of the Chinese revolution a particularly significant form of this was the phenomenon of people who were revolutionaries during the new-democratic stage but turned into counter-revolutionaries in the socialist stage, especially the deeper the socialist revolution went. When the program of the revolution was new democracy (that is, bourgeois-democratic revolution of a new type), there was an inevitable tendency to identify this with the ideology of the Communist Party—though this was fought by Mao and others. But as the revolution advanced to and in the socialist stage, the need to make a radical rupture with bourgeois ideology became all the more pronounced. Most members of the Communist Party did so, of course, but some did not. They went from being participants in, even leaders of, the revolution to becoming the targets of it; they were transformed from bourgeois-democrats into capitalist-roaders. And, especially for those in leading positions, this ideological contradiction was inter-related with the fact that they held positions of great authority in society after political power was seized.

In the midst of the continuing struggle, in the last year of his life, Mao called attention to this phenomenon and summarized it this way:

After the democratic revolution the workers and the poor and lower-middle peasants did not stand still, they want revolution. On the other hand, a number of Party members do not want to go forward; some have moved backward and opposed the revolution. Why? Because they have become high officials and want to protect the interests of high officials.[132]

Mao's point here is not that high officials will inevitably become revisionists—though some will do so at each stage in the revolution—but that if they do not continue to make revolution against the bourgeoisie, if they do not continue to take part in the struggle to advance to communism, they will become bourgeois themselves, in their thinking and being, and attempt to restore capitalism. As explained in the preceding chapter, there is a material and ideological basis for this throughout the entire period of socialism.

The transformation of bourgeois-democrats into capitalist-roaders, while of particular importance in the Chinese revolution, is obviously only one form of the phenomenon of revolutionaries being transformed into counter-revolutionaries and Communist Party members, especially top leaders, being transformed into capitalist-roaders. More generally, the principle that seizing and exercising political power must not be viewed as an end in itself and that it is necessary to continue making the revolution has as its opposite the fact that people who adopt the outlook that socialism is an absolute and an end in itself will take up the stand that the purpose of socialism is to enable them to "have the good life," or at least to "settle down" and "rest on their laurels." They will become conservative, will fear and even oppose the advance of the revolution. For top leaders in the Communist Party, this means that they will become part of the bourgeoisie in the Party, attempting to exercise their leadership position not to guide the masses in the struggle for communism, but to enforce the exploitation of the masses and bring about the restoration of capitalism with themselves as the ruling bourgeoisie.

Mao devoted great attention to this problem and this danger, especially in the last few years of his life. His analysis of it was thoroughly based on materialist dialectics. But some people have argued that if you say, as Mao did, that "the bourgeoisie is right in the Communist Party," then the masses will not follow the Party, because it will be the same as saying that the Party is not the vanguard of the proletariat but a bourgeois party. This, again, is metaphysics.

As Mao explained in "On Contradiction," the nature of a thing, of a contradiction, is determined by the principal aspect. The presence of the bourgeoisie—not the whole but the heart of it—within the Communist Party in socialist society does not in itself change the nature of the Party from proletarian to bourgeois nor of the society from socialist to capitalist. It is only if and when the bourgeoisie in the Party rises to the dominant position and a revisionist line is in command overall that the Party will be transformed from proletarian to bourgeois; and, if this is not reversed, it will lead to the transformation of the society from socialist to capitalist.

Mao's line here is, again, the dialectical materialist one. If there is no bourgeoisie in the Party even when the principal aspect—and therefore the nature—of the Party is proletarian, then how can the Party be transformed from proletarian to bourgeois? It is due to the identity as well as the struggle of opposites that in certain conditions they can be transformed into each other. The contradiction between representatives of the proletariat and of the bourgeoisie exists all along within the Communist Party, even when the proletariat and its Party are not in power. But with the seizure of power and the socialization of ownership, the nature of this contradiction changes accordingly; the basis develops for leaders in the Party to turn the contradiction between the leaders and the led into that between the exploiters and the exploited, and the bourgeois elements within the Party can become actual exploiters even when they do not have control of the Party and power in society as a whole. To deny all this and to act as if the bourgeoisie suddenly appears in the Party only if and at the time it usurps supreme power, is this not the same as the reactionary Deborin school, is it not metaphysics and idealism in opposition to the dialectical materialist line of Mao?

Because the bourgeoisie is constantly regenerated under socialism, and because bourgeois exploiting elements constantly emerge within the Party as the core of the bourgeoisie and commanders of the reactionary social forces in socialist society, Mao summed up, the class struggle against the bourgeoisie is the key link and must be carried out throughout the entire period of socialism, with its main target those in authority taking the capitalist road, the bourgeoisie in the Party. And because every few years a bourgeois headquarters will make an all-out attempt at usurping power, there must be a major struggle every few years. As Mao said in 1966, at the start of the Cultural Revolution:

> Great disorder across the land leads to great order. And so once again every seven or eight years. Monsters and demons will jump out themselves. Determined by their own class nature, they are bound to jump out.[133]

Contradiction, Struggle, Revolution

Here what is reflected again and what is of the most profound importance is not simply the analysis that there will be recurrent major struggles every few years, but the dialectical materialist stand, viewpoint and method that permeate this statement. Order, even "great order," cannot be absolute; it can only be temporary, conditional and relative. Contradiction, struggle, revolution—this is universal, unconditional and absolute.

Far from being idealist, Mao's dialectical view is thoroughly materialist. And as he himself said, "thoroughgoing materialists are fearless." Communism is inevitable, Mao affirmed. But to advance to communism—and to continue advancing even then—struggle is always necessary. The ceaseless emergence and resolution of contradictions through struggle, this is the order, the process and the ever upward motion of all things. In the course of any process, including certainly one so earth-shaking as the advance to communism, there can be reversals and setbacks, but these, too, can only be temporary. The new will supersede the old, the progressive the reactionary, this is an irresistible law.

As Mao put it, applying this law to class struggle, on the eve of the complete victory of the new-democratic revolution and the liberation of China:

> How different is the logic of the imperialists from that of the people! Make trouble, fail, make trouble again, fail again . . . till their doom; that is the logic of the imperialists and all reactionaries the world over in dealing with the people's cause, and they will never go against this logic. This is a Marxist law. When we say "imperialism is ferocious", we mean that its nature will never change, that the imperialists will never lay down their butcher knives, that they will never become Buddhas, till their doom.
>
> Fight, fail, fight again, fail again, fight again . . . till their victory; that is the logic of the people, and they too will never go against this logic. This is another Marxist law. The Russian people's revolution followed this law, and so has the Chinese people's revolution.
>
> Classes struggle, some classes triumph, others are eliminated. Such is history, such is the history of civilization for thousands of years. To interpret history from this viewpoint is historical materialism; standing in opposition to this viewpoint is historical idealism.[134]

Such is the truly immortal contribution of Mao Tsetung to Marxist philosophy and in general, to the revolutionary struggle on this front and overall, to the liberating science and historic mission of the proletariat.

Chapter 5

CULTURE AND THE SUPERSTRUCTURE

Introduction

In 1967, at the height of the mass upsurge of the Great Proletarian Cultural Revolution in China, the following statement by Mao Tsetung was put forward as one of the decisive guiding lines for this unprecedented struggle: "The proletariat must exercise allround dictatorship over the bourgeoisie in the realm of the superstructure, including the various spheres of culture."[1] Here Mao was not only stressing the great importance of the superstructure in general, but of culture in particular. And he was emphasizing not only the need for the proletariat to exercise dictatorship over the bourgeoisie in general but specifically to sweep the bourgeoisie off the cultural stage and defeat its attempts to dominate this sphere, which plays such a major role in the ideological field, in shaping public opinion and influencing the economic base, the fundamental structure of society.

From the very beginning, during the new-democratic as well as the socialist stage of the revolution in China, Mao attached great importance to the role of culture, and he continued to develop and deepen a revolutionary line to guide the struggle in this sphere. Indeed the further development of Marxist theory on and a basic line for culture constitutes yet another of Mao Tsetung's immortal contributions. Specifically, Mao gave great emphasis to the area of literature and art, to their role in the overall class struggle. And, under the guidance of his line, the Chinese people made a qualitative leap in this critical area, beyond anything previously achieved by mankind, including in the socialist countries.

This chapter will focus on this question of culture and specifically on Mao's leadership in developing a revolutionary literature and art serving the struggle of the proletariat to achieve its historic mission of communism.

Of course, in this area as in others, in making his great and immortal contributions, Mao was standing on the shoulders of the great Marxists who preceded him, and especially of Marx, Engels, Lenin and Stalin. It is thus correct to place Mao's contributions against the background of the development of the Marxist theory of art previous to him.

Marx and Engels

The starting point for Marxism is that man's conscious activities, of which literature and art are a part, do not stand by themselves or on their own, and of course do not create reality, but rather, as Marx put it in a famous sentence: "It is not the consciousness of men that determines their being, but on the contrary it is their social being that determines their consciousness."[2]

In other words, the starting point is the material world and the economic activity of people. Material conditions determine the activities, development and products of the human mind, and not the other way around. And as Marx explained further in this same "Preface":

In the social production of their existence, men enter into definite, necessary relations, which are independent of their will, namely, relations of production corresponding to a determinate stage of development of their material forces of production. The totality of these relations of production constitutes the economic structure of society, the real foundation on which there arises a legal and political superstructure and to which there correspond definite forms of social consciousness. The mode of production of material life conditions the social, political and intellectual life-process in general.[3]

In other words, society arises out of the basic need of people to eat, to be clothed, have shelter and so on, and in order to carry this out people have to come together in some particular form so that they can collectively transform nature, to make the various things they need to live. Thus the nature of society is rooted in the material requirements that people have. But society and nature are in a constant process of change—and not a cyclical change, coming out the same way it began, but a process of spiral-like change progressing from the lower to the higher level and marked by leaps.

Thus today we have things undreamed of even 100 years ago, let alone a million years ago or more when the earliest forms of human life were forming the most primitive kind of society. This is one of the basic indications of how society is not only rooted in the organized struggle of people coming together to battle and transform nature, but is developing from a lower to a higher level. And besides this, Marx's great discovery ("the guiding principle of my studies," as he referred to it) was that this development of human society is ultimately determined by the development of the basic forces which human beings have built up in their interaction with nature to produce what they need and want—in other words by the *productive forces* of society. This includes the tools and instruments which people develop, and it also includes, most importantly, the people themselves, with all their skills and abilities, who actually do the producing.

In order to use these productive forces, people have to enter into certain relations with regard to the overall process of production in society. And the nature of these relations will differ and change in accordance with the development of the productive forces of mankind. Thus these relations were termed by Marx the *relations of production* of a society.

As Marx goes on to say in the quotation above, these production relations constitute the economic structure of society. They are also often called the *economic base*. And this base is the "real foundation," as Marx says, of the whole legal, political, ideological and cultural *superstructure* of society. The political institutions, legal structures, habits, customs, artistic conventions, philosophies, ways of thinking and looking at the world, etc., of a given society and epoch all belong to the superstructure. This is true of the philosophy, culture, etc., representing the oppressed class(es) as well as that of the dominant class. But, of course, as Marx and Engels stressed, "The ruling ideas of each age have ever been the ideas of its ruling class."[4] In short, in order to establish its domination in the spheres of ideology, culture, etc., a particular class must first seize political power, establish itself as the dominant class in this most decisive part of the superstructure.

But, again, not just any kind of political power and ruling ideology can be established in any given historical conditions. These things, belonging to the superstructure, will be ultimately determined by the nature of the economic base, which in turn will, in the final analysis, be determined by the level of development of the productive forces.

In other words, as Marx summed it up in a letter early in his development as a Marxist:

Assume a particular level of development of men's productive forces and you will get a particular form of commerce and consumption. Assume particular stages of development in production, commerce and consumption and you will have a corresponding social system, a corresponding organisation of the family, of social estates or of classes, in a word, a corresponding civil society. Assume such a civil society and you will get a political system appropriate to it, a system which is only the official expression of civil society.[5]

And, as Marxism also teaches us, assume a certain social system, civil society, political system, etc., and you will get a certain sort of ideology and intellectual life, including a certain sort of culture, with literature and art a very important part of this. The intellectual life includes, as noted earlier, the ideas representing the oppressed as well as the ruling class—to cite one outstanding example, Marxism itself is a product of *capitalist* society. But, as also emphasized just above, only when an oppressed class rises to the position of the ruling class—only when it overthrows the existing political power and establishes its own state power—can its ideas become the dominant ones in society.

This method of studying and understanding society and history, whose basic principles Marx first laid out, is known as *historical materialism*. Engels summed it up as:

. . . that view of the course of history which seeks the ultimate cause and the great moving power of all important historic events in the economic development of society, in the changes in the modes of production and exchange, in the consequent division of society into distinct classes, and in the struggles of these classes against one another.[6]

This view and method of historical materialism is the basic framework for the correct understanding of the meaning and role of literature and art. Literature and art and culture generally are part of the superstructure. But it should be recalled and re-emphasized that the relationship between the base and superstructure is not rigid, static or one-way. While Marxism is materialist, it is also dialectical. The superstructure is not a passive effect of the base; there is a constant interaction between them. Engels forcefully spoke to this point in combatting mechanical, as opposed to dialectical, materialism:

According to the materialist conception of history, the *ultimately* determining factor in history is the production and reproduction of real life. Neither Marx nor I have ever asserted more than this. Hence if somebody twists this into saying that the economic factor is the *only* determining one, he transforms that proposition into a meaningless, abstract, absurd phrase. The economic situation is the basis, but the various elements of the superstructure—political forms of the class struggle and its results, such as constitutions established by the victorious class after a successful battle, etc., juridical forms, and especially the reflections of all these real struggles in the brains of the participants, political, legal, philosophical theories, religious views and their further development into systems of dogmas—also exercise their influence upon the course of the historical struggles and in many cases determine their *form* in particular. There is an interaction of all these elements in which, amid all the endless host of accidents (that is, of things and events whose inner interconnection is so remote or so impossible of proof that we can regard it as non-existent and neglect it), the economic movement is finally bound to assert itself.[7]

And although the base is overall principal and is the determining thing, it is also true, as Mao points out, that:

When the superstructure (politics, culture, etc.) obstructs the development of the economic base, political and cultural changes become principal and decisive.[8]

In other words, the relationship between base and superstructure must be seen dialectically, not mechanically or metaphysically. This is a point which Mao gave great emphasis to, and further developed, specifically in relation to socialist society. It assumes great significance in looking at Mao's contribution to the theory and basic line for revolutionary culture.

Returning to the founders of scientific socialism, it is important here to note that Marx applied the stand, viewpoint and method of dialectical and historical materialism chiefly to the political economy of capitalism and secondarily to analyzing the class struggle in the political sphere as it was developing, especially in Europe, when he was alive. After his early collaborative efforts with Engels (in *The Holy Family* and *The German Ideology*[9]) Marx did not go on and develop any systematic and all-around theory on the ideological (including cultural) aspects of the class struggle in general, nor of literature and art in particular.

Engels, on the other hand, did devote some systematic work to such forms—notably in parts of *Anti-Duhring* and in his *Ludwig Feuerbach and the End of Classical German Philosophy,* as well as in some other scattered essays (the Introduction to the English edition of *Socialism: Utopian and Scientific* being a good example). But at the same time, Engels, too, did not devote any systematic attention to art. The most that we have from both Marx and Engels on this topic are more or less off-hand comments about past or then-present writers and works.

However, there is the following brief but profound aside by

Marx in one of his works:

> The social revolution of the nineteenth century [Marx means the pro-
> letarian revolution] cannot draw its poetry from the past, but only from
> the future...Earlier revolutions required recollections of past world
> history in order to drug themselves concerning their own content. In order
> to arrive at its own content, the revolution of the nineteenth century must
> let the dead bury their dead.[10]

This statement, with its emphasis on the great difference between
the proletarian socialist revolution and all past revolutions and the
way in which this carries over into the area of proletarian art and
culture, is a theme which is prominent in Mao's contributions on
this subject, and one which will be returned to below.

Lenin

Lenin also cannot be said to have developed a complete and all-
round theory of art and culture. But Lenin *was*, of course, in-
timately involved with a successful proletarian revolution and
therefore with the setting up of a socialist society. And Lenin did
lay out certain basic principles which played a key part in laying
the groundwork for the development of a revolutionary literature
and art serving the struggle of the proletariat.

What Lenin particularly stressed in this regard was the necessity for proletarian culture to be closely integrated with the overall
revolutionary movement of the proletariat. In the upsurge of the
1905 revolution in Russia, for instance, Lenin spoke of the need for
the development of "party literature," and asked:

> What is this principle of party literature? It is not simply that, for the
> socialist proletariat, literature cannot be a means of enriching individuals
> or groups: it cannot, in fact, be an individual undertaking, independent of
> the common cause of the proletariat. Down with non-partisan writers!
> Down with literary supermen! Literature must become *part* of the com-
> mon cause of the proletariat, "a cog and a screw" of one single great
> Social-Democratic [communist] mechanism set in motion by the entire
> politically-conscious vanguard of the entire working class. Literature
> must become a component of organised, planned and integrated Social-
> Democratic Party work.[11]

The same theme was emphasized by Lenin after the establishment of the Soviet Republic, when (in 1920) he drafted a resolution
on proletarian culture, the first article of which read:

All educational work in the Soviet Republic of workers and peasants, in the field of political education in general and in the field of art in particular, should be imbued with the spirit of the class struggle being waged by the proletariat for the successful achievement of the aims of its dictatorship, i.e., the overthrow of the bourgeoisie, the abolition of classes, and the elimination of all forms of exploitation of man by man.[12]

There were, of course, then as now, those who were outraged by and attacked such statements as being incompatible with the "individuality" and "freedom" which is supposed to be necessary for artistic creation. Lenin characterized such a view as bourgeois individualism, and pointed out that such talk about absolute freedom from the mouths of artists in bourgeois society was sheer hypocrisy or self-delusion. He explained:

There can be no real and effective "freedom" in a society based on the power of money, in a society in which the masses of working people live in poverty and the handful of rich live like parasites. Are you free in relation to your bourgeois publisher, Mr. Writer, in relation to your bourgeois public, which demands that you provide it with pornography in novels and paintings, and prostitution as a "supplement" to "sacred" scenic art? This absolute freedom is a bourgeois or an anarchist phrase (since, as a world outlook, anarchism is bourgeois philosophy turned inside out). One cannot live in society and be free from society. The freedom of the bourgeois writer, artist or actress is simply masked (or hypocritically masked) dependence on the money-bag, on corruption, on prostitution.[13]

In a class society, it is impossible for literature and art to rise above classes, impossible for them not to both express some class viewpoint and serve the interests of some class. On the other hand, Lenin pointed out, these classes are not on a par with each other, and the aim of communists is:

. . . to contrast this hypocritically free literature, which is in reality linked to the bourgeoisie, with a really free one that will be *openly* linked to the proletariat.
It will be a free literature, because the idea of socialism and sympathy with the working people, and not greed or careerism, will bring ever new forces to its ranks. It will be a free literature, because it will serve, not some satiated heroine, not the bored "upper ten thousand" suffering from fatty degeneration, but the millions and tens of millions of working people—the flower of the country, its strength and its future.[14]

Stalin

Stalin was the continuator of Lenin's work in leading the Soviet proletariat in the building of socialism and protecting it against

external and internal enemies. He also upheld and applied many of
Lenin's developments of Marxism, including in the theory of art
and literature.

It was under Stalin's leadership that the Soviet Party developed
the concept of *socialist realism,* a concept which conforms to the
viewpoint of the proletariat in literature and art, and which laid an
important part of the foundation for Mao's contributions in this
area.

In 1932, by a decision of the Central Committee of the Communist Party of the Soviet Union, an organizing committee for the
first National Congress of Soviet Writers was set up, which first
formulated the concept of socialist realism. It was defined in the
charter of the Association of Soviet Writers: "Socialist realism,
which is the fundamental method of Soviet literature and letters,
requires the artist to present reality in its revolutionry course of
development, in a true and historically concrete manner."

Note that this definition stresses truth and historical con-
creteness, and links this with "present[ing] reality in its revolutionary course of development" as the main aspect. In other
words, proletarian art is partisan, is part of the revolutionary
struggle of the working class, and is also truthful. In fact, as gone
into in more depth later in dealing specifically with Mao's contributions, such literature and art is truthful precisely *because* it
reflects and serves the outlook and interests of the working class.
It is truthful because it brings out the real underlying course of
development of history and society, which *is* revolutionary.

As the name "socialist realism" implies, there have been other
forms of realism in art—notably bourgeois realism. This had a progressive role to play at one time, just as did the bourgeoisie itself,
when it was still a rising class. But, of course, even at that time its
disclosure of reality was hemmed in by the same limitations as is
the world-view of the capitalists. The most it could ever disclose is
a world of self-seeking individuals, which is by no means the whole
or even the greater part nor certainly the essence of reality. And,
as the bourgeoisie has become a totally reactionary class, its
"realism" has turned into its opposite, into an attempt to portray
people in the most sordid, animalistic and cynical manner, or into
pure fantasy and escapism.

At the same time that socialist realism was brought forward as
the guiding policy of literary and artistic work in the Soviet Union,
it was also emphasized that this was not inconsistent with romanticism, but that it included romanticism of a new type—*revolutionary romanticism*—since to portray reality in its revolutionary

course of development is inevitably to portray the tremendous heroism of the people and the vastest horizons of human progress.

While the emergence of this concept and ideal of socialist realism (including revolutionary romanticism as an aspect of it) was a real advance for the development of proletarian art, there were also certain defects in Stalin's viewpoint in this area. One of these is his idea that the chief thing in the cultural field was to raise the cultural standards of the masses of Soviet workers and peasants— and, moreover, to view this "raising of standards" in purely *technical* and quantitative terms.[15] (This question is specifically dealt with by Mao in his treatment of the contradiction between popularization and raising standards, which will be focused on shortly.) And socialist realism as conceived and applied in the Soviet Union did include weaknesses linked to these errors of Stalin's.

Another and related error of Stalin's in this area is spoken to in the summary of a forum on work in literature and the arts which was convened in Shanghai in early 1966 by Mao's wife, Chiang Ching, to formulate a policy for upholding and more thoroughly applying Mao's line in the arts:

Stalin was a great Marxist-Leninist. His criticism of the modernist literature and art of the bourgeoisie was very sharp. But he uncritically took over what are known as the classics of Russia and Europe and the consequences were bad. The classical literature and art of China and of Europe (including Russia) and even American films have exercised a considerable influence on our literary and art circles, and some people have regarded them as holy writ and accepted them in their entirety. We should draw a lesson from Stalin's experience. Old and foreign works should be studied too, and refusal to study them would be wrong; but we must study them critically, making the past serve the present and foreign works serve China.[16]

Mao on the Importance of the Superstructure

Mao Tsetung made decisive advances in the development of Marxist-Leninist theory in the sphere of literature and art and culture generally. This is closely connected with the overall advance he led in making in the correct understanding of the role of the superstructure, particularly under socialism.

This advance was associated, in turn, with a summation of the theory and practice of Marxist-Leninists, and specifically of certain errors of Stalin, in this area. Thus Mao, for instance, begins his late 1950s "Critique of Stalin's *Economic Problems of Socialism in the USSR*" with the statement, "Stalin's book from first to last says nothing about the superstructure. It is not concerned with people; it considers things, not people."[17]

As pointed out in chapter 3 (on Mao's contributions to political economy, etc.), this work of Stalin's, written in the last few years of his life, did contain some valuable insights into and analysis of important aspects of the advance from socialism to communism, the final goal of proletarian revolution. But, as is pointed out there, Stalin tended to treat these problems ". . . from the standpoint of developing production and raising the material and technical level of the masses and not very much from the standpoint of politics and ideology." (See pp. 91ff.)

Many of Mao's greatest contributions, of course, centered precisely in developing the understanding of the nature of socialist society and in his consequent emphasis on the need to continue the revolution under the dictatorship of the proletariat, even after the socialist transformation of ownership had in the main been completed. This was closely linked with Mao's further development of Marxist theory concerning the interaction of the base and superstructure, especially under socialism.

Mao showed the decisive importance of continuously revolutionizing the superstructure as well as the economic base. He not only upheld the dialectical understanding of the relationship between the base and superstructure—which indicates that overall the base is principal and decisive, but that at certain times the superstructure becomes principal and decisive in determining the nature and development of the economic base. He further summed up and taught that under socialism the role of the superstructure assumes even greater importance and the struggle in the superstructure becomes even more acute and complex. Even while the proletariat holds political power overall in society, the bourgeoisie may actually control certain parts of the superstructure (just as it may control certain units and departments of the economy). Ideology in particular, Mao warned, will be an arena of long and tortuous struggle between the proletariat and the bourgeoisie. As early as 1957, as a crucial part of the revolutionary line he developed in opposition to the revisionists, who preached that "the class struggle is dying out," Mao emphatically stated:

In the ideological field, the question of who will win out, the proletariat or the bourgeoisie, has not yet been really settled. We still have to wage a protracted struggle against bourgeois and petty-bourgeois ideology.[18]

And culture, of course, including art and literature, falls squarely within the ideological field.

As noted, the nature of the relationship between the base and superstructure is a contradiction in which the base is the overall principal aspect, but in which the superstructure may become, under certain conditions, the principal aspect. But, in addition, the superstructure plays the *initiating* role in transforming the base. It is for both these reasons that the superstructure is of crucial importance in any revolution.

But, as also noted, all this applies with even greater force to the *proletarian* revolution and socialist society. For this revolution, unlike any previous revolution in human history, does not aim at bringing a new class of exploiters to power. Rather the goal of the working class is to do away with all exploitation and oppression. Its goal is the abolition of all classes—that is, communism. Thus socialism, in which classes still exist and in which the working class rules society, is *not* the final goal of proletarian revolution, but is a transition stage to that goal.

Because of this transitional nature of socialism, it must be constantly moving forward toward communism. If it does not, then it will inevitably move backward—to capitalism. This can happen most of all because under socialism a *new bourgeoisie* is inevitably generated, and has its core within the communist party itself, especially revisionists in top party leadership, who can seize power from the proletariat and restore capitalism. This is what has happened in the Soviet Union and, following Mao's death, a revisionist coup was carried off in China and the process of capitalist restoration is now being carried out in that country too.

The counter-revolution by a new bourgeoisie begins in the superstructure—here the superstructure plays the decisive as well as the initiating role. And, in preparing the conditions for such a coup, these new capitalist leeches will pay great attention to struggle in the ideological realm, including literature and art. As Mao sharply pointed out in 1962:

Writing novels is popular these days, isn't it? The use of novels for anti-Party activity is a great invention. Anyone wanting to overthrow a political regime must create public opinion and do some preparatory ideological work. This applies to counter-revolutionary as well as to revolutionary classes.[19]

To the degree that the bourgeoisie—in particular top Party persons taking the capitalist road—is not fought in this arena, it will gain in strength and will be in that much better a position to seize political power. Thus the great importance under socialism of class

struggle in the superstructure and of Mao's statement, quoted at
the start of this chapter, that "The proletariat must exercise all-
round dictatorship over the bourgeoisie in the realm of the
superstructure, including the various spheres of culture."

Mao's Line on Literature and Art

In this connection, the quotation earlier from Marx (from the
Eighteenth Brumaire) is worth recalling. There Marx was emphasizing how past revolutions could borrow their poetry from the
past—could cloak themselves in the past precisely in order to hide
from themselves the full meaning of their own revolutionary
nature. This is because they all represented the seizure of power by
a new exploiting class. Although they were, in their period of rise,
instruments of progress for mankind, previous classes, even while
carrying out a revolution and rising to power, could not really be
fully aware of this progressive and revolutionary role they were
playing—because to be fully aware of it would have meant seeing
their own historically transitory nature, their own eventual doom
and extinction.

The proletariat, on the contrary, *must* be aware and conscious of
just what it is doing and of the fact that its own rule is, from an
historical standpoint, only transitory. In fact, the proletariat is the
first and only class in history which aims for the eventual elimination of its state power and all the conditions, material and
ideological, that make that rule necessary. And indeed, if this is
lost sight of, its rule will be overthrown and capitalism restored.
That is why the proletarian revolution cannot draw its poetry, and
its culture generally, from the past—but must constantly strive, in
full consciousness of what it is doing and of its great historic mission, to create something different than mankind has ever known.

Although Mao's main contribution in this area was in connection with the development of proletarian culture and its use in consolidating the dictatorship of the proletariat and carrying forward
the revolution under this dictatorship, he laid out the basic orientation for this even before nationwide political power had been
established and the socialist stage of the revolution had been
entered. He was able to do this, in part, because (as seen in
previous chapters) the Chinese revolution developed in such a way
that it did not consist of the overthrow of the power of the old
regime all at once or in a relatively short time, but through a protracted armed struggle. Actually, this consisted of a whole series
of different wars through which, in the course of more than 20

years, the new base areas liberated from the rule of the reactionaries were built up and then finally an all-out assault was launched to liberate the whole country. During this long process—itself marked by sub-stages—new relations of production and a new superstructure were built up in the liberated areas to serve the developing struggle of the masses. Although the economic, social and political relations were not yet socialist in character—and this was reflected in the realm of ideology and culture—nevertheless, there were aspects of the socialist future, including the leading role of the proletariat and its ideology, which Mao consistently fought for against bourgeois (and feudal) elements, inside as well as outside the Chinese Communist Party.

Yenan Forum on Literature and Art

It was on this basis that Mao developed the fundamental orientation for literature and art. This was concentrated in a series of talks that Mao gave at the month-long forum at Yenan in 1942 on literature and art. (As noted earlier in this book, Yenan was the place where the revolutionary government of the base areas and the leadership of the Chinese Communist Party and revolutionary army were centered.)

Two years earlier Mao had written his basic work "On New Democracy," in which he not only summed up the basic strategy for the Chinese revolution in that stage—the new-democratic revolution—but gave particular emphasis to the fact that, as he said, "For many years we Communists have struggled for a cultural revolution as well as for a political and economic revolution," and that the new China which was being brought into being through revolution ". . . will have not only a new politics and a new economy but a new culture."[20] In this essay he outlined the general characteristics of this new culture, and emphasized that:

Revolutionary culture is a powerful revolutionary weapon for the broad masses of the people. It prepares the ground ideologically before the revolution comes and is an important, indeed essential, fighting front in the general revolutionary front during the revolution.[21]

In general, "On New Democracy" lays the groundwork for Mao's *Talks at the Yenan Forum on Literature and Art*, in which he goes into the specific characteristics which art must have in order to serve as a revolutionary weapon.

First of all Mao spoke to the question of class stand. As has been

In this scene from *The Red Detachment of Women*, Wu Ching-hua, the daughter of a poor peasant, glares in unflinching hatred at the despotic landlord from whose dungeon she has escaped. With this dance drama developed during the Cultural Revolution under the leadership of Chiang Ching, the working class stormed and seized the ballet stage which had been a stronghold of the bourgeoisie, transforming ballet and turning it into a powerful weapon for proletarian revolution.

pointed out, all literature and art have to be guided, and objectively will be guided, by the world-view and stand of some class in
society, whether the person producing it is conscious of it or not.
And Mao pointed out that, in this era, in order for culture to play a
progressive and revolutionary role, it had to serve the proletariat,
because in this stage in human history only the working class is a
revolutionary class in a thoroughgoing way and only the working
class can lead the masses of people in thoroughly transforming
society. And Mao insisted on this, even though the stage of the
revolution then was democratic and not yet socialist. Only with
the leadership of the working class in all spheres, including
culture, could it be a *new*-democratic revolution, capable of
thoroughly defeating imperialism and domestic reaction and advancing to the socialist future.

Closely related to this, Mao also sharply posed the question of
for whom. For whom, he asks the cultural workers at Yenan, are
you producing your works? The basic question here is: should they
be for the elite, should they be for the supposedly "superior
people," or should they be for the masses of people? And Mao
answered that they must be produced for the masses of people,
which in China included not only the working class but also hundreds of millions of peasants, as well as the soldiers (particularly of
the revolutionary army). Art must be produced for the masses of
toiling and oppressed people, Mao made clear. It must be embraced by the masses and taken up as a weapon in their struggle.

In order to fulfill this, Mao insisted, the cultural workers, people
producing literature and art, had to go out among the masses, inte-
grate themselves with them, take part in labor together with them,
and help them to wage the struggle against the enemy. He stressed
that, "Our writers and artists have their literary and art work to
do, but their primary task is to understand people and know them
well."[22] Note that he says that this is not just an important task,
but the *primary* task of revolutionary writers and artists.

What is decisive here, Mao said, is the question of intellectuals
integrating themselves with the masses, transforming their world
outlook and firmly taking up the revolutionary stand, outlook and
method of the proletariat and Marxism. It is in this connection
that Mao describes, in a famous passage, how his own feelings
towards the masses changed as he became a revolutionary. As a
result of bourgeois (even feudal) education, Mao says, he

. . . acquired the ways of a student; I then used to feel it undignified to do
even a little manual labor, such as carrying my own luggage in the

presence of my fellow students, who were incapable of carrying anything, either on their shoulders or in their hands. At that time I felt that intellectuals were the only clean people in the world, while in comparison workers and peasants were dirty.[23]

Mao goes on to recount how his feelings changed:

But after I became a revolutionary and lived with workers and peasants and with soldiers of the revolutionary army, I gradually came to know them well, and they gradually came to know me well too. It was then, and only then, that I fundamentally changed the bourgeois and petty-bourgeois feelings implanted in me in the bourgeois schools. I came to feel that compared with the workers and peasants the unremoulded intellectuals were not clean and that, in the last analysis, the workers and peasants were the cleanest people and, even though their hands were soiled and their feet smeared with cow-dung, they were really cleaner than the bourgeois and petty-bourgeois intellectuals. That is what is meant by a change in feelings, a change from one class to another.[24]

Revolutionary cultural workers, Mao insisted, had to get to know the people—what their feelings were about things, how they saw the world, how they were actually carrying forward the struggle. They had to learn the lively language of the people, had to learn and develop further the cultural works, the song, music, dance, etc., that was produced by the people themselves, especially the more they developed their struggle. Unless this was done, literature and art was bound to be rejected by the masses of people—because it was bound to be alien to them, in form as well as in content.

As the outstanding model Mao pointed to Lu Hsun, a revolutionary writer during the new-democratic revolution who took up the communist outlook and stood firmly with the masses of people, using his pen as a mighty weapon in their revolutionary struggle, until his death in 1936. Lu Hsun was, Mao acclaimed, "the greatest and most courageous standard-bearer" of the new, revolutionary cultural force that had emerged in China in the wake of the May 4th, 1919, anti-imperialist upsurge in China and the spread of Marxism-Leninism to that country and the formation in 1921 of the Chinese Communist Party.[25] In particular, after the Japanese invasion of China, when the task of waging a war of resistance against Japan came to the forefront, Lu Hsun forcefully championed the line of a "literature of the masses for the national revolutionary war," in opposition to the right-wing line of a "literature of national defense," which had currency among influential left-wing literary circles and even within the Chinese Communist Party and

which represented a line of capitulation and subordination to
Chiang Kai-shek. This was a key struggle in the area of literature
and art and was closely linked to and played an important role in
the overall class struggle within the camp of opposition to Japan
and within the revolutionary movement.

In this and other ways, Lu Hsun stood as a titan in China's
revolutionary cultural army. "All communists," Mao said, "all
revolutionaries, all revolutionary literary and art workers should
learn from the example of Lu Hsun and be 'oxen' for the proletariat and the masses, bending their backs to the task until their
dying day."[26]

Mao also took up the question, whom should art extol and whom
should it expose and criticize? His answer was precise and to the
point:

All the dark forces harming the masses of the people must be exposed and
all the revolutionary struggles of the masses of the people must be extolled; this is the fundamental task of revolutionary writers and artists.[27]

Note the emphasis here. This is the *fundamental task* of revolutionary cultural workers. (This does not contradict what Mao had
earlier said, that the primary task of revolutionary writers and artists is to understand the people and know them well, for there he
was talking about what is overall primary, whereas here it is in
terms of their fundamental task in actually creating cultural
works—in other words he is speaking here to the fundamental task
of culture, literature and art in particular.)

Many people in the Chinese Communist Party strenuously ob-
jected to and opposed Mao's line on this question. For a number,
this was part and parcel of opposing his line on culture as a whole
and, in fact, his revolutionary line overall. They said that revolutionary artists should be "objective"—by which they meant even-
handed. We shouldn't always praise the workers, the peasants and
the revolutionary struggle, they insisted; we should also point out
the bad parts, the shortcomings. And if the capitalists do
something good we should give them credit for it; likewise if the
workers do something bad we should point that out, too.

Despite the claims that such a stand is "objective," in fact it is
not. Making proletarian revolution must be a very conscious struggle, and it means a complete exposure and rejection of all the traditional ideas, of all the forces of habit, of all the usual, accepted,
natural ways of doing things. And to be "even-handed" in this
situation means objectively to serve the capitalist class, which has

Lu Hsun, a revolutionary writer who came forward during the anti-imperialist upsurge in China, took up the communist outlook and stood squarely with the proletariat and the masses. He fought for the line that all literature and art must serve the masses' revolutionary cause. Here he gives a lecture at Peking Teachers' University in 1932, struggling against an opportunist line in the Party at that time. "All Communists, all revolutionaries, all revolutionary literary and art workers, should learn from the example of Lu Hsun," declared Mao Tsetung at the 1942 Yenan forum.

the force of habit and the force of tradition on its side.

This question, and struggle around it, came up many times during the course of the Chinese revolution, not only during its new-democratic stage but even more fiercely in the socialist stage. For instance, Tao Chu, a revisionist who was a prominent figure in the Chinese Communist Party's propaganda work at the beginning of the Cultural Revolution, claimed, among many other things, that Party writers should point out the shortcomings of the people's communes which had been created through a mass upsurge in the countryside and represented a further advance of socialism there. Here, like other revisionists, Tao Chu was directly going against Mao's basic line, including the basic orientation he had set for culture. And here, too, we can see again the tremendous role of culture in creating public opinion for one class or another and upholding one system or another.

In response to this, Yao Wen-yuan, a revolutionary who came to prominence during the Cultural Revolution and was one of the Four who heroically fought to defend Mao's line after his death, retorted: "There is a song called *The People's Communes Are Fine.* Is it necessary to modify this title with another sentence 'the people's communes have shortcomings'?"[28]

The point is not that revolutionary writers should tell lies and be one-sided. Exactly the opposite. As Yao explains:

We should distinguish between the main current and the minor currents of life. Only when we focus on the main current can we give a typical presentation of the essence of social advance. Minor currents merely offer a contrast to the main current and can be used as a means to present the essence, forming a subordinate aspect of the whole, and partial and temporary twists in the course of advance, never to be regarded as the main content of life.[29]

Of course everything has both its good and its bad aspect. But which aspect is principal? What is new and vigorous as opposed to decadent and declining? And what is the revolutionary artist's overall purpose? Already in 1942 in his talks at the Yenan Forum, Mao had set forth the basic approach to this question. Yes, he said, "The people, too, have their shortcomings."[30] Yes, the outlook of the exploiting classes has influence. And it is an important task of revolutionary culture to educate the people and help them cast off these burdens. But it must be done on the basis of uniting with them and fully supporting their struggle; it must be done in such a way as to actually help them throw off these shackles, and not so as to attack them or draw no distinction between the people (who are influenced to a certain degree by the ideology and culture of the enemy) on the one hand and the enemy, its system, its exploitation and oppression and its decadent ideology and culture on the other.

Popularization and Raising Standards

Given, then, that revolutionary art should serve the masses in their struggle, the question that arises is, how to do this? And here a critical question that Mao addressed in his Yenan Forum talks was the contradiction between *raising standards* and *popularization*. This was an area in which Mao made important new contributions.

Some people were saying that, while spreading art and culture among the masses was important, the most important things was to raise the standards of revolutionary art—in other words that it was too primitive, dull, stereotyped, etc. But Mao clearly and sharply opposed this view. Popularization, he said, the spreading of art and culture generally among the broad masses, as a key part of the overall fierce revolutionary struggle then raging, was the principal aspect.

But much more crucial was what Mao said about the interrelation between these two aspects, and the relationship of the whole problem to the task of the cultural workers in integrating with and learning from the masses:

We must popularize only what is needed and can be readily accepted by the workers, peasants and soldiers themselves. Consequently, prior to the task of educating the workers, peasants and soldiers, there is the task of learning from them. This is even more true of raising standards. There must be a basis from which to raise. Take a bucket of water, for instance; where is it to be raised from if not from the ground? From mid-air? From what basis, then, are literature and art to be raised? From the basis of the feudal classes? From the basis of the bourgeoisie? From the basis of the petty-bourgeois intellectuals? No, not from any of these; only from the basis of the masses of workers, peasants and soldiers. Nor does this mean raising the workers, peasants and soldiers to the "heights" of the feudal classes, the bourgeoisie or the petty-bourgeois intellectuals; it means raising the level of literature and art in the direction in which the workers, peasants and soldiers are themselves advancing, in the direction in which the proletariat is advancing. Here again the task of learning from the workers, peasants and soldiers comes in. Only by starting from the workers, peasants and soldiers can we have a correct understanding of popularization and of the raising of standards and find the proper relationship between the two.[31]

In other words, revolutionary art and culture must build on

what the masses have already created—their own lively ways of speech and expression, for instance, and the songs, the dances, the music, the folk tales which have come from the people. This is the starting point. And what is the direction? It is the direction in which the masses of people in struggle are already advancing, the direction which they are historically taking and must take—the direction of socialism and communism.

At the same time Mao noted that it was necessary to produce some works of literature and art specifically to fulfill the cultural needs of the cadres. This, Mao said, must of necessity be on a higher level than works produced for the broad masses, since the cadres generally had more education than the masses and were in fact the advanced elements, politically, of the masses. But such literature and art for the cadres must still serve the basic purpose of arousing and enlightening the masses to struggle more consciously and resolutely toward the revolutionary goal. Mao explained the dialectics of this as follows:

Whatever is done for the cadres is also entirely for the masses, because it is only through the cadres that we can educate and guide the masses. If we go against this aim, if what we give the cadres cannot help them educate and guide the masses, our work of raising standards will be like shooting at random and will depart from the fundamental principle of serving the masses of the people.[32]

Radical Rupture in the Sphere of Culture

Why does Mao say that raising standards specifically does *not* mean raising the masses to the so-called "heights" of the feudal and bourgeois classes and the petty-bourgeois intellectuals? What does he mean here and what is the importance of this?

This was in direct opposition to the line that the task in cultural work was to "elevate" the masses to where they could properly "appreciate" the classical works of the "men of genius" of past eras. This, along with the position that the present era and the socialist system should produce a "galaxy" of new "men of genius," is exactly the line of the revisionists—in the Soviet Union, and in China itself, including those revisionists who today rule China—who have consistently attacked Mao's line not only on culture in general but specifically over this point of what "raising standards" means.

Here what is fundamentally involved is whether or not proletarian culture, including literature and art, represents and must represent something qualitatively different from—and advanced beyond—all previous culture. Mao emphatically said yes; the revisionists all, in one way or another, essentially say no. What Mao was basing himself on and applying was the understanding put forward by Marx and Engels in the *Communist Manifesto*: the communist revolution must be the most radical rupture not only with all traditional property relations but with all traditional ideas as well.

This certainly applies to the sphere of culture. It is not possible to carry out the socialist revolution and the transition to communism without creating a whole new culture, including literature and art, which, for the first time in history, puts forward the outlook and promotes the interests of the proletariat in overthrowing everything reactionary and revolutionizing all of society. This cannot be done by supposedly raising "classical" works of art "above class," and treating them as the pinnacle of achievement which the "ignorant rabble" of the masses must be "elevated" to worship. Nor can it be done by creating supposedly proletarian works of art by utilizing the methods of the exploiting classes and their intellectuals: reliance on a few "great men" divorced from the masses and their revolutionary struggles. Instead it must be done by relying on, learning from and unleashing and developing the creativity and the creations of the masses themselves, under the guidance of Marxism.

Does this mean, was it Mao's position, that all art and culture of previous epochs should be indiscriminately negated and simply cast aside as useless or harmful? Certainly not. Historical materialism must be applied to assess the role of such works. Those which played a progressive role in previous epochs should be upheld in that context, while, however, never failing to point out their class bias and limitations. And on this basis, such works can be used as part of educating the masses in historical materialism, so long as this is done from that standpoint and linked to systematic analysis of such works with the science of Marxism. Further, certain artistic devices can be adopted from works which represent the outlook and interests of previous, exploiting classes and systems, but these generally will have to be *adapted* as well to conform to the revolutionary character of proletarian art—since form interpenetrates with content.

Mao spoke to this in his talks at the Yenan Forum:

We should take over the rich legacy and the good traditions in literature and art that have been handed down from past ages in China and foreign countries, but the aim must still be to serve the masses of the people. Nor

Peasant painting from Huhsien County in Shensi Province, "Condemning Confucius at His Temple Gate."

do we refuse to utilize the literary and artistic forms of the past, but in our hands these old forms, remoulded and infused with new content, also become something revolutionary in the service of the people.[33]

This was summarized in the following slogans, which, under Mao's leadership, were applied to culture as well as other fields: "Make the past serve the present and foreign things serve China" and "Weed through the old to bring forth the new."

As part of this basic line, it must be grasped that even works which were progressive in their time—in previous historical epochs—do not play a progressive role in this epoch precisely if they are presented uncritically and put forth as classless "classics" or even staged without systematic Marxist criticism and education of the masses as to their class content as well as their historical role. Here again it must be stressed that the force of habit and tradition weighs heavily in favor of the exploiting classes and against the proletariat. All these works of art of previous epochs, representing the stand and interests of exploiting classes, will, spontaneously, influence the masses in a direction opposed to the proletarian world-view and their own revolutionary interests and, in such conditions, will therefore play a reactionary role. Again, only if the use of such works is combined with systematic education as to not only their historical role but also their class content and world-view, and only if the latter are thoroughly criticized while the former is explained in light of historical materialism, can they play any kind of positive role in regard to the proletarian revolution.

And, beyond that, none of these works, however great they may have been in their own era, can in any way compare to the revolutionary cultural creations achieved in this era under the leadership of the revolutionary proletariat and its ideology. Measured against such proletarian works of art, all previous works pale in comparison. Regardless of their artistic devices, they can never portray the power and grandeur of the self-emancipating struggle of the masses of people under the leadership of the most revolutionary class in history. Only culture guided by the outlook and serving the interests of this class, the proletariat, can scale such heights.

It is on this point in particular that Mao's contribution in the sphere of culture is centered, representing a further advance beyond the previous theory and practice of Marxism and the proletariat in this sphere. And it was exactly under the leadership of Mao's revolutionary line that the Chinese people created works of art representing the highest pinnacle achieved by mankind yet in culture.

Art as a Concentration of the Revolutionary Struggle

Again, it should be stressed that Mao developed this line and made these contributions precisely through keeping uppermost the aspect of class stand in art and culture. This is what Mao stressed again and again, as when he said in his Yenan Talks:

> In the world today all culture, all literature and art belong to definite classes and are geared to definite political lines. There is in fact no such thing as art for art's sake, art that stands above classes or art that is detached from or independent of politics.[34]

This is the essence, and the heart, of Mao's whole basic orientation. Because art is always tied to a definite class, it is also inseparable from politics, from the class struggle.

Now by this, of course, Mao didn't mean that art and culture are the same as politics *per se*, or identical with class struggle in any other form, and that there is no role for art and culture in and of itself. Quite the opposite. Mao stressed that there is in fact the contradiction between political content and artistic form, and that to really be art a cultural work must of course be good in technique, must have proper and appropriate form, and must express its content in this way. He specifically criticized the existence in the Communist Party and among revolutionaries of that time of what he called the "poster and slogan style" of art. For art, in order to fulfill its function as art and play a revolutionary role, must be good artistically. It must perform the function that the masses seek and desire out of art, or else it will not be able to play a revolutionary role.

But what is it, then, that people seek from art? Why is it that although art arises out of life itself, people are not just satisfied with life, but demand art as well? Mao's answer is that, although on the one hand "works of literature and art, as ideological forms, are products of the reflection in the human brain of the life of a given society," on the other hand:

> . . . life as reflected in works of literature and art can and ought to be on a higher plane, more intense, more concentrated, more typical, nearer the ideal, and therefore more universal than actual everyday life.[35]

This is what it means to be art. A work of art must be more intense and concentrated than life itself; it cannot passively reflect life; a play, novel, song, etc., cannot just reflect the minute-by-minute life of someone—there would be no point to it. Art must concentrate and intensify life, must raise it to a higher plane.

But all concentrations of life are not the same and do not serve the same interests. This raises the question of truth and reality. Bourgeois writers and critics (or at least those who still make a pretense of realism) say: "Well, revolutionary art may be more idealistic, but our art is more truthful to reality." However, in fact the exact opposite is the case. All art expresses some aspect of reality, just because it is a social product. But bourgeois art can only portray, at most, the surface of things, whereas revolutionary proletarian art can show the underlying essence, the actual truth. Bourgeois art can only concentrate what is dying; today proletarian art alone can reveal what is new and arising.

As indicated earlier there is no incompatibility between the fact that revolutionary art is partisan and that it depicts reality, nor between the fact that it is a weapon in the struggle of the masses and that it is truthful. For, as Mao says in another famous work:

Marxists hold that man's social practice alone is the criterion of the truth of his knowledge of the external world . . . If you want knowledge, you must take part in the practice of changing reality.[36]

The fact that a work of art is created as part of revolutionary practice, and is used to help change reality, does not mean that it doesn't reflect truth—for in fact truth can only be reflected through the process of changing reality, and the deeper and more essential truths about history, society and human beings can only be arrived at through the process of changing reality in a revolutionary way.

What, then, does revolutionary art do? Mao sums it up succinctly: "Revolutionary literature and art should create a variety of characters out of real life and help the masses to propel history forward."[37]

In connection with the tasks of cultural workers, and specifically in relation to literary and art criticism, Mao also dealt with the dialectical relationship between motive and effect in judging a work of art. Effect, he said, was the principal aspect and, in the final analysis, the criterion for judging motive. But he warned against metaphysics in approaching this question: idealists, he pointed out, ignore effect while considering only motive, but mechanical materialists also err in only considering effect and not motive. In opposition to this, Mao made clear:

> ... we dialectical materialists insist on the unity of motive and effect. The motive of serving the masses is inseparably linked with the effect of winning their approval; the two must be united. The motive of serving the individual or a small clique is not good, nor is it good to have the motive of serving the masses without the effect of winning their approval and benefitting them. In examining the subjective intention of a writer or artist, that is, whether his motive is correct and good, we do not judge by his declarations but by the effect of his actions (mainly his works) on the masses in society.[38]

None of this meant, of course, that any work of literature and art, in order to play a positive role, had to be thoroughly revolutionary or fully reflect the outlook of the proletariat. Indeed there could be, and were, progressive works whose objective effect was mainly to propel the masses forward in struggle against the main enemy, even though the writer or artist might not be a communist. And it was correct to seek to unite with, and to influence, such people. But, precisely in order to do this, as well as to fulfill the basic purpose of creating works guided by the proletarian outlook to meet the needs of the masses (and the cadres) in the fullest sense, it was necessary for revolutionary cultural workers to adopt the orientation Mao set forth in his Yenan Forum talks and to create on this basis literature and art that could "help the masses propel history forward" in the most thoroughgoing way and could serve as models.

Struggle on the Cultural Front
in the People's Republic

Mao's line, the proletarian line, on art, literature and culture generally did not win out in the Chinese Communist Party and the revolutionary movement without struggle. It had to be constantly and fiercely fought for throughout the course of the Chinese revolution. This held true in 1942 and still more so as the Chinese revolution advanced, as it swept away the old exploiting classes and entered the socialist stage with the founding of the People's Republic in 1949. And, further, while the talks at the Yenan Forum had set the basic orientation, further development of this line was needed as the struggle advanced from its first stage, that of the new-democratic revolution, to the stage of the socialist revolution. Thus Mao's line had to be both upheld and deepened through applying it to new conditions, as the Chinese revolution developed.

For instance, in 1951 Mao wrote an editorial (or part of an editorial) for the *People's Daily* calling for criticism of the film *The Life of Wu Hsun*, which was promoted at that time. This reactionary film openly praised this man who, as Mao says, "... living as he did towards the end of the Ching Dynasty in an era of great struggle by the Chinese people against foreign aggressors and domestic reactionary feudal rulers [Wu lived from 1838-96], did not lift a finger against the feudal economic base or its superstructure..."[39] That such a film not only appeared at that time but received lavish praise, including from prominent Party members, indicated that the class struggle was indeed very acute and that bourgeois forces were launching sharp attacks, using culture as an important vehicle for this.

Or again there was, in 1954, Mao's "Letter Concerning the Study of *The Dream of the Red Chamber*," which was a letter to the Political Bureau of the Central Committee of the Party, and which concerned critical essays by two young people on the novel *The Dream of the Red Chamber*, and of the assessment of it by a bourgeois intellectual, Yu Ping-po. Mao comments on how these essays, which seem to have been in the main correct, were suppressed rather than welcomed by the literary authorities.[40]

This incident revealed the underlying class struggle which continued very sharply and how it manifested itself in the field of culture. And indeed this episode proved to be merely a prelude to a very wide-ranging struggle indeed—the Hu Feng affair.

Hu Feng was a Party member and an intellectual figure. Despite his Party membership, he had never actually become a Marxist-Leninist, and in fact espoused bourgeois individualism for writers and artists and opposed putting politics in command of art. In the mid-'50s he began organizing dissident groups, particularly in the universities.

In late 1954 the artists' and writers' federations in China began to repudiate the errors of the literary authorities around the criticism of Yu Ping-po's assessment of *The Dream of the Red Chamber*. Seeing his chance, Hu Feng began criticizing the Communist Party for "authoritarianism" in art. After a struggle, he made a hypocritical self-criticism in January 1955, but in actuality went back to organizing his clique of reactionary dissidents with even greater frenzy. When this came to light, Mao organized a campaign, not only against Hu Feng, but to root out hidden counter-revolutionaries generally. As part of this, the book *Material on the Counter-Revolutionary Hu Feng Clique* was published, which Mao edited and to which he contributed a preface as well as editorial notes.[41]

In his "Preface," Mao goes into the question of why this material was being published and what the importance of the struggle against Hu Feng consists in:

> The masses of the people are very much in need of this material. How do counter-revolutionaries employ their double-dealing tactics? How do they succeed in deceiving us by their false appearances, while furtively doing the things we least expect? All this is a blank to thousands upon thousands of well-intentioned people. On this account, many counter-revolutionaries have wormed their way into our ranks . . . [Success] in spotting and clearing out bad elements depends on a combination of correct guidance from the leading organs with a high degree of political consciousness on the part of the masses, but in this regard our work in the past was not without shortcomings.[42]

In short, as Mao summed up: "We attach importance to the Hu Feng case because we want to use it to educate the masses of the people. . . ."[43]

This case thus brings out at least two important points. First, it shows the close inter-relation of questions and struggles in the realm of literature and art with the class struggle in society in general. And second, Mao's summation and action in this case illustrate how the struggles in this realm can serve as crucial training grounds for the masses in waging the class struggle, particularly under the new conditions of socialism.

In the next several years the class struggle further intensified in China at the same time as events were unfolding internationally, which reacted in a major way on the struggle in China. In the Soviet Union, the revisionists seized power. And in a number of other Eastern European countries there were serious counter-revolutionary disturbances which drew in significant sections of the masses, playing upon discontent over bureaucratic tendencies and other defects in the government and its relations with the people. Emboldened by this, the Rightists in China, with unremolded bourgeois intellectuals playing an influential part, launched an attack in the Chinese Communist Party and the socialist state, also stirring up disturbances. It was in this context, in early 1957, that the policy of "letting a hundred flowers blossom and a hundred schools of thought contend" was put forward.

"Hundred Flowers"

This was advanced as the long-term policy "for promoting progress in the arts and sciences and a flourishing socialist culture in our land," as Mao explained.[44] In this, Mao and the Chinese Communist Party were following a similar line to that argued for by Stalin when he noted that "It is generally recognized that no science can develop and flourish without a battle of opinions, without freedom of criticism."[45] Or, as Mao put it, extending this assessment beyond science to art as well:

We think that it is harmful to the growth of art and science if administrative measures are used to impose one particular style of art or school of thought and to ban another. Questions of right and wrong in the arts and sciences should be settled through free discussion in artistic and scientific circles and through practical work in these fields.[46]

But, of course, this means *struggle* between forms of art and schools in science. And Mao empahsized shortly after the above statement that this is part of the overall class struggle in socialist society:

Class struggle is by no means over. The class struggle between the proletariat and the bourgeoisie, the class struggle between the various political forces, and the class struggle between the proletariat and the bourgeoisie in the ideological field will still be protracted and tortuous and at times even very sharp. The proletariat seeks to transform the world according to its own world outlook, and so does the bourgeoisie. In this respect, the question of which will win out, socialism or capitalism, is not really settled yet. . . .
It will take a fairly long period of time to decide the issue in the ideological struggle between socialism and capitalism in our country.[47]

So this policy was a way of waging the class struggle. Of course, as Mao also mentioned, these two slogans in and of themselves do not have a class character—that is, they can be made use of, of course in opposite ways, by opposing classes. The proletariat will have its own criteria for judging the things that sprout up—for distinguishing, as Mao puts it, fragrant flowers from poisonous weeds. Mao mentions several of these criteria, the most important of which being that they be beneficial to the socialist transformation of society and that they help to strengthen the leading role of the Communist Party.

In other words, not every idea or art work that pops its head up under this policy will be a blossoming flower. Some will be noxious weeds, and they should be rooted out. But the fact that some weeds sprout under this policy does not mean that it is a bad one. On the contrary. For, first, such weeding will have to be done in any case: "Weeds will grow even ten thousand years from now, and so we must be prepared to wage struggles for that long."[48] In other words, there will be bad and harmful ideas under socialism for a long time (and even under communism). The proletariat and the masses of people must be prepared to wage resolute and constant struggle against them.

But besides this, the policy of letting a hundred flowers blossom and a hundred schools of thought contend will often be useful in getting these ideas out in the open so they can be combatted and uprooted. And in fact this was what happened in 1957. The bourgeois Rightists in China indeed seized the opportunity given them by this policy and launched a big offensive. The proletariat and its Party then took *this* opportunity to repulse the offensive and smash these reactionaries.

Some of the Rightists complained that they had been tricked (a theme taken up by many bourgeois China scholars too). But Mao explained:

Some people say this was a covert scheme. We say it was an overt one. For we made it plain to the enemy beforehand: only when ghosts and monsters are allowed to come into the open can they be wiped out; only when poisonous weeds are allowed to sprout from the soil can they be uprooted. Don't the peasants weed several times a year? Besides, uprooted weeds can be used as manure. The class enemies will invariably seek opportunities to assert themselves. They will not resign themselves to losing state power and being expropriated. However much the Communist Party warns its enemies in advance and makes its basic strategy known to them, they will still launch attacks. Class struggle is an objective reality, independent of man's will. That is to say, class struggle is inevitable. It cannot be avoided even if people want to avoid it. The only thing to do is to make the best use of the situation and guide the struggle to victory.[49]

The bourgeoisie is going to exist under socialism and it is going to struggle and launch attacks on the proletariat. Sometimes the best tactic is for the proletariat to let them come out in the open, thus exposing themselves to the masses and arming the people with an understanding of what their real program is—restoration of the old order—so that the people can be mobilized to strike them down.

Battle in Cultural Field Intensifies

Despite this struggle and many others, the bourgeoisie was not, of course, by any means eradicated. Bourgeois forces, concentrated increasingly in the Communist Party itself, especially at its top levels, continued to have vitality and strength, and in fact their strength was centered to a considerable degree in the areas of art and culture. The educational system was one of their strongholds, leading Mao to say later, in reviewing the course of the first year of the Cultural Revolution in 1967:

As I see it, the intellectuals, including young intellectuals still receiving education in school, still have a basically bourgeois world outlook, whether they are in the Party or outside it. This is because for seventeen years after the liberation the cultural and educational circles have been dominated by revisionism. As a result, bourgeois ideas are infused in the blood of the intellectuals.[50]

Here it is significant to note that this assessment by Mao of culture and education as dominated by revisionism for the 17 years after liberation until the start of the Cultural Revolution has all along been sharply attacked by the revisionists in China. Now, since seizing power, they have called this assessment the "two estimates" (on education and culture) and attributed them to the so-called "gang of four" as an indirect but blatant attack on Mao himself and his revolutionary line and as a crucial component part of their reversal of the Cultural Revolution and the Chinese revolution as a whole (there can be no politically aware person in China who does not know that these "two estimates" were actually made by Mao himself).

Before the Cultural Revolution the revisionists were also strongly entrenched in the arts, where they pushed representatives of the old exploiting classes and new elites as models and promoted bourgeois and even feudal values, leading to Mao's famous admonition to the Ministry of Culture that "if it refuses to change, it should be renamed the Ministry of Emperors, Kings, Generals and Monsters, the Ministry of Talents and Beauties or the Ministry of Foreign Mummies."

Mao saw that public opinion (as well as conditions generally) was being prepared for a takeover by these revisionists, and he launched a counter-attack, concentrating at first particularly in the field of culture and especially literature and art. Beginning in 1963 Mao's wife and close comrade, Chiang Ching, along with Chang Chun-chiao, another of Mao's close comrades and member of the so-called "gang of four," led in challenging the revisionists on just this turf, bringing about, through extremely sharp struggle, pathbreaking transformations. One important area of challenge was the traditional Chinese art form, Peking Opera, in which old feudal and semi-feudal works continued to be performed almost exclusively.

During that period Mao himself used the form of poetry to proclaim the inevitable triumph of revolution over reaction, in the face of a revisionist adverse current internationally, centered in the Soviet Union, and of stepped-up attacks from capitalist-roaders in China, in concert with this international trend of treachery and cowardly capitulation to imperialism. Mao ended a famous poem written in early 1963 with the following lines:

The Four Seas are rising, clouds and waters raging,
The Five Continents are rocking, wind and thunder roaring.
Our force is irresistible,
Away with all pests! [51]

Finally in 1965, after giving overall leadership to preparing revolutionary public opinion, and aiming the first few blows in the crucial sphere of culture, Mao made a direct counter-attack politically. Interestingly and significantly, this also was connected with the field of culture.

The revisionists had written and staged a play which was set in the past, but which by analogy very directly attacked Mao Tsetung. The play was called *Hai Jui Dismissed from Office* and ostensibly defended a man who had been dismissed in the feudal past, but by very clear analogy it was actually attacking Mao for knocking down the former Defense Minister, Peng Teh-huai, who had vigorously attacked China's Great Leap Forward in the late '50s. As Mao remarked in December 1965:

The crux of *Hai Jui Dismissed from Office* was the question of dismissal from office. The Chia Ching Emperor [of the Ming Dynasty, 1522-66] dismissed Hai Jui from office. In 1959, we dismissed Peng Teh-huai from office. And Peng Teh-huai is "Hai Jui" too. [52]

So Mao suggested that criticism of this play should be organized. But this could not be done in Peking, so tightly were the revisionists—headed by Liu Shao-chi, Teng Hsiao-ping, Peng Chen (then Mayor of Peking) and others—in control there. It had to be done in Shanghai, where the revisionists also had the upper hand then, but not such tight control as in Peking. Yao Wen-yuan, in close consultation with Mao, wrote a blistering critique of the play ("On the New Historical Drama *Hai Jui Dismissed from Office*"), exposing its real social purpose and essence. This article, as Mao was later to say, was the signal for the beginning of the Great Proletarian Cultural Revolution.

The Cultural Revolution
and the Revolutionizing of Culture

The Cultural Revolution will be discussed in detail in the next chapter. Here the aspect of art and culture is the center of attention. But of course this *was* a central aspect of this revolution—it was called the *Cultural* Revolution for good reason. As the Central Committee of the Chinese Communist Party said, in a decision said to have been personally drafted by Mao, and specifically in a paragraph which deserves to be quoted in full:

Although the bourgeoisie has been overthrown, it is still trying to use the old ideas, culture, customs and habits of the exploiting classes to corrupt the masses, capture their minds and endeavor to stage a comeback. The proletariat must do the exact opposite: it must meet head-on every challenge of the bourgeoisie in the ideological field and use the new ideas, culture, customs and habits of the proletariat to change the mental outlook of the whole of society. At present, our objective is to struggle against and overthrow those persons in authority who are taking the capitalist road, to criticize and repudiate the reactionary bourgeois academic "authorities" and the ideology of the bourgeoisie and all other exploiting classes and to transform education, literature and art and all other parts of the superstructure not in correspondence with the socialist economic base, so as to facilitate the consolidation and development of the socialist system.[53]

Thus, while the Cultural Revolution was certainly not solely concerned with works of literature and art, nor even simply with culture generally, but ultimately (since it was a real revolution) had to center on the political question of who will hold power in society, still the field of culture generally and that of literature and art in particular was a very important arena in which this political question was fought out.

Therefore, the struggle in the field of art was very sharp. A good example is the case of *The White-Haired Girl*, a revolutionary drama created relatively early in the Chinese revolution, which has gone through a number of transformations in the course of that revolution. This opera is based on a true story of an episode during the war of resistance against Japan, which was told of in folk-tales, which were in turn rewritten cooperatively by several writers in the Red Army and then rewritten again on the basis of the criticisms of peasants. During the last years of the war against Japan and during the civil war that followed, it was performed many, many times in the liberated areas. The form that it took then was as follows.

The heroine of the opera is the daughter of a peasant. She is seized by the landlord when her father is unable to pay his debts at New Year's, and is forced to become a maidservant in the landlord's house, beaten and tormented by the landlord's wife. Her father commits suicide. She is raped by the landlord. When she becomes pregnant and threatens to expose him, he plans to murder her. She flees to the wilds and gives birth to the baby, her hair turning white from her hardship and living conditions in a cave. She gets food from a village temple, where the peasants leave offerings, thinking she is a ghost or a goddess. When the Communist Party-led Eighth Route Army comes into the area, they hear of the apparition. Pursuing the "ghost" they find the white-haired girl and her baby. Learning how things are changing, she goes back with the army to her old village and denounces the landlord, who is beaten. The white-haired girl is reunited with another peasant who had been her boyfriend before, and the impression is that they can settle down and live happily now.

Beginning before, and in what constituted an important part of the preparation for, the Cultural Revolution, and specifically under the leadership of Chiang Ching, many changes were made in this work. The opera in many ways reflected the period in which it was made—the new-democratic stage of the revolution, and even more specifically the sub-stage of the struggle against Japanese aggression. As the revolution moved forward through the completion of the new-democratic revolution and into the socialist stage, works of art had to reflect this progress and propel further advances. This work in particular had played a positive and important role in the past, but was far from suited, in its old form, to the needs of the continuing struggle in the socialist stage. In fact, if it were not transformed to keep pace with the advance of the revolution and the growing consciousness of the masses, it would turn into its opposite—it would become a vehicle for promoting ideas and sentiments in opposition to the carrying forward of socialist revolution and socialist construction. It is not for no reason, nor simply out of spite against Chiang Ching, that, since seizing power in October 1976, the revisionists in China have restored the old version of *The White-Haired Girl*, wiping out the revolutionary changes (summarized below) made in it under Chiang Ching's leadership.

One change initiated by Chiang Ching was that the father no longer committed suicide, but was killed while resisting the attack of the landlord's thugs. And likewise the heroine herself is no longer raped, but rather puts up continual resistance to the tyranny of the landlord and his wife and finally has to flee because she is being more and more persecuted for resisting her oppression.

Now many people might say (as indeed they did in China) that such changes make the opera less realistic, that Chiang Ching and those who followed Mao were trying to make it seem that every peasant who had to give up his daughter to the landlord (and this was a very common occurrence in feudal and semi-feudal China), and every peasant girl whom the landlord tried to rape (and this was also common) put up militant resistance, when this wasn't actually true. And of course it *is* a fact that not everyone in those circumstances put up this kind of resistance; there were some who were submissive and some who resisted in a whole range of other, less straightforward, ways than do the peasant father and his daughter in the changed *White-Haired Girl*. But there were also many who *did* resist militantly.

All these different ways of acting could be said to be typical, and portraying any one of them in the drama could be a concentration of one or another aspect of life. But what was being created in China was *revolutionary* art, a revolutionary concentration of life, something, in other words, that will help the masses propel history forward and aid in the revolutionary transformation of society. And for this purpose what is most important to portray is the fierce resistance of the people to their oppression, and how they can break their chains.

Further, this does not mean falsifying things, contrary to the claims that such revolutionary art is "unrealistic." Of course, as was just said, both the peasant who commits suicide and the one who resists are real. But, actually, which one of these most truly presents the essence of what was happening among the peasantry during the Chinese revolution? Wasn't it much more of the essence of things, much more the tendency of where things were going, that the peasants were rising up like a mighty storm, smashing their oppressors and playing a vital part in transforming society? The whole Chinese revolution, like any revolution, seemed unreal, something that was impossible to believe or accept, for reactionaries—and (so long as their outlook was not really remolded) even for people among the bourgeoisie or petty bourgeoisie who went along with the revolution, at least in certain stages. They could not really grasp the essence of what that revolution was about and the actual and decisive role of the masses. And so the portrayal of the reality of heroic peasants was also bound to seem "unrealistic" to these same people.

Also, in line with this socialist orientation, the end of the drama was changed too. Instead of being beaten, the landlord is taken off-stage and executed. The reason is that in the opera the landlord essentially symbolizes the reactionary forces and his execution shows how the Chinese people were rising up and overthrowing these reactionaries by force of arms. (It was found that if he were to be killed onstage, this would create involuntary sympathy for him among the audience.)

Also, in the new version, in the reunion of the white-haired girl with her boyfriend, the love theme is played down and made very secondary to the struggle of the peasants and the Chinese people as a whole. And instead of the two of them going off to live happily ever after, they both pledge themselves to carry forward the revolutionary struggle. This, again, was necessary and correct not only in more accurately portraying the demands of the new-democratic revolution, which was as yet unfinished in the time which the end of the play portrays, but still more so in meeting the requirements of the socialist stage, where, as Mao had summed up, there was the need to continue the revolution and, in line with this, the need to depict in works of art the protracted, ongoing and central role of the class struggle.

The White-Haired Girl was also made into a ballet during this period, one of the great works of art of mankind. In it Western forms of dancing and musical traditions were integrated with traditional Chinese forms, and the effete and bourgeois types of gestures and positions which are almost synonymous with ballet in the West were transformed into militant and revolutionary gestures and positions.

These works of art like the changed *White-Haired Girl* were known as "model works"—that is, pacesetters which the people all over China could use as models in their development of numerous and various artistic works. Further, under the guidance of Mao's line and with the concrete leadership of Chiang Ching and others carrying out this line, not only were model works produced in other areas of literature and art (besides ballet and Peking Opera), such as symphonic music, but there was a tremendous proliferation of revolutionary works, especially creations of the masses themselves, in such fields as film, other forms of drama, short stories, poetry, paintings, music, dance, etc.

And besides this, in an unprecedented way, during this period of the Cultural Revolution tremendous advances were made in mobilizing the masses themselves to wage struggle in the cultural field and develop socialist culture. One of the problems in China is that it is still a backward and relatively undeveloped country. This is particularly true in the countryside, and one of the ramifications of this is that the system of transportation and communication is still relatively undeveloped, especially in the rural areas. Under the leadership of revolutionaries like Mao and Chiang Ching, and especially during the decade of the Cultural Revolution in its different stages and various forms, from 1966 to 1976, new ways were developed to get these new types of culture to the people—such as the development of small movie projectors which could be carried easily into the mountainous regions of the countryside or could be mounted on bicycles, so that films could be taken and shown even in remote and relatively inaccessible areas.

Also, different Peking Opera companies and other performing troupes would tour in the countryside, with bicycles and backpacks, performing in remote areas, helping local groups stage model works, and watching performances of local works in order to learn from them.

These were concrete ways in which the proletariat, its Party and cultural workers strove to break down the differences between city and country in the cultural field, thus helping to transform society under socialism in the direction of communism.

The Arena of Culture in Mao's Last Great Battle

But the Cultural Revolution was not all one straight line of progress, no more than anything is. It was a revolution, and of course it was fiercely resisted by counter-revolutionaries, headed by capitalist-roaders in the Party itself. There were many twists and turns and different stages in which different tactics were required to deal with new conditions.

The final stage of the Cultural Revolution, the stage of Mao's last great battle, began with the defeat of the treachery of Lin Piao, who in the fall of 1971 died in an airplane crash, fleeing the country after having failed in an attempt to assassinate Mao and pull off a coup. But Lin had been identified in many ways with the Cultural Revolution, so his treachery gave an opening for many of those who had been knocked down during the Cultural Revolution and others who opposed it from the start or who later came into opposition to it. Further, the Right was able to take advantage of the fact that during this stage China was entering into certain compromises, establishing diplomatic relations and making certain agreements, with the U.S. and the West in order to keep the Soviet Union off balance, as it had become a direct and immediate threat to China. This last battle ended, after the death of Mao, with the counter-revolutionary coup in October 1976 which saw the arrest

Members of the *White-Haired Girl* dance troupe travel along rugged mountain paths to Wengniu Village in Kwangsi, where they will live, work and study with the masses as well as perform for them. Tours like this across China, including to remote areas far removed from the cities, historically the centers of culture, enabled cultural workers to get to know the lives and the feelings of the masses, so as to be able to produce revolutionary culture in the service of proletarian revolution.

of Mao's closest comrades, the leaders of the forces of the Chinese proletariat who are now vilified as the "gang of four." Revisionism triumphed, for the moment, in China.

In this last great battle, culture and art was once again a crucial field of struggle. The revisionists sought to reverse the gains that the proletariat had made on all fronts, including (and even especially) on this front.

In 1973 they brazenly staged an only thinly disguised remake of a drama which had championed Liu Shao-chi's line in opposition to Mao's before the Cultural Revolution. Around the same time, under the cover of the "opening to the West," and to serve their aims of capitulating to imperialism, they uncritically promoted, and denied the class character and content of, works of art from the Western imperialist countries, in particular "absolute music" (instrumental music with no descriptive title). Along with this they launched a fierce assault on the new, revolutionary works of literature and art brought forward through the Cultural Revolution, including a sharp attack on the model works and specifically on the revolutionization of Peking Opera.

They accused the revolutionaries of suppressing artistic creations and complained that there were not enough "flowers blooming"—attempting to infuse the policy of letting 100 flowers blossom with a bourgeois content and to pose it against Mao's line that "The proletariat must exercise all-around dictatorship over the bourgeoisie in the realm of the superstructure, including the various spheres of culture," which Mao put forward in dialectical unity with the "100 flowers" policy and which strengthened the proletarian basis of this policy. Along with all this, the revisionists struck out at the transformations in education and the fields of science and technology that had been brought about through the Cultural Revolution, whining that these new policies had made a "mess" of things and specifically that they prevented China from "catching up to and surpassing"—in reality they meant tailing after, aping and capitulating to—the "advanced" countries of the world—that is, the imperialists.

Mao and the revolutionary forces he guided, with the Four—Wang Hung-wen, Chang Chun-chiao, Chiang Ching and Yao Wen-yuan—as the active leading core, not only fought back vigorously against these specific attacks but launched a counteroffensive in the realm of the superstructure and the creation of public opinion. Shortly after the Tenth Congress of the Chinese Communist Party (in August 1973), they launched the movement to Criticize Lin Piao and Confucius, a campaign mainly educational in form but constituting an extremely important struggle in the realm of the superstructure. Through this campaign, using the method of historical analogy and based on the application of and education of the masses in historical materialism, the revisionists' counter-revolutionary line and policies and their preparations for a seizure of power, reversal of the revolution and capitulation to imperialism were exposed and mass criticism of them was mobilized.

Later, in the summer of 1975, as the overall class struggle was coming to a head, Mao used literature and art as a sharp weapon in this battle. In particular he focused attention on and called for revolutionary criticism of an historical novel, *Water Margin*, whose hero (Sung Chiang) was actually a traitor to the peasant rebels in whose ranks he had usurped leadership. Similar to those in present day China who joined the revolution in its democratic stage but were never thoroughgoing revolutionaries, never made a radical rupture with bourgeois ideology, Sung Chiang joined the peasant rebels only to fight corrupt officials and not the Emperor. In the end he took the offer of amnesty from the Emperor and enlisted in his service to fight the peasant rebels who continued the struggle and were determined to carry it through.

The criticism of this novel was, Mao stressed, no mere academic exercise or aesthetic pursuit; the merit of the novel, Mao said, was precisely that it would help the masses of people to recognize capitulationists, modern-day Sung Chiangs, who would betray the revolution at home and sell out to imperialism. The targets were those in authority, especially at the top ranks of the Party, who were pushing a revisionist line and taking the capitalist road—people like Teng Hsiao-ping, and behind them, Chou En-lai—veteran leaders who had failed to advance with the continuation of the revolution in the socialist stage and had turned from bourgeois-democrats (bourgeois-democratic revolutionaries) into capitalist-roaders, counter-revolutionaries.

As this last battle further boiled up and broke out into open, all-out struggle, the spheres of education and culture were extremely important battlefronts. Besides focusing attention on the battle in the educational field in late 1975-early 1976 and calling attention to the fact that this was a sharp reflection of the overall class struggle at that time, Mao led the revolutionary forces in the struggle in the cultural field, as another very important arena of the all-around showdown. And one of the main shots fired by Mao was not only about art but was in the form of art. Specifically, as he had done before, Mao used poetry as a salvo in the struggle—in particular two poems, which Mao had originally written in 1965, and which were reissued on New Year's Day in 1976. This was a message to the Chinese people that, just as in the period of 1965, there was a great danger of the revisionists taking over and restoring capitalism, and therefore (even though the forms might have to differ in some respects from the start of the Cultural Revolution) there was also a need for a big, all-out struggle to prevent such a reversal.

One poem "Chingkangshan Revisited" is full of revolutionary optimism, recalling the epoch-making victories of the Chinese revolution over the previous 38 years and pointing the way forward to the fierce struggles that will bring new victories in the future. Chingkangshan were the mountains where the first base area for the revolutionary army had been established, starting the Chinese revolution on the road of armed struggle, in 1927.

The other poem, "Two Birds: A Dialogue," portrays a struggle between a revolutionary and a revisionist, analogized as two birds, the legendary roc and the twittering, frightened sparrow who longs for potatoes and beef (Khrushchev's "goulash communism") and puts his faith in the "triple pact" (the sham nuclear test ban treaty concluded between the U.S., Britain and the USSR in 1963). The revisionist sparrow, like Khrushchev and his counterparts in China, thinks the revolutionary upsurge and turmoil in China and the world is "one hell of a mess." And the answer of the roc, the powerful bird representing revolution, is that the world is being turned upside down, is being transformed through these revolutionary struggles. These poems, along with the struggle on the cultural front generally, played an important part in this last great battle of Mao Tsetung, in arming the masses, including rank and file Party members and revolutionary cadres, to carry forward the revolutionary struggle right into the teeth of the revisionist hurricane being whipped up by the capitalist-roaders in authority.

The triumph of the revisionists in this last battle, their seizure of power, shows precisely the correctness of Mao's line that throughout socialism there are classes and class struggle and the danger of capitalist restoration (as well as attacks by imperialism and other foreign reactionaries) and that therefore it is necessary to continue the revolution under the dictatorship of the proletariat. It shows specifically how correct Mao's line was on the role of the superstructure—not only that it assumes tremendous importance under socialism but that at times it plays the principal and decisive role. The revisionist coup, which constituted the qualitative change and the beginning of the actual process of reversing the revolution and restoring capitalism, obviously occur-

TWO POEMS

Chingkangshan Revisited

May 1965

I have long aspired to reach for the clouds,
Again I come from afar
To climb Chingkangshan, our old haunt.
Past scenes are transformed,
Orioles sing, swallows swirl,
Streams purl everywhere
And the road mounts skyward.
Once Huangyangchieh is passed
No other perilous place calls for a glance.

Wind and thunder are stirring,
Flags and banners are flying
Wherever men live.
Thirty-eight years are fled
With a mere snap of the fingers.
We can clasp the moon in the Ninth Heaven
And seize turtles deep down in the Five Seas:
We'll return amid triumphant song and laughter.
Nothing is hard in this world
If you dare to scale the heights.

Two Birds: A Dialogue
Autumn 1965

The roc wings fanwise,
Soaring ninety thousand li
And rousing a raging cyclone.
The blue sky on his back, he looks down
To survey man's world with its towns and cities.
Gunfire licks the heavens,
Shells pit the earth.
A sparrow in his bush is scared stiff.
"This is one hell of a mess!
O, I want to flit and fly away."

"Where, may I ask?"
The sparrow replies,
"To a jewelled palace in elfland's hills.
Don't you know a triple pact was signed
Under the bright autumn moon two years ago?
There'll be plenty to eat,
Potatoes piping hot
With beef thrown in."
"Stop your windy nonsense!
Look you, the world is being turned upside down."

MAO TSETUNG

red exactly in the superstructure, and naturally could occur nowhere else.

Further, this last battle itself, like all previous struggles in socialist China—and in the earlier period of the Chinese revolution—illustrates the tremendous importance of not only the superstructure in general but of the field of culture and the struggle in that sphere in particular. It shows how correct and what an important contribution was represented by Mao's precise formulation that, upon seizing power, it is decisive that, "The proletariat must exercise all-around dictatorship over the bourgeoisie in the realm of the superstructure, including the various spheres of culture," and the policies and achievements that were developed under the guidance of Mao's revolutionary line on culture and the superstructure. And no revisionist coup and temporary reversal in China can in any way negate or detract from the tremendous and truly immortal contributions of Mao Tsetung, including in the vital area of literature and art and culture as a whole.

Chapter 6

CONTINUING THE REVOLUTION UNDER THE DICTATORSHIP OF THE PROLETARIAT

Introduction

In a famous quotation by Lenin on the dictatorship of the proletariat he states emphatically that:

It is often said and written that the main point in Marx's teachings is the class struggle; but this is not true. And from this untruth very often springs the opportunist distortion of Marxism... Those who recognize only the class struggle are not yet Marxists; they may be found to be still within the boundaries of bourgeois thinking and bourgeois politics.... Only he is a Marxist who extends the recognition of the class struggle to the recognition of the dictatorship of the proletariat. This is what constitutes the most profound difference between the Marxist and the ordinary petty (as well as big) bourgeois.[1]

Today, no less than in Lenin's time, the correct stand toward the dictatorship of the proletariat constitutes the most profound difference between a Marxist and a non-Marxist understanding and guide to action in relation to society and history. In particular it marks the most profound political difference between Marxism and revisionism. And it is precisely in this all-important area that Mao Tsetung made the most important of his immortal contributions to Marxism-Leninism and the revolutionary cause of the international proletariat.

Mao deepened the Marxist-Leninist analysis of what the dictatorship of the proletariat is, deepened it in an absolutely indispensable way, by showing how there continue to be classes under socialism, how these classes continue to struggle, and how the working class must wage its struggle under these new conditions, must continue the revolution under the dictatorship of the proletariat. Just as, at the time when Lenin wrote the above, the

key task of Marxists was to uphold the dictatorship of the pro-
letariat, so today the vital task of Marxist-Leninists is to grasp
and uphold the deepened understanding of continuing the revolu-
tion under the dictatorship of the proletariat which was the
greatest contribution of Mao Tsetung.

Theory of Proletarian Dictatorship

Of course the basic concept of the dictatorship of the proletariat
did not originate with either Mao or Lenin, but was part of Marxism from the first. Marx himself had made a profound statement
on this in a letter, rather early in his development as a Marxist:

As to myself, no credit is due to me for discovering the existence of classes
in modern society or the struggle between them. Long before me
bourgeois historians had described the historical development of this
class struggle and bourgeois economists the economic anatomy of the
classes. What I did that was new was to proove: 1) that the *existence of
classes* is only bound up with *particular historical phases in the development of production,* 2) that the class struggle necessarily leads to the *dictatorship of the proletariat,* 3) that this dictatorship itself only constitutes
the transition to the *abolition of all classes* and to a *classless society.*[2]

It should be noted that this was written before Marx had done his
great and systematic work in political economy, and that what he
is talking about here is his contribution to the discovery of the
general laws of the historical development of human society, and
not about his contributions in the field of political economy. And,
with regard to this field of the laws of historical development,
what Marx emphasizes in the statement above is a basic principle
first elaborated and continually stressed by Marx and Engels, as
for example at the end of the second chapter of the *Communist
Manifesto*:

Political power, properly so called, is merely the organised power of one
class for oppressing another. If the proletariat during its contest with the
bourgeoisie is compelled, by the force of circumstances, to organise itself
as a class, if, by means of a revolution, it makes itself the ruling class, and,
as such, sweeps away by force the old conditions of production, then it
will, along with these conditions, have swept away the conditions for the
existence of class antagonisms and of classes generally, and will thereby
have abolished its own supremacy as a class.[3]

What Marx and Engels emphasize is that the dictatorship of the
proletariat is a *means,* not an end in itself, a means of transition to

communism, to classless society. This does not make the rule of the proletariat one bit less necessary, but it underlines the fact that it is necessary exactly for the achievement of the real goal of the proletarian revolution—the wiping out of *all* class distinctions. As Marx emphatically states in a famous passage:

This Socialism is the *declaration of the permanence of the revolution*, the *class dictatorship* of the proletariat as the necessary transit point to the *abolition of class distinctions generally*, to the abolition of all the relations of production on which they rest, to the abolition of all the social relations that correspond to these relations of production, to the revolutionising of all the ideas that result from these social relations.[4]

Upholding the dictatorship of the proletariat is a cardinal question and a touchstone of Marxism. For without establishing and exercising this dictatorship it is impossible for the proletariat to achieve its historic mission of communism. "We want the abolition of classes." Engels said. "What is the means of achieving it? The only means is political domination of the proletariat."[5]

The Paris Commune

But, although the recognition of the dictatorship of the proletariat was an integral part of Marxism right from the beginning, this does not mean that this doctrine, any more than any other part of Marxism, could be developed all at once and in abstraction from the actual class struggle between the proletariat and the bourgeoisie. At first, in the 1850s, Marx simply recognized the necessity of the class rule (the dictatorship) of the proletariat, without trying to speculate on exactly what form it would take. Even this initial recognition was the product of summing up the class struggle. As Lenin pointed out:

Marx deduced from the whole history of Socialism and of the political struggle that the state was bound to disappear, and that the transitional form of its disappearance (the transition from state to non-state) would be the "proletariat organized as the ruling class." But Marx did not set out to *discover* the political *forms* of this future stage. He limited himself to precisely observing French history, to analyzing it, and to drawing the conclusion to which the year 1851 had led, viz., that matters were moving towards the *smashing* of the bourgeois state machine.[6]

But as the actual revolutionary practice of the working class went forward, it was possible and necessary for Marx's theoretical understanding to progress also. And the revolutionary struggle of the proletariat did go forward, making a qualitative leap in 1871 with the first seizure of power by the working class—the Paris Commune.

The Paris Commune came into being at the end of the Franco-Prussian War when the French bourgeoisie surrendered to Prussia. But the workers of Paris were still armed to fight the war, and they rose up and seized power in Paris, vowing to defend the city both against the Prussian invaders and the French bourgeoisie, who fled to Versailles, set up a reactionary government, and proceeded to collaborate with the Prussian army in attacking Paris. As the Central Committee of the workers' National Guard proclaimed, in its manifesto of March 18, 1871:

> The proletarians of Paris, amidst the failures and treasons of the ruling classes, have understood that the hour has struck for them to save the situation by taking into their own hands the direction of public affairs... They have understood that it is their imperious duty and their absolute right to render themselves masters of their own destinies, by seizing upon the governmental power.[7]

Marx believed that the Commune would not be successful in holding on to its power. In the previous year he had pointed out that conditions were not ready for an uprising by French workers, and he thought after the seizure of power that the proletariat would be defeated after a time. But when the workers did rise and "stormed heaven" (as Marx termed it), he gave them full and absolute support, mobilizing the International Working Men's Association in behalf of the Commune, declaring, "What flexibility, what historical initiative, what a capacity for sacrifice in these Parisians!... History has no comparable example of similar greatness!"[8]

At the same time as he hailed it as the most glorious height yet attained by the working class in its revolutionary struggle, Marx also eagerly studied the Commune in order to grasp its great historic lessons, especially concerning the form which the rule of the proletariat would take. As Lenin said:

> And when the mass revolutionary movement of the proletariat burst forth, Marx, in spite of the failure of that movement, in spite of its short life and its patent weakness, began to study what forms it had discovered.[9]

These forms were many, rich and vital. The Commune itself was composed, as Marx pointed out, mainly of "working men, or acknowledged representatives of the working class." Further, "the Commune was to be a working, not a parliamentary, body, executive and legislative at the same time."[10] All Commune members and officials received workers' wages.

The army and police force were done away with, and in their place the National Guard enrolled all able-bodied citizens. The state subsidy for the church was swept away. Pawn shops were closed down. Crime was met with the iron force of the armed workers themselves, and the streets became safe for the ordinary citizens. Rent was cancelled. The Vendome Column, a monument to France's chauvinist wars of aggression, was pulled down. Schooling was made free and open to all. The factories, whose capitalist owners had fled, were seized and run cooperatively by the workers. The night shift was abolished.

There were other new forms developed by the proletariat in its brief but glorious dictatorship in Paris, before it was crushed with the utmost savagery and revengeful cruelties by the French bourgeoisie. Not all of these forms, of course, were of equal value. Some were "false starts," others were quite correct in the immediate circumstances but were not necessarily models for a long-term socialist society, while others would indeed be features of any society which could really be called socialist. But regardless of all the details of particular features of the Commune, one fact stood out, which Marx summarized as follows:

It was essentially a working-class government, the produce of the struggle of the producing against the appropriating class, the political form at last discovered under which to work out the economic emancipation of labor. . . . The Commune was therefore to serve as a lever for uprooting the economical foundations upon which rests the existence of classes, and therefore of class-rule. With labour emancipated, every man becomes a working man, and productive labour ceases to be a class attribute.[11]

Once again, in other words, the main thing about the dictatorship of the proletariat is its character as a *transitional form* to communism. And in order first to consolidate its rule and advance to communism, the working class must *smash* the old bourgeois state machinery, with its governmental bureaucracy, its police and army, its judicial and prison system, etc. As Marx and Engels noted in their preface to a new German edition of the *Communist Manifesto* in 1872:

One thing especially was proved by the Commune, *viz.*, that "the working class cannot simply lay hold of the ready-made state machinery, and wield it for its own purposes."[12]

Fighters man the barricades of the Paris Commune, the first dictatorship of the proletariat.

Critique of the Gotha Programme

These same themes come to the fore even more explicitly in Marx's other main work on this subject, his *Critique of the Gotha Programme*. This was his criticism (at first sent privately and only published after Marx's death) of the draft programme for the Socialist Workers' Party of Germany (later the German Social-Democratic Party), which was the product of the unification of two working class parties in Germany, one under the leadership of followers of Ferdinand Lasalle, the other led by followers (more or less) of Marx.

In this work Marx marked off clearly what he called the two "phases of communist society," which since that time have come to be called socialism, on the one hand, and communism, on the other. He emphasized that:

> Between capitalist and communist society lies the period of the revolutionary transformation of the one into the other. Corresponding to this is also a political transition period in which the state can be nothing but *the revolutionary dictatorship of the proletariat.*[13]

But, besides emphasizing again the transitional nature of socialism, and the fact that politically this transition must be marked by working class dictatorship, Marx also showed what the crucial difference is between socialism and communism in terms of economic organization. This difference can be expressed in the form of two maxims or slogans.

The maxim of socialist society is: from each according to his ability, to each according to his work. This corresponds to the general level of development of production relations that characterizes socialist society (which in turn is ultimately determined by the level of development of the productive forces). This means that, while provision is made for those actually unable to work, etc., and after a certain amount is set aside for accumulation, public services, and so on, generally each person gets back in the way of consumer goods an equivalent to what his labor has contributed. In all socialist societies that have existed, the exchange of labor for consumer goods has taken place so far through the medium of money—that is, workers receive money-wages with which they buy these consumer goods. This is itself a commodity relation and is an aspect of the situation where commodity relations have not been eliminated in society as a whole. To the degree that this is the case the law of value continues to operate (the law

that the value of commodities is determined by the socially necessary labor time required to produce them) and exerts an influence
on the distribution of means of production and still more so in the
distribution of means of consumption (consumer goods).

Under socialism, because of the transformation of the ownership
system from capitalist to socialist, the operation of the commodity
system and the law of value is restricted. And labor power itself is
no longer a commodity under socialism—no longer can some people appropriate wealth from the labor of others on the basis of
private ownership of the means of production, and instead each
person's income is acquired solely from the labor he or she contributes—so long as socialist relations of production actually exist.
But even so the persistence of commodity relations represents
both a remnant of capitalist economic relations and a contradiction which can be seized on by bourgeois elements in attempting to
restore capitalism.

And, even if the distribution of consumer goods under socialism
were no longer literally in the commodity form, so long as it was
based on exchange of equal values, as Marx explains, the "same
principle prevails as that which regulates the exchange of commodities. . . "[14] And this principle is one which indicates that society
has not yet completely transcended the confines of capitalist relations, although it has made a qualitative leap beyond capitalism
with the achievement of socialist ownership. "Hence," Marx says,
"*equal right* here [under socialism] is still in principle—*bourgeois
right*. . ." [15]

This equality is also bourgeois in that it is still a *formal* equality.
As Marx says: "This *equal* right is an unequal right for unequal
labour. . .*It is, therefore, a right of inequality, in its content, like
every right.*"[16] Different people will differ in their skills, in natural
endowments, in how many others they may have to support, and
so on. So in actual fact, despite formal equality, one person will be
getting more than another, one will be richer than another.

It is this bourgeois right—this equality which is still formal,
bourgeois, and hence really still inequality—which will be overcome in advancing to communist society, a society in which, as
Marx puts it, the principle prevails: from each according to his
ability, to each according to his need.

But this transition to communism cannot be achieved immediately or all at once. As Marx points out trenchantly:

What we have to deal with here is a communist society, [Marx means
communism in its first stage, socialism] not as it has *developed* on

its own foundations, but, on the contrary, just as it *emerges* from capitalist society; which is thus in every respect, economically, morally and intellectually, still stamped with the birth marks of the old society from whose womb it emerges.[17]

Thus Marx sketches here the basic difference between socialism and communism, and therefore what socialism must be in motion *toward.* And it follows from Marx's analysis that the general objective of the dictatorship of the proletariat could be summed up in one phrase: the elimination of bourgeois right. Marx presented this as a question both of overcoming the social distinctions and ideological influences left over from capitalism and of achieving the necessary material abundance for communism, with these two things obviously closely inter-related. As he put it:

In a higher phase of communist society, after the enslaving subordination of the individual to the division of labour, and therewith also the antithesis between mental and physical labour, has vanished; after labour has become not only a means of life but life's prime want; after the productive forces have also increased with the all-round development of the individual, and all the springs of co-operative wealth flow more abundantly—only then can the narrow horizon of bourgeois right be crossed in its entirety and society inscribe on its banners: From each according to his ability, to each according to his needs![18]

But the fact that the "birth marks of the old society" would not only continue to exist under socialism for a long time but also give rise constantly to a new bourgeoisie, that the transition to communism would be a very long one, throughout which there would be classes and class struggle, and that the driving force in moving society forward to communism would be the class struggle of the proletariat against the bourgeoisie—that, as Mao was to explain it, the contradiction between the proletariat and the bourgeoisie would be the principal one all throughout socialism and the class struggle between them the key link—all this was not grasped by Marx, who had only the short-lived experience of the Paris Commune as a concrete instance of working class rule from which to develop theoretical conclusions (in addition to the general lessons he drew from capitalism and previous class societies) concerning the nature of the state in general and the dictatorship of the proletariat in particular. This understanding was developed only later, especially by Lenin and Mao—the former in an embryonic and partial way and the latter as a systematic line—on the basis of further experience in the actual practice of the dictatorship of the proletariat and with Marx's conclusions as a foundation.

Engels as Continuator of Marxism

Engels, of course, was Marx's close collaborator while Marx was alive and the continuator and upholder of Marxism after his death. This is also true with regard to the crucial question of the dictatorship of the proletariat.

During the time when they were both alive, for instance, Engels also strongly criticized the Gotha Programme for its deviation from some crucial Marxist principles. Shortly after Marx's death Engels not only upheld the Marxist principle of the withering away of the state, but also pointed out that:

At the same time we have always held, that in order to arrive at this and the other, far more important ends of the social revolution of the future, the proletarian class will first have to possess itself of the organised political force of the state and with this aid stamp out the resistance of the capitalist class and re-organise society.[19]

Again, in 1890, Engels found it necessary to stress sharply, in correspondence with certain people in Germany, the character of socialism as a transitional society and one in the process of motion and change. He wrote *against* those to whom " . . .'socialist society' appeared not as something undergoing continuous change and progress but as a stable affair fixed once for all . . .'" and stated that "To my mind, the so-called 'socialist society' is not anything immutable. Like all other social formations, it should be conceived in a state of constant flux and change."[20]

And finally, there is the instance of Engel's sharp reassertion of this central doctrine in his "Introduction" to the third German edition of *The Civil War in France,* published in 1891 to mark the twentieth anniversary of the Paris Commune:

Of late, the Social-Democratic philistine has once more been filled with wholesome terror at the words: Dictatorship of the Proletariat. Well and good, gentlemen, do you want to know what this dictatorship looks like? Look at the Paris Commune. That was the Dictatorship of the Proletariat.[21]

It is obvious that Engels is here delivering a sharp blow to certain trends in the German Social-Democratic Party, trends which were to give birth, just five years afterwards, to the full-blown revisionism of Eduard Bernstein. It is significant that Engels' blow against these trends centers here on the question of the recognition of the dictatorship of the proletariat.

But, as has been touched on earlier and will be gone into more fully later, while recognizing the need for the dictatorship of the proletariat and forcefully insisting on this point in fierce struggle against the revisionists of the time, Engels as well as Marx did not recognize the continuation of the class struggle, and its central role, over a long period under socialism and did not recognize that it was not merely a question of the proletariat exercising dictatorship over the overthrown exploiting classes but of continuing the class struggle particularly against a newly engendered bourgeoisie. They tended to see the task of "stamping out the resistance of the capitalist class and re-organizing society" (in Engels' words) as a task which could be accomplished more quickly (and more easily) than has proved to be the case. Thus again, while the theoretical contributions of Marx and Engels, both in general and on the dictatorship of the proletariat in particular, have served as a foundation, they remained to be built upon and further developed.

Lenin

Lenin was able to lead the successful Russian revolution because he kept a firm grip on Marxism and further developed it in the face of the revisionist cancer which infected the revolutionary workers' movement in the beginning decades of this century. This had two aspects. On the one hand, it meant applying Marxism to the ever-changing concrete situation, whose principal feature was the movement of capitalism into a new stage—imperialism. On the other hand, it meant vigorously defending—even resurrecting—some fundamental principles of Marxism which the revisionists were attempting to bury and "forget."

Lenin's initial work with regard to the theory of the dictatorship of the proletariat was centered on the second, which he does primarily in *State and Revolution*. There he pointed out that, due to the growth and influence of revisionism, "...now one has to engage in excavations, as it were, in order to bring undistorted Marxism to the knowledge of the masses."[22] Lenin's "excavation" in this book consists in giving a history (much more thorough than that above) of the evolution of the views of Marx and Engels on the state.

In the course of recounting this development, there are several points which Lenin emphasized as essential to Marx and Engels' teaching on the state. First, as already seen in the passage quoted at the beginning of this article, Lenin strongly pointed out that recognition of the dictatorship of the proletariat was an important difference between Marxism and various forms of bourgeois ideology, including revisionism.

Secondly, he emphasized that this recognition means nothing less than upholding the necessity for violent revolution on the part of the working class and the smashing of the state apparatus of the bourgeoisie. Thirdly, he also underlined the transitional nature of socialism.

And finally, Lenin also emphasized what Marx had said about the persistence of bourgeois right:

> And so, in the first phase of communist society (usually called Socialism) "bourgeois right" is *not* abolished in its entirety, but only in part, only in proportion to the economic revolution so far attained, i.e., only in respect of the means of production. "Bourgeois right" recognizes them as the private property of individuals. Socialism converts them into *common* property. *To that extent*—and to that extent alone—"bourgeois right" disappears.
>
> However, it continues to exist as far as its other part is concerned; it continues to exist in the capacity of regulator (determining factor) in the distribution of products and the allotment of labour among the members of society.[23]

A little later Lenin points to very important aspects of the economic basis for the complete withering away of the state, which requires:

> such a high stage of development of Communism that the antithesis between mental and physical labour disappears, when there, consequently, disappears one of the principal sources of modern *social* inequality—a source, moreover, which cannot on any account be removed immediately by the mere conversion of the means of production into public property, by the mere expropriation of the capitalists.[24]

This is a profound analysis of some of the basic factors involved in the transition from socialism to communism, and one of its implications would seem to be that this transition period, socialism, will cover a relatively long historical period—for, as Lenin notes here, the economic basis for communism is by no means achieved by the expropriation of the capitalists, but only by the resolution of the contradiction between manual and mental labor. (In saying this Lenin was following Marx and Engels, who had pointed out that the division of labor into mental and manual is the basis for classes.) And it is clear that the overcoming of *this* contradiction (between mental and manual labor) will take a fairly long historical period.

Rebellious Czarist troops in Petrograd turn their rifles around and join the workers in insurrection—an insurrection which led to the working class' taking and holding state power for the first time in history.

However, in other parts of *State and Revolution*, it seems that Lenin thought that the period of proletarian dictatorship would be relatively brief. This view that the transition to communism would be relatively quick is also to be found very clearly in Marx and Engels, as for instance in the following sentences from *Anti-Duhring*, which Lenin also quotes:

The proletariat seizes the state power and transforms the means of production in the first instance into state property. But in doing this, it puts an end to itself as proletariat, it puts an end to all class differences and class antagonisms; it puts an end also to the state as state.[25]

This comes through also in a famous statement by Marx, where he says that:

From forms of development of the productive forces these relations [of production] turn into their fetters. Then begins an epoch of social revolution. With the change of the economic foundation the entire immense superstructure is more or less rapidly transformed.[26]

This is correct as a general description of the transition from one system of exploitation to another (though even in such cases there is a generally long period of quantitative change before the final qualitative leap to the firm establishment of the new system). But with regard to the transition from capitalism to communism, this statement errs in two ways. First it does not sufficiently recognize the difficulty, complexity and protracted nature of the struggle to transform the superstructure, tending to view this process as more or less passively tailing in the wake of the changes in the economic base. And secondly, it underestimates the protracted process of transforming the economic base itself, which involves not merely the change in the ownership system but the elimination of the division of labor characteristic of class society and the vestiges of capitalism in the system of distribution. Thus, while Marx and Engels spoke to the necessity to overcome "the enslaving subordination of the individual to the division of labor" and to pass completely beyond the horizon of bourgeois right, and while more generally they stressed that the communist revolution was qualitatively different from all previous revolutions and must involve a radical rupture with both all traditional property relations and all traditional ideas, nevertheless they underestimated the time—and the struggle—that would be required to bring about these radical ruptures.

As noted before, the reason for this is that Marx and Engels, and

Lenin too at the time he wrote *State and Revolution* (in August and September 1917, just before the October revolution), were analyzing the question in advance of any actual extended experience of proletarian rule. As a result, they could correctly grasp the essential features and direction of socialist society, but they could not forsee certain of its most important features and contradictions.

As Lenin says, speaking of Marx's analysis of the state in 1852:

True to his philosophy of dialectical materialism, Marx takes as his basis the historical experience of the great years of revolution, 1848 to 1851. Here, as everywhere, his teaching is the *summing up of experience*, illuminated by a profound philosophical conception of the world and a rich knowledge of history.[27]

In other words, it is a principle of dialectical materialism that, in general and overall, theory sums up practice. This is an aspect of the fact that practice is primary over theory, a fundamental principle of materialism. Human beings can grasp material reality in thought, and sum it up theoretically, but human thought, though it can grasp the laws of motion—dialectics—and on this basis project into the future, cannot thoroughly comprehend things which will only emerge in the future. In other words, armed with a correct science (which is itself the product of theoretical summation of practice), man can grasp the essence of a thing and hence its general course of development, but this does not mean that all the particularities of future development can be predicted by any means. This is a point which is stressed repeatedly by Lenin in *State and Revolution*,[28] who often expresses it by saying that Marxists are not utopians, trying to invent a new society, but are instead theoretically summing up the development of the new society from the old.[29] This basic point was also emphasized by Mao, who said bluntly that Marxists are not fortune-tellers.

And Lenin, of course, *was* to have experience of several years of the dictatorship of the proletariat. In the famous postscript to *State and Revolution* he notes that the book was also to have included a chapter on "the experience of the Russian revolutions of 1905 and [February] 1917," but before it could be written he was "interrupted" by the October Revolution of 1917.

On the basis of the revolutionary practice of the Russian proletariat, led by Lenin and the Bolshevik Party, in exercising its dictatorship in the remaining seven years of Lenin's life, he began to make certain further developments in the Marxist theoretical understanding of the state, of the practice of building socialism and the implementation of the dictatorship of the proletariat.

During these years the Soviet working class fought both internal and external enemies, carrying on a fierce struggle against the bourgeoisie and other exploiters within the Soviet Republic and also against the imperialists and other foreign reactionaries who banded together to try to crush the new proletarian state. From this experience, Lenin drew very important conclusions about the persistent character of the struggle to advance to communist society, about the persistence of the bourgeoisie, bourgeois influences and bourgeois relations, and the regeneration of bourgeois elements under socialism—both from sources within socialist society itself and also from international sources.

Lenin made these points in a number of writings in the early years of the Soviet Republic. Just two years after the October Revolution, he began to sum up the experience of the rule of the working class in an important article in *Pravda*, "Economics and Politics in the Era of the Dictatorship of the Proletariat." Here he points out that classes still exist:

And classes still *remain* and *will remain* in the era of the dictatorship of the proletariat. The dictatorship will become unnecessary when classes disappear. Without the dictatorship of the proletariat they will not disappear.[30]

The classes which Lenin has in mind here are the following. First is the petty bourgeoisie and most especially the peasantry, to which Lenin devotes a lot of attention in this article and others, discussing how the dictatorship of the proletariat must move toward doing away with the class distinction between peasants and workers by eventually transforming the peasants into workers. Secondly, Lenin has in mind the former ruling class of Russia, about which he says:

The class of exploiters, the landowners and capitalists, has not disappeared and cannot disappear all at once under the dictatorship of the proletariat. The exploiters have been smashed, but not destroyed. They still have an international base in the form of international capital, of which they are a branch. They still retain certain means of production in part, they still have money, they still have vast social connections. Because they have been defeated, the energy of their resistance has increased a hundred- and a thousandfold. The "art" of state, military and economic administration gives them a superiority, and a very great superiority, so that their importance is incomparably greater than their numerical proportion of the population.[31]

Some six months later, Lenin returns to these themes, in his famous book on *"Left-Wing" Communism*, where one of his purposes is to sum up the first two and a half years in which the dictatorship of the proletariat has been exercised and socialism begun to be built in the Soviet Republic. Here he particularly stresses the influence of petty-bourgeois production and of the immense force of habit and tradition. He points out:

Classes have remained, and will remain everywhere *for years after* the conquest of power by the proletariat . . . The abolition of classes means not only driving out the landlords and capitalists—that we accomplished with comparative ease—it also means *abolishing the small commodity producers*, and they *cannot be driven out*, or crushed; we *must live in harmony* with them; they can (and must) be remoulded and re-educated only by very prolonged, slow, cautious organizational work.[32]

Here he is particularly referring to the peasantry in the countryside, but also to small traders and other elements of the petty bourgeoisie in the cities. Lenin considered small production to be a prime source of a possible capitalist restoration, and in another famous passage he says:

small production *engenders* capitalism and the bourgeoisie continuously, daily, hourly, spontaneously, and on a mass scale.[33]

Thus Lenin saw the main dangers of a capitalist restoration as coming from the deposed ruling classes and the persistence of petty-bourgeois (small-scale) production. Hence it followed that the main tasks of the dictatorship of the proletariat, in moving socialist society forward to communism and preventing its moving backwards to capitalism, were to crush the resistance of the old landlords and capitalists and to gradually eliminate small-scale production. The class contradictions which the proletariat would have to eliminate before the classless society of communism could come into existence were those with the remnants of the old exploiting classes, on the one hand, and with the peasantry and other petty-bourgeois elements, on the other. And he recognized that two different means would have to be used to resolve these two different types of contradictions—the first antagonistic and the second non-antagonistic.

This is the main thrust of Lenin's view, but it is not the whole of his analysis of socialist society. Lenin also began to deal more extensively with how a new bourgeoisie could begin to develop within socialist society. Thus already in 1918 he says:

Yes, by overthrowing the landowners and bourgeoisie we cleared the way but we did not build the edifice of socialism. On the ground cleared of one bourgeois generation, new generations continually appear in history, as long as the ground gives rise to them, and it does give rise to any number of bourgeois. As for those who look at the victory over the capitalists in the way that the petty proprieters look at it—"they grabbed, let me have a go too"—indeed, every one of them is the source of a new generation of bourgeois.[34]

However, as can be seen, Lenin identifies this danger here almost exclusively with the influence of petty-bourgeois production. And indeed, in the same speech, he makes the flat statement that "in the transition from capitalism to socialism our chief enemy is the petty bourgeoisie, its habits and customs, its economic position."[35] It should be noted that Lenin, as he explicitly says here, is speaking of the transition from capitalism to socialism—that is, from capitalist to socialist ownership—which the Soviet Republic was then undertaking. In other words, he is not here addressing the question of the transition to communism. (And it should also be noted that when Lenin says that the "chief enemy" is the petty bourgeoisie, he does not literally mean that the petty bourgeoisie should be dealt with antagonistically, but that petty production and trading and the petty producer mentality—which is essentially bourgeois—will be the most difficult obstacles to overcome.)

A year later, Lenin referred specifically to "the new bourgeoisie which have arisen in our country." As part of the source for this, Lenin speaks of the fact that "the bourgeoisie are emerging...from among our Soviet government employees"—many of whom were actually bourgeois intellectuals trained in the old society. But he goes on to say that "only a very few can emerge from their ranks" and that the new bourgeoisie is mainly emerging "from the ranks of the peasants and handicraftsmen...."[36]

At the same time Lenin also began to put forward in some writings that the struggle to reach communism, the abolition of classes, would be long and arduous. For instance, in his important article, "A Great Beginning," he stresses:

Clearly, in order to abolish classes completely, it is not enough to overthrow the exploiters, the landowners and capitalists, not enough to abolish *their* rights of ownership; it is necessary also to abolish *all* private ownership of the means of production, it is necessary to abolish the distinction between town and country, as well as the distinction between manual workers and brain workers. This requires a very long period of time.[37]

Here, clearly, Lenin is saying that the period of socialism is transitional, that it must constantly be moving forward to communism, and that the dictatorship of the proletariat must not only stamp out the resistance of former exploiters and eliminate the difference between worker and peasant, but must resolve all the contradictions which give rise to classes—with the consequence that the dictatorship of the proletariat will occupy a fairly long historical period.

In this same article Lenin is also concerned with another aspect of the transitional nature of socialism, and the fact that it is a battleground between the communism which is struggling to develop and the capitalism which resists elimination. In particular, Lenin calls attention to certain "shoots" of the future communist society which were already developing in the first early stages of socialism in the Soviet Republic. In particular these were the "communist subbotniks" (communist Saturdays), in which workers contributed voluntary labor to advance socialist construction in the society overall—not on the basis of being lured with bonuses or forced with guns, nor because they wanted to see their particular unit prosper or profit, but because in fact the workers were in power and were remaking society in their own interests and these "subbotnik" workers in particular were guided and inspired by the communist outlook and the vision of the historic mission of achieving communism.

On the basis of their conscious determination to maintain the rule of the working class and transform all of society, the most class conscious workers, in putting in such unpaid days of labor, began to work, as Lenin said, not for "their 'close' kith and kin, but...[for] their 'distant' kith and kin—i.e.,...[for] society as a whole...''[38] And Lenin correctly summed up that this was a fragile but very important shoot of the future communist society, a sprout of the future production relations (as well as superstructure, in particular ideology) that would be established throughout society.

In this essay Lenin, on the basis of the limited practice of proletarian dictatorship up to that time, began to point to several important aspects of this dictatorship which were later developed much more fully by Mao Tsetung, on the basis of a much more extended and deepened historical experience of the dictatorship of the proletariat. In particular, Lenin pointed to the fact that the task of this dictatorship, of abolishing classes and arriving at communism, will require a long and complex struggle, involving the use of many different means and taking many forms, in order to do away with the underlying contradictions that give rise to classes (notably the contradiction between mental and manual labor).

But at the same time, in Lenin there is only a hint of the view, which was later to be developed by Mao, that throughout this transitional period of socialism there remain antagonistic classes and the antagonistic struggle between the proletariat and the bourgeoisie.

Stalin

This was an understanding which Mao forged on the basis of summing up the historical experience of the dictatorship of the proletariat in the Soviet Union, in China, and in other socialist countries. But before turning directly to Mao's development of the theory and practice of revolution in this most crucial sphere, it is important to make an assessment of the role of Stalin, particularly on this question of upholding and carrying out the dictatorship of the proletariat.

It was Stalin who led the Communist Party of the Soviet Union (CPSU) and through it the masses of working people in the Soviet Union in maintaining the rule of the working class and building socialism for 30 years. And, while providing leadership to such a momentous task under extremely difficult conditions and without any prior historical experience is a truly great contribution of Stalin, it is also true that in this process Stalin made mistakes, some of them quite serious. Therefore a correct summation of not only Stalin's contributions but also his errors, specifically around the touchstone question of the dictatorship of the proletariat, is very important.

In *The Foundations of Leninism,* written just after Lenin's death in 1924, Stalin summed up the basic principles of Lenin's contributions to Marxism, including as one of the main points the theory of the dictatorship of the proletariat. Stalin correctly presented the question of the transition to communist society as one of struggle, a protracted battle both against the remnants of the ruling classes of the old society and against the influences of the petty producers and their outlook—and one which required the transformation of the thinking not only of the peasantry, not only of all the petty-bourgeois elements, but also of the masses of workers, including the factory workers. This struggle, Stalin showed, was part of the basic task of the dictatorship of the proletariat.

And Stalin continued to uphold these principles in leading the working class in carrying out very acute and complicated struggle against class enemies both within and outside the Party. In particular, he led the struggles which defeated Trotsky, Bukharin, and other, especially leading, people in the Party whose lines would in one way or another have wrecked socialism and brought back capitalism to the Soviet Union. (These struggles have been outlined in chapter 3, "Political Economy, Economic Policy and Socialist Construction.")

This was a most important part of Stalin's leadership in carrying out the actual transformation of the ownership system in the complex conditions of the Soviet Union. The transformation of ownership included not only the replacement of capitalist relations by socialist ones but also the advance, through various stages of collectivization, from feudal survivals on a large scale in the countryside to socialist forms of ownership. But after the socialist transformation of ownership had been basically completed, in the mid and late '30s in particular, Stalin drew conclusions which were seriously wrong concerning the nature of Soviet society and the contradictions that characterized it (for background on this see chapters 3 and 4, on political economy and philosophy, respectively).

These errors are exemplified, for example, in the following quotations from Stalin's report, "On the Draft Constitution of the U.S.S.R.," delivered in 1936:

Thus the complete victory of the socialist system in all spheres of the national economy is now a fact.

And what does this mean?

It means that the exploitation of man by man has been abolished, eliminated...Thus all the exploiting classes have now been eliminated.[39]

Stalin goes on to say that there still remain the working class, the peasant class and the intelligentsia, but that "the dividing lines between the working class and the peasantry, and between these classes and the intelligentsia, are being obliterated...," that "the economic contradictions between these social groups is declining, are becoming obliterated," and that "the political contradictions between them are also declining and becoming obliterated."[40] This analysis leads Stalin to say, in his report to the 18th Party Congress in 1939, that:

The feature that distinguishes Soviet society today from any capitalist society is that it no longer contains antagonistic, hostile classes; that the exploiting classes have been eliminated, while the workers, peasants and intellectuals, who make up Soviet society, live and work in friendly collaboration.[41]

It should be clear, after the historical experience of the Chinese revolution and the theoretical summations of Mao Tsetung, that this is incorrect. Antagonistic classes continue to exist under socialism; what distinguishes socialism from capitalism is not the disappearance of hostile classes, but the fact that the working class is the ruling, rather than the oppressed, class.

But, based on his erroneous analysis in the mid and late '30s, Stalin took the position that the only reason for the continuation of the dictatorship of the proletariat was the Soviet Union's encirclement by imperialist enemies. There were others in the Soviet Party who argued that, since (supposedly) there were no longer antagonistic classes in the Soviet Union, then the state should be done away with. But in answering them, Stalin, sharing their incorrect view on the non-existence of antagonistic classes in the U.S.S.R., says only that their view demonstrated "an underestimation of the strength and significance of the mechanism of the bourgeois states surrounding us and of their espionage organs..."[42] Stalin even drew the conclusion that the Soviet Union could, rather soon, achieve communism itself, but even then the Soviet state would still remain "if the capitalist encirclement is not liquidated..."[43]

Of course it was absolutely correct for Stalin to uphold the dictatorship of the proletariat against those who wanted to liquidate it, and it was also correct to point out that the Soviet state was necessary to protect the gains of socialism against foreign imperialists. But it was one-sided and in this sense incorrect to only point to these factors, and consequently to see the internal struggles and contradictions within Soviet society as arising out of the activities of foreign agents and not out of the internal dynamics of socialist society itself.

Thus it can be seen that on the one hand Stalin firmly upheld the need for the dictatorship of the proletariat, but on the other hand, during this period especially, the basis on which he did so was not entirely correct by any means and in fact reflected serious errors in thinking. In a sense, it can be said that Stalin's errors did not lie in seriously deviating from Lenin's specific conclusions on the dictatorship of the proletariat so much as they did in not correctly applying the method of Marxism-Leninism to analyze the new conditions that arose in the Soviet Union with the (basic) socialization of ownership, conditions which Lenin himself (as well as previous Marxists) had no basis to concretely analyze—since they did not exist in their time. When Stalin did deal with these historically new conditions, he drew incorrect conclusions, partly because of the fact that they were in fact new, but also because of a certain amount of metaphysics and mechanical materialism in Stalin's approach. In essence, Stalin one-sidely emphasized the ownership system and failed to deal sufficiently and correctly with the other aspects of the relations of production and the superstructure and their reaction upon the ownership system. This led to his erroneous conclusion (most clearly expressed at the 18th Party Congress in 1939) that once ownership was socialized, antagonistic classes and the *internal basis* for capitalist restoration in the Soviet Union had been eliminated.

Interconnected with these errors is the fact that Stalin did not rely sufficiently on the masses of people and his closely related tendency to rely too much on bureaucratic methods. All of this had the consequence that Stalin made mistakes also with regard to the suppression of counter-revolutionaries. Because of his analysis of socialist society, he thought that all counter-revolutionaries must spring essentially from foreign capitalist sources rather than from the contradictions internal to socialism. Partly for this reason, he failed to rely sufficiently upon the people to ferret out and drag counter-revolutionaries into the light of day, but instead placed almost exclusive reliance upon the Soviet intelligence service. And because he did not correctly understand the source of counter-revolutionary activity (seeing it as coming purely from external sources), he made a number of errors in dealing with it and often wrongly widened the target and confused contradictions among the people with contradictions between the people and the enemy.

During the last part of his life, Stalin did begin to attempt to analyze some of the particular contradictions that still existed under socialism, and in the Soviet Union in particular. This is especially so in one of his last works, *Economic Problems of Socialism in the U.S.S.R.* The strengths and weaknesses of this work have been outlined in an earlier chapter (3) on political economy. For present purposes, what is important to note is that Stalin does here lay stress on the fact that in particular the contradiction between the forces and relations of production continues to exist in socialism and that if not correctly handled this contradiction could become antagonistic and even provide a basis for capitalist elements to arise and drag society backward. But Stalin did not deal with the continuing contradiction between the base and superstructure and still more he did not sum up that the contradictions between the forces and relations of production and the base and superstructure not only constitute the basic contradictions in socialist society but also find expression throughout socialism principally in the existence of the bourgeoisie and the proletariat and the struggle between them, an antagonistic class contradiction.

Chinese Analysis of Stalin

The Chinese Communist Party, under Mao's leadership, seriously and all-sidely addressed the question of Stalin's role in the international communist movement, making an assessment of both his achievements and his mistakes. Thus, after the infamous "secret speech" by Khrushchev at the 20th Party Congress in 1956 and the subsequent anti-Stalin campaign launched by the revisionist usurpers of the CPSU, the analysis of the Communist Party of China summed up crucial lessons at that decisive hour concerning the practice of the dictatorship of the proletariat in the Soviet Union and Stalin's leadership of it.

This summation was in the form of two articles in the *People's Daily* (April 5 and December 29, 1956). Although the revisionists in China did succeed in getting some of their line into these articles (especially the first) and they do contain some positions that are questionable or downright wrong (for example on Yugoslavia), overall these articles defend Stalin and clearly uphold the dictatorship of the proletariat. The first article, "On the Historical Experience of the Dictatorship of the Proletariat," emphasizes that contradictions continue to exist under socialism and that the mass line is key to correct communist methods of leadership. The second article, "More on the Historical Experience of the Dictatorship of the Proletariat," is longer and discusses many topics, but its main thrust is to stress that although Stalin made errors, he was a great revolutionary, whose achievements rather than his mistakes were the primary aspect in summing him up, and to attack those who were using the criticism of Stalin to try to liquidate the dictatorship of the proletariat. It is clear that this attack is aimed not only at Khrushchev but also his revisionist counterparts in China who were bent on doing exactly that.[44]

This is also clear from another of Mao's writings from the same year, "On the Ten Major Relationships," where he says:

In the Soviet Union, those who once extolled Stalin to the skies have now in one swoop consigned him to purgatory. Here in China some people are following their example. It is the opinion of the Central Committee that Stalin's mistakes amounted to only 30 per cent of the whole and his achievements to 70 per cent, and that all things considered Stalin was nonetheless a great Marxist. We wrote "On the Historical Experience of the Dictatorship of the Proletariat" on the basis of this evaluation.[45]

Later that same year, in November 1956, Mao put things even more sharply:

I would like to say a few words about the Twentieth Congress of the Communist Party of the Soviet Union. I think there are two "swords": one is Lenin and the other Stalin. The sword of Stalin has now been discarded by the Russians. Gomulka and some people in Hungary have picked it up to stab at the Soviet Union and oppose so-called Stalinism. The Communist Parties of many European countries are also criticizing the Soviet Union, and their leader is Togliatti. The imperialists also use this sword to slay people with. Dulles, for instance, has brandished it for some time. This sword has not been lent out, it has been thrown out. We Chinese have not thrown it away. First, we protect Stalin, and, second, we at the same time criticize his mistakes, and we have written the article "On the Historical Experience of the Dictatorship of the Proletariat." Unlike some people who have tried to defame and destroy Stalin, we are acting in accordance with objective reality.

As for the sword of Lenin, hasn't it too been discarded to a certain extent by some Soviet leaders? In my view, it has been discarded to a considerable extent. Is the October Revolution still valid? Can it still serve as the example for all countries? Khrushchov's report at the Twentieth Congress of the Communist Party of the Soviet Union says it is.possible to seize state power by the parliamentary road, that is to say, it is no longer necessary for all countries to learn from the October Revolution. Once this gate is opened, by and large Leninism is thrown away.[46]

Mao obviously paid a good deal of attention to making a detailed and objective assessment of Stalin, and as noted, it was especially upon the summation which he reached of both Stalin's achievements and errors that Mao made his own great contributions to the theory and practice of the dictatorship of the proletariat.

Mao of course led the masses of Chinese people in liberating their country from the grip of imperialism, feudalism, and bureaucrat-capitalism, an historic victory which was basically accomplished in 1949. And the particular form of state that was established in China on this basis was what was called the people's democratic dictatorship. This was in fact (if not in name) the specific form which the dictatorship of the proletariat took in China with the founding of the People's Republic, given that the Chinese revolution was initially a *new-democratic* revolution. (See chapter 1, "Revolution in Colonial Countries.") And because of this particular character of the Chinese revolution, the alliance of the working class with the peasantry, which had been a very important question for the proletariat in maintaining its rule and building socialism in the Soviet Union, assumed even greater im-

portance in China, where the overwhelming majority of people
were peasants chained in semi-feudal relations in the old society,
and where the countryside had for a long time been the pivotal
point of the revolution.

But beyond this, part of the character of the new-democratic
revolution was that certain sections of the Chinese capitalists—the
national bourgeoisie—who were also held back by the combination
of feudalism and foreign capital, could be, and had to be, united
with during the first stage of the Chinese revolution, and even (as
far as possible) during the socialist stage, especially during its early years. Under this particular form of the rule of the working class
(the people's democratic dictatorship), it was necessary to restrict
the development of, but at the same time to utilize, the national
bourgeoisie. Mao even insisted as late as 1957 that to the degree
possible it was necessary to handle the contradiction with the national bourgeoisie non-antagonistically—that is, to phase it out as
a class of private owners and at the same time attempt to win over
as much of this class as possible.

And because overall this and other contradictions were correctly
handled at this time, the reactionaries in China, while they seized
on certain grievances of the masses and attempted to turn these into an anti-socialist revolt, were not able to succeed in the same way
and on the same scale as they were in some other socialist countries at that time—most notably Hungary in 1956, where a reactionary rebellion was able to draw in a significant section of the
masses. In fact, when die-hard rightist elements jumped out in
China in 1957 and went head-on against the advances of the
socialist system, the great majority of the masses were politically
aroused in defense of socialism and these counter-revolutionaries
were relatively quickly isolated and beaten back.

By this time, in 1957-58, two very important developments had
taken place in the international communist movement and within
the socialist countries. One was that in China itself by 1956 the
socialist transformation of the ownership system had in the main
been achieved. This meant that in industry, state ownership had
basically been established, while in agriculture a lower form of
socialist ownership dominated the countryside, a collective ownership of the land and the major implements of production by groups
of peasants. And this, of course, was a great advance and a great
victory for the Chinese revolution and for the proletariat
throughout the world.

But at the same time a great reversal was being brought about
in the world's first socialist country. This, of course, was the rise to

power of the revisionists headed by Khrushchev and the beginning of the process of reversing the entire revolution in the USSR and reverting to capitalism. As a necessary and very essential part of carrying out the process of capitalist restoration, Khrushchev launched an attack on the dictatorship of the proletariat. As we have seen already, a central part of this took the form of a virulent and vulgar attack on Stalin, who had led the Soviet working class in consolidating and carrying out its dictatorship. But at the same time, Khrushchev also launched a more general, theoretical attack on the dictatorship of the proletariat, arguing that earlier (under Lenin and in the early part of Stalin's leadership, perhaps) this had been necessary, but now there was no longer a need for it—and therefore the Soviet state could become what he called a "state of the whole people"! The state was no longer to be an instrument of a class, but of everyone, of all classes, in Soviet society. This, which Khrushchev called a "creative development of Marxism," was actually and obviously only the most straight-out form of the ideology of the bourgeoisie, which always tries to make the pretense that the state is above classes precisely in order to exercise dictatorship over the proletariat and disarm it politically.

As noted before, the Chinese Communist Party under Mao's leadership launched a counter-offensive against these attacks on Marxism-Leninism, both by defending the achievements and overall role of Stalin and by defending the basic theory of the dictatorship of the proletariat. But at the same time, as a reflection of the struggle that was going on within the international communist movement as well as the class struggle in China as a whole, there was a sharp two-line struggle raging within the Chinese Communist Party itself. Those within the Party, especially at its top levels, who were bent on taking the capitalist road naturally found support for their position in the revisionism of Khrushchev & Co. and bitterly resisted the efforts of Mao and other revolutionary leaders in the Chinese Communist Party to expose and fight against this revisionism. So at this time Mao was waging fierce struggle against revisionist leaders like Liu Shao-chi and Teng Hsiao-ping, who were arguing that classes and class struggle were dying out in China, and essentially that there was no need for the dictatorship of the proletariat any longer in China either.

As part of this struggle, Mao made two very important statements about the class struggle in China itself at that time, which were also statements having more far-reaching implications about the whole period of socialism in general. In March 1957, in his "Speech at the Chinese Communist Party's National Conference on Propaganda Work," Mao made the important analysis that:

To achieve its [socialism's] ultimate consolidation, it is necessary not only to bring about the socialist industrialization of the country and persevere in the socialist revolution on the economic front, but also to carry on constant and arduous socialist revolutionary struggles and socialist education on the political and ideological fronts... In China the struggle to consolidate the socialist system, the struggle to decide whether socialism or capitalism will prevail, will take a long historical period.[47]

And a month earlier, in "On the Correct Handling of Contradictions Among the People," Mao had stated clearly that:

In China, although socialist transformation has in the main been completed as regards the system of ownership, and although the large-scale, turbulent class struggles of the masses characteristic of times of revolution have in the main come to an end, there are still remnants of the overthrown landlord and comprador classes, there is still a bourgeoisie, and the remoulding of the petty bourgeoisie has only just started. Class struggle is by no means over. The class struggle between the proletariat and the bourgeoisie, the class struggle between the various political forces, and the class struggle between the proletariat and the bourgeoisie in the ideological field will still be protracted and tortuous and at times even very sharp. The proletariat seeks to transform the world according to its own world outlook, and so does the bourgeoisie. In this respect, the question of which will win out, socialism or capitalism, is not really settled yet.[48]

These two passages are of tremendous importance, because in them, for the first time in the history of the international communist movement, it was pointed out explicitly that classes and class struggle continue to exist under socialism, that in particular the class struggle between the proletariat and the bourgeoisie continues even after the socialist transformation of the system of ownership is (in the main) completed, and that this would be true for a long time, with the struggle at times becoming very sharp.

But at the same time, it is obvious that, since proletarian revolutionary practice was still in certain ways only in its beginning stages on this front, and since Mao was only beginning to sum it up theoretically, his understanding of this was also at the beginning stages of development. This is particularly true of his understanding of the nature of classes, and especially of the bourgeoisie, under socialism. But as the class struggle in China sharpened, so did Mao's understanding of that struggle.

And the class struggle did sharpen up in China at this time, particularly around the Great Leap Forward. This was the general movement, of course, out of which the people's communes were born, and the movement in which masses of people, especially the peasants, rose up and did all kinds of things in carrying out socialist revolution and socialist construction that were unheard of and were condemned by reactionary and conservative forces both inside and outside the Party.

The Great Leap Forward has been discussed in previous chapters, and what was said there will not be recapitulated here. But one aspect of this period should be mentioned and highlighted here, and that is the subject of pay differentials. While Mao recognized that wage scales, with people with differing skills and differing productivity being paid different rates, were an aspect of bourgeois right, and hence inevitable during the socialist period, he also recognized that the task of the dictatorship of the proletariat was to *restrict* bourgeois right and, as part of this, to continually restrict these differences in what people received. But in the period of the 1950s, much to Mao's displeasure, such pay-rate differentials had actually been expanded, particularly with regard to Party leaders and full-time Party officials, with large income gaps being created between various levels of officials, and between officials and the masses.

As part of the fight against this—and the revisionist line and policies in general—during this period Mao supported and struggled to get published an article by Chang Chun-chiao, one of those now villified in China as a member of the "gang of four," which attacked the ideology of bourgeois right. The article pointed out that many so-called communists were acting like misers totaling up their cash registers. They were treating themselves like commodities, and if they put in an extra hour working for the revolution they wanted overtime pay for it. And Mao succeeded, during the Great Leap Forward, in leading a fight which cut back on some of this.

Through the experience of the mass revolutionary upsurge of the Great Leap Forward, Mao began to see more clearly the nature of the class struggle and the contradictions in socialist society itself and to develop his basic line and theory of continuing the revolution under the conditions in which socialism had been basically established—that is, the socialist political system, the dictatorship of the proletariat, had been established and the socialist transformation of ownership had in the main been carried out.

This understanding of Mao's had made a qualitative leap by 1962. It was in August and September of that year at the 10th

Plenary Session of the 8th Central Committee of the Chinese Communist Party that Mao put forward what came to be known as the
basic line of the CCP for the historical period of socialism:

> Socialist society covers a considerably long historical period. In the
> historical period of socialism, there are still classes, class contradictions
> and class struggle, there is the struggle between the socialist road and the
> capitalist road, and there is the danger of capitalist restoration. We must
> recognize the protracted and complex nature of this struggle. We must
> heighten our vigilance. We must conduct socialist education. We must
> correctly understand and handle class contradictions and class struggle,
> distinguish the contradictions between ourselves and the enemy from
> those among the people and handle them correctly. Otherwise a socialist
> country like ours will turn into its opposite and degenerate, and a
> capitalist restoration will take place. From now on we must remind
> ourselves of this every year, every month and every day so that we can re-
> tain a rather sober understanding of this problem and have a Marxist-
> Leninist line.[49]

The analysis which is expressed here is a new development in
Marxist-Leninist theory, an analysis which represents a qualitative advance over anything previously achieved in the international communist movement.

Mao in this quotation mentions that "we must conduct socialist
education," and in 1963, following this up, the Party at Mao's in-
itiation began the Socialist Education Movement, which was
meant to combat revisionism and bourgeois practices and thinking. In many ways this movement was the predecessor of the
Great Proletarian Cultural Revolution. On the one hand it actually
prepared the ground for the Cultural Revolution, and on the other
hand it was a first attempt by Mao to develop new forms and
methods for continuing the revolution under the dictatorship of
the proletariat. It was during these years of the early '60s that the
proletariat, particularly under the leadership of Chiang Ching,
launched a sharp counter-offensive against the revisionists in the
crucial sphere of art and culture (see the preceeding chapter). And
it was during this period that the most deep-rooted and hidden of
the new bourgeois forces in China's socialist society began to feel
their position seriously endangered and hence began to jump out in
earnest in their struggle with the proletariat for the rule of society.

It should also be borne in mind that at the same time the Chinese
Communist Party was conducting a fierce struggle internationally
with Soviet revisionism. It was at this time that open polemics
began between the CCP and the CPSU, with the Chinese Communist Party publishing, among other things, the important

documents "A Proposal Concerning the General Line of the International Communist Movement" (June 1963) and the nine-part "Comment on the Open Letter of the Central Committee of the CPSU" (September 1963-July 1964). In particular, the last of the nine-part "Comment," which is entitled "On Khrushchov's Phoney Communism and Its Historical Lessons for the World," is of special importance because in it can be found in concentrated form the basic understanding which Mao had by this time arrived at concerning the class struggle under socialism. Against the thoroughly revisionist line coming out of the Soviet Union at that time, "On Khrushchov's Phoney Communism" stresses that antagonistic classes and class struggle continue to exist under socialism generally and that therefore the reversion from working class rule to a bourgeois dictatorship and the restoration of capitalism in a socialist country is possible—not only through the armed intervention of the foreign bourgeoisie (as had happened in the Paris Commune and the Hungarian Soviet Republic of 1919 and was attempted in the Russian Soviet Republic right after it was founded), but also when "the state of the dictatorship of the proletariat takes the road of revisionism or the road of 'peaceful evolution' [into capitalism] as a result of the degeneration of the leadership of the Party and the state."[50] This article ends with a series of measures which a socialist country can and should take to prevent the restoration of capitalism.

"On Khrushchov's Phoney Communism" served as a weapon not only in the international struggle between Marxism and revisionism which was raging at the time, but also in the same kind of struggle that was raging sharply within the Chinese Party itself as a concentrated reflection of the class struggle in society as a whole. It is also important because on the one hand it shows the unprecedented level to which the Marxist-Leninist understanding of the dynamics of socialism and the class struggle under the dictatorship of the proletariat was being carried by Mao, while on the other hand it shows that Mao's analysis was still developing and had not reached the new levels which it was to attain in conjunction with the Cultural Revolution.

The pamphlet states that:

In the Soviet Union at present, not only have the new bourgeois elements increased in number as never before, but their social status has fundamentally changed. Before Khrushchov came to power, they did not occupy the ruling positions in Soviet society. Their activities were restricted in many ways and they were subject to attack. But since Khrushchov took over, usurping the leadership of the Party and the state

step by step, the new bourgeois elements have gradually risen to the ruling position in the Party and government and in the economic, cultural
and other departments, and formed a privileged stratum in Soviet
society.[51]

Yet despite its many important insights, still, in its analysis of
classes, and in particular the bourgeoisie, under socialism, this
work is not entirely clear, especially regarding the role and nature
of bourgeois elements inside the Party. Nor, along with this, is it
entirely clear regarding the source and material basis of the
bourgeoisie under socialism—specifically after socialist ownership
has (in the main) been established.

In documenting the existence of bourgeois elements in the
Soviet Union, it lays stress on illegal activities, such as profiteer-
ing, black marketing, illegal appropriation of collective property,
etc. And in enumerating the sources of new bourgeois elements
who carry on these and other anti-socialist activities, it mentions
(in addition to the overthrown exploiters and international
capitalism) "political degenerates" that emerge among the working class and government functionaries and "new bourgeois intellectuals in the cultural and educational institutions and intellectual circles" as well as "new elements of capitalism" that are "constantly and spontaneously generated in the petty-bourgeois at-
mosphere" (referring to the persistence of small-scale production
and trade).[52] But it does not identify the revisionists (capitalist-
roaders) in top leadership of the Party and state—including
economic ministries and institutions—as a social stratum constituting a bourgeois class within socialist society itself and with
its core right in the Communist Party. Nor does it sufficiently
place emphasis on the central question that these revisionists can,
in the areas and departments they control, even under socialism,
seize on and expand the capitalist aspects within socialist production relations themselves—the remaining inequalities, the existence of bourgeois right, etc. within and between economic
units—to transform socialist ownership into a mere outer shell and
in this way convert collective property into private property
(capital) and build up their strength in preparation for an all-out attempt to usurp power and then restore capitalism in society as a
whole.

For this and other reasons "On Khrushchov's Phoney Communism" did not represent the full development of Mao's analysis
of the bourgeoisie and the danger of capitalist restoration in a
socialist country, nor of the means for fighting against it. But dur-

ing this same period, Mao did make a number of very sharp and pointed comments, particularly concerning those in positions of authority in China's socialist society, which show the further direction in which his thought was moving. For instance, it was at this time that he made the remark that "leading cadres who are taking the capitalist road have turned, or are turning, into bourgeois elements sucking the blood of the workers." [53] Putting this more directly in class terms, he also said in 1964 that:

The bureaucrat class on the one hand and the working class together with the poor and lower-middle peasants on the other are two classes sharply antagonistic to each other.[54]

Now what Mao was saying was not that every person that worked in an office, or every official or cadre, was a bureaucrat sucking the blood of the workers and a new bourgeois element. In fact, in the main and in most cases, their relations with the workers and peasants were comradely relations of cooperation. But on the other hand, there existed certain actual inequalities between them. They occupied objectively different positions in the socialist system. The cadres, especially full-time leading officials, did a different type of work than the masses of working people, they occupied a relatively more privileged position, they received a higher rate of pay, they tended to have a different sort of outlook—akin to that of the petty bourgeoisie—and the material conditions of their lives tended to foster and strengthen this different outlook. And it was necessary to wage struggle to keep such people from going over to the capitalist way of doing things and following revisionist leaders at the top in carrying out capitalist methods and taking the capitalist road.

Also at this time, in the summer of 1964, Mao had a series of discussions with his nephew, Mao Yuan-hsin (who was a close follower of Mao Tsetung and, as they now call him, a "sworn follower" and "sworn accomplice" of the so-called "gang of four"—he was arrested and/or apparently killed when the counterrevolutionary coup took place after Mao's death). In this series of discussions Mao raises a very important question:

Are you going to study Marxism-Leninism, or revisionism?
Yuan-hsin: Naturally, I'm studying Marxism-Leninism.
The Chairman: Don't be too sure, who knows what you're studying? Do you know what Marxism-Leninism is?
Yuan-hsin: Marxism-Leninism means that you must carry on the class struggle, that you must carry out revolution.
The Chairman: The basic idea of Marxism-Leninism is that you must

carry out revolution. But what is revolution? Revolution is the proletariat overthrowing the capitalists, the peasants overthrowing the landlords, and then afterwards setting up a workers' and peasants' political power, and moreover continuing to consolidate it. At present, the task of the revolution has not yet been completed; it has not yet been finally determined who, in the end, will overthrow whom. In the Soviet Union, is not Khrushchev in power, is not the bourgeoisie in power? We, too, have cases in which political power is in the grip of the bourgeoisie; there are production brigades, factories, and *hsien* committees, as well as district and provincial committees, in which they have their people, there are deputy heads of public security departments who are their men.[55]

Here, what Mao is saying, of course, is that even though we have the socialist form, and everyone claims to be a Marxist-Leninist, the decisive question is the content, the substance—whether the Marxists and the masses of people are in command and leading society in the direction of communism, or whether the revisionists and a handful of bourgeois elements are in command and leading things in quite another direction, back to capitalism. Of course to take socialism back to capitalism requires a qualitative change. It requires having control not just over this or that area of the economy, this or that part of the superstructure, this or that institution or security agency, but rather it means seizing control of society as a whole and completely transforming it. But Mao is pointing out that even within the socialist system there are pockets—and not insignificant pockets—which fall repeatedly under the sway of those who take up the bourgeois outlook, take to the bourgeois style of life and the bourgeois way of doing things, and who therefore implement bourgeois policies and practices, and basically begin to institute capitalist relations under the signboard of Marxism-Leninism.

So this raises the fundamental question, which Mao insisted (with good reason) had not yet been solved: Who is going to overthrow whom? Even under socialism, Mao was saying, it is necessary for the proletariat to *continue* to overthrow the bourgeoisie. Not in the sense, of course, that the bourgeoisie has supreme power and runs society as a whole, but in the sense that continually and repeatedly the working class has to rise up, mobilize its forces and strike down the revisionists in positions of power, and thus regain control of those parts of society which have been usurped from proletarian control. And, of course, there may be certain parts of society where the working class has not yet, at a certain time, been able to gain real control, so in these areas it may be a question of the proletariat's asserting its power for the first time. This was the situation in China in the case of art before the Cultural Revolution (as seen in the preceeding chapter).

This fundamental question was directly addressed in a central part of the Constitution of the Chinese Communist Party at its 9th and 10th Congresses (in 1969 and 1973):

The basic programme of the Communist Party of China is the *complete overthrow* of the bourgeoisie and all other exploiting classes, the establishment of the dictatorship of the proletariat in place of the dictatorship of the bourgeoisie and the triumph of socialism over capitalism. The ultimate aim of the Party is the realization of communism. [Emphasis added.][56]

And, indicating the great significance of this point, when the revisionists did seize supreme power after Mao's death they of course rewrote the Party Constitution, and on this fundamental point—the basic programme of the Party—they took anything about *overthrowing* out of the Constitution, so that now it merely says that they will "eliminate the bourgeoisie and all other exploiting classes step by step."[57]

Now it might seem at first glance that this change is not all that significant, or even that the new version of the basic programme is more correct. It might seem that the task of overthrowing the bourgeoisie and other exploiting classes has been accomplished and now the task is to eliminate them. But that ignores, or really denies, the all-important fact that so long as the bourgeoisie continues to exist it will not only repeatedly attempt to overthrow the proletariat and restore capitalism, but will succeed, as part of this, in usurping portions of power even in the conditions where the proletariat holds power overall in society. And this becomes all the more an urgent question when it is grasped that the core of the bourgeoisie and the commanders of the reactionary forces in society consist precisely of revisionists in the Communist Party itself, especially at its top levels.

In order to deal with this problem and to continue to consolidate its dictatorship and advance toward communism, the proletariat must not merely suppress the bourgeoisie (and other exploiting class elements) but must continually seize back the portions of power usurped by the bourgeoisie. And this means overthrowing those die-hard revisionists who occupy these positions of power and are determined to take the capitalist road. In other words, eliminating the bourgeoisie means repeatedly *overthrowing* it, by mobilizing the masses to seize back *from below* those portions of power the bourgeoisie repeatedly usurps in socialist society. This is the point Mao was stressing when he insisted (in his conversations with his nephew Mao Yuan-hsin) in 1964 that the question of who will overthrow whom was not settled.

It was at this same time that Mao clearly pinpointed who it was that posed the main danger to the continued advance of socialism to communism, and hence who it was that constituted the main target of the revolution at its present stage. Speaking with reference to the Socialist Education Movement then in progress, Mao said:

The main target of the present movement is those Party persons in power taking the capitalist road.[58]

In other words, the main target was no longer the bourgeoisie in society in general, or outside the Party in particular, but had become Party persons in power taking the capitalist road, or "capitalist-roaders," as they came to be called.

It can be seen that this was another significant advance in the understanding of class struggle under socialism. And this understanding was deepened in the course of the next few years, as the class struggle in China sharpened. For of course, with Mao opening the attack on revisionists in the Party, and making them the main target, the revisionists were going to fight back. They tried in every way possible to block the propagation of these policies by Mao and their adoption by the Party, and where they couldn't do that they tried in all sorts of ways to block their implementation. In particular at that time they did everything they could to sidetrack the Socialist Education Movement and turn it into a fight among the masses.

Cultural Revolution

Things were coming to a head, and they erupted two years later with the Great Proletarian Cultural Revolution. It will not be possible here to recount the history of this unprecedented and earth-shaking revolution and the different events and twists and turns which it involved. The important thing for the purposes of this chapter is the theoretical underpinnings of the Cultural Revolution, how the theory that guided it represented the greatest of Mao's immortal contributions to the science of Marxism-Leninism.

Mao explained in 1967 why this Cultural Revolution was a necessity in the following words:

In the past we waged struggles in rural areas, in factories, in the cultural field, and we carried out the socialist education movement. But all this failed to solve the problem because we did not find a form, a method, to arouse the broad masses to expose our dark aspect openly, in an all-round way and from below.[59]

This statement brings out many things, one of which is that the Cultural Revolution was unprecedented, not only in general or in China, but in the history of socialism. It went against all the "norms" of what socialism was supposed to be, what a communist party is supposed to do, and so on. This, of course, is true only in a superficial sense, because in reality the sole purpose of a communist party is to lead the proletariat in making revolution to achieve communism, and this is what Mao was leading the Communist Party of China to do. But it was something that went against all the traditions and the force of habit that had been built up and had in fact become obstacles under socialism. The force of habit cannot be followed in making revolution, including under socialism. Social habit and tradition has been built up by thousands and thousands of years of class society, and following such tradition will not lead toward classless society.

And, of course, it was unprecedented for the chairman of a communist party to call upon the masses to rise up and strike down powerful persons in the party. But revolution does not work on precedent, and in fact within the Party there were two headquarters. The capitalist-roaders had their own machine and their own headquarters, and this was what was necessary to dislodge them in order to prevent China from being taken down the road to capitalism.

Thus Mao summed up that it was not enough to talk about upholding the leading role of the Party, etc. It was a question of constantly revolutionizing the Party as part of revolutionizing society as a whole. Of course overall the Party had to play its leading role. Even when the Party in China was being shaken to its very roots and ceased to exist in many areas, it never ceased to exist nationally, and Mao had every intention of reconstituting the Party. The Cultural Revolution was also the form for reconstituting and strengthening the Party, and doing it unit by unit, area by area, from the base up, by relying on the mass action of the people. And unless such revolutionization of the Party was carried out, unless the masses were mobilized to recognize, to drag into the light of day, and strike down top leaders of the Party who were trying to turn it into a bourgeois party, and to subject to mass criticism and

Peking University, May 1966: China's first Marxist-Leninist big character poster. With Mao's support, newspapers and radio across the country carried this poster's call to uphold Mao Tsetung Thought and unite around Mao and the Central Committee, "break

down all the various controls and plots of the revisionists," and "wipe out all ghosts and monsters and all Khrushchev-type counter-revolutionary revisionists, and carry the socialist revolution through to the end."

The celebration of the founding of the Honan Province Revolutionary Committee in Chengchow. Mao hailed and gave great importance to these new organs of power of the Great Proletarian Cultural Revolution for defending and continuing the revolution under the dictatorship of the proletariat.

supervision the leading cadres in general, then through the force of habit and the conscious action of revisionist high officials the Party *would* become an instrument of the bourgeoisie and society would be taken "peacefully" down the capitalist road under its leadership.

So Mao summed up this most important point from the historical experience of the dictatorship of the proletariat both in China and internationally, particularly the counter-revolution in the Soviet Union, and began to develop the ways and means of reconstituting and revolutionizing the Party, driving out of its ranks those in authority taking the capitalist road. And, again, the form, the method, that was found was basically *reliance upon the masses*. The Party was in fact reconstituted by bringing the Party leaders and members before the masses to receive their criticism and supervision. In this way, together with guidance from the proletarian headquarters in the Party led by Mao, the Party units on the various levels were reformed and linked together according to democratic centralist organizational principles. As indicated above, such a rectification of the Party was, like the Cultural Revolution as a whole, completely unprecedented. For with regard to the Party, as well as the society as a whole, it was determined that the so-called "normal way" of doing things was not sufficient to root out revisionists and shake the upper levels of the Party, in particular, out of the bureaucratic mold into which they were being increasingly cast. A party in power, Mao summed up, must continue to be the vehicle for leading the proletariat in the continuing class struggle under socialism, but it can also become the vehicle for a bureaucratic stratum to pursue bourgeois interests. Only mobilizing and relying on the masses, under the guidance of a Marxist-Leninist line, could solve this problem. (This is very much related to Mao's analysis of the bourgeoisie in the Party itself—which will be dealt with in detail later.)

Through this Great Proletarian Cultural Revolution further transformations were made not only in the Party but throughout society. Here again, the working class and masses of people, led by Mao and other communist revolutionaries, carried out changes which were unprecedented. Divisions and inequalities were reduced between different strata and sectors of society, including between the country and the city. The people rose up in their hundreds of millions, developing and strengthening not only new economic and social relations and the revolutionization of culture, of people's thinking, etc., but also the different forms of struggle so characteristic of the Cultural Revolution—big-character

posters, public mass criticism of persons in power, the organization of brigades of youth, which came to be called the Red Guards,
and so forth.

Mao warmly supported the struggles and initiatives of the
masses and constantly urged them on to persevere in their revolutionary upsurge. He wrote an open letter to the Red Guards, for instance, saying that their actions

> ...express your wrath against and your denunciation of the landlord
> class, the bourgeoisie, the imperialists, the revisionists and their running
> dogs, all of whom exploit and oppress the workers, peasants, revolu-
> tionary intellectuals and revolutionary parties and groups. They show
> that it is right to rebel against reactionaries. I warmly support you.[60]

To provide leadership and guidance to the masses in this
momentous mass struggle, in August 1966 the "Decision of the
Central Committee of the Chinese Communist Party Concerning
the Great Proletarian Cultural Revolution" was issued. (All quotes
below are from this pamphlet of the same name.)[61] Commonly
known as the "16-Point Decision," this was worked out under
Mao's personal guidance and obviously represented a victory of
his line over fierce opposition on the leading bodies of the CCP.
There are many important points in this decision, and it warrants
the close study of all communists. Some of the points it covers
were brought out in previous chapters. What should be emphasized here are the following:

The "16-Point Decision" highlights the fact that "the outcome
of this great cultural revolution will be determined by whether or
not the Party leadership dares boldly to arouse the masses." The
title of this section expresses what might be called the motto of the
Cultural Revolution: "Put Daring Above Everything Else and
Boldly Arouse the Masses." The article points out in the same vein
in the next section: "In the great proletarian cultural revolution,
the only method is for the masses to liberate themselves, and any
method of doing things in their stead must not be used."

The "Decision" reaffirms that "the main target of the present
movement is those within the Party who are in authority and are
taking the capitalist road." It gives basic guidance on correctly
handling both contradictions among the people and the question of
cadres, as well as the policy towards scientists, technicians and
"ordinary members of working staffs" (i.e., those not in authority).
It talks about the line on education and the armed forces. It emphasizes the real connection between revolution and production:

The great proletarian cultural revolution is a powerful motive force for the development of the social productive forces in our country. Any idea of counterposing the great cultural revolution to the development of production is incorrect.

But, perhaps most importantly for the subject of this chapter, the "16-Point Decision" also talks about the organizations created by the masses:

Many new things have begun to emerge in the great proletarian cultural revolution. The cultural revolutionary groups, committees and other organizational forms created by the masses in many schools and units are something new and of great historic importance.
These cultural revolutionary groups, committees and congresses are excellent new forms of organization whereby the masses educate themselves under the leadership of the Communist Party. They are an excellent bridge to keep our Party in close contact with the masses. They are organs of power of the proletarian cultural revolution.

These groups became, through a process of development in the Cultural Revolution, the Revolutionary Committees which were set up at many different levels of society. These creations of the masses were, of course, hailed by Mao. And just as predictably, the capitalist-roaders who have usurped power for the time being in China have hastened to do away with them on the basic levels of society and to transform them into bourgeois-bureaucratic devices where they have been retained in form.

Through the course of the Cultural Revolution, Mao did not stand still, but continued to both sum up the practice of the revolution up until that time and to map out the strategy and tactics for its further advance. The Cultural Revolution itself went through many twists and turns, during all of which Mao provided guidance in the struggle, but what will be concentrated on here is the overall sweep of the revolution and the *general* theoretical lessons which Mao drew from it.

One of the deepest and most important of these lessons is that it is not enough to conduct struggle against revisionists only "at the top"—that is, only on the leading bodies of the Party and state—or only "from the top down"—that is, deal with revisionists and other counter-revolutionaries by decision of the leading bodies first and then conduct education among the ranks of the Party and the masses about why a particular person was purged, what the issues and questions of line, etc., were. Instead it was necessary, as Mao said, to arouse and lead the broad masses to wage struggle and defeat the class enemies *from below*. And the mass upsurge of the Cultural Revolution was an unprecendented example of exactly this. It represented, on a broad and deep scale, a new form and method, as Mao summed up, for defeating die-hard capitalist-roaders and further revolutionizing society, including the Party.

Mao often stated that the Cultural Revolution was "absolutely necessary and most timely." In speaking at the 1st Plenary Session of the 9th Central Committee of the Chinese Communist Party in April 1969, he gave an important indication of why this was so:

Apparently, we couldn't do without the Great Proletarian Cultural Revolution, for our base was not solid. From my observations, I am afraid that in a fairly large majority of factories—I don't mean all or the overwhelming majority—leadership was not in the hands of real Marxists and the masses of workers. Not that there were no good people in the leadership of the factories. There were. There were good people among the secretaries, deputy secretaries and members of Party committees and among the Party branch secretaries. But they followed that line of Liu Shao-chi's, just resorting to material incentive, putting profit in command, and instead of promoting proletarian politics, handing out bonuses, and so forth . . . But there are indeed bad people in the factories . . . This shows that the revolution is still unfinished.[62]

And it follows, as the last sentences make clear, that the Cultural Revolution, while preventing a revisionist seizure of power and capitalist restoration right then, did not and could not solve this problem once and for all. The revolution must be continued under the dictatorship of the proletariat for a long time—in fact throughout the long transition period of socialism, during the entire course of the dictatorship of the proletariat, until the bourgeoisie and all other exploiting classes are completely extinguished and classes as a whole have been abolished along with the basis for them to arise. And, as Mao insisted, many more mass upsurges, like that of the Cultural Revolution in its first few years, would be necessary in the future in order to accomplish this historic mission, together with the people of the entire world.

And this in turn has to do with the deeper purpose of the Cultural Revolution. In 1967, in the midst of this upsurge, Mao had this to say:

Here I'll ask you a question: Tell me, what is the object of the great proletarian cultural revolution? (Someone answered that it was to struggle against the capitalist roaders in the Party.) The struggle against the capitalist roaders in the Party is the principal task, but not the object. The object is to solve the problem of world outlook and eradicate revisionism. The Center has repeatedly stressed the importance of self-education,

Mao reviewing Red Guards in Tien An Men Square on August 18, 1966, showing his backing for the mighty tide of the Cultural Revolution sweeping the country.

In January 1967, proletarian revolutionaries in Shanghai led the revolutionary masses in overthrowing the old capitalist-roader authorities and seizing power from below. This marked a new phase of the Cultural Revolution. Mao supported this whole-heartedly, deciding to have the rebels' proclamation issued to the whole country. Here a message of greetings and support from Party and state leadership is distributed among the citizens of Shanghai, who respond with jubilation.

because a world outlook cannot be imposed on anyone, and ideological remolding represents external factors acting on internal factors, with the latter playing the primary role. If world outlook is not reformed, then although two thousand capitalist roaders are removed in the current great cultural revolution, four thousand others may appear the next time. We are paying a very high price in the current great cultural revolution. The struggle between the two classes and the two lines cannot be settled in one, two, three or four cultural revolutions, but the results of the current great cultural revolution must be consolidated for at least fifteen years. Two or three cultural revolutions should be carried out every hundred years. So we must keep in mind the uprooting of revisionism and strengthen our capability to resist revisionism at any time.[63]

In the course of the Cultural Revolution, and most especially during the mass upsurge of its first few years, the profound truth that Lenin expressed—that masses of people learn in a few weeks of struggle in a revolutionary period what they could not learn in years of "normal times"—was once again powerfully demonstrated and proved to be of decisive importance not just for the struggle in capitalist society but in socialist society as well. All this has everything to do with the fundamental question of who is to be relied on in advancing society to communism. Reliance, Mao insisted over and over, could only be placed on the broad masses. The dictatorship of the proletariat can only be really that if it is dictatorship exercised by the broad masses themselves, which means mobilizing and arming them with a Marxist-Leninist line to fight against the class enemy—and enabling them to distinguish the correct from the incorrect line and the actual interests of the proletariat from those of the bourgeoisie through the course of their own struggle and the study of Marxism-Leninism to master its basic stand, viewpoint and method.

If any other method is used, Mao summed up, then if revisionists seize leading positions and are able to put the official "stamp of approval" on a counter-revolutionary line—in the guise of Marxism—the masses will be in a passive position politically, and, in the name of adhering to the line of the Party and loyalty to its leadership, they will be led back to the hell of capitalism. In short, the dictatorship of the proletariat must not be treated metaphysically—in a static and absolute way—or it will be lost. Exercising dictatorship over the bourgeoisie, Mao showed, means, and can only mean, *continuing the revolution* under the dictatorship of the proletariat, continuing to wage the class struggle against the bourgeoisie and all exploiting classes through reliance on the broad masses. This does not mean that the kind of mass upsurge characteristic of the first few years of the Cultural Revolution is always necessary and possible. What it does mean is that, through different forms, the masses must be politically mobilized and led to wage the class struggle and that, repeatedly through the socialist period, at certain points in the development of the class struggle such mass upsurges will indeed be "absolutely necessary and most timely."

As noted, Mao stressed many times that the Cultural Revolution which began in 1966 could not be the only one if China was to remain a socialist country. At different times Mao gave somewhat different estimates of how often such a thing would be necessary, and possible, but the important thing, of course, is not the exact timetable, which will be determined by the twists and turns of the class struggle both within the country and internationally, but the fact that such a revolution is necessary repeatedly, again and again, throughout the historical period of socialism. And Mao also indicates above *why* this is so. Of course, the people who are the targets at a particular time, individual capitalist-roaders, may be overthrown and cast down—and certain ones may even be won over. But throughout the period of socialism new individuals (or sometimes the same ones again) will come to the fore as revisionist leaders constituting the core of a new bourgeoisie, and they must be continually overthrown. That is why the real object of the Cultural Revolution, as Mao points out here, is not just to overthrow those capitalist-roaders who have, at that time, entrenched themselves in the party of the proletariat; rather, it must be to remold the world outlook of the masses of people, so that they take up the stand, viewpoint and method of the proletariat, Marxism-Leninism, and thus are increasingly armed to recognize, isolate and strike down revisionists whenever they raise their heads, while at the same time strengthening their mastery of society (and nature) and their ability to win over and remold the majority of intellectuals, cadres, etc.

The same point is stressed again when Mao talks, a year later in 1968, of the victories which have been won through the Cultural Revolution:

We have won great victory. But the defeated class will still struggle. These people are still around and this class still exists. Therefore we cannot speak of final victory. Not even for decades. We must not lose our vigilance. According to the Leninist viewpoint, the final victory of a socialist country not only requires the efforts of the proletariat and the broad masses of the people at home, but also involves the victory of the world revolution and the abolition of the system of exploitation of man by man over the whole globe, upon which all mankind will be emancipated.

Therefore, it is wrong to speak lightly of the final victory of the revolution in our country; it runs counter to Leninism and does not conform to facts.[64]

Here Mao makes clear that final victory cannot be achieved for a long time both because exploiting classes still exist in the world as a whole and because the bourgeoisie still exists in China itself. And, with regard to the second point in particular, Mao is not merely describing a phenomenon—that the bourgeoisie still exists in China—but is emphasizing again a fundamental *objective law of socialist society*: that, as he had summed up several years earlier, socialism is not an end in itself or something which can be fully consolidated as such, but is precisely a long period of transition, all throughout which the bourgeoisie will continue to exist and with it the danger of capitalist restoration; and that the key link in continuing the advance toward communism is class struggle, in unity with the struggle of the proletariat and oppressed people the world over.

At this point in the Cultural Revolution—1968-69—Mao also summed up the need for a change in the form of struggle and gave leadership to this process, building on the achievements and transformations that had been made and carrying them forward, further developing and consolidating them. Mao acted here in accordance with the law that the class struggle does not proceed in a straight line and always at the same level of intensity, but in a wave-like fashion, or in spirals. The 9th Party Congress in 1969 represented the consolidation of the struggle, and the achievements of the Cultural Revolution so far, at a certain stage and laid the basis for carrying forward the struggle and building on these achievements in the next period. But at the same time, Mao warned again that, even though the form of the struggle might change, this did not mean that the struggle was over or that there would not again be a need to overthrow a bourgeois headquarters in the Party. In fact, right after the 9th Congress, Mao stated that such an all-out battle would probably have to be fought within a few years.

And indeed a new bourgeois headquarters did arise within the Party within the next few years, this time led by someone who had been closely associated with the Cultural Revolution. The person, of course, was Lin Piao, who tried to pull off a coup in 1971, including a plot to assassinate Mao, and was killed in a plane crash trying to flee the country after his plan was foiled. Mao had recognized quite early that Lin Piao had treacherous characteristics, even though he had played a generally positive role at an earlier stage of the Chinese revolution, and even though Mao felt it was necessary to unite with Lin during the first stage of the Cultural Revolution in order to knock out the strongly entrenched Rightists associated with Liu Shao-chi.

The defeat of Lin Piao's plots and the smashing of his headquarters, although a great victory for the proletariat, also created new conditions—new contradictions and new problems. Many of the veteran leaders of the Party who, in the face of the mass upsurge of the Cultural Revolution and the determined support for it by Mao and other revolutionary leaders, had to one degree or another been won—or forced—to go along, began to back off and oppose it, using Lin Piao's treachery as a rationalization—or pretext—for their opposition.

In effect, Mao's opponents argued that almost no one was more identified with the Cultural Revolution than Lin, and now that he had shown his true colors, one should suspect everything that he had promoted and been involved in. They covered over the fact that there had been many defects in the way in which Lin had promoted the Cultural Revolution, that by the time of the 9th Congress he had begun to attack many of the achievements and gains of the Cultural Revolution, and that he had argued that revolutionary turmoil was fine for a while (namely for as long as it took for him to get on top), but that the time had come for the masses to quiet down, put their noses to the grindstone and just produce. Those who now saw their chance to attack the Cultural Revolution, of course, tried to ignore this, the rightist thrust of Lin Piao's line, as well as its rightist essence, and instead wanted to portray him as a wild-eyed "ultra-leftist," and by implication to smear the Cultural Revolution as a whole with the same brush.

In the course of this struggle Mao made some extremely important summations, which pushed even further forward the Marxist-Leninist understanding of continuing the revolution under the dictatorship of the proletariat. Thus in late 1974 Mao publicly focused attention on the crucial question:

Why did Lenin speak of exercising dictatorship over the bourgeoisie? It is essential to get this question clear. Lack of clarity on this question will lead to revisionism. This should be made known to the whole nation.[65]

With its publication in February 1975, soon after the end of the 4th National People's Congress, this instruction of Mao's launched the campaign to Study the Theory of the Dictatorship of the Proletariat and Combat and Prevent Revisionism. What Mao was stressing in this quotation, and what was stressed in this campaign, is that it is necessary to understand *why*, for what purpose, the dictatorship of the proletariat is being exercised. It is not enough just to understand that there must *be* a dictatorship of the proletariat—it is necessary to understand what the proletariat must accomplish, and in what direction it must be moving, through its dictatorship.

What this direction is, is clarified in another statement by Mao during the same time:

> Our country at present practices a commodity system, the wage system is unequal, too, as in the eight-grade wage scale, and so forth. Under the dictatorship of the proletariat such things can only be restricted. Therefore, if people like Lin Piao come to power, it will be quite easy for them to rig up the capitalist system. That is why we should do more reading of Marxist-Leninist works.[66]

What Mao is talking about here are the remnants—what Marx called the "birthmarks"—of the old society which exist within the socialist economic base—within socialist production relations themselves. Such things—the commodity system, differences in distribution, etc.—can be generally described as bourgeois right, since they belong to the category of economic relations characterizing the bourgeois epoch and signal that the horizons of these relations have not been entirely crossed (to use Marx's words), although these things operate within a different context under socialism, since the exploitation of wage labor is abolished by socialist production relations. These "birthmarks" are closely linked to the continued existence of what the Chinese often called the "three great differences"—between workers and peasants, town and country, and mental and manual labor.

Mao is calling attention to the fact that, on the one hand, bourgeois right—broadly defined as above—continues to exist throughout the period of socialism and that the dictatorship of the proletariat can only restrict it. This is why capitalist restoration continues to be a very dangerous possibility. But on the other hand, he is emphasizing that the proletariat must precisely *restrict* bourgeois right and that the increasing restriction of bourgeois right, in accordance with the material and ideological conditions at each point, must be carried out throughout the period of socialism. Otherwise, the growth and power of the bourgeoisie will be fostered and it will be strengthened in its attempt to seize power, impose bourgeois dictatorship over the masses and restore capitalism, with its supreme bourgeois right—the right to exploit the proletariat.

What exactly the difference between socialism and old China was and in what ways they were the same was further clarified in something else that Mao said at the same time:

> In a word, China is a socialist country. Before liberation she was much the same as a capitalist country. Even now she practices an eight-grade wage system, distribution according to work and exchange through money, and in all this differs very little from the old society. What is different is that the system of ownership has been changed.[67]

This makes a precise and scientific economic differentiation of capitalism from socialism. The system of ownership has changed. It has become basically socialized. But this does not mean that the relations of production have been *totally* transformed, by any means—and Mao is emphasizing that although there has been an advance, it is only the first step.

Further, there is the question of whether the system of ownership itself has been fully socialized. When agriculture becomes collectivized, as it was in China by the late 1950s, with the land and major implements of production being owned collectively by groups of people who also work the land, this is socialization, but it is not full socialization—this only comes when the land and means of production are collectively owned by the whole of society, through the state, and the peasants are transformed into workers. This step in the socialization of agriculture has never yet been completed in any socialist society. Further, as Chang Chun-chiao shows in an important article not long after the publication of these quotations from Mao, even in commerce and industry, state ownership is not complete. Chang points out:

> However, we must see that with respect to the system of ownership the issue is not yet fully settled. We often say that the issue of ownership "has in the main been settled"; this means that it has not been settled entirely, and also that bourgeois right has not been totally abolished in this realm. The statistics cited above show that private ownership still exists partially in industry, agriculture and commerce, that socialist public ownership does not consist entirely of ownership by the whole people but includes two kinds of ownership, and that ownership by the whole people is still rather weak in agriculture, which is the foundation of the national economy. The disappearance of bourgeois right in the realm of the system of ownership in a socialist society, as conceived by Marx and Lenin, implies the conversion of all the means of production into the common property of the whole of society. Clearly we have not yet reached that stage. Neither in theory nor in practice should we overlook the very arduous

tasks that lie ahead for the dictatorship of the proletariat in this respect.

Moreover, we must see that both ownership by the whole people and collective ownership involve the question of leadership, that is, the question of which class holds the ownership in fact and not just in name.[68]

Second, there is the fact that ownership, while it is the most important and basic aspect of the relations of production, is not the only aspect. There are also two other aspects: (1) the relations among people in the process of production, and (2) the relations of distribution. Both of these, under socialism, continue to be infected, to varying degrees, with bourgeois right. We saw that Marx, in the *Critique of the Gotha Programme*, talks about the bourgeois right which is inherent in the socialist system of distribution according to work, and Mao refers to this in the above quotation as well. Bourgeois right cannot be completely eliminated in this aspect of the relations of production under socialism, but it can and must be continually restricted. That was one reason Lenin hailed the communist *subbotniks*—because they represented an overcoming of bourgeois right in distribution relations in a certain respect. Even the eight-grade wage scale represented a restriction—for there had been many more grades in the wage-scale earlier, in the 1950s—but it could not be viewed as a static thing and the final limit of such restriction.

If bourgeois right is not continually restricted in these aspects of the production relations—in distribution and in relations among people in production, the division of labor—then it will grow, and these aspects, together with the influence of the revisionist line, will react back—in a bourgeois direction—on the ownership system. Chang Chun-chiao sums up these important points as follows:

It is perfectly correct for people to give full weight to the decisive role of the system of ownership in the relations of production. But it is incorrect to give no weight to whether the issue of ownership has been resolved merely in form or in actual fact, to the reaction upon the system of ownership exerted by the two other aspects of the relations of production—the relations among people and the form of distribution—and to the reaction upon the economic base exerted by the superstructure; these two aspects and the superstructure may play a decisive role under given conditions. Politics is the concentrated expression of economics. Whether the ideological and political line is correct or incorrect, and which class holds the leadership, decides which class owns those factories in actual fact.[69]

A result of these inevitable contradictions under socialism, both within the economic base (the relations of production), and between the base and superstructure, is that a new bourgeoisie is constantly, and likewise inevitably, generated within socialist society. Mao also spoke to this in the following statement:

Lenin said that "small production *engenders* capitalism and the bourgeoisie continuously, daily, hourly, spontaneously, and on a mass scale." They are also engendered among a part of the working class and of the Party membership. Both within the ranks of the proletariat and among the personnel of state and other organs there are people who take to the bourgeois style of life.[70]

In all these areas, as a result of the contradictions in socialism and the continued existence of bourgeois right, there are people who "take to the bourgeois style of life" and thus become the social base for a new bourgeoisie to seize power. But the leading force, the real bourgeois headquarters, is not here under socialism—at least after socialist transformation of ownership has in the main been completed. Rather, it is actually in the communist party of a socialist country, as Mao points out later:

With the socialist revolution they themselves come under fire. At the time of the co-operative transformation of agriculture there were people in the Party who opposed it, and when it comes to criticizing bourgeois right, they resent it. You are making the socialist revolution, and yet don't know where the bourgeoisie is. It is right in the Communist Party—those in power taking the capitalist road. The capitalist-roaders are still on the capitalist road.[71]

When Mao refers here to those who opposed the co-operative transformation, or in other words the socialization, of agriculture, he is referring to those in the Chinese Communist Party who were revolutionaries in the new-democratic stage of China's revolution, but who wanted to bring a halt to the revolution when it came to moving into the socialist stage and, who increasingly came into opposition to the revolution as it advanced in the socialist stage. In other words, they had never really advanced, in actuality, beyond being bourgeois-democrats, never made a radical rupture with bourgeois ideology. This phenomenon of "bourgeois-democrat to capitalist-roader" had to do specifically with a country like China, where the revolution involved a long democratic struggle as the direct prelude to the socialist stage.

But Mao's remarks are much broader, and have application to any socialist society. The socialist revolution, as we have seen, *must* continue to move forward, and as it does so there will be people who think it has gone far enough and do not want to move forward with it. Mao dealt with this same phenomenon in another important statement during his last great battle:

> After the democratic revolution the workers and the poor and lower-middle peasants did not stand still, they want revolution. On the other hand, a number of Party members do not want to go forward; some have moved backward and opposed the revolution. Why? Because they have become high officials and want to protect the interests of the high officials.[72]

In any revolution there will be people who get some benefits from it and a tendency for some of them not to want the revolution to go further lest their benefits are endangered. As Chang Chun-chiao put it:

> They do approve of the dictatorship of the proletariat at a certain stage and within a certain sphere and are pleased with certain victories of the proletariat, because these will bring them some gains; once they have secured their gains, they feel it's time to settle down and feather their cosy nests. As for exercising all-round dictatorship over the bourgeoisie, as for going on after the first step on the 10,000-*li* long march [i.e., continuing the revolution after the seizure of power], sorry, let others do the job; here is my stop and I must get off the bus.[73]

This does not mean that all such people are hopeless reactionaries. Some may be won over through struggle—but there does have to be struggle. Immediately after the statement above, Chang Chun-chiao goes on to say:

> We would like to offer a piece of advice to these comrades: It's dangerous to stop half-way! The bourgeoisie is beckoning to you. Catch up with the ranks and continue to advance![74]

But it is crucial to grasp that those who are not won over form an important part of the social base for the revisionists at the top levels of the Party in their attempts to mobilize support for the usurpation of power from the proletariat and the restoration of capitalism.

As emphasized several times already, it is precisely the top leaders of the Party who take to the capitalist road that constitute the greatest danger to socialism and must be the main target of the revolutionary struggle. It is they who can give support to more privileged strata in society in resisting further transformations that strike at this privilege and who can play upon the negative aspects—the bourgeois thinking and style of life—that tend to arise among these strata on the basis of this privileged position.

Further, it is they who are in a position to coordinate opposition to the advance of socialism throughout the society, who can unite the forces of such opposition around a common line and program, give them leadership and direction and actually mobilize them for an attempt to usurp power. And, of course, it is they who not only act as the commanders of these forces, but can provide the best cover for counter-revolution, since they are leading members of the Party and can capitalize on the respect that the masses have for the Party and its leadership. This is why Mao called attention to the problem that you "don't know where the bourgeoisie is" and to the answer—"It is right in the Communist Party—those in power taking the capitalist road."

The contradictions of socialist society itself—the remaining division of labor, differences in income, the persistence of commodity relations, etc., as well as the continuing influence of bourgeois ideology—provide the basis not only for bourgeois elements to be constantly generated in society generally, but especially for them to repeatedly emerge at the top ranks of the Party *and* for them to mobilize a social base for counter-revolution. This does not mean that all leading people, by mere virtue of their position, are bound to become bourgeois and turn traitor to the revolution. But it does mean that some of them—in particular those who take to the bourgeois style of life and adopt a revisionist ideological and political line—will do so and that they will then have both the necessity and the opportunity to rally a following for an attempt to seize power and restore capitalism. This, as Mao summed up, will continue to be the case all throughout socialism, until the contradictions of socialism are resolved through the revolutionary advance to communism.

Class struggle not only does not and cannot die out under socialism, but it remains the motive force in socialist society, and the outcome of that struggle—and specifically the struggle between the proletariat and the bourgeoisie—determines whether society continues the advance toward communism or (in the short run) is dragged back to capitalism. As Mao summed up near the end of his life:

In 1949 it was pointed out that the principal contradiction within the country was one between the proletariat and the bourgeoisie. Thirteen years later the question of class struggle was reiterated, and mention was also made of the fact that the situation began to turn for the better. What is the Great Cultural Revolution for? To wage class struggle. Liu Shao-chi advocated the theory of the dying out of class struggle, but he himself never ceased to wage class struggle. He wanted to protect his bunch of renegades and sworn followers. Lin Piao wanted to overthrow the proletariat and attempted a coup. Did class struggle die out?[75]

In concluding this chapter, it is necessary to return in a concentrated way to several points which were touched on earlier and which relate to some major questions that are raised either in the form of uncertainty about, disagreement with or outright attacks on Mao's basic line on classes and class struggle in socialist society and the theory of continuing the revolution under the dictatorship of the proletariat.

Bourgeoisie in the Party

Is it correct to say, as Mao explicitly did, that in socialist society, even after the socialization of ownership is (in the main) completed, the bourgeoisie, as a class, actually continues to exist? Further, is it correct to say, as Mao did, that the bourgeoisie is right in the Communist Party, and how should this be understood?

First, it must be said that the bourgeoisie does not, of course, exist under socialism (after socialization of ownership) as a class which privately owns the means of production, as it does under capitalism. By applying such a definition to socialist society we would have to conclude that indeed the bourgeoisie does not and could not exist after the ownership system is transformed. But by using this same method—which, it must be said, is scholastic and not Marxist—we would also have to conclude that the proletariat no longer exists once ownership is socialized, because strictly speaking the proletariat is by definition a class deprived of all ownership of the means of production. And if this were the case, then naturally it would be ridiculous to talk of the dictatorship of the (non-existent) proletariat—over the (non-existent) bourgeoisie. Thus it can be seen what trouble such a method would quickly land us in—and how it would, in fact, land us in unity with Khrushchev-type revisionists with their theory of "the state of the whole people."

Dialectics teaches that when the struggle of opposites undergoes a qualitative change, each of the opposites undergoes a change as well. This applies to the struggle between the proletariat and the bourgeoisie. When the proletariat seizes power from the bourgeoisie, establishes its own dictatorship over the bourgeoisie and socializes ownership, the proletariat changes from the ruled to the ruling class and from being deprived of all ownership of the means of production to being the collective owner of the means of production. But this does not yet eliminate the proletariat; it continues to exist until communism is achieved with the abolition of all class distinctions and the basis for them. So, therefore, must its opposite—the bourgeoisie—exist, for there can be no proletariat without a bourgeoisie, and vice versa. The bourgeoisie in fact has undergone a change in the opposite direction: it has changed from the ruling to the ruled class and from a class privately owning the means of production to a class deprived of ownership of the means of production.

Let's examine more closely this question of the bourgeoisie under socialism. Here what is meant by the bourgeoisie is the social class and not the specific individuals who make it up at any given time—and, in particular, not merely or even mainly the capitalists who are overthrown when the dictatorship of the proletariat is first established (which, for clarity, can be referred to as the old bourgeoisie). There are instances under socialism where private ownership and the exploitation of wage labor actually take place literally and in the same basic form as under capitalism. It is not generally possible for the proletariat, after seizing power, to expropriate all bourgeois enterprises at once. Further, even after the old bourgeoisie has been stripped entirely of its former capital, there are cases of illegal operations—underground privately-owned sweatshops, etc. Of much more significance, however, is the relationship between the leadership and the masses within the socialist economy. If a Marxist-Leninist line is in command, then these relations, while they involve inequality, will be ones of comradely cooperation—and such inequality will be narrowed step by step. But if a revisionist line is in command, then this turns the relationship between the leaders and those under their leadership into one of oppression, and one that is tantamount to exploitation.

If the leading cadres do not take part in productive labor together with the masses; if at the same time they increase their income relative to that of the masses, through expanded wage differentials, bonuses proportional to wages, etc.; if they put profit in command; and if they monopolize management and planning while the masses of manual workers are effectively barred from these things rather than being politically activated to take part in them and supervise the leading cadres; then in essence how much different is the relationship between the leading cadres and the working masses from that between the workers and the capitalists in capitalist society? And with regard to the high officials who exercise leadership in the ministries, in finance and trade, etc., if they follow the same revisionist line, divorce themselves from the masses and productive labor and effectively monopolize control

The worker-militia of the Peking No. 1 Machine Tool Plant who came to the defense of Mao's line in suppressing the counter-revolutionary incident in Tien An Men Square instigated by Teng Hsiao-ping in April of 1976.

1968 Chinese demonstration of a million people in support of the Black people's struggle in the U.S. Mao stressed that the advance of the dictatorship of the proletariat in China was inseparably linked to the development of the world proletarian revolution. In his famous statement "In Support of the Afro-American Struggle Against Violent Repression," Mao called it "a new clarion call to all the exploited and oppressed people of the United States to fight against the barbarous rule of the monopoly capitalist class."

over these spheres, how much different are they than executives of big corporations and banks in the capitalist countries?

There is, of course, one basic difference—the difference between socialism and capitalism. That is, these revisionists, even if they control important spheres of the economy, portions of political power, etc., under socialism, are still operating in the conditions where overall in society the working class has power and the economy is socialist. This is all the more reason that they must make an all-out attempt to seize power so that they can pursue their bourgeois interests more fully through the restoration of capitalism. This is precisely the process that occurred in the Soviet Union.

This does not, however, change the fact that even under socialism such capitalist-roaders will not only emerge but, where and to the extent that they are able to implement a revisionist line, they will be able to transform the relations between themselves and those under their leadership, especially the basic working masses, into ones of oppression and, in essence, exploitation. These revisionists will seek out each other, form factions and blocs and their own apparatuses within the Party and state (as well as outside them) in opposition to the principles of the Party, its basic line and the revolutionary leadership and forces within it, as well as to the masses of people. Thus it can be seen that they actually constitute a bourgeoisie—or the heart of it—within socialist society and with the characteristics of that class under the conditions of socialism.

In sum: in socialist society, power over the means of production as well as over distribution is concentrated as the power of political leadership. Where and to the extent that power is not in the hands of Marxists and the masses but instead in those of revisionists, then bourgeois relations of production can be generated even within the collective form, although the full development of bourgeois production relations requires the seizure of power by the bourgeoisie—led by the capitalist-roaders in top Party leadership—and the restoration of capitalism in society as a whole.

From this it can be seen why it is not only correct but necessary to speak of the bourgeoisie within the Party—the capitalist-roaders in positions of authority. For the great majority of people who hold leading posts in the economy at the various levels are precisely Party members—it is they who (especially after the first few years of socialism) are overwhelmingly the managers, planners, heads of ministries, etc. And those of them who take to the capitalist road and implement a revisionist line become indeed a bourgeoisie within the Party—with its power deriving from their leading positions. This stems from both the contradictions of the socialist system, as summarized earlier, and from the fact that the socialist economy is a collective one, with the state the decisive economic unit and the Party the leading force.

This does not mean, of course, that the entire bourgeoisie resides in the Communist Party. There are many bourgeois elements generated (or remaining from the old society) outside the Party. But the core of the bourgeoisie under socialism, those in the position to exercise the greatest power with regard to the economy as well as in the superstructure of politics, culture, etc., are obviously those in the Party itself, especially at the highest levels. Analyzing all this, and developing the means for struggling against these forces as the main target of the class struggle against the bourgeoisie, is truly a great contribution of Mao Tsetung.

Mao's Treatment of National Bourgeoisie

This is closely connected with another question that is raised: why did Mao say, as late as 1957, that in China the contradiction with the national bourgeoisie should still be handled non-antagonistically? Was this correct, and if so why—why did it not constitute capitulation to the bourgeoisie?

During the first, the new-democratic, stage of the Chinese revolution, the Chinese Communist Party under Mao's leadership had in fact correctly applied the policy of uniting with the national bourgeoisie—as opposed to the big, comprador bourgeoisie—as far as possible (for more on this see chapter 1). Following that, when the revolution entered the socialist stage with the founding of the People's Republic, Mao recognized that it was correct to attempt to win over or at least neutralize as much of the national bourgeoisie as possible, on the basis of its patriotism and desire to see China overcome the legacy of imperialism and feudalism, which objectively could only be accomplished by taking the socialist road. At the same time, Mao also recognized and pointed out that this policy toward the national bourgeoisie could only be accomplished through struggle and that it might not be possible to handle this contradiction non-antagonistically—that the national bourgeoisie, or sections of it, might very well resist this and pose themselves directly in opposition to the advance of socialism.[76]

And, in fact, there were two tendencies among the national bourgeoisie: some sections of it joined with the camp of counter-revolution in attacking socialism, while others among the national bourgeoisie did basically go along with—or at least did not openly oppose—the socialist system. Mao's policy on this was quite correct—it isolated the enemies, including those among the national bourgeoisie who resisted the policies of the Party and attacked socialism, and it enabled the broad masses to unite more firmly to defeat these enemies.

In fact, especially after the socialist transformation of ownership (accomplished in the main by 1956), the national bourgeoisie in China—which was being phased out of any remaining private ownership—posed much less of a problem than the newly emerging bourgeois elements and in particular the revisionists in the Party itself, especially at its top levels. For with this transformation, the conditions arose whereby the core and most important elements of the bourgeoisie would be within the Party rather than outside it, as explained earlier.

Under these circumstances, while the national bourgeoisie—or remnants of it—still had a dual character and could possibly be united with, this was not the case with die-hard capitalist roaders in authority in the Party and state, who posed the greatest danger to and must be the main target of the proletariat in exercising its dictatorship and carrying forward the class struggle. Again, analyzing these changes in class relations and developing the means and methods for continuing the revolution in these conditions was a truly great contribution of Mao Tsetung.

The All-Round Dictatorship of the Proletariat

Finally, in summing up Mao's contributions with regard to the decisive question of the dictatorship of the proletariat, and in particular the theory of continuing the revolution under this dictatorship, it is ironically appropriate to let his enemies—specifically those in China who have carried out the (temporary) reversal there—point to these contributions. In an attempt to discredit the so-called "gang of four" (and above all Mao), the revisionists in power in China now, in attacking Chang Chun-chiao's article *On Exercising All-Round Dictatorship Over the Bourgeoisie*, cite a statement by a "sworn follower of the 'gang of four' ":

Lenin merely said that only those who recognized the dictatorship of the proletariat were Marxists. When Chang Chun-chiao was writing this article, he found Lenin's words inadequate in driving home his point. As he sees it, only those who recognize the all-round dictatorship of the proletariat over the bourgeoisie are genuine Marxists. But he didn't put it in the article lest others, on reading it, should think Lenin was not a Marxist.[77]

The four top revolutionary leaders overthrown in the October 1976 revisionist coup in China: above, Chiang Ching (left) and Chang Chun-chiao at the rostrum at the Tenth National Congress of the Communist Party of China.

Wang Hung-wen.   Yao Wen-yuan.

To this the revolutionaries in China must plead "innocent as charged." For what is being emphasized in the statement just above—which is clearly expressing Mao's line and not just Chang Chun-chiao's, and which just as clearly is in unity with and a development of Lenin's line—is that, on the one hand, the dictatorship of the proletariat is the necessary product of the development of society through the class struggle at a certain stage, but that on the other hand, it is not an end in itself—it is a transition to communism. It is at the heart of Mao's line on this question that if the dictatorship of the proletariat is treated as an end in itself then it will be turned into its opposite—into a dictatorship by a revisionist new bourgeoisie over the proletariat and masses of people.

As Chang Chun-chiao explained in his article, exercising all-around dictatorship over the bourgeoisie means exercising this dictatorship in all spheres of society and throughout the entire transition period of socialism. To limit this dictatorship to certain spheres can only mean strengthening the bourgeoisie and its attempts to usurp power, and to stop part way along the transition can only mean that the bourgeoisie will overthrow the proletariat and restore capitalism. To curtail this dictatorship and to bring a halt to it at a certain point is, as pointed out earlier, precisely the program of revisionists, especially those in high office, who have secured certain gains from the victories of the revolution and the exercise of the proletarian dictatorship in certain spheres and for a certain time. They do not want the revolution to advance further and the dictatorship of the proletariat to be exercised in an all-around and long-term way, for then the gains they have secured, the privileged position and control over parts of the economy and the superstructure they hold, as well as the basis for these privileges, will be struck at and ultimately eliminated.

Chang Chun-chiao's article explains this point by referring to a famous statement by Marx (cited earlier) where he says that the dictatorship of the proletariat must be "the necessary transit point to the *abolition of class distinctions generally*, to the abolition of all the relations of production on which they rest, to the abolition of all the social relations that correspond to these relations of production, to the revolutionising of all the ideas that result from these social relations."[Emphasis in original][78] Chang Chun-chiao goes on to give the following explanation, wildly attacked by the revisionists in China:

In all the four cases, Marx means all. Not a part, a greater part, or even the greatest part, but all! This is nothing surprising, for only by emancipating all mankind can the proletariat achieve its own final emancipation. The only way to attain this goal is to exercise all-round dictatorship over the bourgeoisie and carry the continued revolution under the dictatorship of the proletariat through to the end, until the above-mentioned four **alls** are banished from the earth so that it will be impossible for the bourgeoisie and all other exploiting classes to exist or for new ones to arise; we definitely must not call a halt along the path of the **transition**. In our view, only those who understand the matter this way can be deemed to have grasped the essence of Marx's teaching on the state.[79]

Again, "our view" clearly refers not just to that of Chang Chunchiao but to that of Mao and the other revolutionaries in China. For it is the essential point of Mao's development of Marxist-Leninist theory on the state and the dictatorship of the proletariat in particular that exercising this dictatorship and carrying through the transition to communism can mean nothing less than *continuing the revolution under the dictatorship of the proletariat.* This theory is the product of Mao's application of materialist dialectics to socialist society, and it represents the greatest of his immortal contributions to Marxism-Leninism and the revolutionary struggle of the international proletariat. Despite what the revisionists in China may say or do, and regardless of the slanders and distortions of reactionaries and opportunists in general, this theory will continue to stand as a powerful weapon of the proletariat and sooner or later will be wielded by it in every country in carrying through the transition to the historic goal of communism.

Conclusion

MAO TSETUNG,
THE GREATEST REVOLUTIONARY
OF OUR TIME

Introduction

The previous chapters have examined Mao Tsetung's contribu-
tions in a number of specific fields, including his greatest contribu-
tion—the application of materialist dialectics to socialist society
and the development on that basis of the understanding that
classes and class struggle exist all during the period of socialism
and the theory of continuing the revolution under the dictatorship
of the proletariat throughout this long transition period, in unity
with the international working class and the oppressed people in
every country, until the final victory of communism world-wide. It
has been shown how Mao enriched and developed Marxism-Lenin-
ism in this most important area, as well as in other spheres, in
dialectical unity with leading the revolutionary struggle of hun-
dreds of millions in China to unprecedented heights, and provided
in this way inspiration and illumination to revolutionary people in
the millions on every part of the globe.

From this it can be seen that Mao Tsetung's contributions are in-
deed immortal. In concluding this book, however, it is important
and necessary to look at Mao's role as a revolutionary leader in a
concentrated and at the same time sweeping way, in order to more
thoroughly comprehend why and how it is that he was the greatest
revolutionary of our time—and in fact since the time of Lenin.

Mao: A Great Helmsman in Uncharted Waters

That Mao led the struggle in China which finally resulted in the founding of the People's Republic, and that this radically altered China and the whole world, are facts which are widely known and which few would (dare) deny. It is also a fact that throughout the course of that protracted struggle, through its different stages and many twists and turns, Mao had to wage a fierce battle against opportunists within the Chinese Communist Party who, from the right and the "left," opposed and attacked the correct line of advance which he led in forging. But beyond that, and as a decisive part of forging the correct line and providing that leadership, Mao also had to challenge and break with the force of convention within the international communist movement. Specifically, he had to fight against the mechanical approach which insisted that the revolution in China must proceed in exactly the same way as that in Russia—that the bourgeoisie must be treated as an enemy rather than as a possible ally, that the cities must be seized first, not the countryside, etc. Had Mao not done so, and instead gone along with those who demanded that the Chinese revolution be a clone of the Soviet revolution, and who invoked the Soviet experience and the Soviet Union itself as a holy icon and treated their association with it as capital, then it can be safely said that there would have been no Chinese revolution and no People's Republic of China.

It can be further said that it is even a law of revolution, and especially of proletarian revolution, that in order for it to succeed in any particular country, the struggle in that country and those leading it will have to depart from and even oppose certain particular conceptions or previous practices which have come to be invested with the stature of "established norms" in the revolutionary movement. This is an expression of materialist dialectics, because every revolution arises out of the concrete conditions (contradictions) in the country (and the world) at the time it is occurring, and every new revolution inevitably involves new questions, new contradictions to be resolved. It is the basic principles and the method of Marxism-Leninism that must be applied as a universal guide for revolution—but these, too, are constantly being developed and enriched, just because scientific knowledge is constantly being deepened, including the Marxist-Leninist comprehension of reality in the fullest sense, and because reality is constantly undergoing change, which requires and calls forth the continuous deepening of this knowledge.

Stalin spoke to this question, specifically in reference to the Russian revolution and Lenin's leadership of it. He pointed out that prior to the experience of the Russian revolution, Marxists generally held the view that a parliamentary democratic republic would be the form in which the working class would rule—a view strengthened by Engels' statements to that effect. Further, Stalin noted, Engels and Marx had concluded that socialism could not be built in one country—and this too was the accepted rule and had acquired the force of dogma among many Marxists. What would have happened, Stalin asks, if Lenin had been bound by the letter of Marxism at that time rather than basing himself on the spirit, applying the method, of Marxism? The Soviets would not have been developed as the form through which the working class actually exercised its rule in that country—in fact there would have been no Soviet Union and no socialism built in that country. It goes without saying what a loss that would have been to the international proletariat.[1]

And so it was in China. Mao consistently argued that the universal principles of Marxism-Leninism must be applied and that the basic lessons of the October Revolution in Russia must be upheld—especially the need for the seizure of power through the armed struggle of the masses and for the leadership of the revolutionary party of the proletariat—but that these had to find different application in China's concrete conditions than they had in Russia. It was on this basis that, as a part of leading the struggle for the seizure of nationwide political power in China, Mao made some of his important contributions which enriched and developed Marxism-Leninism—especially in the formulation of the strategy of new-democratic revolution leading to socialism, in military line and thought, and in laying the basic groundwork of his development of Marxist philosophy.

If it was true that Mao could not have led the Chinese revolution in its first stage to victory, to the founding of the People's Republic, without challenging and breaking with powerful conventions in the international communist movement, this was still more the case with regard to leading the continuing advance in the socialist stage, after the People's Republic was founded. This was so in such fields as political economy and culture and it was most definitely the case with the greatest of Mao's immortal contributions—the basic line and theory of continuing the revolution under the dictatorship of the proletariat.

Most of all, is it conceivable that there would have been a Great Proletarian Cultural Revolution in China, an unprecedented event in the whole history of the communist movement and the socialist countries, if Mao had been unwilling to "go against the tide" (to use his own phrase)—not only to fly into the face of bitter opposition within the Chinese Communist Party itself, most especially from powerful (and, among many, popular) leaders of the Party, but also to depart from, even "violate," certain "norms" which some have come to regard as sacred, in such basic areas as the functioning of the Party and its relation to the masses? Of course, this is inconceivable. And it is also inconceivable that without such "violations"—that is to say, developments—of Marxism-Leninism, the Chinese revolution would have scaled the heights it did, not only making new breakthroughs on the path to communism but inspiring, teaching and impelling revolutionaries all over the world toward the same goal.

Cultural Revolution: A Burst of Light Through the Clouds

After the treachery of Khrushchev & Co. in the Soviet Union and the terrible loss for the proletariat there, it was above all revolutionary China under the leadership of Mao Tsetung that ever more brilliantly shone as a beacon light for revolutionary people on every continent. This was a time when, reaching its high point in the 1960s and early 1970s, there was a tremendous storm of revolutionary struggle in nearly every country in the world, and most especially in the countries of Asia, Africa and Latin America. But, with the reversal in the Soviet Union and Khrushchev's blatant repudiation of revolution and revision of Marxism-Leninism, there was also a great deal of confusion and even demoralization, including within the ranks of revolutionaries. Piercing through the clouds that Khrushchev's betrayal had cast, the experience in China and the Thought of Mao Tsetung not only gave heart to millions of revolutionaries outside China but also kindled their determination to take up and wield the science of Marxism-Leninism.

Was this only or mainly because the Chinese Communist Party defended the revolutionary experience and the achievements of the Soviet people in building socialism before Khrushchev & Co.'s coup? Because they defended Stalin and the dictatorship of the proletariat in the Soviet Union against the completely unprincipled slanders and denunciations of the Soviet revisionists? Because they insisted that the basic lessons of the October Revolution and the banner of its leader, Lenin, were still valid and must be upheld? No, all of these are very important and part of the reason, but they were not the main thing. Mainly it was because

Mao led the revolutionaries in China in summing up the positive experience and the shortcomings and mistakes of the building of socialism in the Soviet Union and the leadership of Stalin, as well as the positive and negative experience of China and other socialist countries in general, and on that basis made a further leap in carrying forward the struggle for communism. This found theoretical expression in the basic line of continuing the revolution under the dictatorship of the proletariat. But most of all, it was the concrete practice of hundreds of millions of Chinese people under the guidance of this theory, particularly in the Great Proletarian Cultural Revolution, which once again (to use a phrase of Mao's) spread the salvos of Marxism-Leninism and the basic truth that it is right to rebel against reaction and that the future of communism will be brought about by the proletariat and masses of people, spread this to every corner of the world.

But, with the revisionist coup in China itself in October 1976, Mao's great contributions and his overall leadership in the Chinese revolution have come under new attacks. First of all, the revisionists in power in China now are intensifying their offensive against Mao's line, concentrating their fire especially on the Cultural Revolution and its achievements, which represent not just the greatest advance of the Chinese people's revolutionary struggle but also the highest pinnacle yet reached by the international proletariat. While these renegades and impostors still must make some pretense to uphold Mao—at least as a national symbol—they are more and more openly trampling on the basic things he stood for and fought for—and indeed they must do so in order to carry out their suppression of the revolutionary masses and the restoration of capitalism.

Reversal in China and New Attacks on Mao

At the same time others, on the basis of the triumph of the counter-revolution in China, have launched assaults on Mao and Mao Tsetung Thought. Some of these even include attacks on Mao's line and leadership in the new-democratic revolution, as well as in the socialist revolution.

But, again, the most concentrated offensive has been against Mao's basic line on classes and class struggle under socialism and the theory of continuing the revolution under the dictatorship of the proletariat—the most important of his immortal contributions. All this has led to a great deal of turmoil in the international communist movement. Some out of opportunism, and others out of ignorance, have taken the position that since there has been a reversal in China, since the revisionists have after all seized power and are rapidly taking China down the capitalist road, then Mao's basic line on classes and class struggle under socialism and the theory of continuing the revolution under the dictatorship of the proletariat, as well as the practice of the Chinese people under the guidance of that basic line and theory, especially in the Cultural Revolution, must have been wrong. Or else, it is said, Mao and the other revolutionary leaders in China must have made serious mistakes, even if their overall line was correct.

As for the first point, what was said in Chapter 4 (on philosophy) speaks directly to that:

This kind of thinking is nothing but empiricism and relativism. The correctness of this theory does not depend on the immediate results in any particular situation; it has been verified in practice, in the mass struggle of hundreds of millions of Chinese people, and will be further verified in the future in the revolutionary struggle not only in China but in every country. (See p. 187.)

And as for the question of mistakes by the revolutionaries, certainly they must have made some—no one can avoid that—but that is not the main thing to focus on in analyzing the setback in China. While it is correct to investigate and sum up what errors they may have made, an all-sided analysis of the reversal, applying the stand, viewpoint and method of Marxism-Leninism, makes clear that any such mistakes were not the cause of this setback.[2]

In this regard, as a general and basic point, it is important to really grasp that the class struggle under socialism is exactly that—and that the bourgeoisie in a socialist country may, especially at certain times, have a more favorable situation than the proletariat, owing to the development of the internal contradictions in that country at that point as well as the international situation and the interrelationship between these two at the time. Here a statement by Mao himself is most relevant:

In social struggle, the forces representing the advanced class sometimes suffer defeat not because their ideas are incorrect but because, in the balance of forces engaged in struggle, they are not as powerful for the time being as the forces of reaction; they are therefore temporarily defeated, but they are bound to triumph sooner or later.[3]

The point here is not to analyze the struggle in China leading up to the revisionist coup of October 1976 and the causes and lessons of this reversal (as suggested in this chapter's introduction, a beginning and basic analysis of that has been made elsewhere, while there remains the task of building on and deepening that analysis—by applying *Marxism-Leninism, Mao Tsetung Thought*). Rather, what is involved here is the analysis—and criticism—of the approach which says that, since the revolution was reversed, then the revolutionaries must be at fault—or must at least have made serious errors. As indicated earlier, this method is pragmatic—and therefore opposed to Marxism. But, beyond that, such an approach also fails to understand the actual process of the Chinese revolution and the development of the contradictions which characterized it, especially after the founding of the People's Republic, and therefore fails to correctly evaluate the tremendous achievements of the Chinese revolution as well as the tremendous obstacles it was up against as it advanced into the socialist stage.

Magnificent Achievements of the Chinese Revolution, Contributions of Mao Tsetung

As pointed out many times in this book, the Chinese revolution first proceeded—and could not but proceed—through the stage of new democracy before it was possible to advance to socialism. In this respect it was in some important ways not that much different from many other anti-imperialist liberation movements that have swept the countries of Asia, Africa and Latin America since World War 2. And the experience of such struggles has clearly demonstrated that, while it is an arduous task to win victory in the struggle to end colonial (including neo-colonial) domination, it is far more difficult to carry forward the struggle to establish socialism and then continue to advance in the socialist stage—and this has proven true even where the struggle has been led by a communist party. The greatest number of these movements, even where led by organizations declaring themselves Marxist-Leninist, have not gone forward to socialism and therefore have, in fact, failed to even win complete liberation from imperialism, falling instead under the sway of one or another imperialist power—generally one or the other superpower in this period.

Viewed in this light, it was indeed a tremendous achievement of the Chinese revolution even to make the initial transition from new democracy to socialism. And this was not accomplished without monumental struggle—including within the Chinese Communist Party.

Many in the Party, including a number of top leaders, did not really want to carry forward the revolution, after the country had been liberated. As Mao said many times, they were keen on over-throwing imperialism, feudalism and bureaucrat-capitalism but not so keen on carrying out the struggle against the bourgeoisie to bring about the victory of socialism over capitalism and the con-tinued advance toward communism. And the further the revolu-tion progressed in the socialist stage, the more that many of these leading people came into opposition to it—not all of them, but not only a few either. What is involved here is the phenomenon of bour-geois-democrats turning into capitalist-roaders in the socialist stage, which has been dealt with several times in this book.

To really grasp this it is necessary to understand that in a coun-try like old China only the proletariat and the Communist Party could lead the democratic, anti-imperialist struggle in a thorough-going way, and therefore many, many people joined the Commu-nist Party—and even became leaders of it—who genuinely desired to carry out the democratic anti-imperialist struggle but were not yet communists in their outlook. Is it not a widespread phenomen-on in many countries today which have not yet been liberated from imperialism, and have not completed the democratic revolution, that there are many people who claim to be socialists, even com-munists, who are in fact nothing of the kind and are (at most) bourgeois revolutionaries? And such was also a widespread phenomenon in old China, including within the Chinese Com-munist Party, which proved to be the only force capable of leading the struggle to victory, even in its first stage. Now many of these people did keep pace with the advance of the revolution and did develop ideologically into communists. But many did not. As noted, the deeper the revolution went in the socialist stage, the more that these latter types came into opposition to it and the more desperate they became in their attempts to turn it around. And for those who became high officials this pull was even greater.

The article in the Revolutionary Communist Party's central organ *Revolution* (December 1978) on Chou En-lai, who may be considered the premier model of such people, explained this phenomenon:

For these bourgeois democrats, the goal of the revolution was to overcome China's backwardness and the near total strangulation of China by the im-perialist powers. Therefore they turned to "socialism"—public owner-ship—as the most efficient and rapid means of turning China into a highly industrialized, modern country. As the socialist revolution advanced, they fought for this development to take place along increasingly bourgeois lines—which under China's conditions would not only restore capitalism but would also lead to bringing China back under the domination of one imperialist power or another.[4]

Further, as also noted several times in this book, such people and the revisionists in general had a social base which, under certain conditions, could be mobilized as a powerful force for the overthrow of the proletarian dictatorship—as indeed happened in 1976.

Again, in light of all this, it can be seen what a remarkable accomplishment it was of the Chinese masses and their revolutionary leadership, headed by Mao Tsetung, that they not only forged their way forward through tremendous struggle to take China on the socialist road, not only broke new ground in building socialism, as for example in the Great Leap Forward, but continued the revolution under the dictatorship of the proletariat, carried out an unprecedented mass revolutionary movement under socialism, the Great Proletarian Cultural Revolution, and through it beat back attempts at capitalist restoration for a whole decade—advancing the struggle of the international proletariat to new heights! All this is not to say that the reversal in China was inevitable, that the proletariat in China was bound to lose power or any other such metaphysical and fatalistic nonsense. But it does provide the correct framework for understanding the actual struggle—the continuing class struggle—that went on in China and both the unprecedented achievements of the Chinese revolution as well as the causes and lessons of its setback. And it provides the correct framework for appreciating the magnificent contributions of Mao Tsetung.

Mao's Role, the Role of Leaders

In discussing, and defending, the contributions of Mao Tsetung and the role of people like Mao, and Lenin, in the revolutionary movement, the point is not to say that great leaders never make mistakes or that history is made by heroes and not by the masses. The greatest revolutionary leaders put on their shoes one at a time like the rest of us, and they eat and empty their bowels in the same way as us.

And it is indeed the masses who make ' way it is the masses who "make" great r the revolutionary struggle of the masses leaders. Leaders do, in turn, play a very si lutionary struggle of the masses. But they role, and in the final analysis can only be o they continue to stand with, and in a fu midst of, the struggle of the masses and o

ward. In this era, in the most thoroughgoing and radical revolution in history, the proletarian revolution, that means they play their role by applying the science of Marxism-Leninism to both learn from and guide the struggle. In this way they can and do exert a tremendous influence on the movement of the masses and can actually accelerate the inevitable revolutionary process (just as they can retard it through errors and deviations from Marxism-Leninism).

Further, just as great leaders carry on the normal functions of life in the same way as the rest of us, they also carry out their role as revolutionary leaders in the same basic way as all class conscious fighters make their contributions to the revolutionary movement. That is, they do it precisely by mastering and applying, in a living way, the science of Marxism-Leninism in light of the concrete conditions in their country and the whole world. The point, then, in focusing on the role and great contributions of such leaders is precisely to learn from them and to strengthen the resolve, and ability, of all in the revolutionary movement to master and apply the science of Marxism-Leninism and to make in this way *their* greatest contribution to the historic mission of the proletariat.

As part of this, it must be understood that no one, no matter how great his or her contribution, can be free of mistakes. This, of course, applies to great leaders as well, including Mao. And, while upholding and learning from their tremendous contributions, and defending these, as well as the overall role of such leaders, from attacks, it is also necessary to understand and learn from their errors.

Specifically with regard to Mao, there seems to have been a tendency to project too much of the experience of the Chinese revolution onto a world scale. In particular, this took the form of giving a national character or aspect to the struggle in (at least some) capitalist, even imperialist, countries in the conditions where such could not play a progressive role. This is an extremely complicated question, and no thorough analysis of it can be made, or even seriously attempted, here. Rather, a few points will be very briefly touched on in relation to this.

All this is closely linked to the question of how to handle the con-iction between defending a socialist country on the one hand the other hand carrying forward the revolutionary struggle ountries, where the proletariat is not yet in power, espe-alist and imperialist countries which do not pose the o the socialist country at a particular time (or are not

part of the bloc of countries headed by that imperialist state which
does then pose such a danger). This becomes especially complex
and acute in the situation where war between imperialist states is
approaching and the likelihood of an attack on a socialist state,
particularly by one imperialist bloc, is seriously increasing.

Specifically, in the last few years of Mao's life it became clear
that the Soviet Union posed the main danger to China and,
especially in the context of sharpening developments toward inter-
imperialist war with the U.S., the Soviet Union was very likely to
launch a large-scale attack, perhaps even an all-out invasion,
against China. In these circumstances, it was quite correct for
China to make certain diplomatic and other moves to keep the
Soviet Union off balance and to make use of contradictions between the imperialist blocs to put China in the strongest position
to deal with a Soviet attack on it. But this has to be done in a way
which, overall, contributes to the development of the revolutionary
struggle worldwide and does not call on revolutionaries in the
countries of the U.S. bloc to give up the struggle for revolution, or
reduce "revolution" to the struggle against the Soviet Union.

On the whole, Mao and the proletarian headquarters he led in the
Chinese Communist Party (with the so-called "gang of four" its active leading core) dealt with this contradiction in a revolutionary
way. They fought for the line of supporting genuine revolutionary
struggles in other countries, including those in the U.S. bloc, while
at the same time warning the revolutionaries not to allow the
Soviet Union to infiltrate and use these struggles and convert
them into their own appendage in the name of "support." Further,
they fought vigorously against the line of depending on—in fact
capitulating to—U.S. imperialism and selling out the revolution in
China itself in the name of "modernizing" the country and
"strengthening its defense" against the Soviet Union. But, on the
other hand, they did adopt the analysis that the Soviet Union was
the most dangerous source of war, on a basis similar to that on
which Stalin declared the fascist imperialist states the main enemy
in the late 1930s. And this included, at least to some degree, the
promotion of the line of "national struggle" against the Soviet
Union in the capitalist and imperialist states that, together with
the U.S., make up its imperialist bloc (just as Stalin had similarly
done, even in the 1930s, with regard to those countries opposed to
the fascist imperialist bloc). As our Party stated at its 1978
memorial meetings for Mao Tsetung:

This error to a certain extent strengthened the revisionists in China, who

were—and are—arguing that the Soviet danger to China justifies and requires writing off revolution at home and abroad. This sort of error by
revolutionaries has, as pointed out, existed in the international communist movement, going back to the 1930s, and there is a real need to more
thoroughly sum it up and criticize it in order to avoid it in the future.[5]

At the same time our Party has consistently, and correctly,
drawn a clear line of demarcation between the line and policies of
Mao and his revolutionary comrades on the one hand and on the
other hand those revisionist traitors who have usurped power
through smashing the proletarian headquarters in the Chinese
Communist Party after Mao's death and are rapidly restoring
capitalism and capitulating to imperialism. And it should be
pointed out that Mao and his comrades in China learned from and
corrected some of the mistakes of Stalin in regard to the contradiction between defending a socialist country and carrying forward
the world struggle. They did not take the stand of subordinating
everything to the defense of China. Most especially, they recognized the importance of leading the class struggle of the proletariat
against the bourgeoisie in China and continuing the revolution
under socialism, and the dialectical relationship of this to a correct
line for defending China. But, more than that, they also continued,
as stated, to fight for support for genuine revolutionary struggles
in other countries, even those within the U.S. bloc.[6]

Thus, despite certain disagreements our Party has with Mao and
his comrades over some questions relating to the international
situation, the character of the revolutionary struggle in various
imperialist countries and the relation of this to the defense of
China, overall we recognize their fundamentally revolutionary role
in this regard and the need to learn from both their contributions
to internationalism and certain errors they made in this sphere.
Most fundamental, however, as stated, is the need to more
thoroughly sum up not merely the line and actions of Mao and the
other revolutionaries in China, but the history of the international
communist movement around this question, its positive and
negative lessons, going back 40 years and more. This is especially
crucial in light of the present international situation, which is
marked not only by the reversal in China and a great deal of turmoil in the international communist movement, but by the deepening crisis of imperialism and the growing developments toward
both world war and revolution.

Learn from Mao Tsetung, Carry Forward
the Cause of Communism

Throughout this book, as well as in this concluding chapter in particular, an analysis has been made of some of Mao Tsetung's most important contributions, including the greatest of these—the theory of continuing the revolution under the dictatorship of the proletariat. These contributions not only tower over any mistakes Mao made, they also mark him as the greatest revolutionary of our time. But the point has further been made that the purpose in examining the contributions of a great revolutionary leader like Mao is precisely to learn from them and carry forward more powerfully the revolutionary cause for which such people have provided such tremendous inspiration and guidance.

Looking, then, at Mao's role and contributions overall and in a sweeping way, what stands out most, what in fact underlies all of these contributions, what is most basic to learn from, is the thoroughness with which Mao applied the stand, viewpoint and method of Marxism-Leninism, and in particular his application of dialectics in opposition to metaphysics. The ceaseless emergence and resolution of contradictions, as against all notions of absoluteness and stagnation—this Mao grasped as the driving force in the development of all things, in nature, society and thought, and this understanding runs like a crimson path through Mao's writings and actions. Can anyone even conceive of Mao as a stodgy bureaucrat or "comfortable veteran" resting on his laurels!

More specifically, Mao's application of dialectics in understanding and explaining the relationship between matter and consciousness, and the constant transformation of the one into the other, led him to correctly place tremendous emphasis on the role of the superstructure, on politics and consciousness, in guiding revolutionary practice to transform the world, including the people. This is a fundamental point which has great importance both in preparing for and carrying out the seizure of power and in continuing the revolution after political power has been gained. It is a point which Lenin also gave great emphasis to in leading the revolutionary movement, as expressed in his monumental work, *What Is To Be Done?* as well as elsewhere. But it is also a point which, in a real sense, Mao revived and further developed in leading the Chinese people and the international proletariat to their highest ascent yet. Whether in class struggle, including warfare, in production or scientific experiment, Mao stressed reliance on the conscious activism of the masses, not on technology and technique; on people, not on things.

For this, of course, the bourgeoisie, the revisionists and opportunists of all stripes, inside and outside China, have labelled Mao an "idealist." But Mao was a thoroughgoing materialist. He based himself on the real world, *in its process of constant motion and change, from the lower to the higher, on the inevitable supersession of the old by the new*. Because of this he never lost sight of but continually grasped the link between the present and the future, the existence of elements of the future within the present, and the fact that the struggle of the proletariat world-wide against the bourgeoisie and all reaction would eventually and inexorably, despite twists and turns and temporary reversals and setbacks, advance mankind to the historic goal of communism, which itself would be propelled forward by contradiction and struggle.

It is this which infuses all of Mao's work and his truly immortal contributions. And it is this, most of all, which all those who are determined to make revolution and aspire to the lofty goal of communism can and must learn from Mao Tsetung.

Mao's line was opposed at every turn by leading Party members who stepped forward to defend the bourgeoisie and fight the revolution, and especially by those who joined the revolution during its democratic stage but opposed continuing it under socialism. However, because Mao relied on the masses and their revolutionary aspirations, and guided them again and again in resolute struggle for their own liberation and the liberation of all mankind, he was able to lead the masses of people in successful battles against these reactionaries. In this way the proletariat's transformation of society advanced to greater heights. In this 1963 photo Mao (in middle) is surrounded by some long-time Party leaders, including three internationally prominent capitalist-roaders: 1) President Liu Shao-chi, 2) Party Secretary Teng Hsiao-ping, and 3) Premier Chou En-lai.

Congolese youth upholding Mao Tsetung.

Above, British riot police fail to break up 1967 protest in Hong Kong as demonstrators hold on tightly to their Red Books, *Quotations from Chairman Mao Tsetung*. Below, scene from January 29, 1979 march outside the White House in Washington, D.C. where 500 revolutionaries led by the Revolutionary Communist Party, USA unfurled Mao's banner in the face of the visit by Chinese revisionist traitor Teng Hsiao-ping.

Above, workers in Guinea study Mao's works at a construction site. Below, Japanese workers on top of a street barricade hold up a red banner inscribed with the words "Long Live Mao Tsetung Thought."

FOOTNOTES

Footnotes are numbered by chapters, and the following abbreviations are used:

MESW   *Marx Engels Selected Works*, Progress Publishers, Moscow, 1973.

MESC   *Marx and Engels Selected Correspondence*, Progress Publishers, Moscow, 1975.

SW   *Selected Works of Mao Tsetung*, Foreign Languages Press. Vol. 1-4, 1975; Vol. 5, 1977.

SMW   Mao Tsetung's *Selected Military Writings*, Foreign Languages Press, Peking, 1967.

HCPSU   *History of the Communist Party of the Soviet Union (Bolsheviks)*, International Publishers, New York, 1939.

CW   Refers to the 45-volume Moscow edition of *Collected Works of Lenin*.

FLP   Foreign Languages Press, Peking.

Chapter 1

1.   Karl Marx and Frederick Engels, *Manifesto of the Communist Party*, Foreign Languages Press, Peking, 1977, pp. 34, 37, 38.
2.   Marx, "Revolution in China and in Europe," *Karl Marx and Frederick Engels on Colonialism*, Progress Publishers, Moscow, 1968, pp. 21-22.
3.   Engels, "Engels to K. Kautsky," *ibid.*, p. 347.
4.   "Engels to K. Kautsky," 1882, *ibid.*, p. 342.
5.   Lenin, "Socialism and War," *Lenin on War and Peace, Three Articles*, FLP, Peking, 1970, pp. 16, 17.
6.   Lenin, "Under a False Flag," *Collected Works (CW)*, Moscow, p. 148.
7.   *Ibid.*, pp. 140, 142.
8.   Lenin, "A Caricature of Marxism," *CW*, Vol. 23, p. 38.
9.   Lenin, "Two Tactics of Social-Democracy in the Democratic Revolution," *CW*, Vol. 9, pp. 86, 87.
10. For the remarks by Lenin summarized in the paragraph above, see Lenin, *CW*, Vol. 9, p. 100.
11. Stalin, "The October Revolution and the National Question," *Works*, Vol. 4, Foreign Languages Publishing House, Moscow, 1953, pp. 169-170.
12. Lenin, "The Second Congress of the Communist International," see "Report of the Commission on the National and the Colonial Questions," *CW*, Vol. 31, p. 244.
13. *Ibid.*
14. Mao Tsetung, *"Report of an Investigation of the Peasant Movement in Hunan," Selected Works of Mao Tsetung (SW)*, Vol. 1 FLP, Peking, 1975, pp. 23-24.
15. *Ibid.*, pp. 28, 29.
16. Mao Tsetung, "Analysis of the Classes in Chinese Society," *SW*, Vol. 1, p. 13.
17. *Ibid.*, p. 19.
18. Mao Tsetung, "Introducing *The Communist*," *SW*, Vol. 2, pp. 286-287.
19. While this set the Chinese Party on the correct road, it was not until years later, in the early 1940s, during a stage of stalemate in the war, that the opportunist lines were thoroughly uprooted in an all-round way. Mao led a rectification campaign within the Party which was aimed against subjectivism and in particular tendencies that failed to combine the universal truths of Marxism-Leninism with the concrete practice of the Chinese revolution. This campaign considerably raised the Marxist-Leninist level of the Party as a whole.
20. Mao Tsetung, "On Coalition Government," *SW*, Vol. 3, p. 252.
21. *Ibid.*, pp. 252-253.
22. See, for example, "The Situation and Tasks in the Anti-Japanese War after the Fall of Shanghai and Taiyuan," written November, 1937, in Mao Tsetung's *Selected Works*, Vol. 2, pp. 61-70.
23. Mao Tsetung, "The Identity of Interests between the Soviet Union and All Mankind," *SW*, Vol. 2, pp. 277, 279.
24. Mao Tsetung, "The Chinese Revolution and the Chinese Communist Party," *SW*, Vol. 2, pp. 326-327.
25. *Ibid.*, pp. 330-331.
26. Mao Tsetung, "On New Democracy," *SW*, Vol. 2, p. 344.
27. See, in particular, "On New Democracy," *ibid.*, p. 349.

28. *Ibid.,* p. 350.
29. *Ibid.,* p. 351.
30. Mao Tsetung, "Some Points in Appraisal of the Present International Situation," *SW,* Vol. 4, p. 87.
31. *Ibid.,* p. 88.
32. Mao Tsetung, "On the People's Democratic Dictatorship," *SW,* Vol. 4, p. 413.
33. Mao Tsetung, "On Practice," *SW,* Vol. 1, pp. 306-307.
34. Mao Tsetung, "On Contradiction," *SW,* Vol. 1, pp. 325-326.
35. *Peking Review,* Number 38, 1976, September 13, 1976, pp. 7-8.
36. *Apologists of Neo-Colonialism,* FLP, Peking, 1963, p. 2.
37. *Ibid.,* pp. 6-7.
38. *Ibid.,* pp. 8, 9-10, 31-32.
39. *Ibid.,* p. 27.
40. *Ibid.,* p. 35.

Chapter 2

1. Mao Tsetung, "Problems of Strategy in China's Revolutionary War," *Selected Military Writings (SMW),* FLP, Peking, 1967, p. 78.
2. Mao Tsetung, "Problems of War and Strategy," *SMW,* p. 269.
3. *Ibid.*
4. Mao Tsetung, "Why Is It That Red Political Power Can Exist In China?", *SMW,* p. 13.
5. *Ibid.*
6. *Mao Tsetung, "A Single Spark Can Start A Prairie Fire," SMW,* p. 75.
7. *Ibid.,* p. 66.
8. *Ibid.,* p. 72.
9. Mao Tsetung, "Problems of Strategy in China's Revolutionary War, *SMW,* p. 111.
10. *Ibid.,* p. 90.
11. *Ibid.,* p. 92.
12. *Ibid.,* p. 89.
13. *Ibid.,* p. 99.
14. *Ibid.,* p. 185.
15. *Ibid.*
16. *Ibid.,* p. 113.
17. *Ibid.,* p. 118.
18. *Ibid.,* p. 121.
19. *Ibid.,* p. 140.
20. *Ibid.,* p. 142.
21. Mao Tsetung, "Problems of Strategy in Guerrilla War Against Japan," *SMW,* p. 153.
22. *Ibid.,* p. 158.
23. *Ibid.,* p. 159.
24. *Ibid.,* p. 181.
25. *Ibid.,* p. 182.
26. Mao Tsetung, "On Protracted War," *SMW,* p. 187.
27. *Ibid.,* p. 201.
28. *Ibid.,* p. 204.
29. *Ibid.,* p. 206.
30. *Ibid.,* p. 255.
31. *Ibid.,* pp. 255-256.

32. *Ibid.*, p. 263.
33. Mao Tsetung, "Concentrate a Superior Force to Destroy the Enemy Forces One by One," *SMW*, p. 317.
34. Mao Tsetung, "On Protracted War," *SMW*, p. 189.
35. *Ibid.*, pp. 217-218.
36. *Ibid.*, p. 228.
37. *Ibid.*, p. 259.
38. *Ibid.*, pp. 233-234.
39. *Ibid.*, p. 239.
40. Mao Tsetung, "Problems of War and Strategy," *SMW*, pp. 269-270.
41. Mao Tsetung, "The Turning Point in World War II," *SMW*, p. 299.
42. Mao Tsetung, "On Coalition Government," *SMW*, p. 301.
43. *Ibid.*, p. 302.
44. *Ibid.*, p. 304.
45. *Ibid.*, p. 306.
46. Mao Tsetung, "Concentrate a Superior Force to Destroy the Enemy Forces One by One," *SMW*, p. 317.
47. Mao Tsetung, "A Three Months' Summary," *SMW*, p. 321.
48. See Mao Tsetung, "The Concept of Operations for the Northwest War Theatre," *SMW*, p. 327.
49. Mao Tsetung, "Strategy for the Second Year of the War of Liberation," *SMW*, p. 332.
50. Mao Tsetung, "The Present Situation and Our Tasks," *SMW*, p. 348.
51. *Ibid.*, p. 350.
52. Mao Tsetung, "The Concept of Operations for the Peiping-Tientsin Campaign," *SMW*, p. 377.
53. Mao Tsetung, "Our Great Victory in the War to Resist U.S. Aggression and Aid Korea And Our Future Tasks," *SW*, Vol. 5, pp. 116-117.
54. *Ibid.*, p. 118.
55. Mao Tsetung, "U.S. Imperialism is a Paper Tiger," *SW*, Vol. 5, p. 309.
56. See Mao Tsetung, "All Reactionaries are Paper Tigers," *SW*, Vol. 5, p. 517.
57. See "Speech at the Group Leaders' Forum of the Enlarged Meeting of the Military Affairs Committee," *Chairman Mao Talks to the People*, edited by Stuart Schram, Pantheon Books, New York, 1974, p. 128.
58. Mao Tsetung, "Reading Notes on the Soviet Text *Political Economy*," *A Critique of Soviet Economics*, translated by Moss Roberts, Monthly Review Press, New York, 1977, pp. 91-92.
59. *Ibid.*, p. 91.
60. Mao Tsetung, "Summing Up After the Ninth Congress," Schram, pp. 285-286.

Chapter 3

1. Mao Tsetung, "Reading Notes on the Soviet Text *Political Economy*," *Critique of Soviet Economics*, p. 110.
2. *Ibid.*
3. Marx, "Letter to J. Weydemeyer," *Marx Engels Selected Works (MESW)*, Vol. 1, Progress Publishers, Moscow, 1973, p. 528.
4. Marx, "The Class Struggle in France 1848 to 1850," *MESW*, Vol. 1, p. 282.

5. *History of the Communist Party of the Soviet Union*, edited by a Commission of the CPSU(B), International Publishers, New York, 1939, p. 262.
6. *Ibid.*, p. 275.
7. Stalin, *Economic Problems of Socialism in the USSR*, FLP, Peking, 1972, p. 60.
8. *Ibid.*, p. 69.
9. Mao Tsetung, "Concerning *Economic Problems of Socialism in the USSR*" and "Critique of Stalin's *Economic Problems of Socialism in the USSR*," *Critique of Soviet Economics*, pp. 130, 135.
10. Mao Tsetung, "Our Economic Policy," *SW*, Vol. 1, p. 141.
11. Mao Tsetung, "On New Democracy," *SW*, Vol. 2, p. 353.
12. Mao Tsetung, "Spread the Campaigns to Reduce Rent, Increase Production, and Support the Government and Cherish the People in the Base Areas," *SW*, Vol. 3, p. 131.
13. *Ibid.*, p. 133.
14. Mao Tsetung, "Get Organized!", *SW*, Vol. 3, p. 154.
15. *Ibid.*, p. 155.
16. *Ibid.*, p. 156.
17. *Ibid.*
18. Mao Tsetung, "We Must Learn To Do Economic Work," *SW*, Vol. 3, p. 191.
19. *Ibid.*
20. Mao Tsetung, "The Situation and Our Policy After the Victory in the War of Resistance Against Japan," *SW*, Vol. 4, p. 19.
21. *Ibid.*
22. *Ibid.*, p. 20.
23. Mao Tsetung, "On the Policy Concerning Industry and Commerce," *SW*, Vol. 4, p. 203.
24. Mao Tsetung, "Report to the Second Plenary Session of the Seventh Central Committee of the Communist Party of China," *SW*, Vol. 4, p. 365.
25. *Ibid.*, p. 368.
26. *Ibid.*
27. *Ibid.*, p. 367.
28. Mao Tsetung, "Reading Notes," *Critique of Soviet Economics*, p. 40.
29. Mao Tsetung, "Report to the Second Plenary Session of the Seventh Central Committee of the Communist Party of China," *SW*, Vol. 4, p. 369.
30. *Ibid.*
31. Mao Tsetung, "On the People's Democratic Dictatorship," *SW*, Vol. 4, p. 419.
32. *Ibid.*, p. 421.
33. Mao Tsetung, "On the Struggle Against the 'Three Evils' and the 'Five Evils'," *SW*, Vol. 5, p. 65.
34. *Ibid.*
35. *Ibid.*, p. 64.
36. *Ibid.*, p. 69.
37. *Three Major Struggles on China's Philosophical Front*, FLP, Peking, 1976, p. 3.
38. Mao Tsetung, "On the Co-operative Transformation of Agriculture," *SW*, Vol. 5, pp. 201-202.

39. Mao Tsetung, "The Debate On the Co-operative Transformation of Agriculture And The Current Class Struggle," *SW*, Vol. 5, p. 217.

40. Mao Tsetung, "On the Co-operative Transformation of Agriculture," *SW*, Vol. 5, pp. 199-202.

41. Mao Tsetung, "On the Ten Major Relationships," *SW*, Vol. 5, p. 286.

42. *Ibid.*

43. *Ibid.*

44. *Ibid.*, p. 291.

45. *Ibid.*

46. *Ibid.*

47. *Ibid.*, p. 292.

48. *Ibid.*, p. 294.

49. "The Theory of Synthesized Economic Base Must Be Thoroughly Criticized," *Three Major Struggles on China's Philosophical Front*, p. 27.

50. Mao Tsetung, "On the Correct Handling of Contradictions Among the People," *SW*, Vol. 5, p. 409.

51. Mao Tsetung, "Speech at the Chinese Communist Party's National Conference on Propaganda Work," *SW*, Vol. 5, p. 434.

52. *Three Major Struggles on China's Philosophical Front*, p. 5.

53. Mao Tsetung, "Speech at the Lushan Conference," Schram, p. 146.

54. Mao Tsetung, quoted in *Report to the Ninth National Congress of the Communist Party of China*, by Lin Piao, FLP, Peking, 1969, pp. 22-23. This report was delivered by Lin Piao but remains Mao's line in opposition to the line of Lin Piao and the report he had attempted to have "delivered" to the Congress.

55. Mao Tsetung, "Reading Notes," *Critique of Soviet Economics*, p. 76.

56. *Ibid.*, p. 79.

57. *Ibid.*, pp. 80-81.

58. *Ibid.*, pp. 111-112.

59. Mao Tsetung, quoted in "The Theory of 'Combine Two Into One' Is A Reactionary Theory For Restoring Capitalism," *Three Major Struggles on China's Philosophical Front*, p. 60.

60. See "On Contradiction," *SW*, Vol. 1, p. 335.

61. Mao Tsetung, quoted in *On Exercising All-Round Dictatorship Over The Bourgeoisie*, Chang Chun-chiao, FLP, Peking, 1975. Reprinted in *And Mao Makes 5*, edited by R. Lotta, Banner Press, Chicago, 1978, p. 213.

62. *Report To The Tenth National Congress of the Communist Party of China*. FLP, Peking, 1973, Reprinted in *And Mao Makes Five*, p. 80.

63. Mao Tsetung, quoted in "Capitalist-Roaders Are The Bourgeoisie Inside The Party," Fang Keng, *Peking Review*, No. 25, June 18, 1976, p. 7. Reprinted in *And Mao Makes 5*, p. 358.

64. Mao Tsetung, "Reading Notes," *Critique of Soviet Economics*, p. 86.

65. Mao Tsetung, quoted in *On The Social Basis of the Lin Piao Anti-Party Clique*, Yao Wen-yuan, FLP, Peking, 1975. Reprinted in *And Mao Makes 5*, p. 196.

Chapter 4

1. "Momentous Struggle on the Question of the Identity Between Thinking and Being," *Three Major Struggles on China's Philosophical Front,* p. 47.
2. Mao Tsetung, "Talk on Questions of Philosophy," in Schram, pp.212-213.
3. *Ibid.,* p. 215.
4. Engels, "Ludwig Feuerbach and the End of Classical German Philosophy," *MESW* Vol. 3, pp. 339.
5. *Ibid.,* p. 340-341.
6. *Ibid.,* p. 342.
7. *Ibid.,* p. 343.
8. *Ibid.,* p. 344.
9. *Ibid.,* p. 354.
10. *Ibid.,* p. 359.
11. *Ibid.*
12. *Ibid.,* p. 361.
13. *Ibid.,* p. 336.
14. Marx, "Theses on Feuerbach," *MESW,* Vol. 1, p. 13.
15. *Ibid.*
16. *Ibid.*
17. *Ibid.*
18. Engels, "Ludwig Feuerbach and the End of Classical German Philosophy," p. 345.
19. Marx, "Theses on Feuerbach," p. 15.
20. *Ibid.,* p. 14.
21. Marx and Engels, "Feuerbach Opposition of Materialistic and Idealistic Outlook," *MESW,* Vol. 1, pp. 29-30
22. Marx, "Theses on Feuerbach," pp. 13-14.
23. *Ibid.,* p. 15.
24. Marx, *Poverty of Philosophy,* International Publishers, New York, 1973, p. 109.
25. Lenin, "Empirio-Criticism and Historical Materialism," *CW,* Vol. 14, p. 329.
26. Engels, "Ludwig Feuerbach and the End of Classical German Philosophy," p. 362.
27. *Ibid.,* p. 375.
28. Engels, "Socialism, Utopian and Scientific," *MESW,* Vo. 3, p. 131.
29. See "Against Pragmatism," *The Communist,* Vol. 2, No. 2, RCP Publications, Chicago, 1978.
30. Lenin, "Materialism and Empirio-Criticism," *CW,* Vol. 14, p. 23.
31. *Ibid.,* p. 20.
32. *Ibid.,* p. 29.
33. *Ibid.,* p. 30,38.
34. *Ibid.,* p. 260.
35. *Ibid.,* p. 260-261.
36. *Ibid.,* p. 261-262.
37. *Ibid.,* p. 261.
38. *Ibid.*
39. Lenin, "Marxism and Revisionism," *CW,* Vol. 15, p. 37-38.
40. Lenin, "On the Question of Dialectics," *CW,* Vol. 38, p. 359.
41. *Ibid.,* p. 360.
42. *Ibid.*

43.   *Ibid.*, p. 362.
44.   See *Ibid.*, p. 359.
45.   Mao Tsetung, "On Contradiction," *SW*, Vol. 1, p. 330.
46.   Mao Tsetung, *A Critique of Soviet Economics*, p. 119.
47.   *HCPSU*, p. 109, (For Lenin quote see "On the Question of Dialectics," *CW*, Vol. 38, p. 360).
48.   Lenin, "On the Question of Dialectics," p. 360.
49.   Lenin, "Conspectus of Hegel's Book *The Science of Logic*," *CW*, Vol. 38, p. 223.
50.   *Ibid.*, pp. 359-360.
51.   *HCPSU*, p. 110.
52.   *Ibid.*, p. 110.
53.   *Ibid.*, p. 111.
54.   Mao Tsetung, "Speech at the Chinese Communist Party's National Conference on Propaganda Work," *SW*, Vol. 5, p. 433.
55.   Mao Tsetung, "On Practice," *SW*, Vol. 1, p. 295.
56.   *Ibid.*, p. 296.
57.   *Ibid.*, p. 297.
58.   *Ibid.*, p. 298.
59.   *Ibid.*
60.   *Ibid.*
61.   V.I. Lenin, "Conspectus of Hegel's Book, *The Science of Logic*," *CW*, Vol. 38, p. 171. (Also quoted in Mao, "On Practice," p. 29.)
62.   *Ibid.*, p. 299.
63.   *Ibid.*
64.   *Ibid.*, p. 305.
65.   *Ibid.*, p. 306.
66.   *Ibid.*, p. 308.
67.   V.I. Lenin, "Materialism and Empirio-Criticism," *CW*, Vol. 14, p. 133.
68.   *Ibid.*, p. 134.
69.   Mao Tsetung, "On Practice," *SW*, Vol. 1, p. 307.
70.   *Ibid.*, p. 307.
71.   *Ibid.*
72.   Mao Tsetung, "On Contradictions," *SW*, Vol. 1, p. 311.
73.   *Ibid.*, p. 345.
74.   *Ibid.*, p. 315.
75.   *Ibid.*, p. 316.
76.   *Ibid.*
77.   *Ibid.*, p. 318.
78.   *Ibid.*, p. 338.
79.   *Ibid.*, p. 343.
80.   *Ibid.*, pp. 319-320.
81.   *Ibid.*, p. 320.
82.   *Ibid.*, p. 343.
83.   *Ibid.*, p. 344.
84.   *Ibid.*, pp. 321-322.
85.   *Ibid.*, p. 320.
86.   *Ibid.*, p. 329.
87.   *Ibid.*, p. 330.
88.   *Ibid.*, p. 325.
89.   *Ibid.*, p. 331-332.
90.   *Ibid.*, p. 333.
91.   *Ibid.*

92. *Ibid.*
93. *Ibid.*, pp. 335-336.
94. Mao Tsetung, "Talks with Mao Yuan-hsin," in Schram, p. 252.
95. Mao Tsetung, "Talks at Chengtu: The Pattern of Development," in Schram, pp. 107-108.
96. Mao Tsetung, "Talks at a Conference of Secretaries of Provincial, Municipal and Autonomous Region Party Committees," *SW*, Vol. 5, p. 367-369.
97. See *Ibid.*, p. 377.
98. See Mao Tsetung, "Be Activists in Promoting the Revolution," *SW*, Vol. 5, pp. 492-493.
99. Mao Tsetung, "Talks at a Conference of Secretaries," *SW*, Vol. 5, p. 377.
100. Mao Tsetung, "On the Correct Handling of the Contradictions Among the People," *SW*, Vo. 5. p. 392.
101. *Ibid.*
102. *Ibid.*, p. 393.
103. See *Ibid.*, especially p. 109.
104. See Mao Tsetung, "On Contradiction," *SW*, Vol. 1., p. 345.
105. "Momentous Struggle on the Question of the Identity Between Thinking and Being," *Three Major Struggles*, p. 31.
106. *Ibid.*, p. 45.
107. *Ibid.*, p. 39.
108. Mao Tsetung, "Where Do Correct Ideas Come From," *Selected Readings from the Works of Mao Tsetung*, FLP, Peking 1971, p. 503.
109. *Ibid.*, p. 503.
110. Mao Tsetung, "On Contradiction," *SW*, Vol. 1, p. 336.
111. "The Theory of 'Combine Two Into One' Is a Reactionary Philosophy for Restoring Capitalism," *Three Major Struggles*, p. 49.
112. *Ibid.*, p. 51.
113. *Ibid.*, p. 60.
114. *Ibid.*, pp. 60-61.
115. Mao Tsetung, "Reading Notes" *A Critique of Soviet Economics*, p. 71.
116. Mao Tsetung, "Talks on Questions of Philosophy," in Schram, pp. 224-225.
117. *Ibid.*, 226.
118. *Ibid.*
119. *Ibid.*
120. *Ibid.*
121. *Ibid.*, pp. 226-227.
122. *Ibid.*
123. *Ibid.*
124. Mao Tsetung, "Where Do Correct Ideas Come From," *Selected Readings*, p. 503.
125. Mao Tsetung quoted in "Firmly Keep to the Orientation of the Struggle," *People's Daily* editorial, April 6, 1976, reprinted in *Peking Review*, No. 15, April 9, 1976 and in *And Mao Makes 5*, pp. 271-272.
126. Mao Tsetung quoted in "The Great Cultural Revolution Will Shine Forever," by the Editorial Departments of *Renmin Ribao, Hongqi,* and *Jiefangjun Bao*, May 16, 1976; reprinted in *Peking Review*, No. 21, May 21, 1976, p. 9.

127. Mao Tsetung quoted in *On the Social Base of the Lin Piao Anti-Party Clique*, by Yao Wen-Yuan, FLP, Peking 1975, pp. 17-18, reprinted in *And Mao Makes 5*, p. 204.
128. Quoted in *On the Social Base of the Lin Piao Anti-Party Clique*, and in *On Exercising All-Round Dictatorship over the Bourgeoisie*, and in *And Mao Makes 5*, p. 196 and p. 209.
129. Marx, "Marx to J. Weydemeyer," *MESW*, Vol. 1, p. 528.
130. Mao Tsetung, "Talks at a Conference of Secretaries," *SW*, Vol. 5, p. 377.
131. Mao Tsetung, "Reading Notes" *Critique of Soviet Economics*, p. 57.
132. Mao Tsetung quoted in "Capitalist Roaders Are Representatives of Capitalist Relations of Production," by Chuang Lan, reprinted in *And Mao Makes 5*, p. 372.
133. Mao Tsetung quoted in "Report on the Revision of the Party Constitution," delivered by Wang Hung-wen, Documents of the 10th Party Congress of the Communist Party of China, p. 45, reprinted in *And Mao Makes 5*, p. 96.
134. Mao Tsetung, "Cast Away Illusions, Prepare For Struggle," *SW*, Vol. 4, p. 428.

Chapter 5

1. Mao Tsetung, "Chairman Mao On Continuing the Revolution Under the Dictatorship of the Proletariat," *Peking Review*, September 26, 1969, p. 9.
2. Marx, *Preface and Introduction to A Contribution to the Critique of Political Economy*, FLP, Peking, 1976, p. 3.
3. *Ibid.*
4. Marx and Engels, *Manifesto of the Communist Party*, p. 57.
5. Marx, "Marx to P.V. Annenkov in Paris," *Marx and Engels Selected Correspondence, (MESC)*, Progress Publishers, Moscow, 1975, p. 30.
6. Engels, "Introduction to the English Edition," *Socialism: Utopian and Scientific*, p. 23-24.
7. Engels, "Engels to Joseph Bloch in Koningsberg," *MESC*, pp. 394-395.
8. Mao Tsetung, "On Contradiction," *SW*, Vol. 1, p. 336.
9. These works have now been translated completely into English and are available in Marx and Engels, *Collected Works*, International Publishers, N.Y., 1975, Vol. 4 (Holy Family) and Vol. 5 (German Ideology).
10. Marx, *The Eighteenth Brumaire of Louis Bonaparte*, International Publishers, New York, 1963, p. 18.
11. Lenin, "Party Organization and Party Literature," *CW*, Vol. 10, p. 45.
12. Lenin, "On Proletarian Culture," *CW*, Vol. 31, p. 316.
13. Lenin, "Party Organization and Party Literature," p. 48.
14. *Ibid.*, pp. 48-49.
15. See Stalin's handling of this subject in his reports to the 16th, 17th and 18th Party Congresses, *Works*, Vol. 12, pp. 307-308, and *Problems of Leninism*, pp. 725-727 and 908-911.
16. *Summary of the Forum on the Work on Literature and Art in the Armed Forces with which Comrade Lin Piao Entrusted Comrade Chiang Ching*, FLP, Peking, 1968, p. 14.
17. Mao Tsetung, *A Critique of Soviet Economics*, p. 135.

18. Mao Tsetung, "Speech at the Chinese Communist Party's National Conference on Propaganda Work," *SW*, Vol. 5, p. 434.
19. Mao Tsetung, "Speech at the Tenth Plenum of the Eight Central Committee," quoted in Schram, p. 195.
20. Mao Tsetung, "On New Democracy," *SW*, Vol. 2, p. 340.
21. *Ibid.*, p. 382.
22. Mao Tsetung, "Talks at the Yenan Forum on Literature and Art," *SW*, Vol. 3, p. 72.
23. *Ibid.*, p. 73.
24. *Ibid.*
25. See Mao Tsetung, "On New Democracy," pp. 371-373.
26. Mao Tsetung, "Talks at the Yenan Forum on Literature and Art," p. 96.
27. *Ibid.*, p. 91.
28. *Comments on Tao Chu's Two Books*, FLP, Peking, 1968, p. 27.
29. *Ibid.*, p. 26.
30. Mao Tsetung, "Talks at the Yenan Forum on Literature and Art," p. 71.
31. *Ibid.*, p. 80-81.
32. *Ibid.*, p. 83-84.
33. *Ibid.*, p. 71.
34. *Ibid.*, p. 86.
35. *Ibid.*, pp. 81, 82.
36. Mao Tsetung, "On Practice," *SW*, Vol. 1, pp. 296, 300.
37. Mao Tsetung, "Talks at the Yenan Forum on Literature and Art," p. 82.
38. *Ibid.*, p. 88.
39. Mao Tsetung, "Pay Serious Attention to the Discussion of the Film *The Life of Wu Hsun*," *SW*, Vol. 5, p. 57.
40. Mao Tsetung, "Letter Concerning the Study of *The Dream of the Red Chamber*," *SW*, Vol. 5, pp. 150-151.
41. Mao Tsetung, "Preface and Editor's Notes to *Material on the Counter-revolutionary Hu Feng Clique*," *SW*, Vol. 5, pp. 176-182.
42. *Ibid.*, pp. 177-178.
43. *Ibid.*, p. 178.
44. Mao Tsetung, "On the Correct Handling of Contradictions Among the People," *SW*, Vol. 5, p. 408.
45. Stalin, *Marxism and Problems of Linguistics*, FLP, Peking, 1972, p. 29.
46. Mao Tsetung, "On the Correct Handling of Contradictions Among the People," *SW*, Vol. 5, p. 408.
47. *Ibid.*, p. 409.
48. Mao Tsetung, "Talks at a Conference of Secretaries," *SW*, Vol. 5, p. 359.
49. Mao Tsetung, "*Wen Hui Pao's* Bourgeois Orientation Should be Criticized," *SW*, Vol. 5, p. 454.
50. Mao Tsetung, as quoted in "Excerpts from *A Talk by Chairman Mao with a Foreign [Albanian] Military Delegation*," *Peoples China*, edited by David Milton, Nancy Milton, and Franz Schurmann, Vintage Books, New York, 1974, p. 263.
51. Mao Tsetung, "Reply to Comrade Kuo Mo-Jo," *Poems*, FLP, Peking, 1976, p. 47.
52. Mao Tsetung, Speech at Hangchow, December 1965, quoted in Schram, p. 237. Also cited in Han Suyin, *Wind in the Tower*, Little Brown, Boston, 1976, p. 266.

53. *Decision of the Central Committee of the Chinese Communist Party Concerning the Great Proletarian Cultural Revolution,* adopted August 8, 1966, FLP, Peking, 1966, p. 1.

Chapter 6

1. Lenin, *The State and Revolution,* FLP, Peking, 1970, pp. 39-40.
2. Marx, "Marx to J. Weydemeyer in New York," *MESW,* Vol. 1, p. 528.
3. Marx and Engels, *Manifesto of the Communist Party,* pp. 60-61
4. Marx, "The Class Struggle in France 1848-1850," *MESW,* Vol. 1, p. 282.
5. Engels, "Apropos of Working-Class Political Action," *MESW,* Vol. 2, p. 245.
6. Lenin, *The State and Revolution,* p. 66.
7. Marx, "The Civil War in France," *MESW,* Vol. 2, p. 217.
8. Marx, "Marx to Ludwig Kugelmann," *MESC,* p. 247.
9. Lenin, *The State and Revolution,* p. 66.
10. Marx, "The Civil War in France," *MESW,* Vol. 2, p. 220.
11. *Ibid.,* p. 223.
12. Marx and Engels, *Manifesto,* p. 2 (the quote within this quotation is from *The Civil War in France*).
13. Marx, "Critique of the Gotha Program," *MESW,* Vol. 3, p. 26.
14. *Ibid.,* p. 18.
15. *Ibid.*
16. *Ibid.*
17. *Ibid.,* p. 17.
18. *Ibid.,* p. 19.
19. Engels, "Engels to Phil Van Patten in New York," *MESC,* p. 341.
20. Engels, "Engels to C. Schmidt in Berlin" and "Engels to Otto Von Boeniek in Breslav," *MESW,* Vol. 3, pp. 484, 485.
21. Marx, "The Civil War in France," *MESW,* Vol. 2, p. 189.
22. Lenin, *State and Revolution,* p. 65.
23. *Ibid.,* p. 112.
24. *Ibid.,* p. 114.
25. *Ibid.,* p. 18.
26. Marx, *Preface to a Contribution to the Critique of Political Economy, MESW,* Vol. 1, p. 504.
27. Lenin, *State and Revolution,* p. 33.
28. *Ibid.,* see pages 36, 43, 66.
29. *Ibid.,* see p. 57.
30. Lenin, "Economics and Politics in the Era of the Dictatorship of the Proletariat," *CW,* Vol. 30, p. 115.
31. *Ibid.*
32. Lenin, *Left Wing Communism, An Infantile Disorder,* FLP, Peking, 1970,p. 32.
33. *Ibid.,* p. 6.
34. Lenin, "Report On The Immediate Tasks Of The Soviet Government," *CW,* Vol. 27, p. 300.
35. *Ibid.,* p. 294.
36. Lenin, "Eighth Congress Of The RCP(B)," *CW,* Vol. 25, p. 189.
37. Lenin, "A Great Beginning," *CW,* Vol. 29, p. 421.
38. *Ibid.,* p. 427.
39. Stalin, "On The Draft Constitution," *Problems of Leninism,* pp. 799-800.